Transforming Gender and Development in East Asia

Edited by
Esther Ngan-ling Chow

ROUTLEDGE
New York and London

Published in 2002 by
Routledge
29 West 35th Street
New York, NY 10001

Published in Great Britain by
Routledge
11 New Fetter Lane
London EC4P 4EE

Routledge is an imprint of Taylor & Francis Group.

Printed in the United States of America on acid-free paper
Design and typography: Jack Donner

Library of Congress Cataloging-in-Publication Data
Transforming gender and development in East Asia / edited by Esther Ngan-ling Chow.
    p. cm.
  Includes bibliographical references and index.
  ISBN 0-415-92491-X — ISBN 0-415-92492-8 (pbk.)
    1. Women in development—East Asia. 2. Sex role—Economic aspects—East Asia. 3. East Asia—Economic conditions. I. Chow, Esther Ngan-ling, 1943–

HQ1240.5.E18 T73 2002
305.42'095—dc21

                                                                          2001057862

With immense indebtedness

to my grandmother,

my mother,

and women factory workers in East Asia.

Contents

Preface

There are four reasons I am compelled to work on this book. The first is to open a critically intellectual space by incorporating gender perspectives in the study of East Asian development in its global context. I intend the book to fill a major knowledge gap and to move women's and gender issues in the development studies in this region into the mainstream. In recent years voluminous literature has found competing explanations as to why and how East Asian economies succeed, particularly in the cases of the economic miracles experienced by Japan, the four "Asian Dragons"—namely Hong Kong, Singapore, South Korea, and Taiwan—and more recently China. Undoubtedly, many thoughtful analyses have advanced our knowledge of the development process in East Asia. However, the prevailing scholarly work in this area is, for the most part, gender-neutral or gender-blind. What is largely omitted is a gender perspective from which researchers and scholars engage in development research and analysis. This omission is surely a serious one since it not only stifles a full intellectual understanding of the very phenomenon of development, which we try so hard to comprehend, but also may misguide development policies and practices. Hence, this book seeks to affirm the value of gender studies, not merely as an alternative vision and analysis, but as a starting point to explore a competing paradigm that parallels and challenges mainstream development thinking.

My profound interest in transforming the consciousness and experiences of women workers into social fact through a text of diverse situated knowledge, both intellectual and illuminating, is the second reason for working on this volume. I firmly believe that such knowledge should be located from the ground up, reflecting everyday lived experiences and standpoints of diverse kinds of women and men. Feminist and Global South scholars with perspectives ranging from liberal to radical and ecofeminist traditions have addressed the androcentric, ethnocentric, and exclusive nature of knowledge in development literature and practices. Their scholarship places socially and differentially situated women, their vantage points, experiences, and realities vis-à-vis men's in the center of a relational, comparative, and historical analysis. This feminist thinking infused with the knowledge of development is not essentially reductionist. It articulates the social embeddedness of gender, not only in power relationships but also in structure, culture, and the process of society. It is intricately linked to the dynamism of macro social forces at work determining normative rules, ideologies, and institutional arrangements and structuring the social locations of people that further shape their identity, subjectivity, behavior, and even resistance.

Related to this is the third reason, which is to give voice. To speak out as a "subaltern other," as Gayatri Spivak has framed it and to encourage workers, especially women, to do so has become my life project so as to dismantle an existence of voicelessness, facelessness, invisibility, and powerlessness. Though my job as a factory worker was brief and seasonal, I witnessed the industrialization of Hong Kong in the 1950s. The indigenous voices of manufacturing laborers as a class, as a group of women, and as subaltern others transformed my being and thinking as a person early on and, ultimately, as a scholar. This underlying motivation has inspired me to do research and promote indigenous scholarship in the field of gender and development to place women at the center, leading me to this anthology. In this volume, many scholars have joined me in an effort to give voice and to develop indigenous situated knowledge from the ground up. I hope that our research and scholarship will help lay an epistemological foundation for future theoretical explorations in gender and development in East Asia specifically and in other parts of the world globally.

The final reason is to underscore an important relationship between knowledge and power, seeing knowledge itself and its process as liberatory and leading to self and collective empowerment. Working on this volume is empowering for those, including myself, who engage in the process of knowledge production, for those who are being studied, and for those who potentially benefit from it. Studies included in this volume have only just begun to lay the groundwork, directly or indirectly, that links theoretical analysis to development policies, programs, and practices in East Asia. This volume serves as an invitation to concerned others to join forces to further the transformation of situated knowledge into liberatory knowledge and the translation of self empowerment into collective empowerment for promotion of global justice, effective social change in society, and for the well-being of its people.

Esther Ngan-ling Chow

Acknowledgments

In working on this book, I have incurred intellectual and personal debts to numerous individuals. Special thanks are given to the contributors of this volume, most of them indigenous scholars and researchers, who have worked diligently and rigorously and with professionalism on each of their book chapters, writing draft after draft to polish their analyses. I would first like to thank Catherine Tang, the Director of Gender Research Programme, who invited me to be a speaker at the International Conference on Gender and Development in Asia held at the Chinese University of Hong Kong at the end of 1997. It was from this conference that two-thirds of the chapters for this volume were obtained. I am indebted to Ching Kwan Lee the most for her tremendous help working with me to formulate the basic ideas of the book proposal. Her thoughtfulness in offering two rounds of chapter reviews provided much needed constructive, yet critical, suggestions and comments to me as well as to the authors. She was also instrumental in obtaining the initial research fund for this project from the Chinese University of Hong Kong.

During the book project, I received much collegial support, encouragement, and advice from Myra Marx Ferree, Judith Lorber, Catherine White Berheide, Marcia Texler Segal, Carla Howery, and Mary Frank Fox. Joan Acker and Patricia Yancey Martin generously shared with me reference information on gendered organizations. Xiaolan Bao, Wu Xu, Nai-hua Zhang, and Christina Gilmartin from the Chinese Women's Studies Society buttressed me with spirited support that energized me when I needed it. Standing by me at American University are Ken Kusterer, Bette Dickerson, and Jenny Verdaguer, who offered office support and consultation, both personal and professional. For years, Ken Kusterer has shared much of his deep sense of knowledge of and experience in the development process in the Third World. He, along with Christine E. Bose, the current editor of *Gender & Society*, spent their valuable time reviewing the first three chapters of this book.

This book would not have been completed so smoothly without the expert guidance and professional advice of the editors, Ilene Kalish and Nicole Ellis, at Routledge. I also owe Kimberly Guinta for her endless patience and concrete assistance in judiciously moving the book project along to meet various deadlines. Thanks are given to the copy editor, Brian Bendlin, for his careful and meticulous attention to the book manuscript.

At the last stage of the project, I am grateful to the efficiency, dedication, and conscientiousness of Deanna M. Lyter, who aided in coordinating and editing the book chapters when I had to leave the U.S. for Tunghai University in Taiwan as a visiting professor in the fall of 2000. Through her valiant efforts at working with me, either in person or via e-mail, this project went smoothly and was completed with intellectual rigor. Elaine Stahl Leo to whom I am always indebted for her friendship, professionally edited several chapters. While I was in Taiwan, Yu-hsia Lu and Ganghua Fan at the Academia Sinica; Ray-may Hsung, Sui-ling Lin, Jenn-Hwan Wang, Chung-Hsien Huang, and Jinlin L. Hwang at Tunghai University lent much support by providing needed references and discussing intellectual issues with me related to the book. Additional references were obtained through assistance from Alvin So, Gina Lai, Pun Ngai, and Shirley Po-san Wan from various universities in Hong Kong. Emily Dempsey, my undergraduate research assistant at American University, was helpful in the early phase of the project, and Ming-Feng Lin, a doctoral student at the Tunghai University, worked diligently in offering research assistance during the last phase of the project.

Last, but certainly not least, I thank my spouse, Norman C. Chang; my son, Paul; and my daughter, Jennifer, for their enduring love and patience, letting me immerse myself deeply and assiduously in this intellectual project.

Introduction

Esther Ngan-ling Chow

Over the past four decades, the spectacular success of the Newly Industrializing Economies (NIEs) of the East Asian–Pacific area has turned the entire region into an economic powerhouse. The well-known stories of these NIEs have repeatedly defied early skeptics about the economic growth and development potential of the region as reported by international agencies in the 1950s and 1960s. A World Bank report (1993) documents that most of this remarkable achievement is attributed to rapid growth from 1965 to 1990 in nine "high-performing Asian economies" (HPAEs). The HPAEs began with Japan and soon included the four "Asian dragons" or "Asian tigers" (Hong Kong, the Republic of Korea, Singapore, and Taiwan), China, and the three newly industrialized countries (NICs) of Malaysia, Thailand, and Indonesia in Southeast Asia. The World Bank Report (1993:2) states that, compared to other world regions, "Since 1960, the HPAEs have grown more than twice as fast as Latin America and South Asia, and twenty-five times faster than Sub-Saharan Africa." They also significantly outperformed the oil-rich Middle East–North African region and some industrialized countries in Europe. Terms such as "The New Asia," "The Asian Miracle," and "The Asian Challenge," have replaced "The Old Asia" and "Stagnant Asia," with some even predicting that the East Asian–Pacific countries will emerge as one of the economic centers of the world system (Frank 1998).

A voluminous body of literature has grown to offer competing explanations of why and how East Asian economies succeed, analyzing the underlying causes, processes, and consequences of their development. Because these economies had neither blueprints nor ready-made ingredients to construct an industrializing and modernizing state, each country has taken its own pathway to development, a path shaped by its own specific historical and social circumstances. To identify commonalities and crucial differences, development studies often engage in mapping the factors associated with a region's capitalist expansion, including historical antecedents, institutional frameworks, cultural conditions, and dynamic processes (Islam and Chowdhury 1997). Existing theoretical models of East Asian development usually revolve around the following explanations: geopolitical factors, colonial legacy, a strong developmental state, cultural values and cohesion, social institutions, and strong links to the world economy (Deyo 1987, 1989; Gereffi 1990; Haggard 1990; Koo 1987; Rowan 1998; Simone and Feraru 1995; So and Chiu 1995; Thompson 1998).

What has been seriously neglected in the field of development, however, is the critical importance of the gender dimension to its theory, analysis, policy, and practice (Benería and Sen 1981; Jackson and Pearson 1998; Kabeer 1994; Moser 1993; Porter and Judd 1999; Sen and Grown 1987; Young 1992). In recent years, there has been a growing literature on gender and development that systematically and insightfully documents how development is gendered and so creates different meanings, processes, and impacts for women and men. Development has a human face and this face is gendered. Gender is embodied and embedded in the process and structure of development. The reality is that development, often not a sustainable one, places a disproportionate burden on women worldwide, and its trickle-down effects are felt primarily negatively by women (Benería and Feldman 1992; Bose and Acosta-Belén 1995; Harcourt 1994; Mehra, Esim, and Sims 2000; Moser 1993; Visanathan, Duggan, Nisonoff, and Wiegersma 1998). As the United Nations (1980:5) once summarized, "While [women] represent 50 percent of the world population and one-third of the official labor force, they [account] for nearly two-thirds of all working hours, receive only one-tenth of the world income and own less than one percent of the world property." Although in certain regions women had seen improvements in the arenas of health and education by the mid-1990s, a greater proportion of women than men in many developing countries of the Global South still consistently had high illiteracy and less education, worked harder and for longer hours, earned less, and lived in poverty (Chow 1996; Heyzer 1995; United Nations 1995, 2000; World Bank 2001). The payoff that development improves women's lives is insufficient, and progress is slow. Gender equality is nowhere in sight since the basic structural transformation of society needed to address gender interests has not been effectively achieved. Neither conventional theories nor policies of development have fully captured the complexity and multiplicity of these gendered realities with their far-reaching consequences for both men and women and their families.

Though feminist critiques and analyses have appeared in development studies for some time, it has only been rather recently that the salience of gender has begun to receive recognition in the literature concerning East Asian development (Brinton 1993; Cheng and Hsiung 1998; Chow 1997a; Hsiung 1996; S. K. Kim 1997; C. K. Lee 1998a; Ogasawara 1998).[1] The regional economic restructuring of the 1980s and 1990s, which had different effects on East Asian women and men of diverse backgrounds (see parts III and IV of this volume), provides renewed impetus for reassessing the so-called economic miracle. In 1997 the financial crisis that rocked Asia exposed dangerous weaknesses in regional and global economies and in development practices that placed more crisis-induced burdens on women than on men (USAID 2000). The impact was not confined to Asian regions but had a ripple effect in other parts of the world.[2] The relative contributions and impediments that globalization has given to the socioeconomic development of the region and the extent to which these global changes have a different impact on women and men regionally and locally beg new questions and demand further examination. Crises, in particular, invoke opportunities for critical analysis, gender assessment, and transformative changes. With this in mind, the importance of bringing gender into East Asian development studies is clearer than ever. The gender gap in our knowledge must be filled, and gender should be mainstreamed in development studies. This book takes on the mission of opening up a critical intellectual space by bringing the centrality of gender to the study of East Asian development in its global context.

With globalization in mind, I raise the following major questions relating to gender in East Asia development in this book: In what way is the process of development gendered? What does development mean to women and men in East Asia? How do women participate as social actors in development processes and practices similarly to and differently from men? How are women and men hierarchically situated in the social structure that in turn affects the way they experience and contribute to socioeconomic development? More specifically, what is the trickle-down effect of industrialization, economic restructuring, and migration on women and men workers? What are the major consequences, positive or negative, of development for women and men?[3] What are some of the inherent contradictions (e.g., dilemmas, oppositions, and resistances) in the gendered process of development?

This book represents an exploratory effort to examine the fundamental transformation of East Asian economies and societies, which have experienced more than three decades of untrammeled growth and remarkable prosperity, and to assess the payoffs and pitfalls of development in women's and men's lives. More specifically, the book offers a unique collection of new research focusing on how three fundamental macro changes—industrialization, economic restructuring, and migration—intricately intertwine to shape a gendering process that influences the organization of human life, social institutions, gender relations, system of meaning individual identities and subjectivity, and collective action. The chapters are grounded in recent fieldwork and empirical studies primarily in the four "Asian dragons," in emergent developing China; and to a lesser extent, in Thailand and North America, both Canada and the United States.

Our overall scholarly goal is to address the major socioeconomic transformation processes in East Asia and thereby to lay a foundation for other scholars, researchers, and practitioners to chart a new theoretical terrain for studying East Asian development, one that recognizes the salient analytical category of gender. Gender matters in the policies, processes, and practices of development because the gender dimension is pervasive and deeply embedded and embodied in human relations, social institutions, culture, and processes of society. It is linked to the dynamism of macro social forces at work in determining normative rules, ideologies, and institutional arrangements and in structuring people's social locations and power relationships that further shape their identity, subjectivity, behavior, and resistance. An ongoing theoretical challenge presented before us is to uncover the social, political, economic, and cultural interplay between the very categories of the global and local and their relationship to a variety of gender phenomena in this region. An urgent need exists to investigate development from the perspective of gender by taking issue with macropolicies and local practices that have led to development successes as well as failures (see Jackson and Pearson 1998) and by stressing how macro-micro linkages differentially shape the lives of women and men. Hence, one focus is on how international development studies have intersected with the field of women and gender studies in the past several decades and what lessons can be derived to build a foundation to authenticize East Asian development through indigenous gender perspectives.

THE ORGANIZATION OF THE BOOK

All of the authors herein, either as indigenous researchers or scholars who have fluent language skills and intimate knowledge of East Asian societies and cultures, contribute to this volume by bringing the indigenous standpoints and voices of East Asian women and men to the forefront of their relational, comparative, and reflexive analysis. Grounded in ethnography, personal narratives, field observations, in-depth interviews, and surveys, their indigenous studies provide richness in data, rigorous interpretations, and insightful analyses that are unique to the East Asian region. These scholarly works are case studies, surveys, ethnographies, and comparative, and historical analyses, reflecting realities of gender and development practices locally, nationally, and regionally in relation to larger and global processes. They were written by authors with a variety of visions and commitment, showing different levels of concerns about equality, empowerment, and sustainable development in the region as well as global justice and resistance. The volume as a whole represents a multidisciplinary approach that incorporates important theory and research from sociology, economics, anthropology, political science, history, demography, women's/gender studies, and area studies to provide insight into the complex phenomena of gendered development.

This book consists of four main parts. Part I sets the stage for the rest of the book by overviewing the history of East Asian development as it relates to industrialization, economic restructuring, and migration as well by discussing mainstream and feminist development theories. As this section shows, when the perspective of gender is infused into development studies, the existing image of East Asia as a region of affluence, with strong states, internal homogeneity, cultural cohesion, and a stable social order must be reassessed. A critical yet balanced view of gender is used to reveal the opportunities and risks that global forces bring and the consequences that these macro changes have in the lives of women and men. Three projects examining mainstream development theories with a feminist critique, internal critiques of feminist scholarship in development thinking, and localized effort to develop an indigenous, situated, and transformative knowledge for studying gender in East Asian development are discussed.

Parts II through IV mirror the three processes of development—namely, industrialization, economic restructuring, and migration. Part II reveals how the divergent pathways of industrialization among East Asian countries have yielded new forms of women's subordination and inequality in work organizations as well as in society, and how women have gained from and contested the process of development. In part III, the authors analyze patterns of gender ordering and changes in economic restructuring that redefine capitalist expansion, reorganize a new phase of the international division of labor, and shape Asian women's and men's consciousness, identities, and strategies in dealing with work and family life at the national, regional, and local levels. Finally, in part IV, the authors explore the mobility and migratory behavior of East Asian nationals as they move either within their own countries (internal migration) or to overseas communities (transnational migration). This set of chapters unravels the gender dimensions hidden in the labor experiences and family life of migrants and discovers how migration strategies are differentiated by class, ethnicity, nationality, culture, and region.

As a compilation, these studies form a nucleus that addresses the major social transformational processes in East Asia by using an analytical gender lens that peers into a global framework. They uncover that export-led industrialization is in fact female-led; that economic restructuring creates a moment when gender, too, is restructured; and that genderization underscores the causes, processes, and consequences of migration. The discussions united in this volume address current debates on how globalization has produced challenges, opportunities, risks, and contradictions risks for societies being transformed and the individuals living through it. Globalization is not devoid of many forums of gender inequality, which raises theoretical questions about the extent to which development has reduced or intensified patriarchal control and transformed gender relationships and inequality. Have people, especially women, been empowered? These questions open the prospect of whether gender empowerment is a prerequisite for sustainable development. Subsequently, the concepts of gender inequality, empowerment, and sustainable development are emphasized throughout this volume to address the macro-micro linkages between gender and development in terms of policies and strategies. Mainstream development models are also challenged by the indigenous gender perspectives offered by the authors, who explore just how varied pathways to development can be.

NOTES

1. Some studies have documented the social conditions and life experiences of women factory workers, but their primary analytical focus was not on gender.
2. According to the International Monetary Fund, worldwide economic growth in 1998 and 1999 was drastically reduced by the ripple effect of the Asian financial crisis.
3. Recently the field of gender and development has begun to focus on women with disabilities as one of the most vulnerable and disadvantaged groups of women being affected. Because our collection of studies does not focus on the issue of disability, I mention it only to sensitize others to its importance.

Part I

EnGendering
East Asian Development

Chapter 1

Globalization, East Asian Development, and Gender

A Historical Overview

Esther Ngan-ling Chow

The dynamism and complexity of East Asian development as it relates to industrialization, economic restructuring, and migration require some historical background to fully understand current situations and future prospects. This chapter offers a historical overview with some national comparisons to comprehend the intricate and ever-changing relationships between globalization and development in the region. When development is interrogated through a gender lens, the phenomenal growth of the region is seen to be beleaguered with inequality, heterogeneity, struggles, and contradictions derived from different hierarchies and the structural transformation of societies.

GLOBALIZATION AND EAST ASIAN DEVELOPMENT IN HISTORICAL CONTEXT

Globalization refers to the compression of the world in spatial and temporal terms, describing the ever-changing and intensifying networks of cross-border consciousness, human interaction, system interdependence, and transformation on a world scale (Chow 1997b). Anthony Giddens (1990) explains that globalization is the intensification of worldwide social relations through time/space distantiation. In a capitalist economy, for instance, the distance and time needed to produce goods and transport commodities from the product's origin to its destination are compressed via technology, telecommunications, and transportation. Globalization has been underway, with continuities and discontinuities, throughout human history, impacting unevenly on different world regions. The process is neither ubiquitously uniform nor linear but rather is construed as a partially integrated, sometimes disjointed, and even contradictory process. Globalization is a multifaceted concept that encompasses a variety of meanings and dimensions. Arjun Appadurai (1990) suggests that current global flows occur in and through the growing integration and disjuncture of different landscapes—finanscapes (e.g., money and trade), technoscapes (e.g., technology and information), ethnoscapes (e.g., people through international migration and travel), mediascapes (e.g., mass media and communication) and ideoscapes (e.g., ideas, images, and ideology). This book focuses primarily on socioeconomic aspects of globalization as they relate to gender.

The global economy refers to the increasingly interdependent system of production, distribution, exchange, and consumption in which flows of capital, labor, raw materials, goods, technology, information, markets, trade, and finance are processed via telecommunication, and transportation across national borders and regions. This economy has accelerated rapidly since the 1950s and early 1960s, when, in the face of international competition, the industrialized countries of the First World sought to expand through economic restructuring and offshore production in order to achieve maximum profit levels and the accumulation of capital.[1] This global force provided an impetus for the socioeconomic development of Africa, Asia, Latin America, and the Middle East. Following is a historical overview of the three fundamental macrolevel changes brought by globalization—industrialization, economic restructuring, and migration—and their gender implications in the East Asian region. I first describe historical and empirical patterns of development in East Asia; then highlight gender-specific aspects of industrialization, restructuring, and migration; and finally explicate any specific East Asian characteristics or anomalies in light of general theories.

Industrialization

Industrialization is commonly known as a complex process involving the transformation from an agricultural society to an industrial one by expanding capital and the labor market, applying innovations in energy and technology, mechanizing production, and augmenting industrial organization with trade and societal infrastructures. Industrialization in East Asia was primarily driven by capitalist expansion, global economic restructuring, and an international division of labor facilitated by a strong state, transnational corporations (TNCs), trade, and financial institutions. As identified by Michael Hsiao (1997), the Asia-Pacific region, including East Asia, has undergone four major waves of development since the end of World War II: the first two relating to industrialization and are discussed in this section while the last two concern economic restructuring with a focus on regional industrial reorganization and integration and are discussed in the next section. The first wave of industrialization started with Japan's continued effort to modernize, beginning in the mid-1950s. Fueled by an abundant labor supply, foreign capital investment, foreign aid, and political stability, the country launched its industrialization and achieved economic recovery from World War II. In the twenty years that followed, Japan sustained a high level of economic growth, surpassing that of major European countries such as Italy and the United Kingdom by 1973. In recognition of its development, Japan has been considered a First World country, or a core member of the world economy, since the late 1960s. The second wave of industrialization is the "economic miracle" experienced by the four "Asian dragons"—South Korea, Taiwan, Hong Kong, and Singapore. Because the former two are nation-states and the latter two are city-states, their pathways of industrialization diverged somewhat. Both South Korea and Taiwan have undergone four stages of development as identified by Gary Gereffi (1990), beginning with the commodity export stage that concentrated on the extraction and export of unrefined or semiprocessed raw materials.[2] During Japan's colonial occupation of Taiwan (1895–1945) and South Korea (1910–1945), their industry, commerce, and production of food were developed to supply the Japanese domestic market. After the defeat of Japan in 1945, Korea was divided into two military zones straddling the 38th parallel. The north, under the control of the former USSR, became a communist state, while the south was initially occupied by the United States but proclaimed its independence in 1948. Taiwan became a province of the Republic of China after World War II and was ruled by Chiang Kai-shek and his party from 1949 until recent years.

The second stage began in the 1950s, when Taiwan and South Korea instigated a somewhat successful land reform policy. In response to global economic restructuring, both countries, which were governed by strong authoritarian states, adopted an inward-looking strategy primarily of import-substitution industrialization (ISI) that entailed a shift from importing to locally manufacturing basic consumer goods. In the third stage, which lasted from the 1960s to 1972, both countries altered their development strategies from ISI to export-oriented industrialization (EOI), which stressed exporting textiles, apparel, electronics, and plastics from their labor-intensive manufacturing sectors. In the mid-1960s, Taiwan was the first country to succeed in establishing export processing zones (EPZs), where a significant number of young, single women workers were employed—a model later adopted in many other Third World countries. After the oil crises of 1973, both countries embarked on their most recent stage and pursued a diversified export promotion and secondary ISI to advance their capital- and technology-intensive industries (i.e. heavy, chemical, and high-tech). By the mid-1980s, they had emerged as newly industrialized economies (NIEs) and were elevated to a semiperipheral position in the world system. Since then, they have experienced sustainable development. Foreign investment, trade liberalization, strong states with political stability, class formation, and local entrepreneurial initiatives and geopolitical factors were the determining forces that propelled the industrialization of these countries (Amsden 1989; Deyo 1987; Gereffi 1990; Gold 1986; Haggard 1990; Islam and Chowdhury 1997; Wade 1990).

However, Tun-jen Cheng (1990) found that South Korea and Taiwan diverged in their approaches to the implementation of development strategies: South Korea followed the classic "rent-seeking" approach that is centralized, hierarchical, unbalanced, and command-oriented, while Taiwan used a "surplus-generating" approach that was decentralized, balanced, and incentive-oriented. State-owned enterprises played a more important role in Taiwan than in South Korea (Gereffi 1990; Koo 1987), although Taiwan has begun to privatize in recent years. In contrast to the preponderance of small- and medium-sized enterprises in Taiwan's industrial sector, South Korea's is characterized by giant, vertically integrated industrial conglomerates (*chaebols*). Labor unionization, though repressed in both countries, has been more active in South Korea than in Taiwan (Frenkel 1993). Finally, Taiwan's economic growth was assisted by its geopolitical alliance with the United States and other Western countries during the Cold War era, which brought foreign aid with relatively low international debt and encouraged Taiwan's active, though unequal, external trading.

Under colonialism, Hong Kong and Singapore were created by the British as entrepot trading posts and shipbuilding and ship repairing bases during the second half of the nineteenth century.[3] Hong Kong is the gateway to trade between China and other parts of the world, whereas Singapore is the hub for commodity exports in the southeast region. Thus international trade has played a pivotal role in their development. In the post–World War II era, the British had a hand in laying the infrastructure for commerce and finance as both countries recovered economically.[4] As small city-states limited in natural resources and agricultural production, Hong Kong and Singapore depend heavily on migrant laborers, trade, foreign investment, and the transfer of technology. Hong Kong began to industrialize in the early 1950s, transforming itself from a free port to a modernized state. Ten years later, a similar process of industrialization took place in Singapore, especially after it attained self-rule in 1959. The economic growth of both countries can be attributed to export-led industrialization that peaked in the 1960s to 1970s, reaching 9 to 10 percent per annum increases in gross domestic product (GDP). Both city-states have sustained themselves economically ever since.

In spite of their similarities, there are some fundamental differences in the development processes of Hong Kong and Singapore. Hong Kong had been subjected to colonial rule by the British, enjoying some political stability but unable to control long-term economic policies and planning. The colonial government of Hong Kong pursued a laissez-faire policy of minimal intervention by putting few restrictions on private ownership, free trade, and currency control (Chiu 1994). Its export-led industrialization process was predominantly focused on local entrepreneurship, a product of grassroots capitalism based on human capabilities (Athukorala and Manning 1999). In contrast, Singapore had the fortune of gaining self-rule in 1959, though it was temporarily merged with the Federation of Malaysia and did not achieve political independence until 1965. Led by the People's Action Party, the government sought nation-building, political stability, and activist policies as foci of its long-term development plan (Quah 1998). Exercising strong state control, the Singapore government launched its industrialization program to attract foreign investment, impose import restrictions protecting infant industries, undertake export drives, and encourage private enterprises. Unlike Hong Kong's reliance on local enterprises, TNCs have largely dominated the export of manufactured goods and are responsible for Singapore's extensive chemical and petroleum industries.[5]

Both globalization and industrialization are neither gender-neutral nor gender-blind. On the one hand, as a country industrializes, globalization undoubtedly creates more consumer goods and job opportunities for many and increased economic growth and wealth for the nation. In studying the impact of industrialization on women in seven Asian countries, Susan Horton (1996) reported that (1) women's participation in the labor force of urban market economies had increased; (2) employment patterns had shifted by industry (from agriculture to manufacturing, commerce, and services), by occupation (e.g., clerical work and some professions), and from unpaid family work to paid employment; and (3) the earnings gap of women relative to men had narrowed as women's education and labor experience increased. Horton found that East Asian countries exhibited some differences from other Asian countries because of their relatively higher women's labor force participation rate and the greater concentration of women in manufacturing and agriculture. Several contributions to this volume (see chapters by Ping, Kim, Gong, Chow and Hsung, Leung, and Lee) provide in-depth analysis of how women's employment and earnings in the market economy are intricately related to their work, family, and personal well-being—providing qualitative additions to Horton's investigation.

On the other hand, globalization-driven industrialization also produces some adverse consequences that are accentuated by macro forces and that may be potentially antithetical to the process of socioeconomic development. Gender is implicated in globalization when consumption by the developed world is built on the cheap labor and and exploitation of workers, particularly through the subordination of women, in developing countries striving to industrialize. As the four "Asian dragons" transitioned from agrarian, subsistence-based, and low-income countries to industrializing, wage-generating, and high-middle-income countries, their process of "export-led" industrialization was, in fact, "female-led." Globalization has meant that waves of women (as well as men) workers have migrated from villages to the slums of global cities and across national borders to work as exploited laborers. Some of them are employed as domestic workers who care for the families belonging to women of a particular class, caste, race, ethnicity, and/or nationality, thus enabling those privileged women to develop their jobs and advance in their careers. Globalization is signaled by the privatization of industries and the state's gradual loss of control over enterprises as the state is forced to concede tax and tariff benefits, by a growth in corporate rights and control over labor by a fragmentation of labor and production, by the suppression of union organization, and by the degradation of the environment. The process allows TNCs and runaway shops (such as sweatshops) to take flight when they recognize the "comparative disadvantages" of remaining in terms of cheap labor costs and larger profit margins that present in other developing nations. Globalization also means a liberalization of trade subsidized by workers' depressed wages, so that their countries can compete economically in international markets. All these issues, though still subject to debate for those who assume business as usual, may potentially become social problems that are in need of solutions and show how globalization has exacerbated rather than amended the adverse effects of industrialization in developing regions like East Asia.

In sum, globalization has fundamentally challenged the notion that East Asian states have omnipotent power and autonomy in orchestrating economic development without external influence. No nation is an island by itself; it is intricately embedded in a web of global links. Several studies in this volume review how global capitalism has unleashed the mobility of capital and labor across national boundaries, how family forms and strategies vary in different nations, and how consciousness has become globalized. Analytical attention is thus redirected toward transnational societal responses, global players like TNCs, cross-national labor markets, transmigrants, and international media. The weakening impact of the state is apparent in the case of socialist China undergoing market reform, as research in this collection demonstrates. Thus, regional economic restructuring has become a testing ground on which many East Asian states are seeking to demonstrate their abilities to achieve sustainable development.

Economic Restructuring

Similar to industrialization, economic restructuring is a regional and local response to globalization and sparked the third and fourth waves in the unprecedented transformation of the Asia-Pacific region. Hsiao (1997) points out that these two waves began in the 1980s with the rising economic growth of China and Southeast Asia and the emergence of various regional growth triangles and regional integration. Economic restructuring refers to the fundamental reorganization of production and economic activities that take place at the global, national, and local levels. Global restructuring means "the emergence of the global assembly line in which research and management are controlled by the core or developed countries while assembly line work is relegated to semiperiphery or periphery nations that occupy less privileged positions in the global economy," resulting in what has been termed the new international division of labor (Ward 1990:2). Fröbel, Heinrichs, and Kreye (1980) point out that capitalist development tends to position developing countries as "industrial enclaves" that supply extremely cheap labor and export manufactured goods for consumption in the developed world. This restructuring propelled industrialization in the developing world, including East Asia, but triggered de-industrialization (e.g., massive plant closings and working-class unemployment) in the developed, modernized West, as the United States experienced in the late 1970s and early 1980s. The end of the Cold War in the late 1980s gave rise to a new urge to seek rapid economic growth, accentuating the trend toward free trade and open market economies and continuing the process of global restructuring.

Similar processes of economic restructuring took place in East Asia regionally, nationally, and locally in interaction with global restructuring. Four major factors contributed to this regional restructuring. First, socialist China promulgated the "one party, two systems" policy in 1978, which commenced its transformation into an open and free market economy after several decades of isolation. Second, the Plaza Accord doubled the yen against the U.S. dollar in 1985 and sent a massive outflow of capital from Japan to Asia, with China and Southeast Asia being the major beneficiaries. Third, a regional bloc, the Association of

Southeast Asian Nations, known as ASEAN, seized this opportunity to provide appropriate incentives for foreign direct investment. And fourth, as the accumulation of capital in the four Asian dragons caught up with their labor supply, wages began to rise above the subsistence level, which adversely affected the surplus of capital and the region's cost advantage in the 1980s. Capitalists responded to these changes with three strategies: exporting capital (i.e., relocating production to countries with lower wages and abundant labor), deepening capital (e.g., adopting new technology to cut costs and upgrade production), and importing cheap labor (Athukorala and Manning 1999). All of this led to a new level of industrialization in China and Southeast Asia, involving regional restructuring with some degree of de-industrialization among the four Asian dragons and regional struggles for integration and cooperation to form growth triangles along the Asia-Pacific rim.[6]

Driven by the capitalist logic of profit, corporations from the "Asian dragons" followed the strategy of Japan and the industrialized West and invested capital in the developing countries in Asia where low production costs, abundant cheap labor, and vast markets worked to their economic advantage. They increasingly set up global factories for offshore production in China, Malaysia, Thailand, Indonesia, the Philippines, and more recently Vietnam, permitting them to exploit less expensive raw materials, land, and overseas labor; to diffuse political, economic, and evironmental costs; to explore diversity in production; to seek greater access to labor markets; and to improve competitive abilities internationally. Backed by state development policies and practices, this microeconomic level of industrial restructuring created its own niche for a regional division of labor in production and for corporate alliances. Labor became subdivided and fragmented in skill level, and sales, research and development could remain in a central location (e.g., the headquarters and main branches of the TNCs), while the piecework of assembly lines could be manufactured in neighboring countries with cheaper labor under special government and business arrangements (e.g., low tariffs and free import duties). For the NIEs, economic restructuring meant downsizing in the manufacturing sector, a decline in the labor-intensive industrial sector due to reallocation abroad, growth in the service sector, and the expansion of capital- and technological-intensive industries.

Meanwhile, China and Southeast Asia were being tapped to make their rapidly growing labor reserves available for production at an ever-decreasing cost. They repeated the process of industrialization with country-specific variations that had been experienced by the four "Asian dragons" in previous decades. The Southeast Asian countries and China underwent their own national and local restructuring marked by five major characteristics: (1) export-oriented industrialization as a hallmark of development, (2) growth in the manufacturing and service sectors as development strategies, (3) feminization of the labor force, (4) economic reforms (e.g., decline of state-owned enterprises in China), and (5) privatizing industries and liberalization by trade—all of which have great implications relating to gender.

There is an ongoing and unresolved debate about how development processes in terms of industrialization and economic restructuring affect Asian women, a debate that parallels the century-old one about the early industrialization of Europe and the United States. On the one hand, the "exploitation" thesis, which dominates neo-Marxist/dependency theory and feminist scholarship, posits that industrialization marginalizes women as exploited laborers, particularly those employed by TNCs in export processing zones (Beneria and Feldman 1992; Mies 1986; Nash and Fernandez-Kelly 1983; Ong 1987; Tiano 1994; Visanathan et al. 1998; Young, Wolkowitz, and McCullagh 1981). Global strategies for capital accumulation see women as secondary wage earners who work for pin money and can be paid less than men and as disposable laborers who can be recruited or laid off depending upon the demands of the labor market. Their presupposed natural womanly qualities of "nimble fingers," docility, and a lack of skills are used to justify low pay and poor working conditions (Elson and Pearson 1981). On the other hand, a contrasting view envisages that the integration of women into the labor market will liberate women from patriarchal control and lead them to economic independence. They are being "pulled" to new opportunities and "pushed" out of the home to earn wages to support their families. Though recognizing some degree of exploitation, Linda Lim (1983, 1990) dismisses the "exploitation" thesis as a stereotype rather than a reality, because it is not the norm for women who are employed in export factories in the Third World. She argues that multinational corporations often provide higher wages and better employment opportunities than jobs in locally owned firms or unpaid work in the home.

The economic reality for women in East Asia, and for Third World women in general, is highly varied and complex; their situations differ significantly by country, industry, culture, and historical era. The trickle-down effects of development on gender are also divided along class, racial/ethnic, and national lines. The impact of development on women, then, may vary by East Asian country and by groups of women, falling somewhere between the two extremes of theoretical debate. Nevertheless, one critical point I argue is that women workers do subsidize the waged labor of men throughout society, making it possible for their countries to achieve development at a lower cost. Capitalist development increasingly differentiates women's jobs from men's jobs, justifying a system of job segregation and unequal pay by gender. Even similar jobs with different titles and tracks for men and women provide men workers economic advantages over women (see chapter 4 by Chow and Hsung). Many employers view men as the primary breadwinners in the family and thus pay men a family wage, providing higher pay for similar jobs and offering higher wage increments. Because women's economic role as breadwinner is deemed secondary, their work is devalued, as indicated by lower pay and limited fringe benefits. When women enter the labor market, they face the double burden of paid production in the labor market and unpaid social reproduction in the family, and in some cases the additional toil of subsistence farming, seasonal employment, and subcontract of home-production. Men seldom take responsibility for household labor. The forms of labor that women undertake in the community, household, and income-generating activities in the informal sector are not counted toward the GDP in their respective countries. Finally, many women workers are affected greatly by unfair international trade between countries of the First and the Third worlds and its accompanying changes in terms of employment, price, consumption, and income effects (Anderson 2000; Benería and Lind 1995).

Study of the impact of economic restructuring and de-industrialization on women and men workers in the NIEs has barely begun. Stephen Chiu and Ching Kwan Lee (1997) point out that little research has been devoted to the subject, but what has been done indicates that the experience of East Asian countries has not been homogeneous (see Committee for Asian Women 1995). In Singapore, Jean Pyle (1994) shows how state policies have shaped the impact that economic restructuring has had on the work roles of men and women. Among the four "Asian dragons," Hong Kong inflicted the greatest "hidden injuries" to women workers during its industrial restructuring; many of whom were middle-aged, married, and unskilled (Chiu and Lee 1997; Leung in chapter 8). As China has stepped onto the capitalist road to a free market economy, the industrial restructuring of state-owned enterprises has led to the devastating effects for women of underemployment, unemployment, and reemployment (see chapters 6 and 7 herein by Gong and Ping; see also Lee 1998b and Summerfield 1994). All of these studies provide evidence to support the critical importance of using a gender lens for rethinking East Asian modes of economic restructuring.

Migration

Migration has recently become an important process of globalization in which flows of people move from rural to urban areas, from one region to the next, and across national borders, demonstrating the structural interconnectedness of societies through globalized space. Demographers define migration "as a change in the place of residence involving movement across a political or administrative border" (INSTRAW 1994:1). Migration is not new, but a centuries-old strategy used to adapt or simply survive, as in the historical case of the Chinese diaspora that spread throughout China, Asia, and abroad. What *is* new is the recent change in its nature, scale, and complexity that is driven by macro forces and not confined by national territory, sovereignty, or identity. Migration has taken on a transnational character, and now the movement of people can be globally linked in time and space. The cultural awareness that is promoted by mass media and modernization, the wide use of telecommunications interconnecting people from afar, the affordability of transportation bringing people in close proximity to each other, and the emergence of global cities expanding into new urban spaces—all of these are developing a global consciousness of interdependence among places and people to facilitate the flow and process of migration.

In addition, the globalization of production across borders has transformed the relationships among capital, trade, and labor. Immigration represents one of the ultimate symbols of the state's sovereignty and control over its citizens. As a result, there is growing tension between the needs of the market and the prerogatives of the state. The impact of immigration on identity, citizenship, loyalty, integration, and cohesion increasingly challenges the very notion of the nation-state and transnationalism. Ong, Chang, and Chew (1995) observe the heterogeneity and increased volume of migration as the most salient features in current Asian transmigration, ranging from economic migrants, professional immigrants, temporary foreign workers, migrant families, tourists, refugees, students, illegal migrants, and most recently return migrants. They particularly point out that women, children, and illegal immigrants are newcomers in the migration literature since they have been overlooked by researchers and policy makers. Feminization is particularly prominent in Asian migration, more so than in other parts of the world. The following discussion will first highlight the history and patterns of migration in East Asia in the context of globalization with special attention paid to issues and problems confronted by women migrants in Asia.

Since the mid-1980s, there has been an unprecedented rise in international migration in the Asian-Pacific region (Ong et al. 1995; Quibria 1997; Stahl 1999). It was unleashed during industrialization and economic restructuring, showing the dynamic relationship between capital and labor as mediated by the state. In both the pre– and post–World War II eras, most East Asian countries had an abundant labor supply, pulled from the subsistence sector of rural areas to the modern sector of urban areas, to support their expanding labor-intensive manufacturing and export-led industrialization. Hence, Japan, Taiwan, and South Korea did not need migrant labor until late in the industrialization process.[7] Rapid growth in productivity, deployment of workers into manufacturing, and a flexible labor market contributed to the momentum of growth in South Korea and Taiwan through the 1980s, despite a tightening of the labor market and increased real wages.

As in many East Asian countries, a major source for a flexible labor supply initially came from young, single women, whom Frederic Deyo (1989) describes as the "super proletariat" because of their concentration in low levels of production with low pay. Large wage differentials based on gender reflected the nature of gendered jobs, occupational segregation, and a bifurcated wage structure as struggling firms took advantage of low-paid female workers. Shortages of young women workers did not occur until later, as low fertility led to a smaller pool of prospective labor and as prolonged schooling and an expansion of the service sector provided more job options. In addition, changes in living patterns induced local workers in increasingly well-off societies to shun jobs at the bottom of the skill and wage distribution. An increasing shortage of unskilled labor became a major problem from the mid-1980s in Taiwan and the early 1990s in South Korea, especially for small and medium-sized firms that were unable to export capital to cope with scarcity of labor and rising wages. Facing slow population growth, an aging population, a less elastic labor supply, a depletion of labor reserves in rural regions and the informal sector, and rising wages, firms chose to import cheap labor from neighboring countries with surplus labor. Facilitated by the state, importing foreign laborers became a viable strategy to cut production costs and to meet keen economic competition.

In contrast, the city-states of Hong Kong and Singapore, lacking agriculture and resources and with a limited population, have developed an elastic labor supply, largely relying on an inflow of migrant workers (mostly from China and Malaysia) for economic production and expansion. In the case of Hong Kong, Ronald Skeldon (1994b) found that geopolitical factors were more crucial than economic ones in affecting migration patterns and experiences in Hong Kong. As a wave of politically induced immigration emerged in the 1980s spurred by a fear of communist China's takeover of Hong Kong and the restriction of inflow migrant labor from China, a serious labor shortage was created by 1987 that was resolved later by a relaxation of immigration policies. Hong Kong's policy toward migrant workers was liberal from the outset, whereas Singapore's government sought to keep the flow of migration and its sectoral distribution in line with national development priorities.

This coincided with the liberalization of reform in China and economic expansion in Southeast Asia, providing opportunities for Japan and the "Asian dragons" to export capital and allocate their manufacturing sectors overseas. While the manufacturing industries had been downsized, these East Asian countries experienced structural shifts characterized by rapid growth in the service, trade, business, and finance sectors with expansions into capital- and technology-intensive industries. In the 1990s, such vibrant economies attracted not only a large number of unskilled and skilled manual and domestic workers with employment visas but also an increasing number of professional and highly skilled migrants. The urban economic restructuring theory argues that the transition to a post-industrial economy creates demand for highly skilled workers, while the replacement hypothesis explains that such a transition also increases the demand for individuals with limited skills and qualifications to fill low-paying jobs (Menahem and Spiro 1999).

In addition to traveling to such traditional migration destinations and regions such as Europe, the United States, Canada, Australia, and New Zealand, recent migration has changed the "ethnoscapes," as Appadurai (1990) calls them, in Asia. Japan, Hong Kong, South Korea, Taiwan, and more recently Thailand and Malaysia. These countries have begun to absorb a growing number of foreign workers, mostly from the less developed countries in the region; though these numbers were small, they grew rapidly in the 1990s. By the mid-1990s, guest migrant workers accounted for over 20 percent of the total labor force in Singapore and Malaysia, over 10 percent in Hong Kong, and 6 percent in Thailand (Athukorala and Manning 1999).[8] Trade unions and the public alike showed concern about the negative consequences of foreign workers. Although some migrant workers were initially sent back to their countries of origin after the 1997 Asian financial crisis, Premo-chandra Athukorala and Chris Manning (1999) are optimistic that the sending countries will continue to use labor exportation to counteract unemployment and that the receiving countries will remain reliant on foreign workers for the survival of firms in many industrial sectors. This reliance is structurally embedded rather than cyclical in the process of economic and social transformation in the East Asian countries.[9]

Overall, traditional migration tended to involve more men as migrants and workers, causing women to be seen as passive migrants or dependent on male migrants and their families. Women migrants' social and economic contributions were also generally considered to be nonexistent or secondary at best. Recent studies in Asian migration have revealed five common trends: (1) an increasing feminization of migration; (2) a prominence of women as autonomous migrants; (3) a shift from a traditional family migration to the migration of individuals; (4) a growing flexibility and diversity of Asian women migrants; and (5) an increasing vulnerability of Asian women migrants that has heightened public awareness and policy concerns. Of the crude worldwide estimate of about one billion lifetime internal migrants and 100 million lifetime international migrants, women account for roughly half of all internal migrants in the developing world and slightly less than half of all international migrants (INSTRAW 1994). In China, the internal migration of women to the south has outnumbered that of their male counterparts (Chow 1998; Davin 1999), and women migrants have entered into the marriage market far more than men (see Gilmartin and Tan in this volume). Asian migration has contributed greatly to the feminization of migration in intraregional movements more than immigration to destinations outside of the region. According to Lin Lean Lim and Nana Oishi (1996), women constituted less than 15 percent of the 146,400 Asian migrants in 1976. By the 1990s, however, Asian migrants had become greatly feminized, with an approximate outflow of 800,000 women migrant workers per year as reported by the countries of origin. One and a half million Asian women are working abroad, and that number is increasing gradually. The number of illegal migrants has been estimated to be equal to or even greater than the number of legal migrants.[10] The major sending countries have included the Philippines, Indonesia, Sri Lanka, and Thailand, and the major receiving countries have been Saudi Arabia, Kuwait, Hong Kong, Japan, Taiwan, Singapore, Malaysia, and Brunei. While men tended to depart for the Middle East in greater numbers, women mostly traveled to East and Southeast Asia during the early phase of migration. In general, women migrants, many employed as domestic workers, tend to outnumber men in the Philippines, Indonesia, and Sri Lanka based on official records and not counting illegal migrations or migration through clandestine means.

Since migration is often a family survival strategy, many Asian women have been willing to respond readily to labor demands by leaving home alone or in groups and becoming labor migrants. Lim and Oishi (1996:88) observe that "the supply of Asian female labor migrants has been very flexible relative both to men from their own countries and to female migrants form other parts of the world." Regardless of marital status, Asian women, particularly young ones and those with a college education, have been attracted to both unskilled jobs (i.e., as workers in domestic service, manufacturing industries, and entertainment) and skilled jobs (i.e., teachers, clerical workers, nurses, doctors, and assorted feminized or "pink-collar" occupations).[11]

Why have women gained prominence in Asian migration? Increasing recognition among scholars and researchers is being given to the notion that migration trends reflect a simultaneous interplay of global and intraregional forces with local sociopolitical and cultural conditions (Finlay, Jones, and Davidson 1998;

Saith 1999). Eight major factors at the macro- and microlevels have contributed to the gradual increase in Asian women's migration. First, the expansion of global capitalism has penetrated Asia, transforming the relationships among capital, trade, and labor in the world system and impacting the international division of labor, including labor demands and migration flows. Second, Asian states have taken on a more active role in dealing with labor supply and demand in the global market by using diplomatic relations to establish policies and legitimize the practices of labor exports. Asian governments see the remittances of foreign laborers as a main source of foreign exchange to help balance international trade. Third, migration is also a direct response to disparities in economic growth, political turmoil, poverty, and related inequalities in a given country or region. The uneven development within Asia has created a pool of proletarian migrant workers, including women. Fourth, the growth of the service sector and tourist industry has created options for women in addition to jobs in the manufacturing industry across national borders.

Fifth, Asian migrant women usually originate from countries with a relatively high female labor force participation rate, and many of them are employed and equipped with labor experience. Hardship, especially when induced by stagnant economic growth and/or structural adjustment (OECD 1999), encourages these women to use labor migration as a family survival strategy. Note that female migrants in domestic service, who are predominantly from the Phillipines, Malaysia, Thailand, and Indonesia, facilitated female labor force participation rates, making it easier for educated women to enter and remain in the job market. Sixth, there have been relatively few social and cultural constraints on norms and values in Southeast Asia and Sri Lanka (e.g., in contrast to Bangladesh and Pakistan) discouraging women from traveling afar (Lim and Oishi 1996). Seventh, social networks have greatly sustained and intensified the nature of Asian female migration flows, since women (especially young women) are more likely than men to move as part of migration chains and to rely on informal social networks. Eighth, private intermediaries in the "immigration industry" in Asia also encourage female migration by facilitating women's job placement overseas and exploiting them with exorbitant fees and control measures. A transnational network of illegal intermediaries in the countries of origin and destination has also arisen to traffic in female slaves and prostitutes at the international level (Kempadoo and Doezema 1998; Matsui 1996; Skrobanek, Boonpakdi, and Janhakerro 1997). This opens up a new, relatively neglected area of migration studies concerning women, children, and illegal migrants as actors in the drama of internal and international migration (Ong et al. 1995).

Migration can be seen as a form of human agency by women that is induced by the process of social and economic transformation globally, nationally, and locally with the purpose of improving the family's survival odds and achieving personal empowerment (see Gilmartin and Tan in chapter 10). Janet Salaff (in chapter 11) points out that migration work is class-based and gendered and that women mediate between families and networks of friends and kin for resource mobilization and exchange. However, the migration process is contradictory and likely to produce both opportunities and vulnerabilities as well as positive and grave consequences for women and men (Cheng 1996; S. M. Lee 1996; Lim and Oishi 1996; Parreñas 2000; Shad and Menon 1997; Yeoh, Huang, and Gonzalez 1999). To begin with, social and cultural attitudes and perceptions concerning women's low social status and traditional reproductive role in the family, workplace, and society are such that women migrants often face gender bias and prejudice that may be different for men in both the sending and receiving countries. Except for professional and highly skilled workers, their relatively lower levels of education, fewer skills, and limited access to information make some women labor migrants more likely than men to rely on informal channels and sometimes illegal practices. Migrant women may fall victim to schemes in the labor recruitment process that force them into occupations that are not what they contracted to do, and they may face underemployment or become embroiled in human trafficking.[12] Women as migrants and foreigners also face labor markets segregated by gender, are isolated in often hostile social environments, work under poor or stressful conditions, have long working hours, are practically indentured to the workplace, have limited job prospects for security, and are subjected to physical abuse and even sexual violence (Shad and Menon 1997; see Lee in chapter 9). Labor migration does not necessarily increase the skills of the women or provide valuable work experience. Women's particular vulnerability to discrimination, exploitation, and abuse has received some policy attention by the governments of sending and receiving countries at the bilateral and multilateral levels, by female migrants themselves, and by nongovernmental organizations seeking to improve the protection, welfare, and human rights of migrant women.

Despite these demographic and social realities, the migration literature reveals more about the characteristics of migrant men, such as factors affecting their migration and its consequences, than about migrant women (INSTRAW 1994; S. M. Lee 1996).[13] The nature, magnitude, and complexity of Asian women's migration in recent times raise social issues and policy concerns that demand rigorous research and theory, to which this collection contributes, in order to advance a systematic understanding in this area. This poses a great challenge to scholars, researchers, practitioners, and policy advocates to explain why the three macro social forces—industrialization, economic restructuring, and migration—discussed above have occurred in response to globalization. Analyses are needed to examine how these forces have led to various pathways and processes of capitalist structural transformation and how their differential positive and negative consequences have profoundly impacted many diverse groups of which women are a part. Finally, good research goes hand in hand not only with a theoretical exploration of new paradigms to explain emergent demographic and social realities, but also with the pursuit of sound and effective policies and programs to address the practical implications of these macrosocial changes in the lives of women and men.

NOTES

1. In the case of the United States, postindustrial society began in the early 1950s (Bell 1956). Globalization of the economy as the result of economic restructuring and the internationalization of the division of labor in various parts of the world coincided with the deindustrialization of the U.S. from the 1970s to the mid-1980s.

2. Gereffi (1990) compared the paths, patterns, periodization, and consequences of different stages of industrialization between Taiwan and South Korea in East Asia and Mexico and Brazil in Latin America.

3. Hong Kong was ceded to the British as a crown colony in 1842 by the Nanking Treaty and remained a colony until 1997, when it became part of China. Singapore became a British crown colony in 1819 and gained political independence in 1965.

4. Because Great Britain as a colonizer had an economic interest at stake in the region, it focused on the infrastructure for economic rather than social development. Hong Kong, for example, did not have nine years of compulsory and free education for its school-aged children under Great Britain's governance until 1981.

5. Although both Hong Kong and Singapore concentrate on export-led manufacturing, Hong Kong relies more on labor-intensive industries such as electronics and garments, while Singapore concentrates more on the chemical and petroleum industries.

6. Whether regional integration constitutes the fourth wave is debatable. Some suggest that economic growth in Vietnam, Myanmar, and China comprises the fourth wave. Allan Findlay and colleagues (1998) argue that regional integration, while more developed than in the late 1960s, is not yet a clear trend. M. G. Quibria (1997) points out that labor integration in Asia is strictly a matter of degree, as is the case with capital market integration. Those writers (Hsiao 1997, Yeung 1999) who argue for the trend of regional integration examine the emergence of numerous so-called growth triangles such as the Southern China Growth Triangle including Taiwan, Hong Kong, and the provinces of Guangdong and Fujian; the JSR Growth Triangle of Johor (Malaysia), Singapore, and the Riau Islands (Indonesia); and the Tumen River Delta Growth Triangle that includes subregional cooperation among six countries (China, North Korea, Russia, Mongolia, South Korea, and Japan). These growth triangles are considered to be natural economic development zones that are basically characterized by geographical proximity, economic complementarity, and political commitment to providing adequate infrastructure to support this subregional cooperation.

7. For a short period from the mid-1970s to the early 1980s, South Korea even had an outflow of male contract workers, who were employed in the construction industry in the Middle East.

8. These figures include some proportion of migrants who remigrated to their countries of origin (e.g., in the case of Hong Kong in the early and mid-1990s).

9. See volume 7 (numbers 2–3) of the *Asian and Pacific Migration Journal* of 1998, which devotes a detailed discussion to Asian migration in a time of crisis in different East and Southeast Asian countries.

10. Note that these numbers were for legal migrants officially recorded as migrating for overseas employment. They do not include women who depart a country for reasons other than work or who enter a country illegally. If Asian women as illegal undocumented workers or aliens had been counted, the numbers would have been higher, but these women's numbers are hard to estimate and may not be accurate.

11. These skilled Asian women migrants originate not only from labor exporting coun-

tries, but also from Hong Kong, Singapore, Malaysia, and even Japan. They go to traditional immigration destinations such as North America and Europe but also to labor importing countries in East Asia and the Middle East.

12. P. Stalker's study (1994) found that 36 percent of Filipino women intending to migrate to work as domestic servants were either college graduates or undergraduates. (See global sex trade studies discussed by Kempadoo and Doezema 1998; Skrobanek et al. 1997).

13. The knowledge gap is contributed to by four main factors: limitations in migration theories, underestimation of women's economic activities and labor force contributions, a general neglect of women in scholarly social science research, and inadequacy in existing data on women's migration (INSTRAW 1994). Even though it was not that difficult to obtain updated statistics on migration flows in certain Asian countries, the data vary greatly by country with no breakdown by gender, making comparable evidence not readily available.

Chapter 2

Studying Development with Gender Perspectives
From Mainstream Theories to Alternative Frameworks

Esther Ngan-Ling Chow and Deanna M. Lyter

In this chapter, we seek explanations as to why and how gender is implicated in East Asia's complex and multifaceted development process and explore alternative ways of studying gender in East Asian development from the ground up. To attain these goals, we propose that three simultaneous projects (the first two were suggested by Mohanty in 1991) are needed: (1) feminist critiques of mainstream theories of development; (2) an internal critique of prevailing feminist thinking on gender and development; and (3) an exploration of an autonomous, indigenous, and inclusive body of situated, transformative knowledge specifically incorporating gender in East Asian development. While the first project strives to deconstruct and reformulate, the other two seek to re-envision and reconstruct. Each serves as a building block, offering the conceptual ideas and analytical tools required to establish a foundation to authenticate analyses of East Asian development through indigenous gender perspectives. These projects form the main underlying concerns of this chapter.

Consisting of five main parts, this chapter begins with a discussion of the definition, meaning, and measurement of development and then moves to a critical examination of how these definitions and meanings are contested and changed when viewed through a gender lens. In the second part, we discuss key mainstream theories used to explain East Asian capitalist and socialist development, followed by a feminist critique. The evolution of feminist perspectives in development with a special emphasis on the Global South feminist perspective is discussed in the third part.[1] In the fourth section, we incorporate gender perspectives in the study of East Asian development by distinguishing the major levels of gender analysis and examining the major themes addressed by all the studies in this volume. Lastly we discuss the development of an autonomous and indigenous gender studies in East Asian development. Key notions of gender equality, empowerment, and sustainability in development are intricately interwoven throughout this volume.

THE DEFINITION AND MEANING OF DEVELOPMENT

Conventionally, development is defined primarily in economic terms because nations are presumed to be in search of high rates of economic growth. The resulting economically based definition states that development is "the structural and behavioral changes that a society undergoes in the process of acquiring an industrial system of production or distribution" (Simone and Feraru 1995:12). Sharing this economic focus, the World Bank commonly uses gross national product (GNP) per capita to classify economies as "low-income," "middle-income," or "high-income" (World Bank 1993:xv). Likewise, in 1979 the Organization for Economic Cooperation and Development (OECD) adopted three criteria, primarily economic ones, to define a developing country as a newly industrialized economy (NIE) by using industrial employment, world export of manufactures, and real per capita of gross domestic product (GDP). And the United Nations uses a set of economic and population characteristics to make an objective assessment of the relative level of development (high developed countries, or HDCs, and less developed countries, or LDCs).

Proponents of a critical discourse in development, such as neo-Marxist and dependency theorists, have tried to redefine development by arguing that it means more than economic expansion, industrial productivity, and income (So 1990). Instead, development should improve the living standard of all people in the periphery, satisfying basic needs of urban dwellers, rural peasants, and the needy. The Brandt Commission of 1980 warned against the persistent confusion of growth with development, and the 1994 independent Commission on Population and the Quality of Life concluded that GNP proves to be an inadequate road map for the quality of life. Over time, the meaning of development has been broadened to include not only economic growth, but also improvement of living standards (Chowdhury and Islam 1993).

Critiques through a Gender Lens

Feminist scholars and practitioners have expanded the meaning of development to encompass improvements in human well-being and in the ability of people to achieve their potential (Weaver, Rock, and Kusterer 1997), as well as the social, economic, political, and cultural betterment of individuals and of society itself (Young 1992). For many, it means choices, self-determination, and the human ability to influence and control the environment, natural or social, as well as the process of change, in accordance with a given society's historical conditions, priorities, and capabilities. This broader meaning of development includes a healthy growing economy undergoing "a transformation of institutions, structures and relations that perpetuate injustice, inequality, and inequity" (Visanathan et al. 1998:29). Implied in this definition is that governance is effective, distribution is equitable, and the environment is preserved (Weaver et al. 1997:13).

A second change appears in the way that development is measured—both quantitative and qualitative tools are required to capture the gendered realities of the process. The Human Development Index (HDI) structured by the United Nations Development and Population (UNDP) Programme began in 1990 to use a simple composite index to compare average achievements in meeting the basic human needs of 174 countries. The *Human Development Report* (UNDP 1999) consistently points out that the relationship between economic prosperity and human development is neither automatic nor obvious. For example, the four "Asian dragons"—Hong Kong, South Korea, Singapore, and Taiwan—made the fastest progress between 1975 and 1997 when they were upgraded from a "medium" to a "high" level of human development. However, when the HDI ranks of Singapore and Hong Kong, two city-states, were subtracted from their real GDP per capita ranks, negative values emerged (–18 and –16 respectively) (see table 2.1). Taiwan followed a similar pattern, although its negative score was not as low (–2) as those for Singapore and Hong Kong.[2]

As Mahbubul Haq, the Special Advisor to the UNDP Administrator remarked, "Economic growth is necessary for human development. . . . But the purpose of development is to help people live longer, more productive and more fulfilling lives. This simple but powerful truth is too often forgotten in the pursuit of material and financial wealth. Economic growth that does not put people at its center is development without a soul."[3] Among the souls missing from traditional development analysis were women. Recognizing this, the UNDP began in 1995 to construct two measures—the Gender-Related Development Index (GDI) and the Gender Empowerment Index (GEI) to address this research issue and gap. Before we examine these indices comparatively in the region, we will discuss first the mainstream development theories that are applied to East Asian development and then provide a feminist critique.

Table 2.1. Human Development Index (HDI) and Real Gross Domestic Product (GDP) Per Capita in Six East Asian Countries (1997)

Country	HDI rank	HDI value	Real GDP per capita (ppp$)	GDP index	Real GDP per capita rank minus HDI Rank
Japan	4	0.924	24,070	0.92	5
Singapore	22	0.888	28,460	0.94	–18
Hong Kong, China (SAR)	24	0.880	24,350	0.92	–16
Republic of Korea	30	0.852	13,590	0.82	3
Taiwan[a]	23	0.874	19,197	—[b]	–2
China	98	0.701	3,130	0.57	6

Source: United Nations, *Human Development Report,* 1999.

[a] Taiwan data were from the Directorate-General of Budget, Accounting and Statistics, Executive Yuan, Republic of China (ROC), 2000 (http://www.dgbasey.gov.tw/dgbas03/STAT-N.HTM).

[b] No available data.

MAJOR THEORIES OF DEVELOPMENT

Why are some countries able to achieve sustainable development while others are not? What are the theoretical explanations for various pathways and differential degrees of development in the case of East Asia? Alvin So and Stephen Chiu (1995) have identified four major theories of development that are relevant to the study of East Asian development—the neoclassical/modernization, culturalist, statist, and dependency/world system theories.[4] We will summarize the main theoretical thrust of each one, explain how it is applied to East Asia development, and offer a general assessment.

Neoclassical Economy/Modernization Theories

Economists who speak in terms of the neoclassical and neoliberal perspective and sociologists who espouse the modernization theory of the 1970s share the same basic assumptions and tenets of the free market approach, which assumes that human beings act rationally in the pursuit of their self-interests and are guided by the principle of maximizing gain and minimizing cost and effort. These approaches also assume that a good society will be stable, promote efficiency, and offer freedom to ensure choices. The free labor market system operates through four mechanisms: (1) private ownership; (2) pursuit of land, labor, and capital; (3) markets for goods and services; and (4) maximization of profits. It is guided by the "invisible hand" of competitive market forces that bring about development. Proponents of the neoclassical perspective believe that short-term, efficient resource allocation (e.g., "getting the price right") to develop a comparative advantage is the key to rapid long-term growth (Wade 1992). Using a laissez-faire approach with limited intervention, government plays an important role in providing public goods, building, and infrastructure to facilitate economic production and trade.

Derived from the theory of social evolution, modernization theory assumes that all societies eventually develop through a linear and progressive series of complex social processes as they move from industrialization to urbanization and, finally, to modernization. Modern societies emphasize free markets and manufacturing, have a rational bureaucratic organization, and are characterized as urban, individualistic, achievement-oriented, and industrialized. In contrast traditional societies have agricultural economies, and are rural, collectivistic, ascriptive-oriented, and kinship-based. The implication is that traditional institutions, values, and practices inhibit economic development. The less developed countries should follow the industrialized West to transform their economic, political, social, and cultural institutions, values, and practices, expecting the potential of the free market economy to raise living standards in poor countries and to modernize their states. Through foreign direct investment, production, marketing, and trade on a global scale, the economy will experience a takeoff stage, and people will share in this growth and reap the benefits of development.

In analyzing the East Asian NIEs, Bela Balassa (1988) points out that export-oriented industrialization in the region has accounted for rising GDP growth rates. He observed four determinants of the NIEs' high economic performance: a stable incentive system, limited government intervention, well-functioning labor and capital markets, and reliance on private capital. What is missing from this neoclassical perspective is a critical examination of the impact of TNCs, interstate systems, and regional dynamics on East Asian development (So and Chiu 1995). Modernization theory fails to acknowledge that there are different pathways to development that may not be linear and that are sometimes country- and culture-specific. Other serious criticisms include its implication of Third World "backwardness" and its failure to acknowledge the detrimental effects of colonialism and imperialism. Neo-Marxist critics, among others, have also condemned modernization advocates for ignoring the exploitation of less developed countries by industrialized ones. The general consensus among scholars is that neither the neoclassical economic perspective nor modernization theory applied well to East Asian countries that did not follow the incremental course presumed to have characterized the West.

The Cultural Perspective

In the 1980s, the cultural perspective emerged to supplement rather than to challenge the neoclassical economic interpretation and modernization theory. It aimed to offer researchers and policymakers a frame of reference within which to view how values, ideology, attitudes, and practices have influenced development policy, institutional arrangements, and the state's role in implementing policy. Cultural values and beliefs also set limits on and shape patterns of development. Unlike modernization theorists, proponents of this perspective treat tradition and modernity not as mutually exclusive, but as co-existing and intermingling.

What the economically high-performing countries in East Asia have in common is the predominantly Confucian-based culture that originated in China and was imported to Japan, Korea, and other parts of Asia. While Western scholars in the Weberian tradition see the Protestant work ethic as having given birth to the capitalist spirit, So and Chiu (1995) point out that Confucian values have promoted education and self-improvement through deferred gratification, intensive study, and the internalization of ethical principles. Confucianism also endorsed the collective orientation and familialism that gave rise to an entrepreneurial spirit and skills, the backbone of East Asian economic success. This religious and cultural orientation, or philosophical principle as some have called it, shaped a new pattern of personalistic corporate management that is different from the Western rational, formal, and bureaucratic one and that created a favorable public attitude to government services. The cultural theory offers an explanation for the transnational economic role the Chinese play in terms of capital investment, entrepreneurship, and business systems in fueling growth not only in East Asia, but also in other countries in the Asia-Pacific region (Redding 1993).

While there is some validity in the cultural interpretation, doubt emerges as to whether culture can be the sole causal factor, especially since it creates contradictions. Confucianism has been a handicap as well as a contributor to development in the region, and non-Confucian countries in Southeast Asia have exhibited similar patterns of development. In sum, the cultural theory generally fails to examine specific historical contexts, the timing of the Confucian impact, and geopolitical conditions through which different forms of Confucianism emerged or failed to emerge in Asian countries (So and Chiu 1995). Finally, the impact that culture has on the gender dimension has yet to be examined.

The Statist Perspective

Emerging as a critique of the neoclassical perspective and modernization, the statist perspective pointedly argues that economic power cannot function effectively outside of the framework of politics provided by the state. Instead of emphasizing free markets, trade liberalization, private enterprise, and a noninterventionist state, the statist perspective attributes economic success to the developmental-oriented state. Because the strong state is politically autonomous from partisan domestic interests, it can provide economic leadership and administrative guidance for market decisions in the private sector and can facilitate global opportunities for economic expansion (Johnson 1982; Simone and Feraru 1995). In particular, the statist perspective focuses on "late industrialization" in which the state intervenes as an economic newcomer to overcome market imperfections and industrial stagnation (Rueschemeyer and Evans 1985). Recent research from the statist perspective (e.g., Onis 1991; Evans 1995) has broadened its concerns by centering on the complex interactions of the state, market, and institutions and addressing which set of social and political institutions is compatible with what mixture of market forces and state interventions.

The capability of a development-oriented state is, moreover, specific to each nation and region. Lai Si Tsui-Auch (2000) points out that the World Bank's 1993 study of the East Asian "miracle" fails to recognize the complementarity between the state and the market, a position that the Bank later revised. She explains,

> The state capability to direct industrial development and to suppress the interests of opposing classes in the case of Taiwan and South Korea [and Singapore and China as well] is attributed to a combination of national and geo-political factors: the felt need to guard against communist penetration; the U.S. provision of massive military and economic aid; the relatively favorable post–World War II global trade regimes; the Japan-led product cycle; and the changing class-state relations. (2000:12)

Particularly in "late development," states are called upon to formulate and implement strategic industrial policies to promote development and to offset disadvantages faced by East Asian firms in international competition in order to make the NIEs' industrial structure more technologically dynamic (Deyo 1987; So and Chiu 1995). While the neoclassical economic perspective is used to justify free markets, investment, and trade, the statist perspective is used defensively by some East Asian states and their apparatuses to justify protectionism and intervention in the economy and society. However, the statist perspective is politically and ideologically driven to support authoritative regimes and ignore the adverse effects of their governance (i.e., inefficiency, corruption, and militarization) and industrialization (i.e., repression of organized labor, human rights violations, and environmental degradation). Yayori Matsui (1996:173) characterizes Asia's state during rapid economic growth as "development dictatorship." An ongoing debate about the state versus market forces is whether the development-oriented state is, in fact, a sufficient condition for sustainable development.

An important fact is that East Asia is not quite as internally homogeneous historically, culturally, and institutionally as has commonly been assumed. Rather, the region is a heterogeneous and diverse one that cannot be reduced to a single model of political economy or development. What is needed, as Meredith Woo-Cumings (1999) has articulated so well, is to fundamentally re-examine the assumptions and frameworks of East Asian growth to convey a sense of time and place in the region. Therefore, it is critical to bring in historical contexts, colonial legacy, geopolitical factors, nationalism, institutions, and regional dynamics to explain the origins and expansion of the development-oriented state to understand where its political autonomy, leadership, and state capacity come from and how it was cultivated. However, the relationship between gender and the state is yet to be systematically examined.

Dependency/World System Theories

Responding critically to the neoclassical economic and modernization perspectives, both the dependency and the world system theories view the process of development within the world context. Both emphasize the concept of power and domination because different nations have different resources and power. Derived from neo-Marxist theories of class domination, dependency theory offers an external explanation of the causes and problems of developing countries such as those in Latin America and Africa (Frank 1967; Rodney 1981). More specifically, this theory examines relationships between the powerful "core" nations and the developing nations on the periphery, relationships that are primarily based on unequal exchange, foreign domination, and economic exploitation. Imperialism has worked to the advantage of rich nations and to the disadvantage of poor ones, systematically underdeveloping the Third World so that it will serve the needs and interests of the former and depleting its resources, both natural and human. The economic overdependency of Third World countries has its roots in their colonization and the practices of TNCs, gradually leading to uneven economic development in different parts of the world. This theory is pessimistic about the future direction of development in the periphery, predicting that it will face further economic backwardness and underdevelopment unless it can free itself from links with the core.

World system theory argues that since the 16th century, the capitalist world system has continued until it now incorporates almost all countries of the world in a complex system of functional relationships. The world system is an economic network that links the noncommunist nations of the world into a single socio-economic unit that works independently of the political systems of the nation-state (Wallerstein 1979). It has three hierarchies and a geographically stratified division of labor among the core, semiperiphery, and periphery. Countries at the periphery provide raw materials to and purchase imported goods and technology know-how from the core countries that, in turn, determine the unequal terms of trade that continue to place the former in a state of dependence and underdevelopment. Moreover, a small number of countries at the semiperiphery serve as buffers between the core and the periphery. They are examples of mobility within the capitalist world system, moving up and down on the development ladder.

While dependency theory tends to see problems of development from the bottom up, world system theory bases its view from the center and regards the role of TNCs and commodity chains as central. The original formulation of these theories did not envision the positive impact of the development-oriented state and domestic capital. However, the ability of the four "Asian dragons" to move into the semiperiphery through the means of strong states capable of mediating between national efforts and global opportunities challenges these theories and requires their further modification (as in the "dependent development" thesis formulated by Cardoso and Faletto 1979). At the same time, the high-speed development of East Asia, perhaps a short-term phenomenon as some have speculated, has caused concern among many scholars because of the dependency of this development on foreign capital and markets and because trade with the economically hegemonic West and Japan is bound to cause problems in the long run. W. Bello and S. Rosenfeld (1990) identify as crises facing the Asian NIEs "the sluggishness of key exports, mounting inflation, faltering growth rates, working-class insurrection, capital flight, and environmental pollution" (So and Chiu 1995). Folker Fröbel and colleagues (1980), the international division of labor theorists, also point out that the transnationalization of assembly processes from TNCs to peripheral countries brought about limited technological transference, skill formation, and knowledge that have not uplifted the developing countries, let alone freed them from dependency and underdevelopment.

Feminist Critiques

Even if we accept that theories of development are gender-*neutral,* as some contend, we must add that the four development perspectives being applied to East Asia are mostly gender-*blind.* Much of the theoretical analysis of the political economy sheds light on the development vision and issues of East Asia and provides signposts for explaining its success and current crisis. Yet, profound as these theories are, significant gender dimensions embedded in the development structure and process are virtually ignored. We offer here seven feminist[5] critiques: the persistence of gender inequality, the sustainability of development, the preponderance of the masculine standpoint and structure of domination, the hegemony of the developmental state, traditional values and gender ideology, the public versus the private sphere, and the neglect of women's agency. We review each of these below.

First, the persistence of gender inequality is not new and yet remains mostly unrecognized and untouched by developmental theorists and analysts, especially those considering the East Asian region. The *Human Development Report* (UNDP 1995) shows that a staggering sixteen trillion dollars is missing from the global economy each year because the value of women and men's unpaid work and the underpayment of women's work in the market are not recognized. Eleven trillion of these dollars represents the invisible contribution of women in unpaid work as reported in economic statistics.[6] The undervaluation of women's work lowers the real value of the national product, undermines women's purchasing power, curtails their rights to own property and land and to acquire credit from financial institutions, and reduces their already low social status.

As previously mentioned, the Gender-Related Development Index (GDI) and the Gender Empowerment Index (GEI) were constructed by the UNDP to capture achievement in basic human development after being adjusted for gender inequality.[7] The closer a country's GDI is to its Human Development Index (HDI), the less gender disparity there is in the country. If the GDI is lower than the HDI, then achievements in human development have not been equally distributed between men and women and an unequal process of building women's capabilities compared to men's is implied. Data in table 2.2 give a 1997 comparison of GDI with HDI and real GDP by gender in six East Asian countries.

UNDP results generally show that greater gender equality depends neither on income level nor on the stage of development of a country. For example, among

Table 2.2. Comparison of Gender-Related Development Index (GDI) with Human Development Index (HDI) and Real Gross Domestic Product (GDP) Per Capita in Six East Asian Countries (1997)

Country	Gender-Related Development Index (GDI)		HDI rank minus GDI rank	Life expectancy at birth (years)		Adult literacy rate (%)		Gross enrollment ratio (%)		Real GDP per capita (ppp$)		
	Rank	Value		Female	Male	Female	Male	Female	Male	Female	Male	Ratio[b]
Japan	8	0.917	-4	82.9	76.8	99.0	99.0	83	86	14,625	33,893	2.32
Singapore	22	0.883	0	79.3	74.9	87.0	95.9	71	74	18,947	37,833	2.00
Hong Kong, China (SAR)	24	0.875	0	81.4	75.8	88.4	96.1	67	64	15,180	32,688	2.15
Republic of Korea	30	0.845	-1	76.0	68.8	95.5	98.9	84	94	8,388	18,708	2.23
Taiwan[a]	23	0.870	0	77.8	71.9	91.1	98.1	87	84	11,659	24,130	2.07
China	79	0.699	2	72.0	67.9	74.5	90.8	67	71	2,485	3,738	1.50

Source: United Nations, *Human Development Report,* 1999.

[a] Taiwan data were from the Directorate-General of Budget, Accounting and Statistics, Executive Yuan, Republic of China, 2000 (http://www.dgbasey.gov.tw/dgbas03/STAT-N.HTM)

[b] Computed by the author, Chow.

the six East Asian countries, Japan, which ranked relatively high on both real GDP and human development, has a score of –4 when the GDI rank is subtracted from the HDI rank; the Republic of Korea shows a similar pattern.[8] Although women generally have a longer life expectancy than men, other measures of GDI show a gender gap in adult literacy rates and gross enrollment ratios.[9]

The Gender Empowerment Measure (GEM) measures gender inequality in three key areas of economic and political participation and decision making, focusing on women's opportunities rather than on their capabilities as measured in the GDI. The GEM ranks for Japan, Singapore, and the Republic of Korea dropped significantly from their GDI and HDI rankings, while the GEM ranks for Taiwan and China were elevated noticeably (see tables 2.2 and 2.3).[10] The lower percentages of "seats in parliament held by women" caused the GEM rankings of the former group of countries to fall, whereas higher percentages of the same indicator contributed to the increased GEM rankings of the latter group. Note that the lower percentage of "female administrators and managers" factored significantly into the low rankings of both Japan and the Republic of Korea. Although the gender-related measures devised by the UNDP in tables 2.2 and 2.3 are more general than specific, they allow comparability of gender inequality politically and economically across countries in the East Asian region.

The second focus of feminist concern is on the extent to which East Asian development is now being and can continue to be sustained. Contrary to the glorification of the East Asian economic miracle, some scholars have drawn attention to the deep-seated problems causing distress and crisis in the region (e.g., Fröbel et al. 1980; Bello and Rosenfeld 1990). The 1997 financial crisis that swept destructively across Southeast Asia (primarily in Thailand and Indonesia and, to a lesser extent, in Malaysia and the Philippines) and South Korea exposed dangerous weaknesses in regional development and the global trade economy.

Table 2.3. Comparison of Gender Empowerment Measure (GEM) in Five East Asian Countries (1997)

Country	Gender empowerment Index (GEI) Rank	Value	Seats in parliament held by women (as % of total)	Female administrators and managers (as % of total)	Female professional and technical workers (as % of total)
Japan	38	0.494	8.9	9.3	44.1
Singapore	32	0.512	4.8	34.3	16.1
Republic of Korea	78	0.336	3.7	4.2	45.0
Taiwan[a]	17	0.558	14.8	14.1	42.4
China	40	0.491	21.8	11.6	45.1

Source: United Nations, *Human Development Report*, 1999.

[a] Taiwan data were from the Directorate-General of Budget, Accounting and Statistics, Executive Yuan, Republic of China, 2000 (http://www.dgbasey.gov.tw/dgbas03/STAT-N.HTM).

The crisis shook the complacency of the development field and alerted it to examine the setbacks, stagnation, and recovery of regional economies.

The evidence shows that women, especially the youngest and oldest, were more severely affected than men, with a greater percentage of women experiencing layoffs, unemployment, falling wages, and poverty (International Labour Organization 1998; USAID 2000). To take South Korea as an example, between April 1997 and 1998, women workers suffered the worst of the crisis-induced job losses; while employment fell 3.8 percent for men, it fell 7.1 percent for women. Employment rates for those in the 15 to 19 age bracket dropped 8.7 percent for men, but 20.2 percent for women; among those in the 55 and older bracket, the rate fell 6.3 percent for men and 14.1 percent for women (USAID 2000). The impact of the Asian financial crisis on women and men and its implication for the sustainability of development urgently need to be systematically and empirically investigated. This directly leads to the following questions: To what extent do theories of development as applied to the study of East Asia reflect gendered realities, experiences, and outcomes of development in the region? How do feminist scholars, researchers, and practitioners respond to these theories?

The third critique is that theories and empirical studies of East Asia's development primarily reflect masculine standpoints and the structure of male domination by muting women's voices, devaluing their worth, and subjugating their position to men's. The definitions, concepts, tenets, and language used in each theoretical discourse are interwoven with masculine meanings and viewpoints and male preoccupations in societal construction and development. Areas in which women are studied and gender is mentioned usually include labor force participation, labor subordination, and the household domain. Yet, even when labor is a topic of concern, reference is usually limited to abstract, universal workers and managers appear genderless. Just as the dominant theories in development are ethnocentric, or biased toward the West, and androcentric, or biased toward men, so are the development policies and practices that are guided by these theories (Chow and Berheide 1994; Jackson and Pearson 1998; Visanathan et al. 1998).

In re-reading modernization and dependency theories, Catherine Scott (1995) discovers that these theories make no explicit reference to gender as a fundamental category of analysis, but are deeply anchored in the social construction of gender differences and display a deep sense of gendered structure. As radical as Marxist and dependency theorists are, they also fail to challenge implicit gender assumptions, elaborating instead on ideas of modernity, development, class domination, colonialism self-reliance, and revolution. World system theory also excludes women/gender as a central construction (Ward 1993) by ignoring the centrality of women's labor to the functioning of the world system, assuming women are only incorporated into households through reproduction and not directly into the world system, and overlooking women's active roles in and resistance to the process of incorporation. A male definition of work has been imposed on women's socioeconomic participation, excluding household labor, home-based production, and the informal labor market in which women as well as other family members makes significant contributions.

The fourth critique is that by focusing on the internal operation of the national economy, the statist perspective fails to acknowledge that the state has many faces. As far as gender is concerned, the state is a public form of patriarchy and embodies a hegemonic masculinity that presumes the values of rationality, detachment, power, and control. It is a gendered institution based on unequal power relationships, giving men authority and control over women. Any state, be it socialist or capitalist, is capable of being either benevolent or violent. In the name of development, the state and its ruling class can impose laws and policies, taking responsibility for affirming the positive human rights of women (e.g., property rights, labor's right to organize) and preventing their violation (e.g., gender-based violence and the trafficking of women; see Lederman and Chow 1996).

Fifth, contrary to development scholars who see Confucian culture as contributing positively to capitalist development, feminist thinking questions whether this religious and cultural tradition has been used to justify the male status quo, women's subordination, and the gendered division of labor.[10] Confucian culture gives patriarchy (meaning that the state is a public form of patriarchy and the family is a private form) an ideological base by justifying the paternalistic authority structure and power relationships that privilege men and subjugate women, especially younger ones. Filial piety as a patriarchal script, although somewhat eroded now, has been used to glorify the three centuries-old principles of women's obedience—obey one's father before marriage, obey one's husband after marriage, and obey one's son while growing old. This lays a foundation of gender ideology that buttresses patriarchal institutions, defines rights and entitlements (such as lineage, residence, inheritance, bride price), prescribes proper roles for women and men, and extorts loyalty from them within the family and kinship system. It affects the degree to which women have access to and control over resources to engage in economic activities (e.g., getting credit for enterprises and saving money for investment) and the extent to which they can bargain with patriarchy (Kandiyoti 1988). It also shapes the division of labor by gender in both the private and public spheres, limiting the extent to which women participate in and attach to the labor market, the kinds of jobs they do, and the wages and/or other benefits they receive.

Sixth, feminist critics and practitioners challenge the dualistic thinking that connects women with the private and men with the public sphere and that underlies development theories. This private/public dichotomy dominating Western thought tends to portray women mostly as homemakers inhabiting the private domain of the household and engaging in reproductive work, while men are assumed to be the breadwinners, occupying the public domain of the economy and politics and doing productive work. This dichotomy does not accurately reflect the realities of women and men in many parts of the world. Compelling evidence shows work and family are intricately intertwined in the lives of women and men, from those laboring in the subsistence and cash-cropping economies in rural areas to urban dwellers working for pay in various industrial sectors. As women actively increase their participation in the labor force in both industrialized and developing nations, work and family in their lives impinge on each other. Gender assumptions about the nature of and split between public and private spheres for women are subjected to a system of domination based not only on gender but also on race, ethnicity, class, sexuality, nationality, age/generation, and disability.

The last feminist critiques is that conventional theories of development generally fail to see either women or workers as social, dependent actors and as being capable of resisting blatant discriminatory treatments, negotiating with unfair employers, and bargaining with patriarchy. Global forces of economic, political, and cultural domination are produced and sustained by different local practices of domination. It takes an organized effort by women to engage in resistance and grassroots movements to subvert local practices of domination and to connect to women's movements that can destabilize global power structures. Under the control of the development-oriented state that suppresses organized labor, workers are rarely able to engage in large-scale union movements. This has given a false impression to outside observers that they are necessarily passive, obedient, mindless victims of capitalist exploitation. Although most labor struggles have been strongly suppressed, union activists have joined forces with radical factions against the state and TNCs in some countries. The involvement of women workers in Hong Kong's union strikes of the early 1950s and union-organized labor struggles in the late 1980s are yet to be documented.[11] Union strikes took place in the late 1980s in Taiwan, but in South Korea labor movements were more noticeable during that decade. The fact is that ongoing struggle and resistance by women workers is commonplace in East Asia as they negotiate and fight for a wide range of issues and concerns (Committee for Asian Workers 1995; Matsui 1996).[12]

In sum, the interrogation of development to include the perspectives of gender is a critical task for those who are interested in East Asian development. It should be a feminist project of paramount importance to reread the major development theories in light of new questions and changing conditions, critiquing their doctrines and examining what is omitted or concealed in the text. In view of the theoretical pitfalls discussed above, there is a great need to move beyond the macropolitical economy to understand the East Asian region as one fraught with inequality, heterogeneity, dynamism, and struggles derived from different hierarchies of inequality—especially those of gender. Meanwhile, a simultaneous project to critique feminist thinking and practice in the field of women/gender and development is in order.

SHIFTING THEORETICAL PARADIGMS TO INCLUDE WOMEN AND GENDER IN DEVELOPMENT STUDIES

In the last section, we began the first project of inquiring into the applicability of dominant development theories to East Asia by using a feminist lens to uncover Western, racial/ethnic, gender, and class biases in the assumptions, concepts, and analysis of the theories, to identify gaps in gender knowledge, and to discuss mainstream gender issues. This section focuses on the second project—the internal critique of feminist thinking, which embarks on a series of successive queries beginning with the incorporation of women's standpoints into development theory and practice. In the industrialized West, or Global North, the incorporation of women in the field of development began over three decades ago with Ester Boserup's pathbreaking book *Women's Role in Economic Development*, published in 1970. The intersection of development studies and women's studies has shifted the theoretical paradigm from women's issues to gender concerns. We will provide a general overview of three changing perspectives with critiques of Western feminism and then discuss a recently developed Global South feminist perspective from which this chapter is derived.

From Women in Development to Gender and Development

Eva Rathgeber (1990) outlines a general framework that represents mainstream feminist debates and discourses on development which are informed by experiential knowledge gained in the field and which incorporate ongoing critiques and current issues as each approach has evolved. This framework consists of three perspectives: women in development (WID), women and development (WAD), and gender and development (GAD).[13] As a policy response to Boserup's concern that women had been left out of development programs, WID represents the Western liberal feminist view that modernization has not trickled down to benefit women and in some sectors has even undermined their social positions (see Bandarage 1984; Scott 1995). WID portrays modern societies as egalitarian and democratic and traditional societies as male-dominated and authoritarian ones that discriminate against women. To solve these problems, women need to be integrated into the economic system and processes through legal reform, education, technology, and income-generating activities. Therefore, women should be factored into development policies, planning, programs, and practices (Moser 1993).

WID has made women's questions visible in theory and practice by advocating for disaggregated data by gender and mainstreaming women's issues into development agencies (Jahan 1995). Yet this perspective challenges neither the problematic notion of development nor the Western biases forming the premise of modernization theory. It characterizes Third World women's conditions as necessarily detrimental, seeks strategies to minimize their disadvantages in the economic sector, and reduces their problems to an oversight by development agencies. Relatively speaking, it tends to focus more on the productive than reproductive aspects of women's lives and it does not stress structural change that would uproot the sources of women's oppression (Visanathan et al. 1998).

Drawing from Marxist and dependency theories, WAD emerged in the latter half of the 1970s from a critique of modernization theory and the WID perspective. Proponents of this approach point out that a lack of economic integration as perceived by WID advocates is not a key question because women have always been part of development. As subsistence economies turned into capitalist economies, the production of goods for direct use was replaced by production for exchange. This shift tends to benefit men more than women. For Marxist feminists, capitalism has produced an oppressive society for the working class, including women, because they are treated like commodities, a part of the wealth and resources controlled by a few. Women's problems will only be resolved when capitalism and the class structure are abolished. Going one step farther, feminists who embraced dependency theory consider the inequality between women and men as part of the workings of the larger global economy caused by capitalist accumulation on a world scale. Existing global structures of inequality based on class domination, imperialism, and the recolonization of the Third World by First World nations affect women. Of particular concern is the exploitative relationship between Third World women and TNCs based in First World countries.

WAD advocates generally place a greater emphasis on classism than sexism, seeing gender inequality as part of class inequality perpetuated by the culprit of capitalism. They do not see gender relations as problematic, downplaying men's roles in women's oppression. As a result, the relationships between different modes of production and patriarchy leading to subordination and oppression of women are not fully examined by the WAD approach. Its proponents generally base their arguments on the shaky assumption that once the international structures become more equitable, women's positions will be improved. They tend to see women's problems as independent of men's. They also focus exclusive concern on women's productive role and give scant attention to their reproductive role in the household.

Representing the convergence of various feminist views, the GAD perspective emerged in the 1980s to challenge the inadequate explanations of women's subordination in WID's liberal feminism and WAD's exclusive focus on class analysis to account for women's oppression. GAD offers a holistic approach to include all aspects of women's lives and sees development as a complex process influenced by political and socioeconomic forces (Young 1992). It does not focus just on women, but on gender as a set of social relationships between women and men in both the production of the labor market and the reproduction of the household. It recognizes women's contribution inside and outside of the household, including both the formal and informal sectors. In other words, GAD deconstructs the public/private dichotomy, uncovering women's oppression in the family. Special attention is given by socialist feminists, a major force in GAD, to both the importance of patriarchy operating within and across classes to oppress women and the role of the state to provide social programs promoting women's emancipation. Seeing women as agents of social change rather than as recipients of development programs, GAD advocates acknowledge women's concern with economic independence, stress political activism, and strategize agendas for community organizing, coalition building, and collective action for empowerment and effective social change.

In general, GAD provides a rich context in which to understand women's issues in the context of gender relations and to view men as potential supporters of women. Visanathan and colleagues (1998) point out that development planners and practitioners are taking the lead in creating a framework of gender analysis, planning, and training for better resources (e.g., power and land) assessment and allocation in households, farms, and communities. Oxfam (the Oxford Committee for Famine Relief) is leading in this effort to bring a focus of gender where designing and implementing their projects. GAD as well as the WID and WAD perspectives are prompted mostly by researchers and practitioners from the Global North working along with some groups and individuals from the Third World. In the mid and late 1980s and early 1990s, new feminist perspectives emanated as an alternate vision and model of development to offer indigenous voices from the Global South.[14]

Global South Feminist Perspectives

In critiquing the ethnocentric and androcentric views, modern values, and presumptive superior positioning of Western traditions, liberal or radical, in development studies and feminist frameworks from the Global North, some Third World feminists have proposed alternative perspectives and strategies for development.[15] One foremost advocate is a research network called DAWN (Development Alternatives with Women for a New Era), which formed in 1984. In their influential work for DAWN, Gita Sen and Caren Grown (1987) point out that the socioeconomic status of the great majority of Third World women had worsened during the U.N. Decade for Women (1976–85) and that the benefits of development have not trickled down to poor people, especially women. According to DAWN, development should start with the perspective of poor women as the most vulnerable group living in the margin where alternative visions are generated. Their viewpoints support the belief that development practices have not adequately addressed this group's needs and interests and are thus blind spots in development analyses, policies, and programs that needed to be reoriented. Self-definition is therefore a key ingredient to alternative development theories and political action.

DAWN's vision is grounded in diverse feminisms and is responsive to the varied needs and issues of women, as defined by women from different societies, times, and cultures. It challenges the monolithic notion of woman and sees gender relations that are compounded by race, class, ethnicity, and nation as being intricately linked to the specific oppression of women. This point was also echoed by Chandra T. Mohanty and her colleagues (1991) in their critiques of Western feminist discourse that constructs "Third World women" as singular, monolithic subjects with a shared oppression and interest and as powerless victims of economic development. They prefer the term "Third World" to "Global South," because the latter consists of a variety of feminisms and discourses on development of which East Asia is a constitutive part (Alexander and Mohanty 1997; Heng 1997).[16] They also point out that Western and white liberal feminist scholars often describe Third World women in conjunction with backwardness, underdevelopment, oppressive traditions, high illiteracy, rural and urban poverty, religious fanaticism, and overpopulation. They offer radical critiques that shed light on how masculine, racialized, class-based, and Western-oriented cultures and structures determine the subjugated position of Third World women, silence their voices, and blur their standpoints in development studies.

As Sen and Grown (1987:20) put it, "Our vision of feminism has at its very core a process of economic and social development geared to human needs through wider control over and access to economic and political power." There is an urgent need to develop and advocate alternative development frameworks, methods, and processes to follow this vision of economic and social development for equality, peace, and justice that is free of all forms of oppression. The Global South feminist framework links macrolevel phenomena such as development and debt crises to microlevel activities and women's lives (Sen and Grown 1987). The struggle of women from the Global South should be understood within the socio-historical context of each country's experience under political, economic, social, and cultural domination by imperialism, colonialism, and neocolonialism, against "a background of national struggles aimed at achieving political independence, asserting a national identity, and modernizing society" (Jayawardena 1994:ix). Peggy Antrobus, the coordinator of DAWN, insists that these perspectives, though varied by country and region, should be holistic in order to integrate social, political, and cultural dimensions into economic analysis (Mosse 1994). Antrobus insightfully points out that the political factors in development that cause underdevelopment lie not merely in access to resources, but in the power imbalances among nations in the political and economic world order. She also suggests that experiences at the microlevel of the community and household should be used to inform macrolevel policies and vice versa, connecting public with private domains, family with economy, and personal with political realities.

The Global South feminist perspectives also stress the importance of both *practical* and *strategic* gender needs and interests, phrases coined by Maxine Molyneux (1985) to differentiate immediate needs for daily provisions from the long-term needs of women as a social group to tackle the structural roots of unequal access to resources and control. These concepts are useful when engaging in transformative politics that start with the everyday life experiences and problems faced by Third World women. Addressing strategic gender interests requires analysis focused on the origins, structures, and processes of women's subordination and inequality and how the processes of change have affected women's consciousness, bringing about their own changes in development. One of the important goals of Global South perspective is the structural transformation of an oppressive society by eliminating gender subordination and all forms of oppression, improving living standards, establishing socially responsible management of resource allocation and usage, and organizing for better change. Short-term strategies are to enhance women's opportunities and participation by increasing their share in resources, land, employment, and income relative to men. These should be accompanied by "long-term systematic strategies aimed at challenging prevailing structures and building accountability of governments to people for their decisions," an increase in women's control over economic decisions, a guarantee that women's voices are entered into the definition of development and the making of policy choices, a cut in military expenditures, demilitarization, control over TNCs, and land reform in rural areas (Sen and Grown 1987:82–86).

Sen and Grown have popularized the term *empowerment* to underscore the human agency of women as social actors to change unequal gender power relations through individual and collective challenges to patriarchal rules and resistance to oppressive conditions. Empowerment is associated with a bottom-up rather than a top-down approach, emphasizing self-reliance and internal strength to transform structures and to work for better change. While recognizing the need for legislative support, Sen and Grown advocate self-empowerment by using grassroots women's organizations as forums to raise consciousness, to offer popular education, to articulate the concerns and voices of diverse people and particularly poor women, to mobilize the masses politically, and to impact policy and legal change, leading from personal to structural transformation through collective action. DAWN also works with international movements of women and the oppressed. Now, many women's groups have actively engaged in diverse kinds of grassroots activism, coalition building, networking, and organizing, linking local and international women's movements (Basu 1995). Kabeer (1994) states that the key achievement of the Women's Decade has been the opening of political spaces for the proliferation of grassroots groups, despite the small size and disparate nature of some, and of nationwide movements for improving the conditions and positions of women. She asserts that women's collective strength, creativity, and empowerment remain the main hope for transformative politics.

Inspired by Global South feminist perspectives, we challenge the conventional knowledge of East Asian development to redirect theory, research, and teaching and practices, by including women's and gender-based concerns and by explicitly recognizing macro social changes and their linkages to the microlevel of social relations and personal life. The Global South feminist perspectives give voice to social actors whose gendered identities, interests, and subjectivities provide clues to their behavior and strategies that are constitutive and transformative of societal development. These perspectives offer a critical viewpoint for examining some of the gender paradoxes in development from the indigenous experiences of East Asian women and men who are situated on the semiperiphery and periphery of the world system. The agency and empowerment of women are adequately addressed in the scholarly literature on East Asian development. Hence, the analysis of such development represents one of the critical dimensions within the Global South feminist perspectives for systematically studying gender relations, institutional transformation, and social change.

ENGENDERING EAST ASIAN DEVELOPMENT

The distinctive feature of this book is its emphasis on the salience and centrality of key gender dimensions in three fundamental macroforces—industrialization, economic restructuring, and migration—that are at work transforming social institutions, gender relations, and people's lives in the global and changing contexts of East Asia. In the last two sections of this chapter, we explore ways to conceptualize an inconclusive, indigenous, and transformative body of knowledge that is grounded in relational, historical, and comparative analyses with gender perspectives in the study of East Asian development. We first define the meaning of gender and its complexity at different levels of analysis. We examine how the contributors make macro-micro linkages at these levels to women and gender in the development process. We then identify three main themes derived from the collection of studies in this volume and draw out these connections between the chapters. Linking the local with the global, we lastly present an ideal to authenticize an indigenous study of gender and development in East Asia.

Gender, as a social construction, is a central category in the analysis of relationships. As Joan W. Scott (1988:42) defines it, "Gender is a constitutive element of social relationships based on perceived differences between the sexes, and gender is a primary way of signifying relationships of power." Gender is relational and social; hence the focus of gender is not on women per se but on gender relations between women and men and among those of the same gender in a variety of settings.[17] It also concerns perceived gender differences, which often signify and enact an unequal and hierarchical power relationship between women and men. Relational analysis helps to problematize the dominant category of masculinity that depends on women as the subordinate "others" in order to buttress the existing gender order and male status quo and seeks to understand how power relations affect the unequal access, control, and distribution of values, resources, and justice. Making power relations the focus of analysis draws on the complex and fluid processes through which women and men negotiate over choices and dilemmas, which are perceived differently by women and men in varying positions and stages of the life cycle.

Gender can be conceptualized as both a process and a structure (Ferree, Lorber, and Hess 1999). On the one hand, gender is a dynamic process, which Candace West and Don Zimmerman (1987) coined the term "doing gender" and which we will here call the *process of genderization*; this means that perceived differences between men and women are socially constructed through human interaction in everyday life. If the process of development is gendered, then an active process of genderization is taking place, constructing fluid gender characteristics as opposed to static ones (e.g., women's work as caring for people and men's work as the production of things) and leading to differential outcomes for women and men. Gender is not seen as a permanent result of early socialization, but as a lifelong process in which people construct, deconstruct, and then reconstruct the meaning, discourse, and accomplishment of gendering. The processes of engendering, degendering, and regendering are constantly evolving in everyday practices and interactions. On the other hand, gender becomes a structure when a variety of gender relationships are institutionalized in the social system, thus forming the basis for gender hierarchy, inequality, and order in society. We argue that gender is embedded in social structures and shapes social processes and is, in turn, influenced by them, with consequences that have implications for women, men, and gender relations. Gender inequality has its basis in materials and ideological realities that underlie many institutional mechanisms, labor regimes, industrial organizations, households, and migration dynamics in East Asia.

Gender is not a monolithic term referring to a general category of women and men; it underscores the diversity and multiplicity of women and men. It is often compounded by other stratifying factors such as race, ethnicity, class/caste, nationality, sexuality, age/generation, and disability. As a result, not all men are equally privileged and, likewise, not all women are unquestionably disadvantaged. Because of class and/or racial privileges, women and men, for example, position themselves differently in society, thus experiencing and benefiting by the development process in varying ways and degrees. Gender cannot be fully understood outside of class, race/ethnicity, and nationality hierarchies, but it should be recognized that the structures of these hierarchical relations are always gendered. Gender relations intersect simultaneously with these social relations, forming a matrix of domination and subordination that serves as a societal base for stratifying people, determining social locations of members, and shaping their identities, behaviors, and subjectivities. Gender inequality is therefore inevitably complicated by hierarchies and other forms of inequalities in different historical and socioeconomic contexts and under various political economies. The East Asian region can be understood as one penetrated by inequality, heterogeneity, mobility, and struggles derived from various hierarchies, especially that of gender.

Because of the complexity of gender, when gender analysis is immersed in a global context it extends beyond the workings of any given society. So, when development is viewed on a global scale, it becomes a multifaceted and inter-linked process built upon the dynamic interaction between macrostructure forces and microlevel interactions that shape inequality, gender relations, and individual experiences. The mainstream development theories used to study East Asian development primarily remain at the macro politicoeconomic level. Global South feminist perspectives on gender point out the failure of development policies and practices to see development from the view below and through the gender lens of poor women. We argue that it is critically important to study these intricately woven macromicro linkages of development as they relate to gender and interact with other social hierarchies.

Gender is highly pervasive in society, operating at multiple levels that are intricately interconnected. The analytical framework used to study gender as both a process and a structure can be organized into five major levels of analysis—the macroscopic, the macroinstitutional, the meso-organizational, the cultural/symbolic, and microinteractions at the individual levels. We adopted the notion offered by Ferree, Lorber, and Hess (1999) of how gender can be revisioned at four different levels. We have departed from it, however, by refining their levels of analysis to include the global and regional aspects and by adding the meso-organizational level to the discussion.

The *macroscopic level* focuses on the macro phenomena or forces that operate at the global and regional levels beyond the unit of analysis of the nation-state. East Asian development, as dynamic and robust as it is, should be analyzed in its global context. The process of industrialization, though rooted in historical and current conditions of nations, is a global phenomenon that is shaped by the dynamism of the politicoeconomic world system. The East Asian region has responded to the persistent force and expansion of world capitalism, and global restructuring has triggered its own inter- and intra-regional industrial restructuring. For example, more research is needed to understand the historical antecedents that shape the landscape of social change, such as Japan's colonial and postcolonial influence on the relatively lower labor participation rates among women in South Korea and Taiwan in comparison to those in Hong Kong and Singapore.

The *macro-institutional level* takes society as a whole and examines the social organization of its interdependent parts including stratification (based on gender, race, class, nationality, and other dimensions), social institutions, social arrangements of groups, and the allocation of resources and power in society as these relates to women and men. Gender is embedded in the structure of macroeconomic and social institutions and subsequently shapes socioeconomic outcomes and impacts gender relations, power, law, ideology, and cultural practices of domination. However, the macrolevel and political economic analysis of institutions that has been prominent in the development studies literature has focused on capital, labor relations, the state, and trade. Feminist perspectives broaden our insight by steering us toward the neglected arena of the patriarchal family and household dynamics, the relationship between gender and the state, and the interplay of culture and religion in the analysis of East Asian development (Blumberg 1994b; Chow 1997a; Chow and Berheide 1994; Dwyer and Bruce 1988; Kabeer 1994; Visanathan et al. 1998; Wolf 1992). The macro-institutional level of analysis is particularly salient with regard to policies that target both practical and strategic gender interests in maintaining one's livelihood and in uprooting the structural causes of sexism, discrimination, and other forms of oppression.

The *meso-organizational level* focuses on interactions and relationships among groups, especially those "collectivities oriented to the pursuit of relatively specific goals and exhibiting relatively highly formalized social structures" (Scott 1998:26). There is a serious omission in sociology as well as in the social sciences when it comes to studying the organization at the meso level. The roles generally of TNCs, industrial organizations, political parties, unions, immigration agencies and intermediaries, correction institutions, and women's national organizations are constitutive elements in shaping and promoting gender interests and needs in East Asian development. As the globalization process unfolds at an ever-increasing rate, the structure of international organizations reveals how the structural adjustment policies and programs of the World Bank and the International Monetary Fund, and World Trade Organization have been detrimental to Third World women (Anderson 2000; Beneria and Feldman 1992; Elson 1992; Osirim 1996). Studying women and gender at the meso-organizational level has just begun, exploding the bureaucratic assumption of gender neutrality and addressing its bureaucratic, hegemonic, and masculine structures, processes, and practices (Acker 1990; Staudt 1997). Research on nongovernmental organizations (NGOs) has revealed the prominent role they play in orchestrating grassroots activism and the political mobilization of women by linking women's participation in local communities to national and international women's movements (Afshar and Barrientos 1998; Basu 1995; Potter and Judd 1999; Townsend et al. 1999; Waylen 1996). This missing link to organizational studies offers hope for strengthening our understanding of the interconnection between globalism and localism. This level of analysis is of paramount importance in the struggle to make organizations accountable to women worldwide and to gain gender equity in terms of the redistribution of values, resources, power, and justice in society.

The *cultural/symbolic level* focuses on the use of symbols, discourses, and culture in constructing and reproducing gender. The gender process is integral to the construction of cultural designs and practices through the use of symbols, images, ideas, texts, scripts, and repertoires that dynamically define and redefine characteristics, behavior, and the relation of women and men. The very meanings of gender often reflect the ideology that supports the interest of the dominant class (or even race and nation) and solidify ruling relations in particular historical epochs and places. Cultural institutions, often neglected in studies, constitute a significant normative force or mechanism for conveying and perpetuating the proscribed meanings and representations of gender through language, social interaction, and everyday practices. In modern times, mass media and popular culture have exerted a powerful influence on how we define social reality and women's and men's roles within it. The simple idea of seeing men primarily as breadwinners and women largely as homemakers clearly places the cultural valuation of the former's social roles and status higher than the latter's, which bears socioeconomic consequences for the women's integration into economic development. Once gender ideology is created, it forms the cultural and motivational bases of inequality not only between women and men, but also among women and men of diverse social backgrounds.

Micro-interactions at the individual level focus on male and female individuals and their interaction, through which gender is constituted, performed, and reproduced in everyday life. To a large extent, gender is determined by culturally prescribed roles and statuses appropriate for women and men with norms and sanctions to regulate behavior. However, the process of gender construction also involves the definition of specific situations, contexts through which women and men interpret their social interaction and shared lived experiences, assess their interests, and select appropriate attitudes and behavior or modify them accordingly. Thus situations, as flexibly defined and redefined, create new meaning in gender relations and increase dynamism in the process of genderization as women and men continuously negotiate their ever-changing realities. The engendering process of interaction is further complicated by women and men in different social locations (be it class, race, or nationality), who bring their standpoints, self versus other identities, and subjectivities as they are related to each other, forming multiple layers of identities, social relationships, and groupings.

The key point is not to study each level of gender analysis in isolation, but to examine systematically how each is intricately related to the others when analyzing gender. Each level can be treated as foreground and background for theoretical analysis or argument (Alford 1998).[18] Two chapters in this book examine the critical role of TNCs in forming globalization of production, international division of labor, organization of work, labor relations, employment, and labor resistance. The chapter by Chow and Hsung uses the mesolevel of analysis of gendered organizations as a foreground argument and examines how this level shapes gender relations, employment patterns, and job outcomes among manufacturing workers in Taiwan within the global context treated as background in the analysis. The chapter by Hyun Mee Kim focuses more on how a group of women workers dealt with their labor dispute with an American firm as they interacted with various interest groups (e.g., the union, the students, the media, the police) and the state by comparing how media representations of gender were culturally constructed and differed within countries and between South Korea and the United States. The micro-interaction at the individual level is analytically related to the cultural and symbolic levels as foreground to the argument, while the globalization of economic restructuring and its TNC agent are treated as the background of the analysis. Most of the chapters in this volume make explicit interconnections between the macroprocesses of industrialization, economic restructuring, and migration; the structural organization of state-owned enterprises, workplaces, and family institutions with microlevel gender relations; family strategies; and personal experiences. While Yin-wah Chu's analysis remains at the macroscopic level and explores both longitudinal changes and intersocietal variations in women's employment in four East Asian societies, Janet Salaff's chapter focuses on the gender and class formation of migration work at the household level transnationally.

Major Theoretical Themes of the Collection

Authors in this volume address and assess the potential to contest and transform gender inequality and utilize a framework of analysis that sees gender, race, ethnicity, class, nationality, sexuality, and age as simultaneous social processes. We have identified three major themes, which can be posited as theoretical propositions that cut across chapters and link together the patterns and complexities inherent in East Asian development. While all of the authors address these themes either partially or fully, we have chosen here those chapters that we feel are the most relevant in highlighting the application of each theme.

Development is a gendered process. As all of the authors in this collection show, women's and men's experiences with the process of development are not mirrored. Gender roles, expectations, and images all impact the way development occurs, what opportunities become available, and what new obstacles arise. Vivien Hiu-tung Leung (chapter 8) found that in Hong Kong, women's employment in the manufacturing sector dropped 70 percent, while men's employment dropped 60 percent from 1987 to 1997. It is clear that both men and women working in this sector suffered increased job instability and deteriorating work conditions during restructuring, but women appear to have been more adversely affected. During this time, the real average daily wage of male workers increased by 8 percent, while women experienced a decline in wage of 7.1 percent. Similarly, Ting Gong's (chapter 6) look at the restructuring in China reveals that women were more likely to be laid off, had to wait longer for re-employment, and earned an income lower than men's. Because women were viewed as less productive primarily due to their familial responsibilities, they were the first to be cut from the workforce as corporations searched for cost-cutting measures.

It should not be assumed, however, that all women experience exploitation and oppression. Chu, in her comparative piece (chapter 3) exploring the changes in Hong Kong, Singapore, Taiwan, and South Korea, points out that industrialization in these countries has led to an increase in women's overall participation in paid employment. Tracking changes from the 1960s to the 1990s, Chu attributes the marked increase of women between the ages of 20 and 49 in the workforce to a decline in the negative effects of marriage and child-rearing on women's paid employment. The author concludes that although equality between the sexes was not reached, improvements did occur nonetheless.

The experience that women, like men, have as restructuring and development occurs is mitigated by other sources of social stratification such as class, ethnicity, national, age, and marital status. These stratifying dimensions intersect and reconfigure forms of social processes, gender relationships, and inequalities. For instance, class intersects with gender to shape the content, range, and meaning of the work that women do when preparing to migrate (chapter 11 by Salaff), particularly the availability of social and economic resource determining. For the South Korean women in Kim's chapter 5, it was their common class position in relation to their corporate employer that became the source for an insurgent collective identity and collective action. These women did not organize solely on the basis of their gender, as mothers and wives, but as workers with a distinct position in the occupational hierarchy. Similarly, nationality was one of the decisive factors influencing the experiences of foreign workers from Thailand who had temporarily migrated to Taiwan (chapter 9 by Anu Lee). While Taiwanese laborers were tracked into gender-typed jobs and women were paid less than men, Thai laborers were paid the same rate regardless of gender, and Thai men were hired to do a "woman's" job, like tending the looms. Here, nationality and legal status combined with gender to create a different standard in treatment, pay, and job allocation than that for Taiwanese men and women.

Gender is embedded in macrostructures and micro-interactions that influence the ways in which women and men participate in and experience development. The second theme focuses on the impact of macrostructures, which include social stratification, social institutions, culture, and organizations—as well as on micro-interactions. The interplay of capitalism and patriarchy as mediated by state, legal, and religious institutions structures the dynamic of work and family life and the dialectic of production and social reproduction. Consequently, the gender regime is continuously molded and inequality between women and men is perpetuated.

The differential effect experienced by men and women during China's transformation into a more privatized economy is partly rooted in the gendered division of labor that existed prior to the reform era (chapters 6 by Gong and 7 by Ping). After reform, a preference for male workers began to arise based on their types of skills, which were attained through gender-segregated occupational tracks, and on the desirability of these skills to privatized firms, which could offer higher wages and better career opportunities. As managers in the remaining state-owned firms began to compete with private firms for valuable male laborers, they encouraged men to stay by offering them jobs that were more marketable and desirable and that provided better access to scarce housing. Women were subsequently funneled into less desirable positions and often found themselves at risk of greater exploitation by management.

In chapter 4, Chow and Hsung further develop the impact of management's control over women workers and the institutionalization of gender in firms. At the management level, authority and power are exercised in the ways that labor is appropriated, coordinated, and regulated. It is management that determines and justifies work arrangements and rewards and perpetuates unequal power relations. The workplace, then, becomes the structural embodiment of gender ideology, tracking women and men hierarchically and placing them in an unequal power relationship in the organizational setting.

How strongly these gender interests are pushed depends at least partly on economic and political forces, which create a fluid construction of gender. In Taiwan (chapter 4 by Chow and Hsung), job criteria in hiring practices would shift according to labor demand and changes in the political economy. Labor shortages would lead to relaxed hiring criteria, resulting in an increase of women workers as well as foreign guest workers. Similarly, when the Chinese government called for increased productivity combined with an acceptance of surplus labor (chapter 6 by Gong), women were targeted for massive layoffs, especially through the application of an extended maternity leave policy and internal retirement ages that were lower than official ages.

As the discussion above illustrates, the interaction of patriarchy and the capitalist system and the state's role in setting policies and national agendas influence the impact and experience of gender. This impact also reaches into the family, as Leung discusses in chapter 8. In Hong Kong, many families maintained a patriarchal form of resource mobilization in which the husband's job preferences and consumption patterns dominated. As Leung argues, the wife's employment was shaped not just by an insufficient level of income, but even more by the husband's determination of how much of the financial burden his wife should share. In some families, a more egalitarian pattern emerged when the wife earned an income. However, because women dominated the service sector and those jobs tended to be unstable and short-term, their egalitarian relationship would often disintegrate when the wife's employment was terminated.

The separation of public and private spheres and the dichotomy of production and reproduction are supported by a gender ideology that places value in the former and underestimates the latter. As Salaff (chapter 11) reveals, the work that women do in preparation for migration has been gendered, unpaid, and invisible.

It lies within the realm of social reproduction, concerned with kinscripts and social networks, and so has remained undervalued and unrecognized as a form of work. In this gendered system, the women become "flexible" spouses who forego careers and education to pursue migration opportunities for their families and, thereby, reinforce their own disadvantaged positions.

This division between productive and reproductive work is again blurred by women who have turned marriage into a market activity in China (chapter 10 by Christina Gilmartin and Lin Tan), although cultural norms serve to reinforce the traditional division. Even though these women have challenged gender norms by traveling far distances or answering newspaper ads to find a husband, few would venture into unknown rural villages and arrange their own marriages. Many of these female marriage migrants have also refrained from entering the public sphere once they have found a husband—perhaps due to an increased dependence on their husband's family, intense feelings of social isolation, and abuse.

As a macrostructure system that secures male privilege, patriarchy embeds itself in multiple institutions, like families and corporations. Termed "corporate patriarchy," the male body, or more specifically a hegemonic form of masculinity, pervades TNCs (chapter 4 by Chow and Hsung). Privileged male characteristics are normalized and institutionalized in the organization's culture, practice, process, and design. Subsequently, male workers are more likely than female workers to be perceived as having the appropriate characteristics and qualifications required by the organization.

Gender images, symbols, and ideology are potent means of shaping politico-economic restructuring, institutional arrangements, personal identity, and activism. As many chapters in this volume point out, women's characterization as docile, patient, detail-oriented, and as having nimble fingers is a way of justifying gendered occupational tracks. In addition, the symbolic meaning of women as keepers of the culture and heroines of the nation invokes tension and even contradiction among the actual roles women play as wives, mothers, and factory workers, as portrayed by a variety of the media with different political interests (chapter 5 by Kim).

As socioeconomic development changes gender relations, women and men may adapt to or even resist these changes, and their behavior, in turn, influences the direction, policies, and practices of development. Socioeconomic development does not necessarily instill positive changes in social relations and the gender hierarchy. Instead, as the macrostructures of patriarchy, capitalist relations, and state policies become altered, new contradictions and forms of oppression are generated. One consequence of such changes, migration, has resulted in mixed experiences for the migrants themselves. As Lee points out in chapter 9, foreign workers migrate with the hope of earning a higher income for themselves and their families, but entered a work environment that controls their job and leisure time activities, provided few protections against exploitation, offers substantially lower pay than for local workers, and fosters negative images of foreign labor. These changes in Taiwan, while having created more opportunities for Thais to increase their wages, also increased the level and forms of exploitation heaped on foreign workers.

In China, as constraints relaxed on the economically motivated migration of unmarried women in rural areas to work for joint ventures and foreign companies that preferred young, single women, the migration of rural women for marriage purposes also increased (chapter 10 by Gilmartin and Tan). With women traveling to urban areas or special economic zones for work opportunities, a sex imbalance arose in rural areas. Millions of women took advantage of these changes and moved from poor rural areas to wealthier ones looking for potential husbands who were more affluent. Evidence suggests, however that these long-distance migrations may have left the women in a more vulnerable position, far from the protection of their natal families. These marriage migrations may potentially be connected to wife battering and high female suicide rates in rural areas.

In both of these cases, women were active agents of change, seeking to empower themselves and improve their lives. Their actions capitalized on changes in state policies, economic conditions, and gender roles and, in the process, triggered new responses and new challenges. Another example is the Chinese women (chapter 6 by Gong) who when faced with a tightening job market opted for self-employment and entrepreneurship. By doing so, the women could enter the market without encountering gender-biased recruitment policies and could also challenge patriarchal beliefs that limit a woman's role to that of homemaker. The unprecedented number of female business owners proves that women do indeed have the skills and vision needed to successfully run their own businesses and to contribute economically to society.

Informed by Global South feminist perspectives, this volume argues that gender interests and subjectivities should be recognized as a central and integral human condition of sustainable development. In particular, women should be seen as active agents, not passive recipients of development, though women of different backgrounds may vary in their abilities to understand their social circumstances or have their understanding obstructed by hidden structures of oppression. We emphasize the potentiality and actuality of women's agency, analyze ways of constructing practical and strategic gender interests and consciousness, explore means of empowering self and others, and discuss how these affect social processes of change. Such recognition allows women to register their resistance at both symbolic and practical levels, develop their oppositional culture, and mobilize collective action to struggle jointly against colonial or neocolonial domination, patriarchal control, capitalistic exploitation, state persecution, and structural inequality.

LINKING THE LOCAL WITH THE GLOBAL: TOWARD AN INDIGENIZATION OF GENDER AND DEVELOPMENT STUDIES IN EAST ASIA

In the early 1970s, feminist social scientists who were deeply dissatisfied with the omission and marginalization of women and gender in "normal science" argued for a paradigm shift, or a transformation in epistemology and methodology in the social sciences (Stacey and Thorne 1985). The fusion of knowledge and scholarship that would ignite the momentum for a paradigm shift lies at the intersection of internationalized gender scholarship and indigenous gender studies. A paradigm shift would entail a fundamental theoretical revelation of the social, political, economic, and cultural interplay between the categories of gender in the global and local realms. Hence, one of the important aims of the third project is to work toward an indigenization of gender and development studies in East Asia.[19]

Ideally, the local project would promote an indigenous, inclusive, situated, autonomous, and transformative body of knowledge that is grounded in the daily experiences of East Asian women vis-à-vis men as they are differentially and structurally located in the process of globalization. Dorothy Smith (1990) pointed out that when scholarship is produced by and from the vantage point of ruling relations and the privileged, the issues and problems of women are largely ignored. Therefore one point from which to begin to understand women involves problematizing the multifaceted aspects of their lived experiences. By developing scholarship from women as knowers and incorporating their standpoints and lived experiences, the analysis of gender will be empirically grounded and "studied up." Porter and Judd (1999:220) expound "Rather than being research done by development organizations and workers on the women affected, 'studying up' would be research done by or with the women affected on the development organizations and on the structure of the encompassing political economy." By studying up, women as subalterns, particularly disadvantaged poor women, are given the opportunity to raise an insurgent consciousness and give voice to elevate themselves and, in this case, other East Asian women, from the realm of invisibility, powerlessness, and the culture of silence. As Kabeer (1994) explains, this is not to imply that excluded, disadvantaged groups are more knowledgeable than others, but rather that they offer a viewpoint from below. It is "a viewpoint that can help to realign development paradigms more closely to 'the real order of things' . . . without the transformation of the lives of the poorest and most oppressed sections of all societies, there can be neither development nor equity" (Kabeer 1994:81). Knowledge generated by excluded groups, such as poor women and all of the oppressed, would provide the missing links and clues needed to reorient development studies, policies, and practices.

Indigenous knowledge is also inclusive and transformative because it embraces all women as gendered, sexual, racial, class, national, and cultural subjects situated structurally in different locations in society. The women's positions closely connect their personal identities, differences, and subjectivities with various types of social institutions and levels of structural hierarchies. These connections are often manifested in such areas as women's subordination and domesticity, class exploitation, racial/ethnic discrimination, colonial/postcolonial domination, structural inequality, and cultural stereotypes. The politics of personal identity go hand in hand with the structural transformation of society because they are not mutually exclusive, though sometimes dialectical. Indigenous gender knowledge is derived from relational, comparative, and historical analyses.[20] It emphasizes the macro-micro links that connect the historical past to the present, the private troubles of women and men (such as being laidoff and unable to pay bills) to public policy issues (such as unemployment and poverty), the practical daily interests of gender to strategic ones, the dimensions of gender to other social hierarchies of inequality, and the independence and development of nations to a discourse on postcolonialism.[21] Hence, the end result of this inclusive analysis will be a wide range of issues, recommendations, options, and strategies to inform a full body of development policies and practices.

Furthermore, autonomy, self-determination, and empowerment are at the core of an indigenous analysis and feminist praxis. To give voice is not enough because it ultimately may be silenced by structural and political forces.[22] As the authors in this volume reveal, indigenous gender studies in the development of East Asia expose some of the deep-seated problems underlying women's subordination and examine the roots and prevalence of different forms of poverty, inequality, and disempowerment. Narrowing gender gaps and improving access to resources are not enough. The very power structure that mutes their voices, obstructs their pathways, and hinders their full participation in the development process must be removed. Reaching beyond a concern for gender equality, we insist on the need for indigenous scholarship to explore the feminist epistemology of agency and the concept of empowerment to demonstrate how women as active agents, as well as collective action and social movements, bring about reform, opposition, resistance, and radical change that democratizes and transforms society.

But what does empowerment really mean? Empowerment to whom, to do what, and for what? Empowerment, a key concept in feminist scholarship and praxis, has been defined and redefined over time (Batliwala 1994; Kabeer 1994; Rowlands 1997, 1998; Sen and Grown1987; Sen and Batliwala 2000; Townsend et al. 1999). The general sense of empowerment is that it means sharing power with, giving it to, or distributing it among people. Analyzing the concept of power as "circulating," "exercised," and "existing in action," Foucault (1980) has raised questions about the possibilities of empowerment, not only the giving of power but also the helping of other to exercise it. Therefore, empowerment is more than a tool or an end result it is an active process.

In the development discourse, empowerment has three identifiable dimensions—personal, collective, and relational (Rowlands 1997). Empowerment involves a self-critical process, embodying the meanings of capacity, internal strength, and potential to take action and to transform power as it is exercised in particular sites. Collective empowerment refers to the ways in which groups are organized, the activities they undertake, and the relationships that exist within and and between them as well as with formal institutions and the wider community. Relational empowerment deals with the ability to negotiate, communicate, defend, and support close relationships with others while maintaining one's own sense of self and dignity. These dimensions of empowerment combine to create four forms of power: "power over" other persons or groups, "power from within" to build strength and respect, "power with" others to enhance social capacity, and "power to" gain access to a full range of human abilities and to potential collective action (Townsend et al. 1999). These power relations are not only between men and women, but also among women of diverse backgrounds and among different groups based on race, ethnicity, class, sexuality, age/generation, nationality, and even disability. To practice gender from the ground up, we need to use the bottom-up approach that the Global South feminists advocate and build strength and assets individually, relationally, and collectively. Through this process of empowerment, East Asian women will be able to develop their autonomy, give voice, exercise their rights to self-determination, actualize their potential, use their power of agency, form solidarity through political alliances, support or develop opposition to dominant discourses, and register their resistance at both symbolic and practical levels. Alternative development thinking, policies, and practices in East Asia will emerge when we recognize the importance of localized indigenous gender knowledge, transform social consciousness, explore ways of addressing gender interests, alter current priorities in resource allocation, change unequal power relations, mobilize grassroots communities and groups, and dismantle structures of oppression.

Consequently, a transformative indigenous analysis of gender and East Asian development should stress the building of a society with a healthy, growing economy undergoing structural transformation to promote a high standard of living, equitable resource allocation among countries and people, effective governance, freedom and human rights, and preservation of the environment (Weaver et al. 1997). Gender interests and perspectives should be recognized as central and integral human conditions of sustainable development. Development must be participatory on an equal, reciprocal, and just basis, with the overriding goal being to improve human well-being and to enable people to achieve their potential. Development should also be gender-sensitive and human-centered so that it empowers people, forms on women's rights and realities, eliminates poverty, secures sustainable livelihoods, forms stable and healthy communities, and promotes peace on a long-term basis.

Once indigenous knowledge is generated, we need to understand its transnational nature by bridging the local with nations and regions and then, finally, with larger global processes. The local is embedded in a web of global links. East Asian women and nations, as part of the global link, should not be seen as a bloc that is immutable. They are inevitably shaped by forces of globalization in terms of industrialization, economic restructuring, and migration as studies in this volume thoughtfully articulate. A fundamental transformation in the study of gender and East Asian development lies in what questions about women vis-à-vis men are asked, how answers or evidence are found, what criteria are employed to define whether these answers or evidence are significant and valid and what the generated knowledge is for. Meanwhile, we need to focus on how the questions we ask ourselves have changed in view of recent global events that have transformed our being and thinking. Collaboration between researchers, advocates, and practitioners with shared perspectives from the North and the South is possible as long as equal partnership, self-determination, and mutual respect are guaranteed.[23] The interlinkages between the global and the local are at the core of indigenous gender scholarship and practice, which opens new frontiers for intellectual adventure and creates a political space for empowerment, solidarity, and change to achieve an equitable, sustainable, and just development in East Asia and worldwide.

NOTES

This introductory chapter is based on two unpublished papers written by Esther Ngan-ling Chow, "Globalization, Gender, and Social Change" presented at the International Conference on Gender and Development in Asia at the Chinese University of Hong Kong in 1997, and an unpublished paper, "Studying Gender and Development in East Asia: A Feminist Critique and Revisioning.

1. The terms *Global South* and *Global North* are discussed in note 14, below.
2. The Taiwan data were taken from the Directorate-General of Budget, Accounting and Statistics, Executive Yuan, Republic of China, 2000.
3. From http://www.undp.org/hdr/1995/hdr95en5.htm.
4. For the purpose of theoretical review, we have grouped theories that share some common ideas into one category. For instance, the neoclassical and modernization theories are grouped into one, and the dependency and world system theories into another category. Note that So and Chiu (1995) and So (1990) treat the latter two separately as distinct theoretical perspectives.
5. Feminism is a term that has been greatly excluded, distorted, and misunderstood in East Asia's social science literature. Feminism comes in a variety of forms characterized by different meanings, theoretical ideas, concepts, methods of thinking, approach to analysis, and praxis. Scholars in the East Asian region have yet to explore the profound meaning of the term and to come up with their own feminist definition, perspective, and analysis.
6. In industrialized countries, roughly two-thirds of women's total work burden is spent on unpaid activities and one-third on paid activities. For men, the shares are reversed. However, in the developing countries, two-thirds of women's total work time is also spent on unpaid labor, while less than one-fourth of men's work is unpaid. The disparity by gender between rural and urban areas is alarming (UNDP 1995).
7. Bardhan and Klasen (1999) offer a critical review of the UNDP's Gender-Related indices. Some researchers also argue that quantitative measures are objective indices and suggest that qualitative measures should be added to capture fully the phenomena of gender.
8. Although Japan is not one of the countries being discussed in this book, I include it for comparison to point out that as economically advanced as Japan is, the severity of its gender gaps on some measures remains striking (see tables 2.2 and 2.3).
9. The brain drain of well-educated and professionally trained Chinese who emigrated to other countries and the in-flow of the less educated from mainland China may have potentially lowered the educational level of its residents in recent years.
10. While there are cultural variations within Asia, Confucian tradition and culture originating in China, were spreading to Japan, Korea, and other parts of Asia, and have remained dominant forces in the East Asian region.

11. I observed several incidences of labor disputes and confrontations with police when I was growing up in Hong Kong in the early 1950s. Some women union workers often behind the scenes or marched alongside men labored in the street to support labor strikes.

12. Besides the case study discussed by Kim in chapter 5, other cases were reported of Korean women workers' resistance against factory closures and dismissals in Korea Sumida and the city of Masan.

13. Several attempts to classify different feminist theories and practices in gender and development (Bandarage 1984; Kabeer 1994; Moser 1993; Rathgeber 1990), have different foci, concerns, and frameworks. To some extent, these various classifications have created some ambiguity and overlapping. For the purposes of introducing the field, Rathgeber's classification was chosen for it is a straightforward one that combines theory with practice.

14. At the 1955 Bandung Conference of "non-aligned" African and Asian nations, the adoption of the term "Third World" was premised on these nations' solidarity that emerged from the anticolonial struggles in Vietnam and Algeria. It has been used to designate the developing countries vis-à-vis the countries of the First World (U.S., the Western European countries, and Japan) and the Second World (e.g., the former Soviet Union, the East European bloc, and China) to replace the derogatory connotations of the LDC and HDC terms. After the Cold War, the term Third World became less meaningful and useful, though some scholars still use it when referring to an imagined community for the purpose of political identity, alliance, and solidarity against the hegemonic West or North. In recent years, "the North" and "the South" are used more often in substitution for the First and Third Worlds, simply because most of the developing countries are located in the Global South. However, some researchers argue that not all developing countries are in the Global South, especially those in East Asia; and some developed countries such as Australia and New Zealand are, in fact, located in the Global South. In the absence of better terms, the Global South feminist perspectives appear to be more appropriate theoretically and practically in the analysis of women and men in East Asian development.

15. Unlike others, Visanathan et al. (1998) and Mosse (1994) view the Global South feminist perspectives as distinctively different from the other three perspectives. Some argue that DAWN is not an alternative development perspective because some of its key concepts have been incorporated by GAD and other frameworks.

16. In comparison with terms like "North/South" and "advanced/underdeveloped nations," M. Jacqui Alexander and Chandra T. Mohanty (1997: 7) still prefer the term "Third World." They explained that it "retains certain heuristic value and explanatory specificity in relation to the inheritance of colonialism and contemporary neocolonial economic and geopolitical processes that the other formulations lack." Geraldine Heng (1997) expanded the notion of multiple Third World feminisms and discussed how the nation state disciplines certain women, prostitutes, and lesbians and writes them out of the nation's script.

17. Some scholars question the common notions of sex, gender, and compulsory heterosexuality. They advocate the deconstruction of the fixed binary categories of sex and gender to include a variety of sexual orientations such as lesbians, gays, bisexuals, intersex, and transgender.

18. Alford (1998:32) maintains that the three aspects of theoretical claims depend on the particular research question being asked (the foreground of the argument), the kinds of assumptions being made (the background of the argument), and the kinds of evi-

dence being sought. For example, the multivariate analysis can be in the foreground of the argument, with historical backdrops as its background to specify the context of analysis.

19. Taking a strong anti-racial, anti-colonial, and anti-capitalist stand, M. Jacqui Alexander and Chandra T. Mohanty (1997) have advocated comparative, relational, and historical analyses of feminist genealogies and colonial legacies to understand the globalization of capitalism and recolonization and to empower women and organizations with autonomy and self-determination in order to build future democratic movements.

20. For the discussion about the relationship between private troubles and public issues, see C. Wright Mills's (1959) discussion of the sociological imagination and the central mission of sociology.

21. Gayatri Chadravorty Spivak (1988a, 1988b) raised a critical question: Can the subaltern speak? See her insightful analysis to address various complex and intricate aspects of this issue.

22. Marilyn Porter, Ellen Judd, and a team of feminists (1999) from the North and the South discussed extensively the pros and cons of their collaboration including problems of ethnocentric assumptions, misunderstandings, project constraints, and tensions that may have undermined an inclusive feminist agenda for development. They concluded that an equal partnership and openness are critical to continuing reflexive critiques of development practices in an attempt to identify ways in which feminists, North and South, can do development in genuine and transformative ways.

Part II

The Process of Industrialization

Institutional Embeddedness, Control, and Resistance

Chapter 3

Women and Work in East Asia

Yin-wah Chu

The industrialization of developing countries has given rise to a phenomenal growth in female employment. But has paid employment freed women from their subjugation? A prominent line of argument, known as the "exploitation thesis," answers that question in the negative. It maintains that Third World development has been fueled by the expansion of labor-intensive manufacturing industries, which require workers who are manually dexterous, obedient, and willing to work long hours, and for little pay. Young women in these developing countries, most of whom have received limited formal education and are expected to marry in their early 20s, are the perfect recruits for these semiskilled manufacturing jobs. Furthermore, employers have deployed, consciously or otherwise, patriarchal practices to gain the compliance of women workers. The result has been not to tear down patriarchy, but to reinvigorate it; the participation of Third World women in the labor force has been exploitative rather than liberating (Beneria and Sen 1981; Hartmann 1976; Nash 1977; Nash and Fernandez-Kelly 1983; Tiano 1987; Ward 1988).

The thesis has been influential and used with great success to analyze the subjugation of working women in Hong Kong, Singapore, Taiwan, and South Korea (Greenhalgh 1985; Kung 1983; Lim 1983; Salaff 1981). Recent research has moved beyond this thesis by examining in depth the cultural and institutional practices of domination, exploring the subjective experience of women workers, and registering their resistance at both the symbolic and practical levels (Hsiung 1996; Lee 1998a; Ong 1987, 1991). This chapter intends to contribute to the understanding of female employment by taking a different approach. It will adopt a macroscopic perspective, exploring both the longitudinal changes as well as the intersocietal variations of female employment in these East Asian societies.

The first part of this chapter will provide an overview of the changing structures of female employment in the four societies. The second part will try to account for the observed patterns. The author will argue that "patriarchy" and the "capitalist world economy" have continued to shape the employment opportunity of East Asian women. However, these forces have only defined the boundary conditions. Patriarchy is not invincible and it has expressed itself in a variety of gender role specifications and institutional arrangements. Similarly, core countries within the capitalist world economy do not exert unqualified domination over the system. The governing elite of a country can choose within limits their strategy of development. In East Asia, there has been more than one path of capitalist development. The path followed by a specific country has shaped the economic opportunity structure and the labor systems, which in turn account for variations in the patterns of female employment.

CHANGING STRUCTURES OF FEMALE EMPLOYMENT IN EAST ASIA

The structure of female employment in the four East Asian societies has undergone massive changes over the last three decades. While some of the changes are across the board, others are idiosyncratic. A summary of the salient patterns is presented in table 3.1. The following will examine the points in greater detail under the headings *labor force participation, sectoral distribution,* and *occupational representation.*

Labor Force Participation

Industrialization in East Asia has led to a general increase in women's paid employment. In 1961, the female labor force participation rate (LFPR) was 36.8 percent in Hong Kong. In 1966, the figure stood at 24.2 percent in Singapore, 32.6 percent in Taiwan, and 31.5 percent in South Korea. By 1996, comparable rates for the four societies had increased to 49.2 percent, 51.5 percent, 45.8 percent, and 48.7 percent, respectively (see table 3.2). In all these cases, however, the male LFPR remained nearly 30 percent higher than that of the female.[1]

The four cases also share another characteristic in the relationship between industrial growth and female labor force participation. Specifically, the early stage of export-led industrialization, which took place around the mid-1950s in Hong Kong and mid-1960s in the other three cases, was associated with the massive entrance of women between 15 and 19 years of age into the labor market. At its zenith, about 50 percent of women within this age group in Hong Kong, Singapore, and Taiwan and 40 percent of those in South Korea were active economically (see table 3.3).[2] Since the 1980s, there has been a reduction in their level of participation, and in 1996 only between 13.6 percent and 22.8 percent of women were in the labor force.

The decline in teenage women's labor force participation took place in tandem with an unfettered increase in the participation of women between 20 and 49 years of age. This tendency is apparently linked to the decline in the adverse impact of marriage and child rearing on women's involvement in paid employment. In Hong Kong, the level of labor force participation among married women increased from 28.5 percent in 1961 to 45.5 percent in 1996.[3] Singapore and Taiwan also saw a commensurate increase from 14 percent in 1957 to 48.4

Table 3.1. Patterns of Female Employment in Hong Kong, Singapore, Taiwan, and Korea

Similarities	Differences
Labor Force Participation	
1. Increase in the overall female labor force participation rate (LFPR)	1. An increase in female LFPR in the four cases
2. Rapid initial increase followed by gradual decline in the LFPR of women 15–19 years of age	2. Reversal during the 1990s of the increase in LFPR of women 50 years or older in Hong Kong
3. Persistence, albeit decline, in the dampening effect of marriage on female LFPR	3. Persistence of the M-shaped, age-specific, female LFPR in contemporary South Korea
Sectoral Distribution	
1. Sectoral shift from "agriculture, fishery, mining" to "manufacturing" and, subsequently, "finance, real estate, insurance, business service"	1. Simultaneous expansion within South Korea of "commerce, wholesale, retail" and "manufacturing"
2. Disproportionate impact of the decline in manufacturing employment on women	2. Male domination of "manufacturing" in South Korea and, until the 1990s, female domination in the other cases
	3. Drastic decline of "manufacturing" in Hong Kong after the mid-1980s
Occupational Representation	
1. Increasing representation of women in "clerical," "associate professional," "professional," and "administrative" occupations	1. Greater progress among women in Hong Kong and Singapore in the "administrative" occupations
2. Feminization of "clerical" occupation	2. Higher absolute number and portion of Taiwan women than men in the "professional" occupations in 1996
3. Continued male domination in "administrative" occupations	3. Women in South Korea lag ostensibly behind in the "professional" and especially "administrative" occupations

percent in 1998 and from 31.7 percent in 1981 to 46.0 percent in 1996, respectively. As for South Korea, the rate of married women's labor force participation actually grew more rapidly than that of single women between 1985 and 1991. In 1996, the LFPR of married women was 50.5 percent (Hong Kong Census and Statistics Department 1961, 1996; Pyle 1994; Singapore Ministry of Manpower 1999; ROC Executive Yuan 1996; ROK National Statistical Office 1997a; Park 1995).[4]

These common trends notwithstanding, the four cases exhibit considerable longitudinal and intersocietal variations. The first intersocietal variation has to do with the increase in women's labor force participation. Among the four, Hong Kong saw the earliest expansion of female employment. Its rate of female labor force participation increased most rapidly in the 1960s and 1970s, had stabilized by the early 1980s, and has been declining since the 1990s. In the other cases, the rates did not start to rise steadily until the 1960s, and this climb was sus-

Table 3.2. Women's Labor Force Participation by Age (in percent)

Age	Hong Kong			Singapore			Taiwan			South Korea		
	1961	1981	1996	1966	1980	1996	1966	1981	1996	1963	1980	1996
15–19	47.9	42.7	22.8	25.5	50.7	18.5	40.1	41.3	18.0	34.5	34.4	13.6
20–24	51.1	80.0	76.9	40.9	78.4	77.6	38.2	58.3	60.8	43.4	53.5	66.0
25–29	} 33.9	61.3	82.1	25.9	58.7	81.4	26.1	41.2	66.5	36.2	32.0	51.1
30–34		49.2	68.7	21.0	44.2	68.0	24.9	39.6	60.0	39.2	40.7	49.1
35–39	} 38.0	52.3	58.1	19.2	37.1	60.5	29.5	42.7	60.2	41.6	53.0	60.1
40–44		54.1	57.0	21.9	33.2	56.9	27.7	42.3	59.6	48.4	56.7	65.6
45–49	} 42.1	49.4	54.7	20.4	26.5	53.9	24.9	38.9	53.5	44.9	57.3	62.2
50–54		44.6	44.2	24.4	20.4	43.7	17.8	31.1	41.8	38.5	54.0	57.2
55–59	} 28.2	36.9	28.4	23.2	14.5	28.5	12.4	22.7	30.9	32.5	46.2	53.3
60–64		31.4	14.3	18.5	11.3	14.9	5.8	12.2	21.0	18.9	} 16.9	29.2
65&above	9.9	13.7	3.8	7.4	6.4	5.2	1.9	1.9	4.0	6.5		
Total	36.8	49.0	49.2	24.2	44.3	51.5	32.6	38.8	45.8	36.3	42.8	48.7

Sources: Hong Kong: Hong Kong Census and Statistics Department 1961, 1981, 1996. Singapore: Singapore Ministry of National Development 1967; Singapore Department of Statistics 1993; Singapore Ministry of Manpower 1998. Taiwan: ROC Executive Yuan 1996. South Korea: Lee 1993; ROK National Statistical Office 1997a.

Note: Most tables in this chapter have reported statistics taken from noncomparable years. Strictly comparable data for the 1960s and 1980s are either unavailable at the original source or inaccessible to the author. Readers have to be cautious in drawing comparative analysis of longitudinal changes.

tained throughout much of the 1980s. In Taiwan, the growth rate leveled off in the mid-1980s, but in Singapore the rise did not slow down until the early 1990s. In South Korea, the increase had become even more rapid during the late 1980s (Hong Kong Census and Statistics Department, various years; Singapore Ministry of Manpower 1999; ROC Executive Yuan 1996; Lee 1993; ROK National Statistical Office 1997c).

A second intersocietal difference has to do with the employment experience of women between 50 and 64 years of age. Women in this age category from Hong Kong were moving out of the labor market between 1981 and 1996, yet similar women from Singapore, Taiwan, and South Korea were actually increasing their involvement in paid employment (see table 3.2). As the next section will try to establish, the idiosyncrasy of Hong Kong in this respect and the aforementioned difference in the pace of women joining the labor force are related closely to the societies' trajectories of industrial expansion.

The third and most intriguing irregularity has to do with the impact of marriage. In general, unmarried women were more likely than married ones to engage in paid employment. However, the four cases exhibit a considerable difference in the gap between the LFPR of married and unmarried women. In Hong Kong, the LFPR of married women was 22.4 percent lower than that of their unmarried sisters in 1996. The situation in Singapore was similar, with the comparable figure standing at 16.9 percent in 1998. The gaps were much smaller in Taiwan and South Korea. Over the years in Taiwan, married women's LFPR increased while those of the unmarried women actually declined. In 1996 compared to married women in Taiwan, unmarried women were only 6.0 percent more likely to have joined the labor force. As for South Korea, married women in 1996 were actually 1.0 percent more likely than single women to be in the labor force (Hong Kong Census and Statistics Department 1996; ROC Executive Yuan 1996; Singapore Ministry of Manpower 1999; ROK National Statistical Office 1997a).

The differential impact of marriage is also manifested in whether women have to quit their jobs immediately after marrying. In 1996, the median age of first marriage of women was about 27 in Hong Kong, Singapore, and Taiwan and 25 in South Korea (Hong Kong Census and Statistics Department 1996; ROC Ministry of the Interior 1997; Singapore Department of Statistics 1998). In the same year, only in South Korea was age 25 the cutoff point after which women's labor force participation tended to drop sharply. In Hong Kong, Singapore, and Taiwan, the cutoff point was postponed for about three years, to age 30. In addition, while the LFPRs of women in Hong Kong, Singapore, and Taiwan tended to undergo perpetual decline after reaching their peak at age 30, the LFPR of South Korean women picked up again after 35 years of age. Indeed, Korean women age 40 to 59 were more likely than their counterparts in the other cases to be attached to the labor market. The pattern seen in South Korean is known as an M-shaped labor force participation. The same pattern can also be found within Hong Kong, Singapore, and Taiwan during the 1960s, but it has disappeared gradually in these places. South Korea is the only case where the M-shaped, age-specific, female LFPR formed in the 1960s and showed no signs of wavering in 1996 (see table 3.2).

From the data, it appears that women in contemporary Hong Kong and Singapore have not found marriage itself a major deterrent against paid employment. Child rearing, however, has remained a mother's responsibility and has continued to dampen women's labor force participation. In Taiwan, marriage and child rearing as such appear to have exerted a relatively mild impact on women's employment. The difference in the LFPR of married and unmarried women was small and, in 1996, the LFPR suffered only a mild decline between the peak years and neighboring ones. One decisive factor appears to be the low level of labor force participation among women between 20 and 34 years of age. This, however, is a puzzle that remains to be solved. Of the four cases, marriage exerted the greatest impact on the working lives of South Korean women; many had to quit their jobs immediately after marriage. Two factors help to explain the apparent paradox of the aforementioned narrow gap between the LFPR of married and unmarried women in South Korea. First, a substantial number of married women re-entered the labor market after the age of 35. Second, keen competition in the Korean labor market and the prospect of a short occupational life discouraged some young women from looking for jobs at all (Lee 1993).

Sectoral Distribution

East Asian industrial development has also been associated with the intersector transfer of workers. At a very general level, their experience appears to conform to the textbook case of a two-phase transition wherein workers are transferred from agriculture to manufacturing and, later on, to the service sector. Thus one can observe in the 1960s and 1970s, the rapid contraction of agriculture in Taiwan and South Korea, and in all four cases the surge of manufacturing as the locomotive of employment expansion. Economic restructuring,[5] which commenced around the 1980s for most of these cases, has brought about the rise of social and financial services as an important source of female employment (see table 3.3).

A general trend notwithstanding, the cases have differed in a number of

Table 3.3. Gender and Industrial Sector (in percent)

Industrial Sector	Hong Kong 1961 Male	Female	1981 Male	Female	1996 Male	Female	Singapore 1966 Male	Female	1980 Male	Female	1996 Male	Female
Manufacturing	37.6	45.7	34.7	53.1	19.3	18.2	19.0	20.0	24.7	40.4	23.0	23.6
Construction	10.8	2.4	11.2	1.4	12.3	1.7	7.5	2.3	9.3	1.4	9.6	2.2
Commerce, wholesale, retail	12.9	6.3	20.7	16.5	23.3	27.3	25.8	15.8	21.4	21.1	22.9	23.7
Transport, storage, communication	9.2	2.4	10.3	2.5	14.0	6.2	11.8	2.2	14.3	5.1	14.5	6.5
Finance, real estate, insur., bus. serv.	} 18.7	} 31.3	4.5	5.5	13.3	13.7	} 30.1	} 55.1	7.1	9.2	12.2	16.7
Social, personal, community services			14.4	17.8	16.0	32.0			20.0	21.7	16.9	26.9
Public administration	N/A	N/A	N/A	N/A	N/A	N/A	N/A	N/A	N/A	N/A	N/A	N/A
Agriculture, fishery, mining	7.5	9.6	2.1	1.9	0.7	0.5	3.7	2.1	2.1	0.8	} 1.0	} 0.3
Utilities	1.9	0.8	0.9	0.2	1.0	0.3	1.7	1.0	1.0	0.3		
Others	1.4	1.5	1.3	1.1	0.2	0.2	0.3	0.1	0.1	0.0		

Industrial Sector	Taiwan 1961 Male	Female	1981 Male	Female	1996 Male	Female	South Korea 1966 Male	Female	1980 Male	Female	1996 Male	Female
Manufacturing	17.7	18.5	28.8	39.6	26.7	26.8	5.1	3.5	23.0	21.9	24.0	20.3
Construction	4.7	0.5	12.1	2.0	14.8	3.1	1.1	0.1	8.6	1.0	14.3	2.4
Commerce, wholesale, retail	11.2	12.9	15.6	18.7	18.9	26.3	6.3	6.3	17.6	29.5	22.2	34.3
Transport, storage, communication	5.7	1.5	6.6	2.1	7.0	2.5	2.1	0.1	6.4	1.2	8.0	1.4
Finance, real estate, insur., bus. serv.	} 13.5	} 18.7	2.2	3.1	5.0	8.1	} 8.7	} 3.6	3.2	2.8	8.3	8.9
Social, personal, community services			9.2	14.7	11.3	22.1			11.9	10.8	8.1	17.2
Public administration	N/A	N/A	3.9	2.9	3.7	3.3	N/A	N/A	N/A	N/A	4.0	1.7
Agriculture, fishery, mining	44.9	47.0	21.0	16.9	12.0	7.6	76.3	86.4	29.0	32.7	10.4	13.6
Utilities	1.0	0.2	0.6	0.1	0.5	0.1	0.3	0.1	0.3	0.1	0.5	0.1
Others	1.3	0.7	N/A	N/A	N/A	N/A	N/A	N/A	N/A	N/A	0.1	0.0

Sources: Hong Kong: Hong Kong Census and Statistics Department 1961, 1981, 1996. Singapore: Singapore Ministry of National Development 1967; Singapore Department of Statistics 1993; Singapore Ministry of Manpower 1998. Taiwan: Chou 1994; ROC Executive Yuan 1996. South Korea: ROK Economic Planning Board 1962, 1984; ROK National Statistical Office 1997c.

Note: The Korea statistical yearbooks for 1980 and 1981 have relied on a very crude classification of industrial sectors; this table therefore reports 1983 data instead. See the note at table 3.2 for other reasons why the table reports statistics from non-comparable years.

important ways. The first area of contrast is related precisely to the sequence of sectoral transition. The two-phase transition fits the experience of Hong Kong, Singapore, and Taiwan very well, but does not describe the South Korean case accurately. In South Korea, commerce expanded simultaneously with manufacturing and, between 1983 and 1996, provided the single most important source of employment for women (ROK Economic Planning Board 1984; ROK National Statistical Office 1997b).

The second intersocietal variation lies in the gender composition of the manufacturing workforce. Until recently, the portion of women in manufacturing was higher than that of men in the cases of Hong Kong, Singapore, and Taiwan. But the reverse was true for South Korea. In 1981, for example, 53.1 percent of women in Hong Kong, 40.4 percent of women in Singapore,[6] and 39.8 percent of women in Taiwan were employed in manufacturing. Comparable figures for men were 34.7 percent, 24.7 percent, and 28.6 percent, respectively. In South Korea in 1983, however, 23 percent of men contrasted with 21.9 percent of women were so engaged (table 3.3). Indeed, this pattern was formed in South Korea in the 1960s and was continuing in 1996 (ROK Administration of Labor 1978; ROK National Statistical Office 1997c).

The pattern is related to the release of the workforce from the agricultural sector, because a comparable difference existed in the gender composition of the agricultural labor forces in Taiwan and South Korea.[7] For three decades in South Korea, the portion of women in agriculture was higher than that of men, though the absolute number of men in the sector was more substantial. In 1996, the sector employed 13.6 percent of women, but 10.4 percent of men (table 3.3). It appears that industrial development in the country tempted men, to a larger extent than women, to move out of agriculture. Between 1966 and 1994, the male population in farm households had decreased by 54.6 percent, while the female counterpart had only decreased by 39.6 percent (ROK Administration of Labor 1978; ROK Ministry of Labor 1995). The experience of Taiwan has been different. Only for a brief period of time, up to the early 1960s, had proportionately more men than women showed the tendency of moving out of agriculture. With the growth of export-oriented industrialization, women overtook men in the rate of outward movement. In 1996, agriculture engaged 7.6 percent of employed women, but 12 percent of men (see table 3.3; see also Chou 1994).

A third intersocietal variation has to do with the timing and magnitude of economic restructuring. The four societies went through economic restructuring and, as a result, faced either a slowdown or decline in manufacturing employment. But the decline began at different points in time. The trend began in Hong Kong in the early 1980s, Taiwan in the mid-1980s, and South Korea and Singapore in the 1990s.[8] The varying extent of restructuring in the economies and their differential impact on women can be observed by comparing the 1996 data with those of the year in which manufacturing employment was at its peak in each of the cases. In Hong Kong, the portion of women in manufacturing dropped by a glaring 34.9 percent after 1981. The portion of women in manufacturing decreased by 6.6 percent in Singapore after 1992, 14.0 percent in

Taiwan after 1987, and 8.7 percent in South Korea after 1989.[9] With no exception, women have borne the brunt of economic restructuring. The corresponding decline in male manufacturing employment amounted to 15.4 percent, 2.8 percent, 5.1 percent, and 3.0 percent, respectively (Hong Kong Census and Statistics Department, various years; Singapore Ministry of Labor 1995; Singapore Ministry of Manpower 1998; ROC Executive Yuan 1996; ROK National Statistical Office 1997a).[10]

Occupational Representation

Three decades of industrial development also transformed the occupational distribution of East Asian women. The most prominent source of occupational change has to do with the replacement of agricultural occupations by positions of production and clerical work. Since production occupations are related to the sectoral shift discussed above, this section will only examine the passage of women into white-collar occupations.

Clerical work is the white-collar occupation that attracted the largest inflow of women. Between the 1960s and early 1990s, the portion of women employed in the occupation increased by 8.7 times in Hong Kong, 2.3 times in Singapore, 3.2 times in Taiwan, and 46 times in South Korea (see table 3.4).[11] Clerical work used to be a male-dominated occupation. It became female-dominated in Hong Kong, Singapore, and Taiwan in as early as the 1980s. By 1996, women made up 69.7 percent, 76.7 percent, 75.8 percent, and 51.6 percent of the clerical workforce within Hong Kong, Singapore, Taiwan, and South Korea, respectively (see table 3.5). One can safely conclude that there has been a feminization of clerical occupation in East Asia.

Women also increased their presence in the professional and technical occupations. Between the 1960s and early 1990s, the portion of women as professional and technical workers increased by approximately 2.3 times in Hong Kong, 1.3 times in Singapore, 1.5 times in Taiwan, and 20.8 times in South Korea (see table 3.4). The 1996 data on occupational distribution relied on a more refined classification scheme. It indicates that, in the cases of Hong Kong, Singapore, and Taiwan, the portion of women working as associate professionals (e.g. nurses, social workers, and high school teachers) either exceeded or was similar to the portion of men in such occupations. When it comes to professional occupations (e.g. architects, engineers, and accountants), however, men clearly outperformed women. Taiwan is exceptional in having had a higher portion and absolute number of women in the professional occupations. Among the four cases, South Korean women did least well. Their representation in both the associate professional and professional occupations was inferior to that of men in both absolute and relative terms (see table 3.5).

Among the occupations that carry high status and high remuneration, women made the least progress in administration and management. Between 1966 and 1991, Hong Kong and Singapore registered a respectable increase in the portion

Table 3.4. Gender and Occupation (in percent)

Occupation	Hong Kong						Singapore					
	1961		1981		1991		1966		1980		1990	
	Male	Female	Male	Female	Male	Female	Male	Female	Male	Female	Male	Female
Professional and technical	4.6	6.3	5.6	6.3	13.8	14.3	5.0	13.6	11.5	11.9	15.7	15.5
Administrative and managerial	4.0	0.7	3.5	1.0	11.8	4.9	2.3	0.4	8.6	1.9	11.7	4.0
Clerical	6.9	3.3	8.8	18.0	8.0	28.8	12.4	11.8	7.5	25.8	5.7	24.2
Sales	15.7	8.6	11.5	8.0	6.0	7.3	17.6	9.9	} 15.0	} 13.9	} 14.2	} 13.3
Services	11.4	24.3	15.9	15.0	17.1	22.1	17.7	36.5				
Agricultural and fishery	6.6	9.2	2.2	1.9	0.9	0.7	3.5	3.9	2.0	0.8	0.4	0.1
Mining, transportation, production	49.4	47.2	51.7	49.3	42.0	21.9	41.3	23.9	47.1	44.6	46.1	42.2
Others	1.4	0.4	0.8	0.5	0.4	0.0	0.2	0.0	8.3	1.1	6.2	0.7

Occupation	Taiwan						South Korea					
	1966		1981		1991		1961		1983		1991	
	Male	Female	Male	Female	Male	Female	Male	Female	Male	Female	Male	Female
Professional and technical	4.6	5.7	5.2	6.3	7.4	8.8	1.6	0.4	5.3	4.1	7.1	8.3
Administrative and managerial	4.4	1.4	1.2	0.2	1.5	0.3	1.3	0.1	2.1	0.1	2.6	0.2
Clerical	7.3	6.1	11.2	17.5	12.0	23.7	3.0	0.3	11.4	9.1	13.0	13.8
Sales	10.4	12.4	12.9	12.8	14.8	15.4	6.3	6.7	13.4	18.6	12.9	17.1
Services	5.1	9.8	6.6	9.3	7.8	12.7	2.7	2.6	6.7	15.4	7.5	17.3
Agricultural and fishery	42.4	46.6	19.7	16.4	14.4	10.3	75.4	85.7	27.5	32.5	15.2	18.6
Mining, transportation, production	25.9	18.1	43.1	37.5	42.3	28.8	9.8	4.3	33.8	20.2	41.7	24.8
Others	N/A	N/A	N/A	N/A	N/A	N/A	N/A	N/A	N/A	N/A	N/A	N/A

Sources: Hong Kong: Hong Kong Census and Statistics Department 1961, 1981, 1991. Singapore: Singapore Ministry of National Development 1967; Singapore Department of Statistics 1993. Taiwan: Chou 1994; ROC Executive Yuan 1996. South Korea: ROK Economic Planning Board 1962, 1984; ROK National Statistical Office 1992.

a. See the note at table 3.2 for reasons that this table reports statistics from noncomparable years.

b. Starting in the 1990s, the governments of Hong Kong, Singapore, Taiwan, and South Korea adopted the "1988 International Standard Classification of Occupation" promulgated by the International Labor Organization (ILO). To facilitate longitudinal comparisons, this table is confined to data classified according to the 1968 ILO standards. More recent information on gender and occupation is reported in Table 3.5.

c. Hong Kong's 1991 data have been tabulated manually by applying the 1968 ILO standards to the 1991 census data, which were collected relying on the ILO's 1988 standards. In general, the number of professional and technical workers as well as administrative and managerial workers are slightly inflated.

of women in managerial occupations, but the percentage for South Korea increased very moderately, while that of Taiwan actually decreased. In 1996 in Hong Kong, Singapore, Taiwan, and South Korea, men were 2.2 times, 2.8 times, 4.3 times, and 14 times more likely than women to engage in an administrative occupation (see table 3.5). A comparable figure for the United States in 1996 was 1.1 times (U.S. Bureau of the Census 1997). If one considers control over corporate and government assets as the most important source of power in a modern capitalist society, men in East Asia have clearly remained dominant (see Brinton 1988).

Table 3.5. Gender and Occupation in 1996 (in thousands of persons; percent)

Occupation	Hong Kong				Singapore				Taiwan				South Korea			
	Male		Female		Male		Female		Male		Female		Male		Female	
	No.	%	No.	%	No.	%	No.	%	No.	%	No.	%	No.	%	No.	%
Legislators and administrators	282.9	15.4	86.3	7.1	172.0	16.8	43.3	6.0	373	6.8	56	1.6	524	4.2	25	0.3
Professionals	100.1	5.5	51.4	4.3	79.1	7.7	49.5	6.8	264	4.8	278	7.8	657	5.3	357	4.2
Associate professionals	201.4	11.0	167.7	13.9	177.1	17.3	130.4	18.0	1376	15.1	545	15.3	1,363	11.1	612	7.3
Clerks	155.5	8.5	357.2	29.5	61.4	6.0	201.9	27.9	223	4.0	699	19.6	1,241	10.1	1,323	15.7
Service and shop sales workers	256.1	14.0	163.6	13.5	130.2	12.7	100.0	13.8	715	13.0	815	22.9	1,881	15.3	2,791	33.1
Craft and related workers	328.1	17.9	45.1	3.7	134.4	13.1	10.5	1.4					2,455	19.9	774	9.2
Machine operators, assemblers	211.7	11.6	48.2	4.0	152.4	14.9	87.4	12.1	2,459	44.6	903	25.4	1,875	15.2	295	3.5
Elementary occupations	280.1	15.3	284.6	23.5	56.8	5.5	99.9	13.8					1,112	9.0	1,184	14.0
Agriculture, forestry, fishing	N/A	N/A	N/A	N/A	N/A	N/A	N/A	N/A	642	11.7	264	7.4	1,222	9.9	1,073	12.7
Others	17.2	0.9	6.3	0.5	60.2	5.9	1.6	0.2	N/A	N/A	N/A	N/A	N/A	N/A	N/A	N/A

Sources: Hong Kong: Hong Kong Census and Statistics Department 1996. Singapore: Singapore Ministry of Manpower 1998. Taiwan: ROC Executive Yuan 1996. South Korea: ROK National Statistical Office 1997c.

Note: Data reported in this table rely on the ILO's 1988 code of occupational classification and are not comparable to those reported in table 3.4 above.

EXPLAINING FEMALE EMPLOYMENT: PATRIARCHY AND DEVELOPMENT

The above discussion has led to two general observations. First, although thirty years of economic development did not allow East Asian women to gain equal footing with men in the world of employment, some improvements were achieved and female employment cannot be described one-sidedly as exploitative and subordinate. Second, while women from Hong Kong, Singapore, Taiwan, and South Korea have differed in their employment experience, they have made improvements to varying extents and in different dimensions. The question becomes, How to account for the longitudinal changes and intersocietal variations?

An adequate account of the change in female employment in East Asia will most likely be multivariable. This chapter emphasizes two major explanatory variables: patriarchy and capitalist world development. With regard to the former, the author maintains that patriarchy has structured institutions and shaped the normative context within which employers and women have determined their priorities. The institutions and beliefs have, more often than not, worked against the economic betterment of women. However, patriarchy is not impregnable and women are able to change their social and economic positions through individual and collective endeavors. At the same time, patriarchy has been played out in disparate ways. There is evidence that the four societies have attached different meanings to femininity, maintained diverse family structures, prescribed different role relations in marriage, provided dissimilar levels of institutional support for child rearing, and upheld distinct legal and political codes on gender equality. All of these have contributed to the diversity of employment opportunity for women in East Asia (Liew and Leong 1993; Phongpaichit 1988; L. Wang 1995). The bulk of analysis in this chapter falls on the second major explanatory variable, namely, capitalist world economy and its interaction with patriarchy.[12]

The capitalist world economy is the second factor that has shaped the employment opportunities of women. The search for profit has been the impetus behind the global expansion of industrial production. However, world economic development is not a zero-sum game controlled by players from the center. Subject to constraints by the social and political structures of their societies as well as regional alignments that take place from time to time, the governing elite of the developing countries do have room to frame their development strategies. The four cases being examined have differing trajectories of development, as measured by the sequence of sectoral development, extent of government intervention, emphasis placed on light or heavy industries, relative domination of large or small firms, and the geographical distribution of industries. These trajectories have also been associated with diverse labor systems, which are "differentiated by . . . changing and politically contested distributions of economic property rights" (Deyo 1989:154). A given labor system affects the legitimate input that workers can make in the labor process, the right of workers to claim economic subsistence, and sanctions that workers and management can deploy to enforce such rights.

Table 3.6 presents an outline of the trajectories of development as well as the labor systems in these four societies. The limitation of space has prevented the

Table 3.6. Pathways of Development and Labor Systems in Hong Kong, Singapore, Taiwan, and South Korea

	Hong Kong	Singapore	Taiwan	South Korea
Government Intervention	Low	High	High	High
Sequence of Development	1950s: Export-led industrialization	1950s: Import substitution 1960s: Export-led industrialization	1950s: Import substitution 1960s: Export-led industrialization	1950s: Import substitution 1960s: Export-led industrialization
Industrial Mix	Labor intensive	Labor intensive/skill intensive	Labor intensive/skill intensive	Labor intensive/heavy and chemical/skill intensive
Engines of Industrial Growth	Small- and medium-sized firms	State enterprises/multinational corporations	State enterprises/small and medium-sized firms	Family-controlled conglomerates (Chaebol)
Geographical Distribution	Dispersed in the compact territory	Dispersed in the compact territory	Dispersed in the western part of the island	Concentrated in major cities
Labor Systems	Bureaucratic paternalism/stable proletarian/communal paternalism/patriarchy	Bureaucratic paternalism/stable proletarian/hyperproletarian	Bureaucratic paternalism/stable proletarian/communal paternalism/patriarchy	Patrimonial/stable proletarian/hyperproletarian/communal paternalism

author from providing an overview of the development processes of East Asia and describing the characteristics of the labor systems being used. (Interested readers may refer to Amsden [1989], Cheng [1990], Deyo [1989], Gereffi and Wyman [1990], Gold [1986], Haggard [1990], Hamilton and Biggart [1988], Lim [1985], and Wade [1990] for detailed analyses.) The following will try to account for the intersocietal variations and some of the longitudinal changes in female employment by examining the interactions among (a) trajectories of development, (b) labor systems, and (c) patriarchal values and institutions.

Industrial Growth and Female Labor Force Participation

In Hong Kong, Singapore, Taiwan, and South Korea, industrial growth has been associated with the expansion of labor force participation among women, particularly those between 15 and 19 years of age. One set of contributing factors has been the structure of Asian families as well as beliefs about gender roles. The need to feed large families, the economic and ceremonial import of male offspring, as well as the belief that women will be homemakers for a large part of their lives have induced parents to sacrifice their daughters' education and send them to the factories at an early age. The massive expansion of women's labor force participation also occurred because of the nature of industrial development and the fact that the industrial division of labor has not been gender neutral. In particular, the surge of female employment has been associated with the rise of labor-intensive industries. Production tasks in these industries, such as sewing and assembling, have been considered women's work. Such beliefs have been utilized and perpetuated by the management to enhance production efficiency and maintain labor control. These issues have been analyzed in great depth and with tremendous insights (S. K. Kim 1997; Lee 1998a; Ong 1987; Salaff 1981); there is no need for repetition here.

Yet the momentum of increasing female labor force participation is not uniform in the four cases. Among other things, Hong Kong witnessed the most rapid increase in the 1960s and 1970s. During the same period of time, Singapore, Taiwan, and South Korea had only started to embark on the trend. This and related differences occurred in part because of the differential sequence of industrial development. Hong Kong began to export labor-intensive manufactured goods in the mid-1950s as a means to overcome economic setbacks induced by the United Nations 1950 embargo on China. At that time, Singapore, Taiwan, and South Korea were prompted by political and/or military considerations to promote import-substitution industrialization. It was in the mid-1960s, when Singapore was separated from the Federation of Malaya and Taiwan and South Korea were cut off from U. S. military and economic aid, that these countries turned to export-led industrialization. The time when export-led industrialization commenced correlates with the entrance of women into the labor market.

Gender Composition of the Manufacturing Workforce

Rapid industrial development resulted in a general increase in female employment in manufacturing. Nonetheless, data in the above section have found on the one hand a lack of uniformity in the extent of female manufacturing employment among the four societies and on the other a difference in the extent to which the economic restructuring affected women.

In the first place, men rather than women dominated South Korea's manufacturing sector, while the reverse was true for the other cases. Similarly, unlike Taiwan, where men were predominant in agriculture, proportionately more South Korean women than men were employed in the agricultural sector. The idiosyncrasy of South Korea can be comprehended as an interaction among patriarchy, the country's industrial mix, and the geographical distribution of industries.

Beginning in the mid-1960s, industrial development in South Korea was concentrated geographically in a few cities such as Pusan, Taegu, Seoul, and Inchon. In the early 1970s, politicomilitary concerns also induced the government to launch a "heavy and chemical industry drive." Workers needed to make a long-distance, permanent migration from the countryside so as to capture the expanding employment opportunities in industry. This worked against women, who are generally less geographically mobile. Together with the tendency to associate heavy industrial jobs with men, these forces gave rise to male domination in the South Korean manufacturing industry. By comparison, Hong Kong and Singapore are geographically compact, while Taiwan's industries have tended to be dispersed widely in the western part of the island. In all three cases, employment in manufacturing did not entail long-distance, permanent migration. Additionally, labor-intensive industries had continued until the late 1980s to play an important part in the manufacturing industries of these societies. In all three cases, both the industrial mix and the geographical distribution of industry allowed women to capture the expanding employment opportunities in manufacturing.

A second dissimilarity among the four cases is the impact of economic restructuring on women's employment in manufacturing. To be sure, economic restructuring has in general hit women hard in Hong Kong, Singapore, Taiwan, and South Korea. In the 1980s, labor-intensive industries started to move out of these societies and into those offering lower costs of production. Because most women workers were concentrated in the labor-intensive industries, they were invariably affected more severely. In addition, some employers maintained the stereotypical view that women are secondary breadwinners. They sometimes chose to dismiss female workers and asked the men to take on jobs performed previously by the women (Kim and Kim 1995; Lai and Lam 1988; Pyle 1994).

This general trend notwithstanding, the impact of economic restructuring has been far from uniform, with women in Hong Kong being affected most severely. Significantly, there has been a decline since 1981 in the labor force participation of Hong Kong women between 50 and 64 years of age. During the same period, women of the same age group from the other three societies actually increased their labor force participation. The extent of government industrial support, the society's industrial mix, and patriarchal practices have again accounted for these differences.

The governments of Singapore, Taiwan, and South Korea have devised strategies and injected resources to upgrade the technological levels and to maintain the viability of the manufacturing industries. Specifically, Singapore has enticed multinational corporations, Taiwan has established a science-based industrial park, and South Korea has worked through the family-controlled conglomerates (*chaebol*). Although not all of their policies have succeeded, the result has generally been favorable and the manufacturing industries have become more technology intensive. The strategies have slowed down the speed with which manufacturing has withered and allowed a more gradual displacement of the labor-intensive industries and their workers.

In contrast, the Hong Kong government has adopted a noninterventionist industrial policy and provided very limited industrial support. The bulk of small- and medium-sized firms, having spearheaded the early phase of industrial development, have not been able to upgrade their technological levels. Many have tried to reduce their costs of production by taking advantage of China's open-door policy and transferring manufacturing production to Mainland China. This explains the drastic decline of Hong Kong's female employment in manufacturing since the early 1980s.

Although the Hong Kong government has attached much hope to the service sector, the latter has not created enough employment to compensate for the loss in the manufacturing sector. More importantly, service sector jobs usually demand basic literacy as well as impose hidden requirements such as youthfulness and feminine demeanor (Wu 1995). Most of the former factory women had received limited education, tended to be older, and were not accustomed to wearing cosmetics at work, and as a result faired poorly in the competition for service sector jobs. Many displaced women workers gave up after a period of unsuccessful job searching.[13] After all, patriarchal values have stipulated a domestic role for women, which makes it easier both socially and psychologically for women to seek "early retirement." Hence, the drastic decline in female manufacturing employment has not boosted the unemployment rate of Hong Kong, which has stayed around 3 percent since the 1980s (Hong Kong Census and Statistics Department, various years). Instead, the problem manifests itself as a secular decline in the labor force participation rates of women aged 50 to 64.

MARRIED WOMEN: LABOR FORCE PARTICIPATION
AND SECTORAL DISTRIBUTION

In general, married women from Hong Kong, Singapore, Taiwan, and South Korea have been less likely than their unmarried counterparts to take on paid employment. However, the impact of marriage has differed. As the above discussion has shown, the gap between the labor force participation rates of married and unmarried women in Taiwan and South Korea has been smaller than that in Hong Kong and Singapore. Furthermore, while the female labor force participation rates in Hong Kong, Singapore, and Taiwan entered into a steady decline after women turned 30, in South Korea the rate began to erode around age 25 but then picked up again after age 35.

The normative context of patriarchy and gender-informed employment practices have played an important role in deterring paid employment among married women. More often than not, the government, corporations, the general public, and the women themselves have considered household tasks and child care to be women's responsibilities. Very few institutional supports have been developed to free married women from such constraints. Most women would consider paid employment desirable as long as work is compatible with their household duties and/or generates an income that covers the cost of child care and domestic service. Given such a general background, the labor system becomes a crucial determinant at the microlevel that influences the ease with which married women may take on paid employment and juggle the responsibilities of home and work.

Frederic Deyo (1989) has identified six labor systems in these four Asian societies. They include the hyperproletarian system, the stable proletarian system, bureaucratic paternalism, patrimonialism, communal paternalism, and the patriarchy (see table 3.6). In the hyperproletarian labor system, workers are not shielded from the capitalist wage system by any communal ties and they maintain minimal control over their labor, the products, and profits. The stable proletarian system involves a greater measure of job security, better income, and higher skill levels. In turn, bureaucratic paternalism provides job ladders, internal labor markets, fixed annual wage or salary increments, and seniority inducements. Role expectations are spelled out formally, while work and nonwork domains are demarcated clearly. The patrimonial labor system relies on loose networks of dyadic exchange in order to manage workers. In such a system, the immediate superior has discretion over promotion, job assignment, and conditions of work. As for communal paternalism, it is defined by the greater embeddedness of labor recruitment and control in dialectal and other communal associations. Workers are said to have greater claims on the firms with matters of training, job placement, and economic security. Finally, the patriarchal labor system has governed production relations and labor rights through elaborate sets of personal, familial, and kinship obligations.

In Hong Kong, most of the small- and medium-sized industrial enterprises have employed the labor systems of patriarchy and communal paternalism. As white-collar occupations have become predominant in recent years, the labor of the stable proletarian system and bureaucratic paternalism have surged in importance. As for Singapore, multinational corporations have deployed stable proletarian systems and bureaucratic paternalism to manage white-collar workers, and hyperproletarian systems to manage industrial ones. Both the stable proletarian system and bureaucratic paternalism are formal and uncongenial to flexible work arrangements. It is thus understandable that women in Hong Kong and Singapore have tended to quit the job market after they turn 30, when the burden of child rearing has intensified.

As for Taiwan, small- and medium-sized family firms played a pivotal role in the early stage of industrialization and, until very recently, their significance has not been reduced by the introduction of technology-intensive industries. With deficient resources, these firms have relied on the labor systems of patriarchy and communal paternalism, which utilize flexible management and intimate management-labor relations as a means to recruit good workers and gain compliance. Together with the geographical dispersion of industrial enterprises and a short commuting time, the labor systems have made it relatively easy for married women to juggle between home and work (Brinton, Lee, and Parish 1995; Cheng and Hsiung 1992).

South Korea has presented the most interesting case of all. Its age-specific female LFPR has remained M-shaped since the 1960s, which is related in no small way to the economy's bifurcation into two sectors. On the one hand, the conglomerates have been able to offer superior pay and benefits. Assembling, clerical, and managerial tasks in such companies are considered prime jobs. These firms have been able to pick and choose their workers from the long labor queues. Furthermore, these conglomerates tend to rely on patrimonialism, the stable proletarian system, and the hyperproletarian system, all of which are against flexible labor deployment. Women occupying such positions have, more often than not, been compelled to leave as soon as they marry. This helps to explain why female participation in the labor force suddenly drops around age 25.

On the other hand, South Korea has had a substantial number of small- and medium-sized manufacturing firms as well as small enterprises in its commerce sector. Furthermore, the commerce sector has also provided ample opportunity for self-employment. Because smaller firms are less competitive, they have resorted to the labor systems of patriarchy and communal paternalism. Needless to say, self-employment provides an even higher level of employment flexibility. These small and medium enterprises in the manufacturing and commerce sectors have generated employment opportunities for women who can no longer find primary sector jobs. In 1989, for instance, 82 percent of women in the commerce sector worked in establishments employing one to four persons. The same pattern was followed by 54 percent of women in social and personal services (Bai and Cho 1996). Furthermore, women in service and sales occupations tended to be older than women employed in the clerical and production work. This supports the argument that the presence of a large commerce sector and an informal economy have provided the opportunity for married women to re-enter the labor force (Lee 1993). Finally, given the nature of these service sector jobs, they have only been able to attract women who have to work out of necessity. In South Korea, married women with more educational have been less likely than their less educated counterparts to participate in the labor force. Similarly, college educated Korean women have had the highest hidden unemployment rate (Bai and Cho 1996; Lee 1988; Lee 1993).

OCCUPATIONAL REPRESENTATION: IS WOMEN'S STATUS ENHANCED?

Finally, the above suggests that East Asian women have moved gradually into the clerical, professional, and managerial occupations. However, women from these four countries have not performed equally, and it is important not to overemphasize the extent of improvements. Among high status and high remuneration occupations, East Asian women have done best in professional and associate professional occupations. Even here, however, a high level of sex segregation can be found. Significantly, women are poorly represented in engineering, architecture, law, and medicine at the professional level (Hong Kong Census and Statistics Department 1996; Singapore Ministry of Manpower 1999; ROC Executive Yuan 1996; ROK National Statistical Office 1997a).

Yet it is within the administrative and managerial occupations that women have faced the greatest obstacles. According to some studies, employers believe that most women will place their families before their careers. They also fear that women have a harder time gaining the respect and trust of their customers. Some male employees have also been found to resent their subordination to women administrators, which results in the development of stressful relations at work. Finally, social attitudes have not been supportive of women's assertiveness or their attempts to mingle socially with their male customers or superiors. This has resulted in the exclusion of women from the real power networks and prevented them from realizing their potential (Bai and Cho 1996; Chan and Lee 1994; Cheng and Liao 1994; de Leon and Ho 1994; Lai 1999; Westwood 1997).

Of all white-collar occupations, clerical work has been most receptive to women. (Incidentally, clerical workers—and female clerical workers in particular—have tended to be younger than people working in other occupations. In South Korea in 1996, 68.2 percent of female clerical workers were between 20 and 29 years of age. The comparable figure for Hong Kong in 1996 was 45.3 percent, 33.2 percent for Singapore in 1998, and 47.5 percent for Taiwan in 1996 (Hong Kong Census and Statistics Department 1996; Singapore Ministry of Manpower 1999; ROC Executive Yuan 1996; ROK National Statistical Office 1997a). One may argue that the youthfulness of female clerical workers is a function of their recent mass entrance into the occupation. This argument does not hold for Singapore nor, to a lesser extent, for South Korea and Taiwan, because the expansion of women's representation in the occupation has come gradually. A more plausible postulation is that clerical work has become deskilled and largely devoid of opportunities for promotion to administrative positions. Employers also find it cheaper to hire young female clerical workers. Given the exacting atmosphere, women would quit either when they have the means to, or when their familial obligations compel them to do so. But this remains a hypothesis to be verified.[14]

To the extent that this postulation is true, it is tempting to argue that clerical work has replaced production as the most "appropriate" occupation for women.

In fact, the gender stereotype that was associated with female production workers now applies to women clerical workers (Ong 1987). In an interview with the *Economic Journal,* a newspaper in Hong Kong, the personnel manager of the Hongkong Bank remarks that women are more courteous in serving the customers and dexterous in handling office machines. They are, in his opinion, very suitable to be tellers, secretaries, programmers, and to take on a number of jobs in the personnel, accounting, and other supporting departments (Association for the Advancement of Feminism 1993). In these East Asian countries, the nimble hands of women, though no longer required to perform assembling tasks, have been deployed to handle typewriters, computers, and other office machinery. Their patience and meticulousness are now utilized to deal with the tedium of paper work.

CONCLUSION

This chapter has tried to examine the longitudinal changes and intersocietal variations in female employment within Hong Kong, Singapore, Taiwan, and South Korea. The data suggest that the pattern of female employment has become increasingly complex. These East Asian women are no longer confined to production tasks in manufacturing industries. A number of them have moved on to clerical, professional and, to a lesser extent, managerial occupations. Equally important, women in these four societies have performed differently in the labor market, making it quite impossible to talk about an "Asian model" of female employment.

The chapter has tried to use patriarchy and capitalist world development as two major variables to account for both longitudinal changes and intersocietal variations. The author maintains that patriarchy has manifested itself in different ways. The four societies appear to have differed in meanings attached to femininity, the structure of family and kinship networks, institutional support given to married women, and the political and legal codes on female status. Given the lack of good comparative research, the author has only been able to explore the general implications of patriarchal practices on female employment in East Asia.

In this chapter, the author has examined in greater detail how differences in the trajectories of development and in labor systems have resulted in varying patterns of female employment. In particular, it is suggested that the governments of Hong Kong, Singapore, Taiwan, and South Korea have provided divergent levels of industrial support and that these economies have differed in industrial mix, geographical concentration of industries, and domination of small or large firms, and that they have relied on different types of labor systems. Altogether, these have helped to explain the differences in timing of women's entrance into the labor market, their relative domination in the manufacturing sector, the ease with which they faced the challenge of economic restructuring, and their chance of being able to work after getting married.

This chapter has left unanswered many questions. They include the low level of labor force participation among unmarried women in Taiwan and South Korea, the superior performance of Taiwanese women in the professional occupations, and above all the systematic differences in the nature of patriarchal beliefs and institutions in these four societies. It is the author's earnest hope that concerned scholars will pursue these issues in the future.

NOTES

1. Men's 1996 labor force participation rates in Hong Kong, Singapore, Taiwan, and South Korea were 77.6 percent, 78.7 percent, 71.1 percent, and 76.1 percent, respectively.

2. The discussion concerning the trends of female LFPRs is based on a tracking of data between the 1960s and 1990s. It has covered data not reported in table 3.2.

3. The LFPR of married women in Hong Kong reached 47 percent in 1986, but subsequently declined (Hong Kong Census and Statistics Department, various years.)

4. ROC refers to the Republic of China, which is also known as Taiwan, and ROK is the Republic of Korea.

5. "Economic restructuring," understood as the reorganization of a society's fundamental economic activity, has taken place at many points in history. Researchers have used the term more specifically to refer to the "deindustrialization" of the United States in the 1980s and the phasing out of labor-intensive industries in the East Asian societies.

6. The Singapore figures were for the year 1980.

7. Hong Kong and Singapore are city-states with negligible agricultural sectors.

8. Singapore's manufacturing industry suffered a decline in 1985 and 1986, but it picked up again in 1987.

9. The decline in the portion of female manufacturing employment is calculated by subtracting the figure in 1996 by that of the year in which female manufacturing employment started to decline. In Hong Kong, for example, 53.1% − 18.2% = 34.9%.

10. It is notable that the year in which female manufacturing employment declined does not necessarily correspond to the year when manufacturing employment as a whole declined. In South Korea, female manufacturing employment started to decrease in 1989, that of men continued to increase until 1995. For the country as a whole, manufacturing started to drop in the year 1991.

11. Because the base years of these four cases are different, the figures presented have only indicative value. They should not be used for comparative purposes.

12. It would have been ideal to sort out the systematic differences between the patriarchal institutions of these four societies and identify their specific impact on the patterns of female employment. There is, unfortunately, a lack of good comparative research and a study from scratch is beyond the scope of the present chapter. The author will therefore resort to a general discussion of patriarchy, analyzing prescribed roles for women at different stages of their lives as well as the gender-based division of labor both at home and at work.

13. A representative of the Hong Kong Women Workers' Association made this point during an informal communication back in 1995.

14. The comparable figure for male clerical workers was 32 percent in South Korea in 1996, 36.6 percent in Hong Kong in 1996, 23 percent in Singapore in 1998, and 27.8 percent in Taiwan in 1996 (Hong Kong Census and Statistics Department 1996; Singapore Ministry of Manpower 1999; ROC Executive Yuan 1996; ROK National Statistical Office 1997a). That male clerical workers tend to be older than their female counterparts suggests that men either view the occupation as an interim step toward an administrative job or that, in the worst case scenario, they have to hold on to it.

Chapter 4

Gendered Organizations, Embodiment, and Employment among Manufacturing Workers in Taiwan

Esther Ngan-ling Chow and Ray-may Hsung

As globalization of national economies has proceeded, entities such as transnational corporations (TNCs) have become prime sites in which the logic and practices of capitalism are articulated in production relations and labor processes to create and perpetuate class-based power relations and inequality in the workplace. The logic of late twentieth-century capitalism has been to achieve profit maximization and capital accumulation on a world scale (Braverman 1974). To achieve these goals, beginning in the early to mid-1960s, the First World nations—Japan, the United States, and those in Western Europe—sought economic expansion in the form of global markets for cheap labor, land, and natural resources. TNCs were established to embark on this economic deployment by setting up offshore production, thus restructuring industrialization globally and creating the international division of labor and global assembly lines. Taiwan, then a less developed nation, responded to these economic initiatives by shifting its import-substitution strategy to export-oriented industrialization, which has been its primary policy and strategy for propelling its economic growth since the mid-1960s (Chow 1997a; Hsiao 1987). Special "export processing zones" (EPZs) were established to house the TNCs and their global factories, following what Rae Lesser Blumberg (1994a:5) has called "the latest development gospel for those promoting national income growth." Hence, the industrial establishment of these zones provides a social context in which class relations and divisions are produced and reproduced in the segmented labor market and the workplace.

Undergirding the "economic miracle" of Taiwan, which has claimed the status of a "newly developed country" since the mid-1980s, has been a "quiet revolution" marked by the gradual increase of women's labor force participation to support its economic development process. One prime characteristic of the EPZs is the high proportion, ranging from 60 to 80 percent, of female laborers in manufacturing industries such as those of electronics, textiles, garments, plastics, and household appliances (Ngo 1989). These young women constitute a cheap source of labor that has attracted foreign capital investment and an ever-growing number of firms, particularly TNCs, to Taiwan. Research has pointed out that the process of economic development is highly gendered, with female and male workers having different labor experiences (Benería and Roldán 1987; Blumberg 1994b; Nash and Fernandez-Kelly 1983; Visanathan et al. 1998). Arguing the theoretical importance of using a feminist analysis, Maria Mies (1986) suggests that the interplay between patriarchy and capitalism has been integrated into a world system of accumulation and exploitation that divides and oppresses workers, particularly women. Aihwa Ong (1987) also points out the effect of capitalist logic and interest for disciplining workers through work organization. Given the gendered process of development, this chapter specifically deals with the bureaucratic work organization as one of the critically important locations in which this intricate interplay is articulated. Such a bureaucracy is also a site in which class relations are socially constructed through gender relations that in turn intensify class division and inequality.

Recent feminist scholarship has challenged some of the basic assumptions and tenets of traditional theories that tend to see organizations as gender neutral and disembodied. In fact, organizations are highly gendered and embodied, characterized by the differential positioning of men in higher ranks and women in lower ones within the hierarchy and the systematic patterning of male-dominated power relationships, forming a gender regime in the organizational context. Authority relations are structured on class and gender lines, with jobs performed by male and female bodies that are highly regulated and controlled by management.

In this study, we adopt the gendered embodiment perspective to examine how the gendering process in work organizations and its institutional embeddedness affect the employment patterns and labor experiences of female and male workers in manufacturing industries in Taiwan.[1] Although we recognize that gender is imported into organizations from such broad contexts as the segmented labor market and sex-segregated occupations, our primary focus here is on the gendered organization. We first highlight the theoretical perspective used to analyze an organization as a gendered and embodied space. We examine how gender is embedded and embodied in the structure as well as the process of the work organization. We then discuss how such gendered embeddedness and embodiment (1) greatly influence women's and men's employment and situate them differentially in the division of labor, the bureaucratic hierarchy, ruling relationships, promotion decisions, and the reward system in the workplace, and (2) are intimately connected to sexuality, family, and work.

THE ORGANIZATION AS A GENDERED
AND EMBODIED SPACE

How are women and gender issues dealt with in conventional organizational theories? In what ways have feminist critiques of these theories advanced the situated understanding of the gendered nature of organizational structures and processes? The Weberian tradition sees the organization of work as a rational coordination of many sets of roles and activities performed by its job incumbents to attain specific purposes or goals through a division of labor, a hierarchy of authority, and a governance of rules and regulations (Scott 1998). Marxist and radical analyses conceptualize the workplace as a class-based structure grounded in production relations that divide workers into capitalists and proletarians, managers and workers. This structure uses mechanisms of control to regulate labor processes, to extract surplus value from exploited laborers, and to suppress opposition. Both of these classical traditions have made theoretical contributions but have tended to use an opaque gender lens, viewing job and position as abstract categories filled by universal and generic workers.

Feminist scholars suggest that a gender-embodied subtext underlies both the classical and contemporary social and organizational theories. Specifically, feminist critiques point out four major questionable assumptions in conventional organizational theories: (1) that the organization is gender neutral; (2) that the "job" is an abstraction that is filled by a disembodied and universal worker; (3) that the organization is asexual, ignoring the importance of sexuality; and (4) that the "social" and "personal" categories are excluded from analysis (Acker 1990; Calas and Smircich 1992; Savage and Witz 1992). Thus, the focus of an organizational analysis rests on impersonality and rationality rather than on personableness and emotionality in social relationships in the organizational context. In fact, gender is a *personal, relational,* and *sexual* analytical category that is situated in a social field.

In this study, we argue that gender relations are embedded in the organizational structure, processes, and practices as a constitutive part. Organizations are a kind of patriarchal structure characterized by a form of masculinity within which are built systemic sets of ruling relations of male dominance and female subordination. The concept of rationality itself is built upon a particular form of masculinity that excludes the *social* and the *personal.* Hence, gender interests are obscured by the neutrality vested in bureaucratic rules, regulations, and procedures. The positing of a job as an abstraction is an essential move in creating jobs as mechanisms of compulsion and control over work processes to conceal a gender substructure in which men's and women's bodies fill the jobs. Drawing insight from the work of Michel Foucault (1980), we see that sexuality, as part of the ongoing production of gender, sexuality, and power, is intertwined in everyday social interactions in bureaucratic organizations (see also Adkins 1995; Cockburn 1991). For example, Catharine MacKinnon (1979) points out that some jobs include sexualization of female workers as part of the job. Sexual harassment, an overt form of control over women in the workplace, can be understood often as a condition of the job, both a cause and a consequence of gender discrimination.

Explorations of human embodiment in social relations in recent years have led scholars to recognize the significance of embodiment in gendering processes and its institutionalization of gender and sexuality in the organizational context (Acker 1990; Adkins 1995; Butler 1993; Cockburn 1991; Price and Shildrick 1999; Schilling 1996; Scott and Morgan 1993). Chris Schilling (1996) conceptualizes the body as a theoretical space that is simultaneously a social and a biological phenomenon. Because our concern is with embodiment in the organizational context, we see the body as a social rather than a biological category (Kerfoot and Knights 1996). Given the physical makeup of the body, the body is not only transformed by social forces, but also forms a basis for and enters into the construction of social relations.

According to David Morgan (1998), embodiment refers to different modes of being in bodies. He explains that within the capitalist system, "class consciousness is not only frequently symbolized by bodies of workers both sharing and challenging a common fate but is based upon a recognition of the sharing of physical and symbolic space by embodied workers" (p. 655). These complex divisions of labor and hierarchies are represented in bodily terms as embodied behavior and lifestyle interacting with social and economic status and other divisions, including gender. Gender rests not only on the surface of the body, in performance and doing, but becomes embodied deeply as part of who we are physically, psychologically, and socially (Martin 1998).

More specifically, Joan Acker argues that the nature of organization is actually premised on a type of embodiment associated with men's and women's bodies. She (1990) elaborates that

> . . . the abstract worker is actually a man, and it is the man's body, its sexuality, minimal responsibility in procreation, and conventional control of emotions that pervades work and organizational processes. Women's bodies—female sexuality, their ability to procreate and their pregnancy, breast-feeding, and child care, menstruation, and mythic "emotionality"— are suspect, stigmatized, and used as grounds for control and exclusion. (p. 152)

Once we see organizations as embodied systems of social relations, Witz, Halford, and Savage (1996:175) explain that "both gender and sexuality are inscribed on, marked by and lived through the body" via everyday interactions and the structural design of organizations. When embodiment is routinized, it becomes a relatively autonomous system, taking on a life in its own right. The organization is therefore an embodied, situated system; one that provides the material and cultural (i.e., symbolic and ideological) bases for power relations based on class, gender, and sexuality to be discursively constructed, contested, and reconstructed through organizational designs, processes, and practices.

Slightly departing from Acker's gendered organizational theory, we focus on TNCs as representing a form of corporate patriarchy that privileges not just the male body, but one particular version of it and one specific form of masculinity—"hegemonic masculinity," as Robert Connell calls it (1987). The interests and logic of capitalism and patriarchy are ensured and practiced in TNCs to impose rationality, efficiency, predictability, and stability in the economic sector and to control labor processes in production and social reproduction to guarantee interests and continued profits (Burawoy 1985; Edwards 1979; Mies 1986; Ong 1987). Since the capitalist class is primarily under the control of men, the bureaucratic organization of TNCs as corporate patriarchies was set up to enhance and protect the corporate and men's class and gender interests. Although not all managers are men, male domination of most hierarchical levels within management pervades the corporate structure, excluding women, who experience a glass ceiling on their job advancement. Men and senior executives are frequently depicted and portray themselves as "hard men" and "flamboyant entrepreneurs." They are the "disciplined body," as Arthur Frank (1991) calls it, a highly controlled one with a masculine management style. Hence, these organizations are embodied with images of male bodies and hegemonic masculinity in TNC structure and processes which marginalize women in invisible, lower-level positions, segregated in certain jobs and occupations. Female bodies are basically cheaper sources of labor than male bodies. Female bodies are perceived naturally to have nimble fingers, to be docile and unskilled, and to be willing to accept tough work discipline and to do tedious, repetitive, and monotonous work (Elson and Pearson 1981).

The gender regime of TNCs greatly determines the ways of organizing and ordering masculinities and femininities, male and female bodies, in a valued hierarchy. While managers have numerous functions, our analysis concerns the gendering process and embodiment discourse by which managerial control and labor practices have an impact on human resource matters such as recruitment and hiring, division of labor, work assignment, promotions, and earnings for female and male workers. Management has the upper hand, exercising authority and power in appropriating, coordinating, and regulating labor and gendered bodies. Managerial control is accomplished through the use of rules and regulations, task categorization and segregation, job routinization, authority hierarchy, and the depersonalization of relationships within the work organization (Chow 1994). These means of control define and legitimatize what female and male workers actually do and how they do it; they justify existing work arrangements, positions, and rewards; and maintain unequal power relationships. At the same time, organizations construct ideology, symbols (e.g., language and gesture) and images (e.g., dress and slogans) that explain, express, and reinforce the existing structure, ruling relations, and culture that influence greatly the identity, subjectivity, and behavior of the workers. Thus, the privileged characteristics of male embodiment are normalized and institutionalized in organizational design, practice, process, and culture, meaning that male workers are more likely than female workers to be perceived to match and to qualify for the requirements of the bureaucratic organization.

In recent work on sexuality in organizations, G. Burrell (1984) suggests that attempting to suppress sexuality in the place of capitalist production is in the interests of organizational control of its members and their activities, thus limiting women's organizational participation and excluding them from certain areas of work activity and rank positions. Insistence on heterosexuality is a way to take sexuality out of the workplace and legitimize the home as the location of sexuality. The conceptualization of the disembodied job symbolizes this separation of gender and sexuality and of work and family, thus making it easy to disqualify women from holding high-ranking positions in which the homosocial nature of male embodiment is guarded, maintained, and controlled (Pringle 1989; Kanter 1977).

Almost all of the research on gendered organizations using the embodiment perspective has been done in the context of the West and the First World. In this study, we apply this theoretical approach to analyze the employment patterns and job outcomes of manufacturing workers employed in TNCs and local firms in Taiwan. Among Asia's "little dragons," Taiwan has the largest proportion of its labor force participating in the manufacturing industries, which have more workers who are women than men (see Chu in chapter 3). Several studies in Taiwan have reported that a greater proportion of women cluster in segregated jobs at low-ranked positions, earning substantially less than their male counterparts (Brinton, Lee, and Parish 1995; Chang 1996; Chen and Yang 1994; Hsu 1989; Tan and Yu 1996; Tsai 1987). The number of female workers decreases substantially as the job level increases. However, most of these studies are primarily of a quantitative nature, treating gender as a variable. Responding to Tsung-Kuo Hsu's plea (1989) to conduct qualitative research in Taiwan, we integrate both quantitative and qualitative data in the analysis.

THE RESEARCH STUDY

This study is part of a large-scale comparative study of the impact of economic development on workers' employment and family life in Taiwan and China. At each site, we conducted a survey study and field research to collect both quantitative and qualitative data to cross-validate and substantiate research findings and analysis. We collected 569 survey interviews and 48 in-depth interviews from the nine factories in an EPZ and an industrial park in Taiwan.[2] The survey sample cases were randomly selected by using a stratified random sampling method. The stratifying factors used were type of ownership and size of factory, forming six substrata from which one factory in the EPZ was randomly selected. Types of ownership, determined by the ownership registered in government documentation, were foreign, joint, and Taiwanese. Factory size was divided into large (more than 200 employees) and small (fewer than 200 employees) by using average firm size. In addition, we randomly selected three factories according to ownership type from another industrial park for purposes of comparison.

Within each of the nine factories, we chose respondents randomly and proportionally with regard to worker's gender and job rank (i.e., high, middle, or low). Since most factories had very few female managers in high-ranked positions, only a few of these women were included in the quantitative data, but many of them were secured in the qualitative field data. For this reason, we primarily ground our present analysis in the sample of 48 in-depth interviews, which were controlled by the same stratified factors as those in the survey sample. All of the interviews were conducted in either Mandarin or Taiwanese. Each in-depth interview took one to two hours to complete. Interviews were conducted at the place the workers found most convenient (e.g., factory, home, or public place). Personal narratives about their experience as employees in gendered organizations were systematically coded and analyzed.

RESEARCH FINDINGS

Gendered Jobs and Gendered Tracks

Division of labor by gender is one of the widely pervasive mechanisms in the design of organizational functions. It intersects dynamically with class to divide workers into different job categories with various assigned tasks, options, and activities for women and men. In general, women have similar job assignments as laborers of the working rather than the managerial class, their assignments inevitably affected by sex-based ascription via specific personnel practices and power dynamics (Reskin and McBrier 2000). Consistent with the culturally defined gender ideology, the organization of work structures gender relations by assuming that certain jobs are appropriate for women and men and by segregating the genders accordingly into different occupations and job positions. However, jobs are more gendered than occupations (Acker 1990; Baron and Bielby 1984; and Bielby and Baron 1986), and organizations design different gates to facilitate the entry deemed appropriate for gendered bodied workers.

Gendered jobs can occur in two main types: men's versus women's work, and identical work with different titles (Martin 1992). In both types, categorization, separation, and differential compensation tend to favor male workers. A great proportion of women consistently experience disadvantages by concentrating in jobs that are generally low in rank, social status, and pay.

The first type is based on gender assumptions concerning the physical capabilities of male and female bodies; these assumptions are socially constructed to justify perceptions of jobs appropriate for either men or women. In the factories studied, management perceived certain jobs as supposed to be occupied and performed by gendered bodies, seeing the male gender primarily in managerial, technical, and skilled positions and the female gender on the assembly line and in clerical and unskilled positions. Most workers interviewed easily identified a clear division of labor by gender in the jobs they did. Men performed primarily heavy manual, mechanical, technical, and professionally skilled types of tasks and activities, while women did mostly light manual, dexterous, simple, minute, routine, and unskilled (or at most semiskilled) jobs that were basically of an operative, clerical, or administrative nature.

The second type of gendered job involves identical work activities that are given different job titles so that men and women do not appear to do equal work and thus can be given different rewards. Management's strategy is to separate jobs for women and men and to justify the perception that men are endowed with innate abilities to rule and thereby to provide these jobs with a higher status and pay rate. One middle-level director offered a concrete example of this practice:

> One of my colleagues recently finished his military service. When he entered the firm, he was given a foreman's position with authority to supervise workers. However, he was assigned the same job tasks as those done by female operative workers who taught him how to do a basic assembly-line job before he could start to super-

vise them. It makes it difficult for him to deal with female workers because his work does not match his actual job title.

We asked the workers when in their experience with the organization the categorization and separation of gendered jobs began. Most of the workers said that a clear division of labor along gender lines started when workers entered the firm. A high-ranking male manager explained further,

> Clearly a separation of gender in the division of labor at all levels started from the very beginning, as workers arrived. Work abilities vary between men and women. It really depends on the type of job that they do. Job content that requires manual labor such as machinery is better suited for male workers, whereas work that requires careful and meticulous attention (such as desk and production jobs) is better suited for female workers.

One female worker from a Japanese firm remarked, "A female worker has a weaker body than a man. What the male body can handle, the female body cannot." We asked respondents to specify the attributes of gendered bodies. On the one hand, they described the distinctively male body as strong, hard, and active, tending to be competitive, to use rational thinking in decision making, to be willing to engage in dangerous activities, and to be equipped with "black hands" that do dirty and oily tasks. On the other hand, they characterized the female body as weak, soft, and passive, tending to be gentle and emotional in ways that might color their judgment and decisions, to be less capable of handling complex tasks, and to be equipped with "white hands" that do less dirty things. Because a woman's body is supposedly weak, it needs to be protected. One female worker pointed out to us that even the Labor Standard Law did not permit women to work the night shift from 10:00 P.M. to 6:00 P.M. unless certain accommodations were provided.[3]

A male general manager from a Taiwanese firm observed, "We don't hire women to work in our division because women do not like to do technical and maintenance kinds of work. . . . They don't know how to fix machines and don't like to do it as well. Most women are production workers. They came to our office and didn't stay long. They quit, either moved to other firms or got married." Thus, women are temporary bodies. Jobs done by female bodies are ones from which they may be easily transferred and replaced, especially when employers used foreign guest workers from Thailand, the Philippines, and Indonesia as cheaper sources of labor to replace them (see Lee in chapter 9).

As workers engaged in an engendering process that assigned different task arrangements for women and men, they invoked meaning for gendered jobs that can be classified into three main views—the "absolute," the "physically exceptional," and the "constructionist."[4] Slightly over half of the workers interviewed held the "absolute" view that used biological explanations of supposed differences in innate abilities, intelligence, cognitive thinking, and personality between men and women. A female worker from a Japanese factory said, "I think that there are some gender differences in men's and women's abilities. . . . Men are able bodies and they are more dependable. There is work that women can't do, and men can take it over and do it well." Fearing the accusation that they discriminate against women, managers used a "separate but equal" rationale to maintain the appearance of treating the two genders equally. So long as workers remained tracked in doing their gendered jobs, they would be treated equally within their own track.

About one-third of the workers held to the "physically exceptional" view that they generally saw few gender differences between male and female workers except with regard to their physical abilities. One female supervisor explained,

> Male workers tend to be more physical, with endurance. Mental abilities are more or less the same for both genders, but men tend to be absentminded, and they sometimes need to be reminded to get their work done. It really depends on individuals and their intelligence, keen observation, and comprehension. . . . The IQ of a girl is not lower than a boy's. We need to help girls to develop their potential and make them as good as boys.

The "constructionist" view was held by about one-eighth of the workers, who saw basically little or no gender differences in workers and their abilities. Critical of patriarchal ruling relationships that indoctrinate the notions of men's superiority and domination and women's inferiority and subordination, a high-ranking female manager perceived gendered jobs and embodiment as a result of the social construction of power relationships between men and women. She pointed out that Japanese firms were more patriarchal than U.S. firms, and offered this analysis:

> Actually, I think that men and women do not differ in their abilities at all. Any observed differences lie in individuals rather than gender. I feel that women are generally in disadvantaged circumstances when competing with men in this man-made society. We are expected to yield more and take less so that men will have a competitive edge over women. This is the present prevailing gender-biased ideology that tends to favor men. It really costs more to be a woman.

A male supervisor agreed with this view, saying that female workers were as good as male workers. Another female supervisor from an American firm summed up the "constructionist view":

> Gender differences in men's and women's abilities are gradually diminishing because schooling has become commonly available to all who receive some education. The traditional gender ideology of separate spheres for men and women is outmoded as the society becomes advanced and modernized. Female workers are allowed to enter the factory. I see very little gender difference in workers and their jobs nowadays.

These various perspectives of gendered jobs call to mind Robert Connell's (1987) analysis of reproduction of gendered bodies, in which he argues that the production of gender differences is due to the fact that similarities between male and female bodies are neglected, their differences are exaggerated, and the meanings of biological features are changed into new sets of oppositional gendered categories as represented by the first view discussed above. The second view reflects how gendered bodies are transformed by social and labor practices except with regard to the "cult of physicality." The dominant notions of masculinity and femininity become embodied through practices of gendered jobs and tracks that are routinized in daily operations through labor processes and are further institutionalized into work structure. Embodiment can itself serve to further justify the original social categories of men as "the stronger sex" and women as "the weaker sex." A self-fulfilling prophecy may be at work here as gendered bodies operate in ways that support the validity of original gender images and practices. The "constructionist" view, though held by a minority of workers, implies that gendered typing in jobs is not always fixed, for it can be modified as labor market conditions, ideology, and society change.

RECRUITMENT AND HIRING OF EMBODIED WORKERS

How are embodied workers recruited into the work organization? First of all, women and men do not arrive at the organization's door as equals. Women's and men's backgrounds, qualifications, and experiences, along with assumptions and preferences about men's versus women's suitability and commitment to paid employment combine to situate men and women differently as they enter the workplace. Recruitment and hiring policies and practices become an important mechanism for screening them to determine whether they are desirable for employment. However, we found that job criteria, including gender, in hiring policies have been and can be altered according to the changes in labor demand and in the political economy of a given time in Taiwan. In general, manufacturing factories follow the labor stipulations as officially stated in the Labor Standard Laws. One union representative said that TNCs, especially those located in EPZs, do not dare to violate stated labor regulations. Local firms and TNCs outside of the EPZ might find loopholes in the labor laws or engage in different labor practices that are not clearly regulated in the labor statutes.

Personal characteristics such as age and marital status historically and presently have shaped female bodies more than male bodies in the workplace. Presently, the legal working age is set at 16 years old. Some firms had hired student interns who worked full-time during the day and went to vocational schools for training in the evening after their work hours. While age limitations have not been clearly imposed on male workers, an informal perception, we were told, is that good employment prospects have been limited for female workers who are above 30 or 35 years old. Reduction in fertility had deceased the reproduction of labor by the 1980s. Since the early 1980s, regional economic restructuring that has prompted industrialists to move their production units to China or Southeast

Asian countries has re-created a decline in the manufacturing jobs in Taiwan. Postindustrial Taiwan has also attracted some women to enter the fast-growing service sector that provides better working conditions than those in the manufacturing sector. As women have increased their schooling and training, many have preferred to enter semiprofessional and technical fields. When the labor shortage in manufacturing industries was severe, criteria for recruitment and hiring were relaxed. In addition, foreign guest workers, particular those young and single, were recruited to fill the vacant positions. Older women were also recruited for trivial and dead-end jobs, such as in the cases of the female middle-aged cleaning and line workers we interviewed.

In Taiwan's early phase of industrialization, employers sought women as a cheaper source of labor than their male counterparts. The corporate image of female bodies is that they are young, single female workers with nimble fingers, docility, and manual dexterity, all desirable traits for doing assembly-line jobs. Single women were preferred to such an extent that there was a prohibition against hiring married women. Due to the high demand for labor in the 1970s and labor shortages in the early 1980s, however, many firms in Taiwan eliminated such prohibitions. In our sample, the overwhelming majority of male managers (89 percent), slightly over half of male workers, and one-third of female workers were married. Evidence suggests that being young and single tends to be favored more in the hiring of production workers in Japanese than in American firms (Chow and Hsung 2000).

Workers informed us that the preference for hiring single women was still implicit, not so much in terms of personnel policy, but as a presumed labor preference that did not apply to men. One female manager recalled several years ago that when applying for a job with a computer firm she was asked to sign a contractual agreement to remain single. She complained that the male managers ". . . were very chauvinistic in requiring only women to sign a contract specifying that they would quit their jobs if they got married. This clearly shows a mistrust between the management and vulnerable female workers." Another woman told of a similar experience that happened to her a long time ago, when she had to give up her job in a Japanese firm when she got married. However, we were informed that this blatantly gendered labor practice does not exist any more. An examination system that some workers considered to be fair required testing those who applied for technical and professional jobs. A male manager described the present situation:

> There is no restriction in hiring. I do not think that the company nowadays rejects hiring female workers if they are married. However, single women will be asked whether they can continue working if they get married. They may be asked whether they can take care of their children and continue working at the same time. This personal factor reduces women's chances of being hired.

Ethnic tension, overt or subtle, sometimes constrains social relationships at work in ways that may affect the processes and practices of recruitment and hiring, depending on the political context of the time. One woman worker from a Japanese firm recalled some discriminatory hiring practices by Japanese management in the 1970s which favored Taiwanese workers over non-Taiwanese, although she believed that this had not been the case in recent years.[5]

In the factories we studied, the lower-level positions were filled mostly by internal succession and promotion, whereas the higher-level positions were usually filled by external recruitment of qualified personnel. Workers interviewed pointed out that sources of human capital (a labor supply factor) such as education, skills, and work experience, which workers brought with them, together with the types of job demand (a labor demand factor), were the most important factors in recruitment and hiring (Becker 1964; Brinton 1988). In our sample, the average educational level of male workers was slightly above high school graduate and that of female workers was around high school graduate. Men and women who were not in managerial positions tended to be young, with fewer years of work experience. Among them, women on average had approximately two years more work experience than their male counterparts. The main reasons were that women sacrificed their education to work to support family and/or to allow their brothers to have more education, while men prolonged their schooling to attain a higher level of education, spent time in military services, and had a higher probability of having been promoted to higher level positions.

The most common rationale used to justify men's advantages in obtaining highly ranked and paid positions in the manufacturing industries was that of men's reputedly greater technical skills and competence. When we asked whether this also applied to female applicants, one middle-level manager shook his head and said, "It is rather rare for a woman who has just completed schooling and technical training to apply for top jobs. The only exception is the case of family connections."[6] A female division chief sympathetic to gender equity for women recognized that women are stereotyped as less competent:

> Of course, the company is practical in recruitment and hiring. If we have a vacancy for an engineer, I would consider hiring women because, proportionally speaking, there are very few female engineers. This is an obvious gender inequity. I encourage women to apply. Gender discrimination in job recruitment is not common, but gender inequity does exist in the ways that female applicants are treated. A general notion is that women are not as strong in quantitative types of things as men are.

Patriarchal control of male privilege constrains women, even educated ones, from obtaining jobs commensurate to their education, training, and skills. Hence, human capital investment in male and female bodies differs, and the returns on such investment diverge.

The types of job demands that male and female bodies must meet when jobs and tracks are gendered seem to exert a greater influence on employment than human capital factors from the recruitment stage onward. Factories do not generally set up explicit regulations for the differential recruitment of men and women. However, implicit, taken-for-granted beliefs about the sex-typed job suitability for men and women track them accordingly into different gendered jobs, thus producing and reproducing disadvantageous work conditions for women. Men were thus assumed to be suitable for managerial, technical, sales, and heavy manual-labor-oriented jobs, whereas women were presumed fit for jobs on the assembly line and in quality control, accounting, bookkeeping, clerical, and administrative areas. In the gendering process, workers conformed to presumed beliefs concerning job suitability by actualizing stereotypical beliefs in their job-seeking behavior.

Embedding Gendered Bodies in Hierarchy

Typically, men and women are differentiated simultaneously by both bureaucratic and gender hierarchies, with the result that official rank and gender status are confounded, inserting gendered embeddedness and embodiment hierarchically into a work structure under patriarchal control. In the factories studied, it was clearly evident that men dominated the authority structure of the workplace. Men predominated at the upper echelons, numerically and positionally, and most women, even those in management, occupied low- or at most middle-ranked positions in the organizational hierarchy. Differences in hierarchical location gave men the advantage of being conferred with more opportunities, options, power, resources, and rewards (Kanter 1977). Because men tended to have more valuable job opportunities and organizational resources, including required technical experience, they occupied more powerful positions with higher pay.

A middle-ranked male manager acknowledged the powerful force of tracking jobs by gender once jobs are structured into different hierarchical positions, generating effects that are not necessarily irreversible but which are endurable, because they are hard to alter once set in place. He explained,

> Abilities of men and women are more or less the same. The important key is whether the workers are given the opportunities and resources to develop themselves at the onset when they enter the firm. If a female worker is only offered a clerk's position without any chance and resources to develop her full potentials, there is no way that she can be promoted to a manager, to bear such a heavy burden of the management. On the contrary, if a male worker is placed in a favorable condition close to the manager to whom he can readily demonstrate his capabilities and competence, promotion to a managerial position will be soon within his reach. That means that what they are assigned to do at the entry point makes a whole lot of difference later on.

Social and cultural resources embedded in gendered social networks are critical for goal attainment of individuals and organizations (Erickson 1996). Employers value the importance of good networks and personal ties as the by-products of workers' cultural resources. Men at higher level jobs in the factories tended to have greater accessibility to a wide range of resources than women; therefore, men had a greater ability to enhance (or impede) organizational goal attainment and to control high-level positions. As a senior male manager said this,

To be a manager is more than a matter of ability; it also depends on other factors such as experience, resources, and connections. Female managers tend to be weak in handling business. Quite to the contrary, male managers can socialize with other CEOs and managers to lobby for external resources. Women depend on their own abilities to secure positions and to fit themselves in the corporate world.

Regardless of firm type, management was clearly a site of hegemonic masculinity; very few women were located in upper management positions.[7] A glass ceiling reinforced the logic of capitalism and patriarchy concerning the place of women in TNCs. Men were more likely to supervise women than vice-versa. Workers generally perceived men as better suited to be managers than women. Confronting personnel problems constantly at work, even some female supervisors openly admitted, perhaps with regret, that men made better managers than women because men commanded workers' attention and obedience more easily and readily. Employees of various ranks tended to characterize male managers as having masculine traits and female managers as having feminine traits in much the same way as they attributed sex-linked capacities (or traits) to gendered jobs (see previous discussion). In addition, male managers were described as authoritative, powerful, carefree, broad-minded, rational in giving clear directives, and firm in decision making, whereas female managers were depicted as consultative, careful, narrow-minded, receptive to workers' needs and interests, and anxious to use close supervision. A middle-ranked male manager made typical distinctions of this type, noting, "There are gender differences in management style. Female managers tend to be kind-hearted. When they face dilemmas, they have a hard time handling them. But male managers tend to be decisive in this regard. . . . The tenderness of women can be appropriately utilized . . . for matters of consultation. I seldom see them doing conflict resolution." While some male managers were labeled as temperamental, some female managers were portrayed as emotional. However, female managers and supervisors sometimes engaged in emotional labor to enhance the well-being of work groups, showing the nurturing quality of femininity. A male supervisor commented, "Male managers tend to think of the company's production and profit earnings rather than workers' well-being. Our female manager is not like them, for she is receptive and responsive to the needs of the workers."

Even in mixed groups, men and women seldom work together as equals. A female division chief pointed out, "Female workers are quite idealistic, naive to some extent, for they believe in hard work to secure their positions, while male workers are practical and know how to bargain to enhance their advantages. . . . For example, my female subordinates often complain that male workers give them things to do that should be done by the men themselves." On the whole, the gendered organization dominated by a male managerial regime was molded in the image and with the characteristics of the male body to rule power relationships in the workplace.

Promotions, Gendered Job Ladders, and Wages

Internal labor markets are job ladders and hierarchies along which workers can advance in seniority, status, and pay. However, the internal labor market is highly gendered with material, symbolic, and sociopsychological consequences for both female and male workers. In many cases, male managers did not admit that discriminatory promotion policies and wage disparities by gender even existed in the factories, despite objective evidence to the contrary. Quantitative measures of promotion and wage yielded the following results: (1) the managerial class had a greater likelihood of having been promoted than the other classes of workers; (2) men were promoted to a greater extent than women; (3) women were less likely to be promoted at all ranks; (4) very few female managers were promoted to upper-level positions; (5) separate and multiple job ladders existed for men while women's options were limited; and (6) significant wage gaps existed between men and women at all job levels. Gender inequality embedded in these observed patterns is institutionalized, consciously or unconsciously, in everyday work practices and even constituted an explicit personnel policy in some firms that we observed. A highly ranked female manager remarked, "The promotion policy is extremely unfair. Men are promoted more quickly than women, who may not be promoted unless they have special social backgrounds and/or personal connections with powerful persons inside the company who mentor them."

Explanations for women's lack of promotion are numerous. First of all, gender assumptions in culture and society view men as breadwinners and thus as more deserving of work and higher wages than women are. Women are viewed as less qualified than their male counterparts and as needing costly extra training to bring them to the men's level. Perceiving them as a temporary labor force, employers may be unwilling to invest the time, training, and resources to enhance women's prospects for promotion. Gendered tracking in work assignments, which places women workers in the peripheral and men in the core units, lessens women's abilities to obtain direct authority, to gain visible power, and to accumulate valuable resources important for promotion. In addition, failure to gain promotion is often due to a self-perception that opportunities are blocked, and thus women do not aspire to advance. Their inability to seize power through organizational activities and alliances, their limited access to and control of valuable resources, and their low self-esteem also affect their work performance and give them less opportunity for promotion to key positions. Many female managers and supervisors perceived and complained about men's sense of superiority and men's fear of women attaining the same level of achievement. While many high-level female managers/directors and middle-level female supervisors strongly sensed discrimination in promotion and rewards, female workers at lower levels who found their jobs dead-ended were indifferent to or alienated from consideration of how they could improve their lot.

Men perceive that working alongside women involves psychological, economic, and social costs to themselves. Employment in a mixed or female-dominated work setting may threaten men's masculine identity, lower their self-esteem, and reduce their privileges if they have to share them with women (Wharton and Baron 1987). Male managers' strategy of mentoring men rather than women bears positive results for same-sex alliances and solidarity within the work organization (Cohen, Broschak, and Haveman 1998). Realizing their own vested interests in the face of competition from women, men discriminate against them to maintain their advantageous work positions. Women possessing expertise, high status, and authority are often targets of discrimination. "Homosocial reproduction" is a common tactic for recruiting men who share male managers' goals and values and protect their status quo in the organization. Men exercise control in choosing their successors and exclude the "dissimilar others."

In the case of Taiwan, military service works as an exclusionary vehicle to qualify men's bodies and disqualify women's bodies for climbing a special job ladder set aside for men only. At the entry level, men and women learn the basics as production workers. In our research we were told that normally it would take workers three years to move up one position level with a slight increase in pay. However, almost all men are required to enter military service between 18 and 20 years of age and receive at least two years (three years for special units) of military training. A female worker complained, "Upon their return to the labor market, military service gives men a competitive edge over women. As new entrants, the men are not given job positions at level one but at least at levels two or three. It is not fair to us who have to start at the first level and work our way up. We'll never catch up with them in rank and pay simply because of their military privileges." Openly admitting this preferential treatment, another senior male manager justified this labor practice, saying, "Men were promoted much faster after they fulfilled their military requirements. While they were in the military, they acquired skills that were important for their job search, and they sacrificed their years of training for the country." This example illustrates vividly how organizations and society make rules in favor of men, widening gender gaps that place female workers at a further disadvantage.

Once the gendered bodies are tracked and trapped in the work structure, their social locations in the organizational hierarchy have material, social, symbolic, and psychological consequences for both women and men. Rationality-based incentive systems are supposedly legitimized as institutional rules and accepted by employers as well as by workers, determining job assignment, wage, promotion, and job advancement. Most social scientists found that the major cause of a wage gap between women and men is their segregation into different occupations, jobs, and positions (Bielby and Baron 1986; Reskin and Padavic 1994). It has been men's propensity to maintain their privileges by constructing certain rules, such as paying a family wage only to male household heads, thereby justifying the unequal distribution of rewards to guarantee men's economic interest and devalue women's worth. Hence, employers see women as a cheaper source of labor than men; women cost less to be trained to do assembly-line work and can be replaced as needed. They perceive the job interruption in women's labor experience as problematic and consider it not to be cost effective to hire women for higher-level positions with greater levels of job responsibilities that are rewarded by higher pay rates. Misogyny also accounts in part for how women's promotion and pay are determined. Even some women doubt the competence of other women as supervisors and managers.[8]

Differential reward systems can be observed at three levels. First, the same job does not necessarily receive the same pay. A male union representative clearly illustrated this by explaining,

> When men first enter the company, their salaries are generally N.T.$1,000 to $2,000 [in new Taiwan dollars, equivalent to U.S.$37 to $74] more than those of women. The fact is that there is no equal work for equal pay, putting female workers in a disadvantageous position. Since women do not complain much about this gender-based wage gap, we don't have to deal with any wage adjustment for them. This is quite commonplace in every firm; it is not our problem alone in this company.

Another worker complained that she was offered an entry-level job at an annual pay of N.T.$13,000 (U.S.$481), which was lower than what student interns received (N.T.$15,000, equivalent to U.S.$555) at that time. In addition, one female operative worker reported that the Japanese management used biological explanations of sex/gender differences to justify how gendered work for women and men was translated into gender worth. She also complained that male workers automatically received $10 extra each month as a productivity bonus for doing jobs comparable to those done by women workers who received no bonus.

Furthermore, salary increments also differ by gender. One woman director explained, "The pay scales for male and female employees are not the same. Men receive about N.T.$5,000 (U.S.$192) in every salary increment, whereas women get only about N.T.$3,000 [U.S.$115]. I think this is, more or less, a norm that is difficult to correct in Taiwan." In other words, women's salary increments were about two-thirds of men's for production workers based on a percentage of current wage. Hence, the overall wage disparities widened as the ranks and positions differed when men moved up the job ladder faster than women. In our sample, the average annual wage of men was about N.T.$7,000 (U.S.$259) more than that of women. The earnings gap between all male and all female workers was about 32 percent, meaning that for every $100 men earned, women only earned $68. Gender-based wage disparities were much larger in the Japanese-managed rather than the American-managed firms (Chow and Hsung 2001). Needless to say, male managers earned substantially more than female managers and other classes of workers did. Men's privileges in job type, rank, position, and pay were also accompanied by better fringe benefits, greater power, more accessibility to diversified social and cultural resources such as information, contacts, networks, trust, tastes, and lifestyle. Most women were located in lower status positions and had fewer fringe benefits, little power, and fewer social and cultural resources. For example, going out to eat and singing karaoke have become the most popular forms of entertainment for business as well as social purposes in Taiwan (e.g., it is used in business to smooth work relationships, to attract new clients, to get a promotion or a pay raise). Affordability of such social resources is closely tied to class and gender.

Sexuality, Family, and Work

Sexuality might seem to be antithetical to the rationality, impersonality, and efficiency of the modern organization. In fact, the gendered organization is highly sexualized, and the politics of the female body is suspected, stigmatized, controlled, and excluded. Women's bodies are sexualized in how they are perceived, addressed, touched, and talked about (e.g., in sex jokes). To some extent, the sexualized bodies of female workers threaten the very existence of the masculine regime and strike one of the main nerves of the gender order. Illustrating how the female body was sexualized in everyday interaction in the workplace, one senior female manager recalled,

> I was young and did not know such a term as *sexual harassment* existed. I was harassed into signing a single contractual agreement specifying that I must resign if I got married. . . . I often suspected that my top boss checked on us and closely monitored our job activities. . . . When I came to this area looking for a job, I went for a job interview at a local Taiwanese firm. I was very hurt when the boss, along with his wife, came to conduct a personal interview for the job that I applied for. She tried to ferret out the reasons why I remained single with fear that I might be involved in their personal life as a third party. I felt that women were treated neither seriously nor equally. When the boss's wife found out that my work is the central interest of my life, she attempted to depress my wage, for I had no one but myself to support. Men who seek young mistresses here and there are considered desirable, whereas women can't do the same and seek young men as their companions.

While sexual seduction of women was suspiciously guarded as the last example demonstrated, the sexually unattractive woman was ignored. Another woman worker revealed to us confidentially that, "In this factory, male managers do not treat female workers equally. Some male managers like pretty girls and they take special care of them." Her own unattractive body made her not one of their favorites, as she regretfully admitted.

Sexuality is intimately linked to women's reproduction of labor in which their capacities for menstruation, pregnancy, childbirth, breast-feeding, and child rearing are stigmatized and controlled. For example, the only female manager in the firm was rather unpopular among the workers in lower positions. One young male worker questioned her emotionality and speculated about whether her emotional outburst was due to a concurrence with her menstrual cycle. Managers in general pointed out that marriage and especially parenthood remained barriers to women's employment, promotion, and equity in the workplace. One senior male manager stated,

When female workers at the entry level are pregnant, their productivity will slow down. If they take two months of maternity leave, they will shorten their job tenure. . . . Taking such a long maternity leave is definitely not good for them or for the firm. A midsize company cannot function with the absence of a manager for such a long time. Men have no such problems of pregnancy and childbirth. I think the biological difference of procreation is the main gender difference, not their abilities. I have seen outstanding female workers, but they don't last long.

Related to sexuality, family is the factor most frequently mentioned by both male and female workers that is viewed as legitimizing gender inequality in work arrangements, promotion, and wage disparities. Since a man's principal family role is to be the major breadwinner, the work world becomes men's main public domain, whereas a woman's primary role is as homemaker, and women's "proper place" is thus the private domain of the home. Because the workplace is a gendered space that is embodied in the image and practice of men, work organizations segregate work from family and keep sexuality out of the work domain as much as possible. When women enter the labor market for gainful employment, they are expected to experience the burden of a double day, to juggle the demands of both work and family (Hochschild 1989). If promoted, women should supposedly have a decent chance to strive for upward mobility. However, the higher the position on a job ladder, the more privileges as well as responsibilities workers tend to have. Family support becomes more of an issue for women than for men if they seek to prevail in the workplace and be promoted to top jobs. Both male and female managers acknowledged that family may pose a constraint on promoting female employees. As one male manager explained,

> The higher the position is, the less promotion probability the female employee will have. The major factor is the family. The high-ranking manager is expected to take the interests and the goals of the company to heart. This means that he or she will work long hours, handle crises as they emerge, patrol the whole factory throughout the day or even at night for the sake of efficiency and security. These may pose limitations for women.

Most of the women we studied rejected the "superwoman" label because of its negative connotation implying that women try to do it all. Incentive systems at work and in society neither encourage nor reward women with high motivation to succeed occupationally and economically. Balancing work and family is not at all easy for young, professional women, causing them stress, role conflicts, guilt, and resignation. Female employees gave in to the societal values of womanhood and the culturally defined roles for women by cooling themselves off. Family constraints were not only the burden of household chores, but also child bearing, child rearing, management of family life, and maintenance of kinship ties and support networks (Moore 1990). A middle-ranked female supervisor expressed anguish that she failed to get a promotion due to family pressures. She was aware of familial constraints and tried to adapt to her situation by changing her self-identity, giving priority to her family's stability rather than her job mobility, and by lowering her role expectations regarding how she managed both work and family life.

Female workers sometimes received some family support from their spouses, children, kin, and friends in coping with work and family demands. While the higher-ranked female employees tended to have greater bargaining power when negotiating for spousal and kin support in sharing housework and child care, lower-ranked women had to tolerate the burden at home as well as deprivations in the workplace. Most of the low-ranked working women—assembly-line, operative, and clerical employees—tended to be young and single with less education and skills. When they entered the industrial zones, they generally were not aware of worker's rights and promotional policies in the factories. With low expectations and personal aspirations in their work, they tended to have little awareness of unfair personnel policies and discriminatory labor practices affecting women in particular. They internalized the shared logic of the superiority of male bodies, accepting the false gender consciousness that supports the male status quo. They were busy with work and family demands and had little time and energy to comprehend how institutional arrangements and processes in both the public and private spheres had created dialectical forces, hindering them simultaneously. In addition, they had few cultural and socioeconomic resources with which to bargain with others for the enhancement of their work and family lives. Childbirth and child rearing also restrict young married women.

While employed women gained some benefits from the convenience and assistance of altruistic members residing together in extended or "stem" families, they also experienced continuous subordination within these patriarchal households that inevitably disadvantaged them. These women struggled to survive and endured because the cost of quitting was, relatively speaking, too high for them. Some did resist these circumstances (e.g., through personal protest, joining a union, and/or striking), showing resilience and tenacity (Brinton 2000; Chow and Hsung 2001). For example, there has been an increase in the number of women who either joined or ran for official positions within the company union to express their practical gender needs and interests rather than strategic ones (Molyneux 1985). However, most female workers tended to be acquiescent, obedient, and tolerant of whatever vicissitudes they experienced in everyday living.

CONCLUSION

Given the gendered process of development, we demonstrate the theoretical utility of focusing on the bureaucratic work organization as one of the critically important locations in which the intricate interplay between capitalism and patriarchy is articulated. Our critiques of the classical organizational theories challenge the basic assumptions that organizations are gender neutral and disembodied; in fact, organizations are both highly gendered and embodied. They are characterized by the engendering processes of labor practices and the systematic patterning of male dominance in power structures and social relationships; these form a gender regime that simultaneously interacts with class to intensify gender inequality within the organization. To a large extent, the gendered nature of the development process has intensified the patriarchal structure as well as its ideology through the functions, practices, and processes of the gendered organization, producing more disadvantages for women as exploited laborers than for their male counterparts.

In his social theory of the body, Chris Schilling (1996:203) concludes that we need ". . . to examine more precisely the conditions that affect the degree to which the body is constraining and enabling for different groups of people at particular historical conjunctures." Indeed, industrial organizations such as TNCs and local firms provide an organizational context that enables us to understand theoretically how gender as a principle of social organization and a system of meaning are constitutive parts. Conceptualizing gender as an embodied, situated system, we have explored empirically how it is manifested in bodily terms. Gendered embodiment furnishes the material and cultural (i.e., symbolic and ideological) dimensions for power relations based on class, gender, and sexuality to be discursively constructed, contested, and reconstructed through organizational designs, processes, and practice. Given the division of labor by gender and class in many of the factories studied, male and female bodies were recruited and hired to fill gendered jobs, and then entrapped in the gendered tracks based on the logic of job suitability, sex typification of work arrangements, presumed proper place in the hierarchical structure, blocked opportunity in promotion, segregated job ladders for men, and differential rewards for working men and women.

One of our important findings is the dynamism of the way gender is historically and socially constructed in accordance with the changing labor force structure and the political economy of a given time. The first wave of global restructuring in the 1960s, which propelled the early industrialization of Taiwan, attracted the first generation of workers, many of them women who were young, single, unskilled, and migrating from rural to urban areas for employment. The high labor supply created a situation in which employers could pick and choose labor sources, building dormitories adjacent to the factories as housing. High labor demand also necessitated that the government and employers lift the marriage ban in the 1970s to allow married women to work. The changing demographic, social, and economic realities in the 1980s and 1990s have shaped a new labor force that is more educated and technically trained to meet the expansion of service and professional sectors in postindustrial Taiwan. When employers faced the economic restructuring of the 1980s, labor shortages in the manufacturing sector required them to relax their job criteria in recruitment and hiring policies and practices. As a result, a great proportion of the second generation of women working in manufacturing that we studied were older, married with or without children, and slightly better educated; with some of them held semiskilled positions. Job criteria, including gender, for hiring policies have been and can be altered in response to changes in the labor market and in the economic situations of different times in Taiwan.

Furthermore, our analysis offers some ideas for further research and some suggestions for personnel policy and practices. Firstly, gender differences and relations within certain ramifications, are somewhat fluid and not as fixed as they appear to be. Influenced by the patriarchal society, the majority of workers still held to the culturally defined gender ideology that essentialized the traits, work abilities, roles, and positions of women and men. However, as social actors they constructed various meanings to characterize gendered bodies and their jobs and positions. In our study, the constructionist view, though held by a small number of workers, implies that gendered typing in jobs is not always fixed, for it can be modified as labor market conditions, ideology, and society change. A few workers thought that education, training, and technology hold promise for reducing significant gender differences at work. This insight opens the prospect of ways to empower working women. It also suggests that researchers need to explore the crucial factors that may lead to degendering processes within organizations and for human resource personnel managers to seek ways to eliminate gender biases in existing labor policies and practices.

Secondly, we suggest bringing sexuality back to the gender paradigm, since the sexual dimension is an integral aspect of embodiment and a pervasive element of organizational life. Sexuality is part of the ongoing production of gender for it intimately shapes social interaction, gender relationships, and the politics of gendered bodies. Thirdly, we detected substantial differences in managerial regimes (e.g., Japanese-owned, U.S.-owned, and local firms) that affected most of the various employment patterns and job outcomes that we examined in this study. How the transference of different globalized managerial regimes such as those in TNCs interacts with local cultures to create unique styles of management and control of labor policies and practices deserves attention in future research (Chow and Hsung 2001). How gender further compounds these managerial regimes' control of labor is no less important a topic for investigation. Lastly, we found that both the content and the process of embodiment vary by rank and by gender. The characterization of gendered bodies differed greatly not only between men and women but also between male managers and workers and female managers and workers. Further differentiations of masculinity and femininity, such as the hegemonic and marginal ones suggested by Robert Connell (1987), may yield a refined understanding of the social construction of gender embeddedness and embodiment in the workplace.

NOTES

Data collection for this project was funded by the American Sociological Association/National Science Foundation Fund for the Advancement of the Discipline Award and by research grants from the Chiang Ching Guo Foundation in North America and the National Science Council in Taiwan. We are grateful to Mei-Chi Chen for her dedicated support and research assistance. Special thanks also go to Elaine Stahl Leo for her editorial help.

1. This paper is based on the theoretical framework developed in Chow (2000).
2. We also collected data from six focus groups. Only certain relevant aspects of this data set are mentioned in this analysis.
3. The protective labor legislation regarding the night shift for women workers was abolished in August 2000.
4. Both the "absolute" and "physical exception" views echo Schilling's discussion (1996) of the "naturalistic" view of the biological and physical dimensions of the body, which are both constraining and enabling in shaping social relations.
5. In view of the heightened ethnic consciousness recently in Taiwan, ethnic antagonism has been revived. How ethnic tension has spilled over to the labor competition and practices is an important, yet subtle issue for further investigation.
6. We were told that a highly ranked female manager secured her position because her family owns part of the firm.
7. In the organizational pyramid, we found plenty of women in low-ranked positions and very few female managers to fill our sampling requirements regarding gender and rank.
8. This view was generally held by men and women in lower-level positions and many of them preferred male to female managers.

Chapter 5

Power, Media Representation, and Labor Dispute
The Case of Women Workers in South Korea

Hyun Mee Kim

The new international division of labor, emerging during the last half of the twentieth century, has become a mode of international production, utilizing simple assembly and processing in which production depends quite extensively on the so-called nimble fingers of low-paid women in developing countries. Innumerable lower-class women from urban and rural areas, through employment in the light manufacturing sector, have been rapidly incorporated at the bottom of the global capitalist economic system (S. K. Kim 1997). Beginning in the early 1970s, South Korea established free export zones in Masan and several other cities and provided regulatory privileges, including a five-year tax exemption and a ban on labor union activities, within these zones.

This chapter is based on a case study of labor disputes arising in one U.S.-owned multinational corporation in Korea, referred to here as Company M (a pseudonym).[1] Korean workers, mostly middle-aged women, had formed a union to fight for the improvement of their working conditions and wages in the summer of 1988; a time marked by a sharp increase in labor costs and the rise of militant labor activism in South Korea, beginning in mid-1987.[2] In February of 1989, these women workers faced a classic "runaway shop" when the company closed down without notifying the workers and left Korea without paying their wages.

It was also the time when the Korean government announced plans to restructure the country's economy in the name of progress. The first targets in the cutbacks of bank loans and other monetary sources were the so-called declining industries, such as those of textiles, footwear, and electronic assembly where women workers had a strong union presence. Likewise, employers who regarded their businesses as less profitable than before reduced their lines of operation or closed down factories. Many Korean factories, as well as foreign plants, moved to Indonesia, China, and numerous other less developed countries that offered cheaper labor. Women workers in the light-manufacturing industries actively participated in the labor movement. However, no matter how women workers actively engaged in union organizing, their efforts did not always directly enhance their collective power as laborers, since faked factory closures, layoffs, and relocations in both domestic and foreign industries were common practices in response to workers' demands for better working conditions.[3] In 1989, 13 foreign factories, most of which were Japanese- or U.S.-owned, were closed and 8,000 factory workers were discharged (C. B. Kin 1990; S. Y. Yi 1990:102).

This is one of the first instances where women workers of a multinational corporation sought reparation from a U.S. corporation under the jurisdiction of the U.S. legal system (*Korea Update* 1990:8). After the factory closed down, workers protested despite overwhelming odds. Their prolonged public protests, replete with antagonistic encounters with the notoriously violent police, received no sympathy from the Korean government. As a result, the union sent its leaders to the U.S. company's headquarters to negotiate directly with its president. The union finally took its case to the United States District Court for the Northern District of New York but lost its suit and, consequently, terminated its four-year-long struggle in 1992.

Company M's labor dispute, along with labor disputes in other multinationals in Korea at the time, received considerable attention from the media, both in Korea and the United States. In fact, in terms of media coverage and scholarly analyses of labor strikes, struggles waged by women workers have been almost invisible, in contrast to the well-publicized image of those waged by skilled male workers working for large companies. However, reports of the labor strife in foreign corporations involved powerful and emotional charges. It was claimed that these foreign industries tended to take the lion's share without taking responsibility for Korean laborers. Some members of the media expressed great concern about the economic crisis that large-scale, foreign divestment would create in South Korea and exhorted workers to show restraint in union activism. Others portrayed the situation of women workers in an attempt to elicit emotional anxiety in Koreans who held a strong sense of national identity.

This chapter seeks to examine the process of how women workers' labor struggle against one multinational company's factory closure was presented in the realm of the media and other writings. I examined a range of reports on this event, both from South Korea and the United States. In addition, this particular case of global labor conflict shows how gender, class, and national identity are complexly integrated. By comparing women's collective subjectivities with the media's representation of this labor dispute, the chapter shows how a multinational corporation became the site for a political struggle that involved varied local groups in South Korea and the United States.

The comparative analysis of the media's representation with the women workers' narratives shows how working-class women workers were being constituted in the discourse and how the media's framing of the dispute hindered lower-class women workers from standing as political actors. First, the chapter shows how the relationship of gender and class played out in the politicization process; second, it critically examines the media's representation by illustrating these women workers' structural relationship to the Korean political economy and to global capital.

"OMMA NODONGJA" (WORKING MOTHERS)

Since the 1960s, Korea's modernizing project has promoted capitalist industrialization based on labor-intensive and export-oriented industries. From the beginning, it dramatically mobilized the Korean masses into a productive and nationalist collective. The Korean government mobilized young, single women who had been branded as obedient and disciplined because they were considered to be a stable supply of cheap labor as well as an inducer of foreign capital.[4] In the mid-1980s, the supply of young, single women was exhausted, and married women, who had earlier had difficulty entering the labor market, became a large component of the labor force in Korea. Married women's employment in the manufacturing sector grew from 13 percent in 1983 to 19.8 percent in 1989; it reached about 22 percent of all workers by 1992 (Korean Women Development Institute 1994).[5]

For women only, marriage and age became markers of cheaper labor, regardless of individual differences in skill. Married women workers in their late 30s, 40s, and 50s were mostly channeled into the cheapest, most arduous, and contaminated factories and labeled as temporary, unskilled labor. This trend has continued more than a decade later as married women, who lack a "marketable skill" but need money to educate their children and to maintain their livelihood, are employed by small factories with poor working conditions while single workers are preferred by large, clean factories.

Company M's female workers were no exception in this regard. Married women workers whom I interviewed metaphorically compared the harsh factory work to "grinding one's flesh and bone." However, they told me that "while single women should stay young and fresh until married, we already have given birth to children and have overworked ourselves." They hardly differentiated between their bodies having been exhausted from housework or rapidly deteriorated by factory work. Some women workers took pride in themselves for persevering and not easily giving in. These married women workers' conception of their bodies was, in fact, the origin of the surplus profit produced by the company. On the other hand, it also enabled them to stand as "dauntless fighters" against the violent police at later stages of the struggle.

Before the labor strife began, their gender identity as married women was sometimes in conflict with the externally imposed social title of factory worker. Many women stated that they did not regard themselves as "laborers" during their employment at Company M. These women emphasized that they worked to earn money for their children's education and that they would not work for long. These remarks demonstrate that they tried to maintain their higher cultural status by identifying as mothers and housewives rather than as factory workers, which was associated with a low social status in Korean society.

One of the reasons why these women workers had decided to unionize was that their wages were far below minimal levels, let alone being close to what other workers in that sector were paid, but a more important reason was that they were no longer able to endure coerced, overtime work. Daily production quotas were on the rise, but no additional workers were hired. So they were required to work either overtime or through the night to meet production quotas, which became a threat to their identity as working mothers. As one woman stated, "We started out working to pay for our children's education. But we could not find time to take care of them, having to leave home for work at dawn and come back home at midnight." Forced overtime work conflicted with the married women's sense of balancing the distribution of energy between home and factory.

Many workers indicated that they unionized without prior knowledge or experience but had high expectations for the union, which was first organized by married women workers in the region. One woman worker, Ms. Yu, explained,

> We used to say that we would make the union help save the company, not ruin it like the radical kind we saw on television. We thought if we worked harder after unionization, the company would have more revenue, and then we would not hear that the company closed down because of the union. We really worked diligently, hoping that our wages would increase that January, as had been promised in the collective bargaining in November the previous year. We typically had one shipment per week before unionization. But after that, the number of shipments increased to two to three.

Six months into unionization, Company M closed down without paying its employees or even giving them notice. That was when these women came to identify themselves as "laborers."

BECOMING LABORERS

The mode of divestment utilized by most foreign corporations was similar in that workers experienced unnotified and sudden factory closures, while management disappeared without paying wages or severance pay to workers. Workers attempted to seek justice against this illegal practice by visiting embassies and demonstrating in front of the Office of Labor, but to no avail. Without any institutionalized means for articulating their demands, the workers often vented their grievances through wild street struggles which made them targets of the blunt force of the state. For Company M workers, the reality of the closing hit them with a wave of shock and confusion. From the outset of their struggle, the women workers had anticipated good intentions by and commitment from educated elites such as lawyers and politicians—those whom they believed were able to help them out of this traumatic situation. In the beginning stages of their struggle, publicity, which many workers saw as important to resolving their problem, was actively sought. They distributed 60,000 fliers to explain their situation and generate public interest. During their 14-month struggle, workers came to the factory almost daily, camped out for two months at the factory, and often visited the U.S. Embassy. Getting few results, workers turned to more active measures to "politicize" their case by waging a petition campaign directed toward the government. Workers who asked the state to issue a legal order against such lawless factory closings were often dragged away by the police on charges of disrupting the order.

Company M workers, the so-called full-time protesters or ever-striking workers due to their protracted negotiations with the U.S. company's president, had made alliances with other workers in two ways. First, they conducted a collective struggle on a regional basis with other workers from neighboring factories. Second, they sponsored collective struggles against any particular foreign enterprise experiencing labor disputes. This kind of cooperation greatly helped Company M workers as well as other participants in transforming their consciousness into something akin to a "working-class consciousness."

Even though the workers were at times loosely organized as a union due to their multiple roles as mothers and housewives, their shared, lived experience became the union's strength. As Ms. Chu explained,

> When we first started our protests, going to the Labor Office, for example, it took almost two hours for all *ajummas* [middle-aged women] to finally show up there. When we were just about to leave, some ajummas rushed to the restroom, and others said they would come right back after making lunch for their children returning from school. So it seemed to me that we'd never go anywhere together forever. Moreover, these middle-aged women were not likely to listen to each other's orders when pushed. They just acted if they felt it was right. So, thanks to this "power of action" [*haengdongnyok*] shown by the ajummas, as other unionists called it, there was always "order in this apparent disorder."

When this new perception of worker solidarity took root among workers, it encouraged them to accommodate the laborers' oppositional culture. The process of identifying as laborers was built upon education efforts, their common struggle to build alliances, and the formation of emotional and personal friendships through a sharing of life stories. During their 14-month struggle, workers traveled to the factory almost every day, camped there for a 60-day period, staged a two-month sit-down demonstration at the headquarters of an opposing political party, and participated in numerous street fights and protests. When not protesting, they usually taught themselves about the Korean labor movement and the workings of multinational corporations. But most of the time, the women continued to inform themselves about the struggle's background and the goals of their actions. It helped them to gain a systematic understanding of their case.

During their unpromisingly long sit-down protest at the factory, many ajumma workers did piecework knitting for export, which was one main source of income for married women in Korea, or made *kimch'i* (Korea's popular vegetable dish) to be sold to nearby unions. Therefore, some workers were able to recover some of the financial losses from their extended protest, albeit only partially. Despite having been often evaluated as the weakest segment of workers in terms of consciousness and durability, these middle-aged housewives gained the potential to become long-term protesters through their flexibility in shifting jobs and the mutual understanding acquired from their marginal experience as lower-class, married women.

Sometimes their transformation into laborers was generated by an array of organizational paraphernalia, such as banners, and Company M flags and T-shirts. In the Korean labor movement of the late 1980s, where workers' allied street struggles were not unusual phenomena, items like banners, flags, and T-shirts were dominant paraphernalia used to generate among the workers themselves as well as to the outside world a vivid, visual presentation of their struggle. For Company M workers, the process of becoming laborers included being organized in ensemble.

Although they always emphasized the "pure-mindedness" of their motivation, in order to fulfill their unadulterated intentions the women workers took on an "aggressive" or "radical" tone in their mottoes and slogans and wielded violent measures against the state's force. Ms. Chon, who saw herself as a typical housewife, explained her understanding of this debate as it related to her own transformation,

> I just wanted to live as quietly as possible while at the same time saving money for my family. I just didn't like the union. I was more sympathetic to the company side, to be honest with you. But after the company shut down, I really felt guilty for my indifferent attitude toward the union. The only thing that I thought was to do my best to reach a settlement. But as I got involved in the fighting, I realized how much I had been cheated by the company and the government. There was no way but to become "radical." As I looked at my change from being dumb and timid to being radical, I could see the reason why many "enlightened people" always fight radically. Just being "pure-minded," you never get anywhere.

Because of their lived experiences, these middle-aged women regarded themselves as representatives of Korean laborers who were engaged in political struggle; however, the outside world did not recognize them as such. One woman recounted, "They said, 'What did ignorant housewives like us know about multinational corporations?' and that we had better go home and take care of the children." These workers participated in every protest rally to which they were called and took an active part in them in order to be recognized, not as "ignorant housewives without class consciousness" but as degendered laborers. In order to fit the image of the ideal laborer, the women workers did not reveal their fear of violence but engaged in a vehement physical struggle with riot policemen.

LABORERS AS AGENTS OF VIOLENCE, WOMEN WORKERS AS VICTIMS OF VIOLENCE

In this section I examine the changing process of the media's representation in Korea and abroad by tracing the discourse of women workers within the movement, that of the press, and literature on Company M's labor dispute. The tenor of these articles, as will be seen, illustrated the political predilections of each source.

The labor struggle at Company M became widely known to the public when they waged a sit-down strike at the U.S. Chamber of Commerce. Mainstream media discourse stressed the "illegal, violent, and hence undemocratic" behavior of union workers. Because a politicized labor movement was considered a threat to the stability of the Korean regime, such press coverage was not uncommon. An article from the *Journal of Commerce*, which was no less unfavorable to labor than the conservative Korean papers, defined the workers' protest at the U.S. Chamber of Commerce as a riot. The article stated,

> Employees of an American-owned company Wednesday wrecked the offices of the U.S. Chamber of Commerce in Seoul to protest against the disappearance of their employer. They barricaded themselves inside and smashed computers and other equipment. Police later broke through an office and seized the *60-odd workers and 10 student activists* who accompanied them. The workers, mostly young women, have been frustrated in their attempts to get back wages and severance pay. The problem, Mr. Hughes [a pseudonym for the president of the company] said, is that the workers belong to a militant union and have threatened bodily harm to several company representatives, from American and Korean managers of M Korea to the company's Korean law firm. (Moore 1989)

Similarly, an article that appeared in the *Los Angeles Times* (Schoenberger and Yoshinara 1989) also identified the workers as young female assemblers. It was no accident that both the Korean and the American newspapers distorted the workers' identity. Despite the different political settings of the two countries, the tenor of the articles bore a striking similarity. They shared the same capitalist interest for discipline and highlighted the workers' violence and their inferiority as independent actors. The crude media characterization of the unionists, as being violent and disruptive to social life, often generated widespread public disapproval for the labor movement in South Korea. While the discourse in U.S. newspapers consistently ignored gender and placed greater emphasis on racial or national differences as an explanation for the Korean workers' so-called excessive radicalism, Korean newspapers never failed to miss the gender aspect of the company's labor struggle.

The American media consistently depicted workers as agents of violence who wrecked offices and smashed computers and other equipment (Moore 1989) or captured them breaking down a thick glass door and sending panicked office workers scurrying out of a window. Thus, it characterized the riot police's incursions as a means of restoring order. The narrative, targeted to an American audience, conveyed that the incident was emblematic of militant Korean workers' radicalism. Consequently, its readership was expected to readily accept that the police should have been called out to control the workers, a rationale that justified the extreme exercise of South Korean state power and, thus, made it seem reasonable and legitimate.

In contrast, some Korean newspapers, both conservative and progressive, reported this incident in a manner that was meant to arouse a sense of frustration in their audience. The focus here was on the workers' identity as married women who were subjected to the blunt force of the state. The *Chosun Ilbo* initially blamed the few unionists for their violent sit-down strike, but later contradicted itself by becoming an ardent critic of state force. Given that the paper in previous years had blamed the state for lacking the will to deal with numerous such cases, it seemed to have changed its position. The headlines read "The Police Indiscriminately Assault the Protesting Workers," and the article stated, "The riot police, in the process of routing workers, protesting against the American company president, who ran away without paying their back wages and severance pay, wounded about 10 workers, most of whom are married women in their 30s and 40s, while assaulting these women workers indiscriminately" (*Chosun Ilbo* 1989). It continued to describe the situation, gave details about the number of troops involved, and printed a vivid photograph of the scene of violence:

> The police, including one unit of the Seoul Special Task Force [the so-called *paekkoldan*] and another unit of regular riot police, totaling 300 troops, were sent to the scene, where they broke down the wall and iron door, and dragged out all resisting workers. In this process, the police snatched the wooden bars carried by workers for defense, wielding them against the women workers, trampling and dragging them down by the hair. Most of these women were *punyoja* [married women, usually housewives]. When the police started to randomly attack, some women protested violently, crying, "Is it a crime to ask for the wages we've earned?" A few of those women who cowered in the corner were soon taken down by the police. (*Chosun Ilbo* 1989)

This account gave the audience the impression of the state's excessive use of force on married women and housewives who were plainly troubled by their situation and, therefore, visited the U.S. Chamber of Commerce to appeal. The tenor of the article was such that it portrayed the incident as a confrontation between the victimized housewife workers and the excessive and indiscriminate exercise of state force. Therefore, much of the narrative focused on how the workers were beaten and how their intentions were simple and economic, rather than radically and politically motivated.

By repeatedly using the term *punyoja* for the workers, the article expressed a paternalistic concern for the women workers as victims of male violence by the state. It urged the state to view these women as non-threatening to society and distinct from radical and politicized workers. This paternalistic discourse easily portrayed women as *victims*. Once the workers' identity was manifested as women, they were no longer considered to be striking laborers or political actors. In this way, the term *women,* as a symbolic marker, determined the way in which they were represented. Scant attention has been paid to the process of how these women struggled to stand as actors, anxiously transforming themselves into equal partners with more renowned male activists.

The discourse reflected its patriarchal character in the desire to see women as subordinate and domesticated beings. It was very unusual for a conservative newspaper like the *Chosun Ilbo,* whose previous coverage of labor protests had expressed a disciplinary tone by advocating the exercise of state force, to later represent state violence in such a graphic manner. By portraying the scene of masculine violence unleashed on women in such detail, the newspaper transformed the incident from a type of oppression of laborers by the state into one that represented gender persecution.

While these articles illustrate how a capitalist narrative was sometimes at odds with a patriarchal narrative of protesting women workers in South Korea, they also demonstrate that the Korean media viewed the incident as a domestic affair. There was consistency in the *Chosun Ilbo*'s voice regarding labor strife in multinational corporations, which argued that South Koreans themselves were responsible for dealing with and solving this structural problem. Regarding Company M workers' protest in the United States, the newspaper criticized the Korean government for neglecting its role as a protector of its citizens and for not resolving the problem, thus making it necessary for Korean workers to visit the U.S. headquarters. The newspaper indicated that the struggle of the Korean workers should have been conducted within the national political arena, which implied that the South Korean government was the party responsible for not only controlling foreign companies, but also for conducting diplomatic negotiations with the United States on this matter. Furthermore, the paper went on to assert that the key to resolving the problem depended on the union's volition in being rational and reasonable (*Chosun Ilbo* 1990).

This article evidently seemed to be concerned about social disturbances that may have occurred because of the Korean workers' excessive demands from foreign businesses, possibly resulting in a decline of foreign investment in South Korea. By linking workers' demands directly to an economic crisis that the nation potentially faced, the state-controlled media criticized the workers' union for pursuing its own narrow self-interest without having considered its possible impact on the image of South Korea and its national economy. Until recently, this image of a potential national crisis has successfully hindered union activism to a great extent.

As a matter of fact, the *Chosun Ilbo* covered neither Company M workers' repeated appeals to government-related organizations nor the subsequent treatment they received at the hands of the police. By not reporting these disruptive realities the media produced a contradictory discourse that was at once capitalistic, patriarchal, and nationalistic. The same workers became violent agents making excessive demands when portrayed as unionists and, simultaneously, they became the victims of state violence as married women workers.

These women workers never failed to point out the outrageous nature of terror they felt the first time they faced the police at the U.S. Chamber of Commerce. They told me that this became the major turning point of their union activism and the nature of social awareness in relation to their labor dispute. Before this incident, the women workers thought of their labor dispute as a simple matter that could be solved through the good will of the powerful. The unexpected terrorist attack by the *paekkoldan* [the White Skulls] instigated the women workers to think of their case in relation to both national politics and the international power hierarchy. As one worker, Ms. Kim, said, "It was a total change of my worldview." Many women who were radically disenchanted about state ideology became more dauntless. To fight for their lost justice, they implemented violent practices in the name of defense and as an expression of the moral justification of their cause. They spearheaded street struggles with other laborers in the face of the police. As another worker, Ms. Han, stated, "When the laborers from Haean City demonstrated, they put us on the front line. As we marched, we swung bats, iron pipes, and firebombs to scare off the riot police. We got the strength from our frustrations. We fought hard, saying, 'What have the police and the government done for us?'"

KOREAN WORKERS AS ANTI-AMERICAN, AJUMMA WORKERS AS NATIONAL HEROES

Ms. Chu explained why their labor case had drawn so much attention from the media, in the context of rising anti-American sentiment among Korean opposition groups in the late 1980s. She said that those who did not like America were willing to keep their case in high profile, as an example of American wrongdoing. This rhetoric of anti-Americanism was brought up frequently by the president of Company M to identify these women workers as communists or as anti-American. By labeling these workers as such, he hoped to appeal to an American audience that found communist stereotypes repugnant. In fact, projecting the workers as anti-American enabled Company M executives to protect their economic interests. Indeed, when applied to political transformations in other societies, an anti-American discourse has led to an omission of and disregard for those complicated, internal contradictions that shape people's political consciousness, as well as the different groups or agents involved.

As shown below, the U.S. media also highlighted the discourse of anti-Americanism. The *Wall Street Journal* showed great interest in the Company M case, which was headlined as follows: "Plant's Closing Raises Tensions in South Korea"; "Plant Closing Aggravates Anti-Americanism in Korea"; and "Abrupt Exit From South Korea Could Inflame Anti-American Sentiment" (Manguno 1989a, 1989b). These articles focused on the plant's closure in relation to anti-American sentiments as indicated by their almost identical narrative structure and content. By making reference to Korean officials, labor representatives, and foreign businessmen, these articles shifted the emphasis away from the specifics of the case, having focused instead on the rise of anti-American sentiment. The articles often affirmed the interconnection between the company workers' militancy and rising anti-American sentiment. Such articles like "Welcome to South Korea, Where Xenophobic Rhetoric and Actions Have Seeped into the Realm of Labor Relations" (Maass 1989) do not explain how workers' anti-American sentiment had led them, supposedly, to *attack* the Chamber of Commerce and how labor militancy had harbored antiforeigner feelings. The article explained that Company M made the situation worse for other American corporations by not paying back wages, and this evoked extreme nationalistic emotions, or what the Korean worker described as *minjok kamjong* (national sentiment).

By articulating issues related to labor protests in foreign corporations in the idiom of feelings and sentiments, the article was able to justify ending the discussion without having mentioned any structural issues surrounding labor-capital relations in multinational corporations. Here we see how labor disputes in foreign (multinational) corporations were reduced to references of workers' so-called retrograde nationalism and antiforeign sentiment. Through the use of such narrative, the real nature of the dispute, which was structural, was muted and pushed into oblivion. This created the context in which the labor dispute was portrayed, judged, and handled by the media, which, both unconsciously and intentionally, catered to the capitalist class' interests and, therefore, effectively safeguarded the persistence of illegal practices by multinationals in other countries.

Reporters, in fact, made a concerted effort to build up anti-American discourse surrounding labor strife in U.S.-owned multinational corporations, as we can see in the women's narratives. Their discourse, full of anti-American sentiment in Company M's case, echoed the American reporters' confusion. The latter tended to identify the radical student activists' discourse as identical or similar to the South Korean workers' political activism. As one worker, Ms. Song, explained about the first day women workers publicly protested in front of the U.S. Embassy,

> We were very pissed off when they [the American reporters] came and asked us, "Is this anti-Americanism or not?" We don't know what anti-Americanism means. But I hate the American company president for sure, since he cheated us. How could we like a person who ran away, leaving us so miserable like this? But they [the reporters] don't want to listen to us when we gave details on how much money we are entitled to receive.

Once presented in this way, anti-Americanism became more forceful and obliterated the dissenting and contradictory voices of the concerned people. This, in turn, increasingly made the people involved adopt an anti-American idiom. Company M's union newsletter, written by the workers, commented on the demonstrations in front of the U.S. Embassy as follows: "How could we not develop anti-American feelings after being robbed by an American? Anti-American sentiments have grown ever since we came to know [the president of the Company]" (Company M Labor Union 1989). Simultaneously, their slogans and mottoes took on anti-American characteristics in their representation of the struggle, and anti-Americanism became the major theme for their protests afterward.

The nationalist emphasis found in South Korean media and writing ran a parallel course with the U.S. media's stress on anti-American sentiment. A drastic turn in the media's presentation of Company M's labor struggle occurred when the workers traveled to the United States and waged a three-month long protest at the company's headquarters. After a rather long silence in the national political arena regarding the women workers' numerous protests, there was a surge of newspaper articles in major Korean daily newspapers beginning in April 1990. The press began to take note of interesting events in this labor dispute case, as indicated by their headlines: "[Company M's Union Workers] Go to the United States for Negotiation" (C. B. Kim 1990); "[Company M's Union] Visits the U.S.A." (H. Y. Yi 1990); "[Company M's Factory] *Ajumma* Goes to the U.S.A. to Protest" (Chong 1990a). *The Hankyoreh*, while still under the control of government press censorship, was considered the most outspoken and antigovernment in their production of oppositional discourse in Korean politics:

> These ajummas laid aside household matters and visited the American Chamber of Commerce and the U.S. Embassy in appeal, only to be dragged to police cars and the police station. The only thing that awaited them was not a solution but fierce violence. The matters of the [Company M] labor dispute lie not in their fight against the tyranny of one American multinational corporation but in the fact that their struggle becomes an emblem wherein Korean workers who want to regain their own rights bravely confront the gigantic U.S. capital. (Chong 1990a)

Evident in this narration is the expression of the workers' self-image as powerless in Korean society; an identity that underwent a drastic transformation into a symbol of victimized and yet still heroic actors struggling against U.S. capital. Four articles from *The Hankyoreh* (Chong 1990b, 1990c; Yu 1990; S. G. Kim 1990), which covered the process of the workers' protest in the United States, characterized their fight as one for national pride against an arrogant capitalist. Thus, from the perspective of the oppositional press, this case and other labor disputes against U.S.-owned multinational corporations were instances of the U.S. hegemonic order existing in the Korean peninsula and about which the Korean audience needed to be informed and persuaded. This labor dispute was seen as an effective tool to arouse anti-American sentiment and advocated by left-wing groups, but suppressed by the ruling elite.

The emphasis in this presentation was primarily on the process of the transformation of *ordinary housewife workers* into *fighters* against the power of U.S. capital. By doing so, the oppositional press provided the reader with a new perspective on the seemingly politicized idiom of American imperialism. It constructed the workers' position of subjection to U.S. tyranny as *real* rather than an abstract and distant image created by the activists' discourse. Thus, the articles' descriptions tended to highlight the *ajumma* workers as agents involved in an anti-American struggle. This illustrates how ordinary housewife workers became victims of U.S. imperialism and, subsequently, questioned the people's memories and ideology of the United States as the savior of South Korea.

Left-wing literature and newspapers often described foreign capital as arrogant and insolent, while powerless Korean workers were portrayed as oppressed but dauntless fighters. This mode of representation instigated readers to position themselves as anti-American. More significantly, there was a major difference between conservatives and the left in their use of gender images in their representations. The difference lay in their use of different gender terms for women workers. As we have already seen, the *Chosun Ilbo* identified them as *punyoja* (wife), while *The Hankyoreh* and the left-wing literature identified them as *ajumma* (a familiar term of reference for middle-aged women) or *omoni* (an honorific, meaning mother). There is a curious difference in the use of language that viewed women as glorified mothers, evident in the left-wing literature's use of the word *omoni* as opposed to *punyoja*. While *punyoja* conveyed the notion of a domesticated woman within the home, the symbolic use of the term *omoni* in describing these women workers called to mind a glorified maternal figure, one that has often been emphasized in Korea. The left wing wished to project these women workers as nationalist subjects, given its mission of opposing U.S. imperialism. Therefore, the workers were used to serve the ends of the political elite rather than their own interests. It was not the women workers themselves, but the spectacle of their struggle that was included and projected as part of the historical mission of the leftist elite's nationalist project.

As some feminist scholars have argued, gendered narratives of nationalism position women as guardians and keepers who preserve the core of the nation and thus encompass and presuppose the everlasting, emotional bonding of the nation to women (Parker, Russo, Sommer, and Yaeger 1992; Yuval-Davis 1993). Likewise, *The Hankyoreh* and other left-wing literature's laudatory tributes to the struggle of Company M *ajumma* workers against their formidable enemy, U.S. capitalism, established an emotional bond between Korean mothers and their nation. This is significant because the Korean mother has been a symbol of collectivity and inclusiveness at the national level. Through this gendered representation of Company M workers and their struggles, nationalism and anti-imperialism were projected.

The emphasis on the everlasting bond of the nation with the mother contrasts with the representation of young working women as feeble, unmarried women who were violated by foreign capitalists. The young workers were treated in the media as having had their virginity violated by foreign capital. This strong sexual metaphor contributed to evoking a collective, male-oriented, nationalist sentiment that pointed to women's vulnerability to foreign forces (H. M. Kim 1997). Company M workers became political embodiments of the national will by being repeatedly described as outspoken patriots, confronting the enormous power of U.S. capital and fighting for national pride.

In contrast to the rhetoric of nationalism, these workers' experiences failed to speak for the true identity of the nationalist subject. Their newly claimed identity as Korean laborers in the international political economy encompassed their evolving perception of a common struggle with workers all over the country and, simultaneously, a realization of their powerlessness as a class. The workers' nationalist narrative did not always include the positive prospect of being allied to other Koreans who were in different class positions in their own struggle against the American multinational company.

These women workers' understanding of anti-Americanism also displayed an ambiguity that comes from various sources. The profoundly conflictual narrative, evident in their discussion of anti-Americanism, was due to several factors. Some women workers were reluctant to adopt this politically charged term to describe their own actions, while others had moved toward becoming anti-American in a political sense. However, most of the women workers told me that their experiences with the long-term struggle led them to reinterpret their deeply rooted, historicized memories about the role of the United States in a stereotypical sense. Consequently, some women redirected their interpretations and understandings of their past and current lives:

> Ever since we learned how to read at school, we heard that America was our *ubang* [ally] or *hyolmaeng* [blood ally]. We expected too much of it, and [now] every ajumma says she would never go to a U.S.-owned factory (Ms. Song)

> I used to think that anything American was good; that it was the best and all Americans were friendly. That's what I've heard from childhood. They helped us during the war and so on. But now, whenever I want to buy something American, I tell myself that I'd rather not, thinking of our farmers. I'm not anti-American like the typical college student activist. I'm not like that at all, but I'm not too crazy about America any more. Not all Americans are angelic, preaching democracy. I know that there are people like [Hughes] and there are good people too. That's about it. (Ms. Im)

> Just because we were oppressed by an American company doesn't mean that we hate every single American. This was a problem between the workers and the capitalists which could happen in any other country. But after we lost this trial, I thought it means that the American law is also one that oppresses the workers in the world, the same as in many other poor countries. (Ms. Yi)

In many cases, it was also a fact that the workers' experiences affected their perception of themselves as subaltern gender and class subjects (Spivak 1988a: 246; 1988b). Class domination in South Korea constituted a major part of the workers' life experiences. The strikingly national or anti-American explanation could not address the nature of this labor dispute, let alone the women's subjective identity. Workers, in fact, identified themselves as experiential subjects who refused to marginalize their own identity in opposition to any elite discourse.

When the representatives of the union went to the United States, they also entered a new arena of representation. Suggesting the victimization of workers, the union's struggle was highlighted as a case typical of a Third World situation. Non-Western women workers have had a strong historical presence in international capitalism, as markers for poverty, submissiveness, and victimhood. Therefore, the focus often has been on how many cents the Korean workers were paid per hour, and how terrible their working environment was rather than on the process of their extensive struggle in the national arena. The perception of the protesting workers by the American labor groups was expressed in terms of this same hierarchical positioning, as the groups called for support for these poor workers who were relegated to the bottom of capitalist accumulation.

While so-called Third World industrial workers have been invisible in Western scholarly debates on working class consciousness, Company M workers were overly drawn as the victims of capital accumulation by their supporters. When workers were referred to as *women workers* in the non-Western world, the term tended to lose the political image of women workers as a class, and, instead, a strikingly victimized image emerged. Often, a dichotomous classification of the masculinized image of First World capital and the victimized portrayal of Third World women failed to induce any discussion of female workers' sense of sovereignty and independence, manifested through their actions in specific historical contexts. The making of the Korean worker as "an average third world woman" (Mohanty, Russo, and Torres 1991:56) was in line with U.S. labor groups' ideas about Korean women workers. Without regard to time, region, space, and nationality, all Third World women workers were viewed as mere victims of either capital or the sexist cultures of their own societies, without being class/gender/national subjects.

WOMEN SUBJECTS IN THE INTEGRATED CIRCUIT OF GLOBAL CAPITALISM

"What started as a 200-*won* [about 26 cents] raise a day turned out to be a fight between David and Goliath," Ms. Sim explained of the origin of their fight. The verdict in 1992 finally announced that the union lost the suit. The main reason given to the workers by the jury was insufficient proof that the headquarters "intentionally" closed the Korean subsidiary against the union:

> M Products' action must be viewed as a purely economic based decision, the type of action expressly sanctioned by New York law. M Products action was motivated by its desire to protect its economic interests, not out of disdain for unionism. As the New York courts have held, such a motivation is justifiable. (The Verdict on the Labor Union of the Company M, Ltd., et al., vs. M Products, Inc. of New York, No. 90-CV-774, p 11).[6]

Each worker presented various interpretations of her loss:

> Our chances seemed so promising. Even during the trial, the prosecuting attorney said, "Why make a big deal? Proper wage will be given." But strangely enough we ended up losing. I think the attorney was probably pressured because it looked to become a national scandal. If we set a precedent, every foreign worker would bring his or her cases to the U.S court. (Ms. Yi)

Since our government didn't have power, it couldn't help us get our wages back
from the American company. Someday our country will be stronger than now and
there won't be any people in our situation. (Ms. Im)

If our government cares for its own citizens equally and humanely, outsiders will
treat us with certain respect. And if all are treated equally under the law, we Korean
people know how to treat outsiders that way. (Ms. Kim)

The Company M workers felt that their strong militancy, which was often
identified with their resistant spirit and power as working mothers, could not
bring them real gain if it was not supported by legally guaranteed labor rights
that had not yet been established with globalized capital.

A critical understanding of Company M workers' sociopolitical positions and
lack of representational power created a dilemma concerning how to locate these
women's agency in social transformation (Spivak 1988b). Neither a simple evo-
cation of the women's marginalized voices nor the treatment of these women as
uncontaminated, native subjects accounts for the political space the Korean
women workers encountered (Loomba 1991).

The workers largely pictured themselves as naive victims and middle-aged,
housewife workers while they appealed to a shared nationality. The manner in
which these women highlighted the issue in order to reach a wider audience
involved a considerable struggle. The women workers also took advantage of the
images attached to them to attract more support from outside elites. Sometimes,
internal disputes over the portrayal of their identity and struggle arose among the
workers and their supporters. The workers' encounters with varied public reac-
tion also drove them to present their case not as a national question but as one in
which they were exploited; this made their case a matter of international concern.
Ms. O, the chairperson of the union, talked about the suppression of her voice
on national issues by outsiders:

What I say and all that I say is from my own experiences, naturally. I'm not a band-
wagon person. I might agree with what others say, but I do have my own opinions.
The people have shown their scorn to me. There were so many people, both in
Korea and in the United States, who said that I shouldn't say things like "national
pride." But, I say those things not because I was told by someone, I only say what
I think and feel. When I was protesting in the United States, everything I said was
received, as if I was supporting and taking sides for certain factions within the
group.

Ironically, since the concept of the Korean masses (*minjung*) as a national subject was an elite construction, neither the unofficial nor oppositional discourses
(Abelmann 1996), the *minjung* or subaltern, could claim their emerging social
consciousness as their own. A subaltern representation indeed has its own paradox, as shown in Ms. Hong and Ms. Yu's narratives:

They said that Chu did it. She is young and educated. She told the story like a practical, intelligent person of how they took off without paying us. No one paid attention, as a result. If we talk about the Foreign Capital Inducement Law, we're not going to be able to reach out and touch people. It's not that I don't know anything. It's just that when I talk about how we didn't receive the money, we find it hard to win people's hearts. So, if we talk intelligently, people won't respond. Chu is like that. Yeah. When she talks, I heard that it's not very effective. (Ms. Hong)

As you know, Yi is an excellent speaker. Whenever I heard her explaining our situation, one I know but find so hard to put down in language, I was very impressed by her. But others are saying that she is too articulate. They even say that she lacks sincerity. Some people question whether she is talking about her own experience or something she heard from other people [implying the student activists]. That's what some people in the audience said. There's always something wrong; you're either too good or too bad. (Ms. Yu)

For the women workers to speak for themselves, to address the elite, they necessarily had to reinforce an image mirroring the popular masses who were not yet affected by, and were unknowing of, the intellectual elite discourse. Moreover, they themselves recognized that, although they had become conscious of their plight to a great degree, they would have defeated their own purpose if they were to appeal to the public in a sophisticated way rather than as the uneducated masses they were perceived to be. This, in fact, was the dilemma faced by women workers who were in the process of becoming socially aware subalterns and who experienced multiple axes of domination.

CONCLUSION

This case illustrates what the globalization process meant to Korean working-class women when it was revealed in the form of foreign plant closing in the manufacturing sector. This case highlights diverse aspects of the condition of the women workers' struggle; cutting across dimensions of gender, class, and nation, this case study offers an arena for understanding the female subject in the process of globalization. I have argued that gender images account for a large and important part of the politics of representation when it comes to relations between labor and capital in the new international division of labor.

The historical reality and experience of these South Korean women workers is partially revealed in their narratives about moments during their active resistance, alternating between heroism and victimhood. As such, those who are actually engaged as subjects in history do not exclude the complexities of their own experiences of multilayered domination. The ambivalence, contradiction, and resistance illustrated in their narratives, in contrast to elite discourses, challenge us to account for what constitutes Korean, working class, female subjectivity. In this chapter, I have sought to show how the Korean women workers' labor struggle became the grounds for discourse formation, reflecting diverse political interests. I have also sought to show that gender images operate as core symbols of labor activities and constitute an important symbolic framework for the international division of labor.

When women workers are no longer passive in demanding their labor rights, they gradually enter male-dominant arenas of labor and politics in Korean society. However, their different, gendered images, as *punyoja, omoni,* and Third World women, which dictate defining these women's activism into prescribed categories, serve to reinforce the masculine point of view of women as a homogeneous category. While highlighting the resistance of women workers in their struggle with the multinational company, this chapter also reveals the impasse faced by this subaltern group. This is particularly evident in that this group was unable to acquire an adequate voice to represent its own case and to benefit from its strong activism, both in national and international arenas.

NOTES

This is a fully revised version of the article "Power and Representation: The Case of South Korean Women Workers," included in *Asian Journal of Women's Studies* 4, no. 3 (1998).

1. One of the ethical issues in anthropological research is to use pseudonyms to protect the company and the workers being studied. Korea and South Korea are used interchangeably throughout the chapter.
2. The multinational corporations workers were permitted to unionize in 1986 and their demands started to become increasingly strident in the late 1980s.
3. These foreign industries have been characterized as *ch'olsae kiop* (migratory, runaway shops), meaning that they have continuously relocated their capital in search of cheaper labor for greater profits and, subsequently, have not made long-term investments in personnel or the working environment (S. Y. Yi 1990:125).
4. Female-dominated light manufacturing accounted for 70 percent of total exports. The number of female industrial workers had increased from 360,000 in 1970 to 1,090,000 in 1978, while male industrial workers numbered 1,080,000 in 1970 and 2,910,000 in 1978.
5. In 1997, single women workers numbered 2,093,000, while married, widowed, and divorced women workers added up to 6,546,000 out of the total 8,639,000 women workers (ROK National Statistical Office 1997b).
6. A Supreme Court decision was also made on Nov. 16, 1992, rejecting the union's appeal.

Part III

The Impact
of Economic Restructuring
on Employment and Family

Chapter 6

Women's Unemployment, Re-employment, and Self-employment in China's Economic Restructuring

Ting Gong

China's sweeping economic reform since 1978 has greatly affected all its social groups. Some have gained, others lost, and still more must make extensive adjustments to accommodate the social and economic changes. What has happened to women in terms of employment? What adjustments do they have to make as reform reshuffles the workforce? Are they affected to the same extent as men by the changing employment policies? And, perhaps more importantly, how do women themselves respond to the changes that have had a drastic impact on their careers and lives?

The existing literature has come up with some answers to these questions. Most scholars extend the notion of "unfinished liberation" (Andors 1983) or "postponed revolution" (Wolf 1985) to the reform period and argue that the economic reforms have not only failed to help bring women to full equality with men but also have created new and different, if not more, discrimination against women. This can be seen in the degree to which the labor force is stratified by gender, forcing women to engage in low paying occupations (Liu 1995), in women's "double burden" of full-time work and family responsibilities (Bian 1987), in the correlation between women's low level of education and their lack of employment opportunities (Bauer et al. 1992), and in the increased discrimination against women in hiring and layoffs during the periods of economic reform (Dalsimer and Nisonoff 1984; Summerfield 1994). I concur with the argument that changes in labor policy since the reform have had a profound but not always positive impact on women. I also agree with Gale Summerfield that the cost of reform has fallen disproportionately on women.

Using interview data and statistics on women's employment, I illustrate in this chapter how and why gender-biased unemployment and re-employment practices have taken place during China's economic restructuring. In addition, I will show how women themselves responded to the disadvantageous changes in their employment prospects as they sought self-employment or individual entrepreneurship. The three related employment issues—women's unemployment, re-employment, and self-employment—represent a clear picture of the dilemmas and opportunities facing women in the economic restructuring process. They are living embodiments of China's painful transition from a rigid, centrally planned economy to a competitive market economy. These issues have received some scholarly attention, though there is no lack of media coverage.

FROM UNDEREMPLOYMENT TO UNEMPLOYMENT

For several decades after 1949, China proudly claimed that unemployment did not exist. This denial was largely based on the government's commitment to the communist ideology, if not so much on the support of facts. According to this ideology, unemployment exists only under capitalism, which treats labor as a commodity, and the capitalist system itself is incapable of solving this great social affliction. On the contrary, in a socialist society where workers are masters of the nation and fully entitled to a job, there is no question of any being excluded from employment. Thus, for prereform China, full employment was not only a socio-economic policy but also a political manifestation that differentiated itself from capitalism.

As a result of this political credo, China carried out a "low wages, high employment" labor policy and an egalitarian income distribution policy between 1949 and the late 1970s. Under the prevailing slogan of "jobs for everybody, food for everybody," jobs were assigned by the government to everybody eligible to work in urban areas, with cradle-to-grave security. Workers were not subject to layoffs, while personnel mobility was kept at a minimum. The government took the responsibility to mitigate the income inequality caused by different incomes and number of children.

Under the "iron rice bowl" system, women workers enjoyed dual protection. They were part of the working class and thereby regarded as the masters of the state. In addition, they were a special social group whose status was believed to reflect the commitment of the party to equality, a core concept of communism. Women's participation in the labor force was considered the key to the liberation of women, since the party could not afford to lose the support of women for nation building and political consolidation. Thus, despite that many women were in fact employed in the less privileged collective sectors, they were entitled to employment and income protection. The government sometimes even assigned quotas to work units to hire a certain number of women. Consequently, female participation in the labor force in urban China has always been among one of the highest in the world (Wen 1993).[1] The years between 1949 and 1965 were a "golden period" for women's employment, when the sex ratio between men and women in the labor force decreased from 108.2:100 to 104.4:100 (Research Institute of the All China Women's Federation 1991). In the three years from 1958 to 1960 alone, the number of women workers in state-owned units increased more than three times, from 3.28 million to 10.08 million (Jinling Wong 1992). This higher employment rate among women could be attributed, to a large extent, to the centralized economic system in which everything, including the sex ratio of its labor force, was decided by the government.

China's economic restructuring has led to significant changes in every facet of society. The "iron rice bowl" was among the first targets hit in the transition to a market economy. To create more incentive for innovation and production, the previously government-sponsored employment was gradually marketized, giving employers and employees the freedom to choose one another. In addition, individual work units were entitled to more personnel power in recruitment and dismissals, promotion and demotion, and wages and benefits. At the same time, productivity was replacing political and moral considerations to become the most important criterion for evaluating industrial performance, and prompted enterprises of different ownership systems to compete with each other. And unemployment has been accepted as an integral part of the working of a competitive and healthy market economy. These market-oriented changes, however, have put women at a disadvantage as indicated by the massive layoff, or *xiagang* in Chinese terminology, of women workers in recent years.

Xiagang has long been a Chinese euphemism for unemployment. In a strict sense, however, it is a narrower concept than unemployment, as it refers to the layoffs due only to redundancy or bankruptcy. In addition, xiagang only happens to workers in state owned or urban collective enterprises who were employed on a permanent basis rather than on contract; it therefore is different from a termination of contract. Consequently, employers are often obligated to provide xiagang workers with some compensatory benefits such as medical insurance and minimal wages.

Xiagang emerged as a solution to underemployment or "on-the-job unemployment," a chronic problem facing post-1949 China. Gary Jefferson and Thomas Rawski (1992) distinguish two types of underemployment, *administered* and *transitory.* The former refers to a "labor packing" situation in which enterprises were asked to employ unneeded workers to avoid open unemployment, while the latter refers to idle workers caused by shortages of production needs such as energy or materials. As reform began to hold enterprises accountable for their losses as well as profits, how to appropriately handle surplus and idle workers when reducing labor expenditure became a dilemma for most state-run enterprises.

Xiagang first appeared as a solution in 1986 when the government called upon all enterprises to conduct the so-called optimal labor reorganization (*youhua laodong zuhe*) with a view to increasing productivity. Many workers were asked to change jobs or even stay home with significantly reduced wages in order for their factories to lower production costs and to achieve "optimal productivity." Although women were not singled out for xiagang, they became the de facto target as they were often seen as less productive at work, particularly if they had to bear and then raise young children and, thereby, take long-term leave from work at the employer's expense. Propped up by government subsidies, however, state-owned enterprises still confronted very limited market competition at that time and remained capable of keeping a certain amount of surplus labor and of tolerating idle workers. Many enterprises also experienced difficulties in finding outlets for laid-off workers, and had to stop. As a result, the scale of xiagang was kept fairly small. Statistics show that while the number of underemployed women workers had in fact reached as many as 9.75 million by 1993, only about 400,000 women were receiving unemployment compensation (Chang 1994).

Redundant labor in the state sector has become more of an open problem since 1992, when as many as two-thirds of the state-owned enterprises were found to be operating in the red (Xiao, Jiang, and Hu 1997). About one-third of these enterprises did not have enough work for their employees but still paid regular wages to them. To reduce the financial burden of these enterprises (and thereby that of the state) and enable them to compete more effectively in the market, xiagang became an officially endorsed practice. The government issued the "Rules for Reforming the Operational System of the Industrial Enterprises of Public Ownership" in 1992 and then the "Regulations Regarding the Placement of Surplus Workers" in 1993, aiming to establish a "modern enterprise system" in the state sector. Both documents sanctioned xiagang as a solution to the problem of state surplus labor. Women were badly hit by two government-supported practices. The first of these practices was extended maternity leave or family leave, and the other was "internal retirement," which retired workers before they actually reached the official retirement age. The new rules also left plenty of leeway for implementation by local authorities, leading to the emergence of many local policies for xiagang. The Coal Bureau of Pingdingshan stipulated, for instance, that all pregnant women who could not keep up with their regular schedules had to take a three-year leave at partial wages. It also requested that all mothers with children under two-and-half years of age stay home with a 40 percent wage reduction (Yang, Wu, and Chang 1993:124).

The practice of "internal retirement" (*neitui*) was an arrangement to retire workers at an earlier age but to allow them to maintain connections with their enterprises. While applicable to both male and female workers, this policy actually had more impact on women. This is because the age for internal retirement was set at 45 for women, ten years younger than that for men, while the original difference in the official retirement policy had been only five years (55 for women and 60 for men). The policy made it easier for factories to ask women to leave the labor force. As a matter of fact, many employers were eager to retire people at about age 45 because, as the generation of the Cultural Revolution, they had received little formal education that enabled them to compete in the job market. Thus, women became the de facto targets of internal retirement. The benefits associated with internal retirement might have been better than formal xiagang, for it at least allowed a "retiree" to keep his/her employment status. However, it has deeply hurt many women who were forced to depart from their work while physically still strong and relatively young.

Currently, xiagang as an exit for redundant workers from the labor force takes three forms: off-duty (*daigang*), early retirement (*tiqian tuixiu*), and voluntary resignation. The form matters because it decides how much income and for how long a xiagang worker can receive the income after she leaves the post. Off-duty workers remain affiliated with their work units, and are still entitled to minimal wages and benefits. The amount depends on the economic efficiency of the enterprise—the better its economic performance, the higher the wages for xia-gang workers. In reality, many enterprises are running up debt and often fall into arrears with off-duty wages and other benefit payments. A survey conducted by the Women Workers Department of the All-China Federation of Trade Unions (1998a:14) revealed that among 6,413 xiagang women in 20 provinces, 35 percent did not receive any income, 42.3 percent could not get their medical expenses reimbursed and 66 percent lost medical coverage for their children.

Under the second form of xiagang, pension for early retirement comes mainly from the government, with enterprises providing a supplementary contribution. Enterprises usually welcome this kind of nonemployment settlement with their workers since the government shoulders the major responsibility for pensions, thereby reducing the enterprise's financial burden. For the retirees, the early retirement arrangement might be a little bit better in the sense that a certain amount of pension is guaranteed, but they lose many of the subsidies workers can get, and their pensions often fail to keep pace with the rising cost of living. Early retirement can also easily cause a sense of psychological loss among those who are still young and able to work. The Shengli Petroleum Management Bureau once conducted a survey of 500 women workers and found that 82 percent believed that early retirement was imposed upon them (Sun, Chen, Gao, and Liu 1998:184).

Voluntary resignation takes place when a worker, in the shadow of an approaching layoff, quits her old job to embark on a new one. This serves as the best solution for the worker and the enterprise. The worker actually is not out of employment as she has a new job awaiting, while the enterprise only needs to provide a once-and-for-all compensation. The problem, however, is that workers are sometimes forced to accept "voluntary" resignation before they have new jobs, causing them to experience a painful period of joblessness.

Xiagang, in varying forms, has been widely practiced in recent years. The latest statistic shows there were 16 million xiagang workers at the end of 1998 (*Ming Pao Daily News*, 1999). Women were disproportionately affected as they accounted for more than 60 percent of xiagang workers nationwide, while making up 38 percent of the country's workforce (Xiao et al. 1997). Statistics from individual cities also concur with this rate.[2] The hardest hit industries are textile and electric machinery, where female labor is traditionally concentrated. In order to survive the heavy pressure stemming from market competition, factories in these industrial sectors experienced agonizing restructuring and massive layoffs: some of them were completely shut down (*guan*) or temporarily suspended (*ting*) and others were merged (*bing*) or transferred into other industries (*zhuan*). In Shanghai alone, 17 textile and electronic machinery factories went under in 1997 and 40 percent of the 55,000 textile workers had to accept xiagang (X. Chen 1997).

A fundamental cause of women's xiagang lies in the centralized labor policy of the prereform period which led to the structural surplus and underemployment of women's labor, especially in those female, labor-intensive sectors mentioned above. However, the disproportionate exit of female workers from the labor force merits further explanation. It is, in a sense, an unintended consequence of the reform policies seeking to force enterprises to compete in the marketplace. To survive, enterprises must reduce production costs, especially those unnecessary elements of the workforce. Women, thereby, tend to become the first target for layoffs, as they are conventionally considered less productive. For example, a textile factory with 1,362 women workers in the Hubei province blamed the various kinds of leave and compensation female workers received for its annual loss of 700,000 yuan (Fang 1998). Enterprises in the Guangxi province claimed that the annual average productivity of their male workers was 1,898.8 yuan more than that of female workers and 10, 739.1 yuan more than nursing mothers (Xiao et al. 1997). Reports such as these often lead to the conviction that women are less competitive than men and should be laid off first.

Education also plays an important role in decisions about layoffs. In China, women generally have lower education levels than men. Official statistics show that women account for 70 percent of China's illiterate population and 23.24 percent of women aged 15 and above are illiterate and semi-literate, while the rate is only 9.58 percent for men (State Statistical Bureau 1998:116). Enterprises tend to lay off first those who have less education and are unskilled. According to a survey in Shanghai, among approximately 121,220 female xiagang workers in 1996, 66.9 percent had education at primary or middle school levels and 91.7 percent of them had no special skills (Zhao 1997). A report from Chongqing City confirms the same: about 64 percent of the laid-off female workers surveyed had middle school or lower education (Chongqing Women's Federation 1997:34).

What should also be noted is that the gender disproportion in layoffs has much to do with the deeply rooted patriarchal values in China. At the bottom of the social pecking order, women are considered less able than men. Old prevailing doctrines such as "men in charge of external affairs and women internal ones" (*nanzhuwai, nuzhunei*) and "men's superiority and women's inferiority" (*nanzhun nubei*) have continued to influence Chinese society to the present. A nationwide survey conducted by the All China Federation of Trade Unions (1997:44) in 1994 and 1995 showed, among all the xiagang female workers surveyed, that while 42.8 percent were redundant labor and 21.4 percent went home due to health or other reasons (e.g., factory closure, voluntary resignation), 35.8 percent of them became xiagang workers simply because they were women.

Xiagang tends to have multifaceted, negative consequences for laid-off workers and their families. Most obviously, it reduces a family's income and worsens its financial condition. In a survey of laid-off women workers in the Luwan district of Shanghai, 91.9 percent of the respondents said that the financial situation of their families had worsened after xiagang (Women's Federation of Luwan District 1997). Their reduced wages fell far behind the rapidly rising cost of living. The Labor Department reported that at the end of 1995 about 72 percent of xiagang women nationwide did not live up to the local average living standards, 42.3 percent had to pay for medical expenses out of their own pockets, and 35 percent did not have any income (Chen 1998).

The negative impact of layoffs on women also lies in the reduction of a woman's status within a family, though many of them are reluctant to accept the role of a dependent wife. According to the survey conducted by the All-China Federation of Trade Unions (1997:98), among 1,607 xiagang women in the Hebei province, 71.8 percent had to stay home and relied on their husband for a living, while 97 percent of them were actually eager to return to work. It is alarming to note that some women even became the victims of discrimination and domestic violence after xiagang. Among 6,106 laid-off women surveyed by the Chongqing Women's Federation (1997:35), 22.5 percent claimed that they had been somewhat discriminated against by their family members and relatives; 10.1 percent were battered by their husbands; and 2.1 percent were divorced because of xiagang.

Finally, xiagang can generate a negative psychological impact on the women workers and their families, as they consider themselves or are considered by others as socially unneeded or abandoned. This is particularly true for young xiagang workers, many of whom are only in their 30s and still able-bodied. These women actually account for a majority of xiagang workers. Statistics show that the percentages of xiagang women workers under 40 years of age were 60 and 65 in Shanghai and Wenzhou, respectively (Chang 1995).

For many xiangang workers, the loss of identity can easily cause frustration, depression, pessimism, and desperation as their future livelihood becomes dim. The survey by the Chongqing Women's Federation (1997) reveals that 35 percent of the respondents said that they could not understand and accept the reality of being laid off and that 34.8 percent felt at a loss and did not know what to do next.

Xiagang has indeed become a social problem in China due to its prevalence and many negative consequences. The actual xiagang experience and the looming possibility of becoming unemployed have generated strong pressures upon women, pushing them to seek alternatives for survival (Xue 1998).

SEEKING SURVIVAL: WOMEN'S RE-EMPLOYMENT

Like the term xiagang, *zaijiuye* (literally, "re-employment") has become another familiar phrase to Chinese people in recent years, referring to a laid-off worker who re-enters employment at another enterprise. Re-employment is important for the government as well as the dislocated workers themselves. While massive layoffs are unavoidable as a necessary price for restructuring the economy to a more rational and market-driven economy, a social security net is not yet in place in China. Many of those laid off are not able to make ends meet unless they become breadwinners again. Thus, re-employment is the immediate demand of millions of xiagang workers. For the government, finding new jobs for laid-off workers is also urgent since it helps ease social tensions caused by massive unemployment so that it will not threaten the existing political order and stability.

The Re-employment Project (*zaijiuyie qongcheng*) thus emerged as a nation-wide governmental effort to help xiagang workers return to work. Varying in forms with localities, the Re-employment Project entails a major responsibility upon governments at different levels and for co-operative efforts on the part of industrial sectors, trade unions, women's federations, and other social organizations. These institutions pool services and funds to assist laid-off workers with re-entry into jobs by providing them with job training and placement information. In many cities, re-employment service centers have been established to accommodate the needs of xiagang workers for information on employment policies, skill training programs, and job referrals.[3] These job centers sometimes even push for job interviews by making direct contact with potential employers on behalf of applicants.

However, the assistance from job centers does not necessarily bring about rosy prospects for female xiagang workers. First, these centers themselves are under serious financial constraints, relying on a very limited budget allocated by the government and dependent upon contributions from the industrial sectors, many of which are in the red themselves. Second, job centers have no way of guaranteeing that women will be treated as fairly as men in the very competitive job market, where women often fall victim to unfair recruiting practices. Sex discrimination is not rare in today's China; many job advertisements explicitly request "men only." Employers are able to do so because the labor supply in China currently far exceeds the demand for labor. As the economy gets further marketized, individual enterprises virtually have power to decide whom they should hire. According to the survey conducted by the All-China Federation of Trade Unions in 1997 on the re-employment of xiagang workers, among 423 heads of enterprises surveyed, 71.6 percent said they would prefer men if their enterprise needed to recruit additional workers. The survey also revealed that some factories gave re-employed female workers lower wages than their male counterparts (All-China Federation of Trade Union 1998a). The jobs introduced through the re-employment centers tend to be unskilled, low paid, fatiguing, and tedious. Most of them are in the service sector and often require irregular or long working hours. Examples include vending, street cleaning, laundering, babysitting, caring for the elderly, and food preparation. Although the new term *irregular employment* (*feizhengui jiuye*) has been introduced to include these practices and other domestic services into the traditional concept of employment, women are reluctant to accept such positions as they do not contain formal or contractual labor relations and, therefore, lack legal protection. The same survey mentioned above found that among those who once declined job offers, 57.6 percent did it because of the irregular nature of the offer. Those who had to accept low-status jobs often felt further marginalized by the gendered job market.

Given the limited role of government-sponsored re-employment centers in meeting the demands of massive layoffs, it is not surprising to see xiagang workers seeking re-employment in the booming private sector on their own. As has been well noted, the rise of the private economy and its contribution to national economic growth are the major achievements of China's market reform. Accordingly, the private sector has demonstrated a great potential to absorb unemployed labor. From 1989 to 1998, the number of employees in the private sector increased by 13.6 percent annually, while the workforce in both state-owned and collectively owned enterprises shrank by .01 percent and .06 percent on average (Zhang and Ming 1999). In Shanghai alone, some 100,000, or 15 percent of 660,000 re-employed xiagang workers, were absorbed by the private sector in recent years (Sun et al. 1998:247).

Private enterprises tend to welcome xiagang workers because their salary expectations are usually lower than other applicants. The cost of hiring a xiagang worker, especially a woman, is even lower than that of a migrant worker whose lodging often adds to the financial burden of the enterprise. The massive layoff in the state sector in recent years has provided the private sector with a low-cost reserve of labor and made it possible for them to offer low wages.

Xiagang workers themselves tend to have mixed feelings about working for private enterprises. They like it, on the one hand, because it provides them with career opportunities and makes them regular income earners again, thereby getting out of the unemployment plight. This is particularly true for women because they have less chance than men of getting re-employed through state sponsored channels. For example, the survey conducted by the All-China Federation of Trade Unions in 1997 revealed that, among more than 50,000 respondents, 12.1 percent of the laid-off male workers received re-employment training sponsored by the government, but only 8.8 percent of women had such an opportunity. The same survey also indicated that 83 percent of female xiagang workers had the experience of being turned down in their initial job applications (Policy Research Institute 1999:53).

Under such circumstances access to the private sector brings them new hope. Zhao's case is very telling: at 31, she became unemployed after her state-owned factory went bankrupt. She soon found another job at a state-run department store. However, as a result of lacking special skills, she was once again laid off after six months when the store downsized. Frustrated, Zhao turned to the private sector. She tried many different types of private businesses such as street vending and cooking and ended up working for a wedding service center. She put it very frankly that xiagang, as a serious crisis in her personal and familial life, has forced her to rely on nobody but herself (Yu 1998). This feeling is not rare among xiagang workers. For example, one woman worker expressed, "In the past we had secure life-time employment, but nothing is guaranteed now. We should look for new opportunities" (Yang et al. 1993:174).

Working for the private sector, however, may mean tough working conditions, strict regulations, and lack of fringe benefits. Statistics show that working conditions in the private sector are the worst among the four existing types of enterprises—state-owned, collectively owned, private, and foreign—in China. According to the report by the All-China Federation of Trade Unions (1997: 38–39), 83 percent of women workers surveyed in the private enterprises did not have any maternity benefits, 81 percent could not get government-required labor protection when engaging in toxic work, and 35 percent were even deprived of the right for maternity leave. As for working hours, 44 percent of women workers in these private enterprises had to work for more than 44 hours a week. All this can cause women to flinch at taking a job offer by a private enterprise. Although the All-China Women's Federation has spared no effort in its struggle to improve women's working conditions, the actual effect remains to be seen.

SELF-EMPLOYMENT: ANOTHER WAY OUT OF THE PLIGHT?

Self-employment is a third option for xiagang workers. The rise of self-employment in China resulted from the reform policy "being rich is glorious." Pioneer *getihu* (self-employed) began their businesses in the first individual-business boom of the early 1980s, when millions of youths who, rusticated during the Cultural Revolution, flooded back to the cities to set up their own businesses. More women, however, set out on their business journey in the later and even larger business mania of 1992. Stimulated by Deng Xiaoping's much publicized tour of the southern "special economic zones," which signaled the leadership's determination to push economic reform forward, hundreds of thousands of new businesses, small or large, then surfaced.[4] As the party appeared more willing to accept market mechanisms such as free pricing, stocks, and private ownership, more people were anxious to try their luck at self-employment. From the business boom a new social stratum has emerged of rich, private business people, or *dakuan* (literally, "big money") in Chinese popular terminology. Initially, through self-employment and by gradually expanding their businesses, these people have brought themselves great fortune through hard work and good business skills. Many of them pull an extremely high income (often several hundred times that of public-sector workers) and enjoy a good living.

While self-employment is a bridge toward significant personal financial advancement for some, it is for many merely a way to salvage oneself from a job crisis or a means to make ends meet. This is particularly true for state-sector workers who live in the shadow of layoffs. The government has designed preferential policies to encourage laid-off workers to start their own business as *getihu*, either individually or collaboratively, thereby reducing the demand for government-sponsored employment. At many localities, for example, the self-employed businesses of xiagang workers are exempt from the cumbersome bureaucratic procedures of registration and, perhaps more importantly, enjoy significant tax reductions. When qualified, xiagang workers can also obtain low-interest loans from the government to get their businesses off the ground. According to Shanghai's official statistics, among the more than one million xiagang workers, 105,000 had become self-employed by 1997 (Sun et al. 1998:69).

Self-employment attracts female xiagang workers because it enables them to venture in the market without being confronted with gender-biased recruitment policies. As a writer in the *Shanghai Labor Movement*, the official magazine of the Shanghai Municipal Trade Union, puts it, "getting self-employed perhaps is the best outlet for older xiagang women, because it helps them avoid gender and age discrimination, which is still prevailing in the labor market" (Lu 1999:15).

For many laid-off women, the business world is mystifying, but it is a path worth pursuing in order to become breadwinners again. In Hubei province, 75,000 xiagang workers became self-employed after being laid off (Women's Federation of Hubei Province 1998). In Jiangshu province, 30 percent of the 113,000 self-employed are women; in Shanghai, the number is 40 percent out of 227,000 (Deng 1998; Lu 1999). According to an official estimate, in 1995 there were about four million female business owners in China. This is a significant number, compared with the total number of women, 56 million, in the urban labor force (Si 1995). However, this is hardly an accurate figure since many individual businesspeople simply do not register.

Today, the economic environment in China is perhaps at its best for conducting business because opportunities abound. For many women, however, to start up as self-employed in the traditionally male-dominated business world is certainly not an easy undertaking. This is particularly true for xiagang women who lack cash and capital, special skills, and business networks. As a result, they often have to choose businesses that require less capital, technique, and marketing networks, such as food, lodging, and cleaning services. These are also areas where women are believed to have an "advantage" because they are caring, patient, and persistent (Lu 1999:14).

These feminized businesses demand hard work—especially long, irregular working hours. This is a big challenge for many working mothers who shoulder the work-and-housework double burden and who, in their own words, "are racing men while carrying a baby."[5] They do not mind working long hours or harder than others, which is often the case to compete in the business world when self-employed, but they do feel pained when they have to sacrifice family life for business. The self-employed women we interviewed told us that they often felt guilty about not being able to spend more time with their families. A 40-year-old woman manager said, "I hate the term 'strong woman,' which I and other businesswomen are sometimes referred to. I am not strong at all; I always feel tired. I also feel suffering because, though successful in business, I am not a qualified mother and wife" (Xia 1995:35).

To make things worse, there is also a lack of social understanding about self-employed women. Social prejudice against female self-employment is deeply rooted in Chinese society, as the following story from Shanghai's popular evening daily, *Xinmin Wanbao,* indicates. Chen, a xiagang woman, opened a streetside breakfast shop. One day a well-dressed lady passed by with her child. She pointed to Chen and her store and told the child, "You must study hard; otherwise, you will do the same thing that this woman is doing when you are grown up" (Tang and Sun 1997). Women like Chen are deeply hurt by this kind of prejudice. In my study, one interviewee described the gender bias against women this way: "If a woman has a job of her own and her husband stays home to take care of the children, people around them would look down upon the family. However, if vice versa, the wife stays home and the husband works, people would say this is a happy family."

Despite social prejudice and the stereotype that women are less able to run a successful business, self-employed businesswomen have emerged in China. Many of them were once laid-off workers and are now prosperous. Tang, a Sichuan xia-gang woman, for example, spent several months seeking re-employment after being laid off. She visited almost all the re-employment centers in the city but was still unable to find a job. Consequently, she had to embark on a restaurant business as self-employed. Her business went very well and she quickly accumulated a total of 400,000 yuan in assets. In order to help other xiagang women, she employed only xiagang workers, and five of her employees later became individual businesswomen themselves. Zhuang's case is another example. Zhuang and her husband both became unemployed four years ago. They borrowed 30,000 yuan from relatives and friends and set up a food processing factory. Their business has been very successful, thanks to their hard work and Zhuang's good management as chief operator. The Madam Zhuang Food Processing Center now earns a net profit of more than 20,000 yuan per month.[6]

These cases indicate that xiagang women, while compelled to take part in market competition, can succeed. Self-employment has led to a change in the lives of many laid-off women and, especially, to a shift in women's role from dependent wife to independent breadwinner. More significantly, individual businesswomen represent a new social identity that is rising from the reform in which private capital is allowed to run parallel with public ownership and in which individual producers, whether male or female, are encouraged to compete with each other in the marketplace. Traditionally, Chinese women did not have a highly visible economic role in society and were merely confined to the domestic sphere, doing household chores, or better, engaging in agricultural or subsidiary work not far from home. It was rare for a woman to conduct a business on her own. Thus, women's self-employment today comes as a direct challenge to the traditional patriarchal value that regards women as *neiren* ("inside people") whose main activities take place within the home. The rise of an unprecedented number of female business owners indicates that women have the vision and skills required for running businesses and can make a much greater economic contribution to society than was traditionally thought.

During our interview, one woman told us that she was a very shy person and had relied on her husband to the extent that she needed his company every time she went out. "Now I have my own business and a network of good friends that I can rely on when I have difficulties in business. I now understand that my husband needs time for himself, since he has his own career. And I love him even more than before, even though we don't go out together as often." A survey conducted in the Luwan District of Shanghai asked a group of self-employed women what satisfied them most about their work. More people chose "having work autonomy" than anything else, including "earning income" and "increasing abilities" (Lu 1999:15).

Women's self-employment is also significant because it reflects xiagang workers' self-salvation efforts. Women's social and economic status in China is far from satisfactory even after the "women's liberation" movement in 1949. This can be seen in women's low level of education, low wages, limited access to new technologies and skills, and their lack of representation in political affairs. These factors have interacted with discrimination against women to reinforce traditional female roles. In the prereform period, the structure of labor institutions generally discouraged people from seeking alternatives to changing the status quo because it did not allow free labor movement. Consequently, even if women were conscious of and unsatisfied with their low status, they could do little to make a change. Reform has provided women with opportunities as well as incentives to change their status by allowing them to explore new roles in society. If we can say that before reform women mainly relied on the help of the government to improve their living conditions, then today many of them have to learn how to look after themselves, with or without government assistance, in an increasingly competitive but still largely gendered labor market.

This said, running a self-employed business is still very challenging for women in China as they are confronted not only with acute market competition but also with the deeply rooted social prejudice mentioned above. Individual businesswomen must have special aptitudes, including a psychological fortitude, to bear the biases and risks. The individual stories of our interviewees all point to the fact that women often have to work much harder, spend more time, and deal with worse conditions to accomplish the same as men do. One respondent explained, using a figure of speech, "If a woman and a man each have to carry 50 kilos of stuff to a certain destination, the man can do it all at once, but the woman may have to make three trips." Individual businesses owned by women can also easily be victimized by government corruption. Because these businesses tend to be small and weak, they are sometimes forced to provide free services for corrupt officials in order to stay in business. Yang, a xiagang woman, had a small restaurant open for more than two years and should have earned a net profit of at least 20,000 yuan. However, she was still deep in debt. The reason was that the town government officials frequently came to eat on credit and never paid a single yuan to her. She finally had to close the restaurant when it became too hard to eke out a living (Deng 1998).

CONCLUSION

Indeed, economic restructuring has a very real and gendered bearing on women, as reflected by their dilemmas and opportunities in unemployment, re-employment, and self-employment. In other words, for many women, whether they are able to maintain a job, how they enter and exit from the job market, and what kind of jobs are available to them have been largely determined by the reshuffling of the labor force as a result of economic restructuring.

In recent years, unemployment in China has soared as bloated, inefficient state-owned enterprises are shut down. In the economic restructuring process, women, as a conveniently elastic segment of the labor force, are hardest hit. They are more likely to be asked to exit from jobs, while having fewer opportunities to re-enter the workforce. It is true that women's overrepresentation among the unemployed is the result of prereform labor policies, which absorbed more workers than needed into the labor force to support the radical egalitarian ideal. Protected by the "iron rice bowl," the unemployment problem appeared only in the form of workers' underemployment. As reform breaks the "iron bowl" and replaces it with market competition, this old problem takes a new form in xiagang. In other words, reform has merely changed the form of the problem from underemployment to unemployment rather than having created a new problem.

Nonetheless, while China's economic restructuring attempts to establish a competitive job market, little effort has been made to degender it. The cost of economic restructuring is disproportionately borne by women, and especially by xiagang women. This is evident in that more women than men are laid off, that women tend to wait longer for re-employment, and that their incomes after xiagang lag behind men's.[7] In addition, after women have successfully re-entered jobs, they tend to engage in low-pay, low-status, and irregular work. Xiagang has marginalized their social and economic status, leaving little choice for them but to take less desirable positions in the job market. This is particularly true for those laid-off women who have passed the prime of youth, have low levels of education, and lack professional skills.

Self-employment is an outlet for women to avoid the gendered job market, since one does not have to go through possibly discriminatory hiring processes and can, to some extent, choose the type of business. Allowing women to transcend their traditional family roles, self-employment has contributed to the rise of a considerable number of prosperous individual businesswomen in China. However, this has proven to be no easy undertaking for women because, under China's current conditions, traditional gender roles in the family are yet to be reconstructed. Individual businesswomen are often caught in a dilemma: on the one hand, they have to be strong-willed, smart, and very hard working to compete in a still largely male-dominated business world; on the other hand, they are often expected to play the traditional motherly and wifely roles in the family, though many of them cry out for understanding from society and their families.

Moreover, one's chances in the business world are selective—not all who are brave enough to strive for individual success can achieve it. Successful businesswomen are, after all, small in number. In addition to timing and business strategy, managerial skills closely related to one's education level are required. In China successful businesswomen are usually at least high school graduates, and some of them even have college diplomas.[8] This significantly differs from the general profile of xiagang women, more than 36 percent of whom only have an elementary or junior-high level of education, and only 32 percent of whom have reached the high school level. The question remains to what extent the salvation efforts of a few successful individual businesswomen can save the fate of hundreds of thousands of women being laid off. Not all xiagang workers can easily enter the business world by themselves, whereas not all of those who have already entered can prosper.

For Chinese women, both challenges and opportunities have come in the wake of economic restructuring. While women's unemployment is an inevitable outcome of the transformation of China's labor institutions from pro-equity to pro-efficiency and from rigidly and centrally planned to productivity-driven pragmatic institutions, successful reemployment and, particularly, self-employment of xiagang women workers indicates opportunity. As reform deepens and the market develops further, there surely will be more such opportunity. What needs to be done, however, is to degender the labor market and people's perceptions of xiagang women workers. The government needs to help enhance women's abilities to compete in the marketplace. This, to say the least, involves two difficult but fundamental undertakings. First, more attention should be brought to women's education, the key to the promotion of their social status; this includes vocational retraining for middle-aged women so that they can reenter the labor market if a layoff becomes unavoidable. Second, women's family responsibilities should be reduced in order for them to have a greater chance for career advancement. For example, more social services, such as child care, should be established to help reduce household chores so that when women are competing in the marketplace, they do not have too many concerns back home. In short, with reform going on, there should be more choices available for women, and women should have the ability to make the best choice for themselves.

NOTES

Research for this chapter was funded by an earmarked competitive grant from the Research Grants Council of Hong.

1. Women accounted for 44.5 percent of China's labor force in 1990, a rate higher than those of the developed nations such as Italy (32 percent), Japan (34.7 percent), Germany (36.9 percent), France (38.7 percent), Canada (40.4 percent), and the United States (42 percent). See Wen 1993:8–14.

2. The percentages of women among the total number of xiagang workers in several individual provinces or cities for roughly the same period are: Shanghai, 58 percent; Guangxi, 55 percent; Guangdong, 70 percent; Nanjing, 54 percent; and Hebei, 63 percent.

3. In Beijing alone there were about 290 job centers in 1998 (Wang 1998).

4. It was reported during the month of July 1992 alone that more than 2,000 new economic entities were registered in Beijing; this means that on average three new businesses emerged every hour.

5. The data came from interviews with 70 self-employed business women in 1996 and 1997 in Shanghai. The author participated in the interviews as the principal research collaborator. Hereafter, quotes from self-employed businesswomen in the text are from those interviews unless otherwise noted.

6. Zhuang and 29 other xiagang women were praised by the Shanghai Women Federation as Model Workers of Re-employment in December 1997.

7. A survey shows that the average monthly income for xiagang women workers is only 245 yuan in six major Chinese cities, 32 percent less than that of xiagang men workers, 423 yuan. In Shenzhen, while women account for 67 percent of xiagang workers, the percentage rises to 73 percent among those who have been out of employment for more than a year (Women's Committee of Zigong Party 1998).

8. The author participated in the interviews of 70 self-employed business women in the summer of 1996 and February 1997 and found that all those successfully self-employed had at least a high school diploma and about half of them had received some higher education.

Chapter 7

State Women Workers in Chinese Economic Reform

The Transformation of Management Control and Firm Dependence

Ping Ping

Academics are more and more concerned about the gender impact of economic reform in China. Studies have found in the midst of the reform that, compared to men, women workers as a group were subjected to disadvantaged situations, which were manifested in different ways, such as through wages, employment status, and welfare benefits offered by firms (Feng and Xu 1993; Meng 1995; Rai 1992). However, lacking an institutional perspective, the present description of women workers' experience in the postreform era is far from clear. Most studies so far focus on women's situation from 1978 onward—namely, after economic reform. Yet I believe that there exists an inherent connection between the prereform (1949 to 1978) and postreform periods. An analysis of women workers in the prereform era is indispensable for a comprehensive understanding of women's workplace encounters in the postreform era. Therefore, this study analyzes women workers' relations with state-owned enterprises before and after the reform.

This chapter argues that it was the social arrangement of women workers in firms in the prereform era that shaped their disadvantaged status in the postreform era. It begins with a description of women workers' experiences during the prereform era with job arrangement, distribution of political resources, and scarce welfare resources in order to depict the women's distinctive condition of dependence on state-owned firms in the prereform era. It then discusses changes in the gender strategy of control by management when responding to institutional change during the economic transformation. It concludes that the unified pattern of workers' dependence constructed by Andrew Walder (1986) needs to be reconsidered to include women workers' gendered condition of dependence on their work units.

First, I need to clarify some concepts. The worker's situation, according to Walder (1986) and Yanjie Bian (1994), refers to the worker's status and treatment in the distribution of economic, political, and welfare resources. Economic resources consist of jobs, types of skills, and levels of wage. Political resources include opportunities for development, authority, and honor, such as party membership and model worker entitlement. Welfare resources (mainly those that are scarce) refer to provisions of housing only. Besides these factors, dependence—or the extent of worker dependence—is defined by two aspects of the employment relationship. One is the proportion of workers' needs that are satisfied in the workplace, and the other is the availability of alternative sources for the satisfaction of these needs (Walder 1986:14). In addition, dependence implies power that the workplace wields over its dependents (Blau 1964). Gender strategy refers to the conscious priority of management in using gender as an important dimension in the labor process (C. K. Lee 1995) and in resource allocation.

LITERATURE REVIEW

Walder's (1986) profound generalization of the political authority of industrial sectors in socialist China can be problematic in failing to see gender relations in the workplace, which contributed to a certain extent to the state's successful political control over workers before the reform. According to the logic of a resource-dependence framework, Walder conceptualizes the essence of the employment relationship in Chinese state work units—that is, workers' full dependence on work units both rationally and emotionally. He puts forth an enormous effort to show that "organized dependence" is the central state's designated institution for practicing and maintaining the party-state's domination. The institution is realized through the state's monopoly over all kinds of resources; workers have been unified to depend on work units in many areas. Therefore, the system discourages workers from organizing themselves, so they have to submit to the only source of power at the workplace, which is management. This serves to maintain a steady political system. My study on women workers in state enterprises in the prereform era departs from Walder's theoretical track, which assumes that all workers fall into the same unified structure of dependence and have shifted to the same level of dependence found in the prereform era. My data show that Walder's assumption is not true for women workers even in the prereform era.

Moreover, the reward and incentive system in factories revealed by Walder work in the same way for women workers. Walder emphasizes that cultivating vertical ties among a devoted minority of workers is an important way to maintain control effectively. Activists are formed in this kind of vertical tie, and they have priority in career opportunities and in many other benefits and privileges. Yet curiously, women workers are most likely to be indifferent to playing the role of activists. Why are they indifferent? Walder believes that even though rank-and-file workers have an unprivileged status with regard to resource allocation, they usually develop personal relationships with individual superiors who are in control of the allocation of scarce goods. They give gifts to their superiors, and, in exchange, their superiors provide them with scarce goods. Women workers, however, are seldom found to have this kind of personal exchange with superiors. The reason women are indifferent to being activists or to developing personal relationships with superiors is that the reward system and allocation of scarce goods have a negative institutional bias against women workers.

In general, Walder's evidence exposes both political loyalty and deep-seated personal loyalty as being the principles behind resource allocation; in other words, the one who obeys is rewarded and the one who disobeys is punished. When I tested this principle against women workers' life experiences, I found that it explains little of the women's encounter in enterprises even in the prereform era. Accordingly, it is reasonable to say that the extent of women workers' dependence differs from the universal model constructed by Walder, which is mainly based on men's working experiences. The reason may be due to a different structure of dependence for women workers.

This study questions Walder's model based upon his gender blindness in viewing work and authority in Chinese industry. I have tried to formulate an appropriate application for studying state women workers. The study will specify the condition (or situation) of women workers' dependence. It will focus on the institutional shift of the living sources of women workers before and after the reform and show how that affects their relationships with the firms. In response to Walder's theory about authority in Chinese state-owned enterprises, this study argues that, aside from the principle of particularism in state-owned factories, gender still serves as a dimension of control that has been missed. My field data show that management shifted the focus from political control in the prereform era to economic control in the postreform era. Women's working behaviors became diverse during the reform period, because their degrees of dependence on the firms were uneven.

Using gender as an observational perspective, the study finds that a woman worker's dependence was shaped by her family's economic situation, while a male worker's dependence could seldom be predicted by his family's economic situation to the same extent. This was especially significant in the postreform era. If a woman's family economic situation was strong enough, she would depend on her family economically and would not care about the factory job's wage. I call this kind of situation "family dependence." However, if a woman's family economic situation was not that strong, she depend on her work unit or seek alternative resources in the market. If she had marketable skills and extensive social networks, she would depend on the market to gain more money in spite of the payment from her formal work in the firm. I call this kind of situation "market dependence." If her market situation was poor, she would depend on the firm. For the woman with no social networks and marketable skills, it would be necessary to depend on the work unit to support the family's survival. Such a woman would work hard and care much about her payment by the firm. I refer to this type of situation as "firm dependence."

Based on empirical evidence, I hypothesize that, along with the rising of the market as a new institution for reallocating economic resources after the reform, the living resources of people, which used to be confined to the work unit only, are much more diverse than before. Accordingly, the economic situations of families become heterogeneous. Thus, three types of dependence of women workers were formulated in the process of reform. Their dependence on work units was mainly determined by the combination of their family economic situations, social networks, and marketable skills.

RESEARCH METHOD

I conducted in-depth interviews in two state-owned enterprises in Guangzhou from 1994 to 1996. One is the South Machinery Group Firm (SMGF) and the other is the Exactitude Optical Instrument Firm (EOIF). My interviewees were on-duty women employed as permanent workers. The reasons for choosing them were that they witnessed the transformation in the state's policy on employment, wage, and welfare from the prereform to postreform eras and that they were also the most experienced group able to enjoy the complete and permanent welfare services offered by the state enterprise.

I interviewed 30 women workers in total. Half of them came from the SMGF and the other half from the EOIF. I chose the samples based on differences in job, age, and family background, which was based on the kind of ownership of work unit for which their husbands labored. The average age of the female interviewees was 39.83, which matched the actual average age of women workers in the firms.

In general, this generation of women workers entered the factory before 1980 and were mostly born and raised in Guangzhou. Twenty-three of the interviewees piece-rate workers in skilled and semiskilled jobs, and the rest were non-piece-rate workers who mainly hold unskilled jobs. As to their marital status, except for two who are unmarried, one is divorced, and the other 23 workers are married. Nineteen of the interviewees' parents (both or one spouse) are workers, and the other 11 were originally from cadres or peasants families. Sixteen of the women's husbands work in the state system just as they do, while the remaining seven husbands work in private or joint venture firms. In addition, I interviewed 16 managerial staff members in the two firms and had informal interviews with some male workers. Both the women workers and the managerial staff have provided a comprehensive understanding of the labor system.

STATE-OWNED FIRMS: TWO RESEARCH SITES

The two firms are similar in that they are both under the control of the Guangzhou government, but they differ in the proportion of women workers found in their work force. Women workers comprised 33 percent of all workers in the SMGF, and they accounted for 65 percent of the whole work force in the EOIF. The sex composition of the workforce in the two firms is shown in table 7.1.

The SMGF was set up in 1948 and consisted of several privately owned factories in the same industry. During the time of the study, the chief administrator of the SMGF was the Economic Commission of Guangzhou. The SMGF is located on the south shore of the Pearl River in Guangzhou and spans 560,000 square meters. It produces centrifuges, pressure vessels, general machinery, light industrial machinery, and, in 1996, mainly served the domestic market despite the fact that 30 percent of its products were exported. It has retained its own technical secondary school; hence, it enjoys the fame and prestige of its well-

**Table 7.1. The Composition of Employees
and Women Workers in the Two Firms**

	SMGF	EOIF
Size	Large	Medium
Overall employees[a]	4,503	550
Female employees	1,484	283
Overall workers	3,183	358
Women workers	1,052	233
Proportion of women workers	33%	65%

Source: Statistical Forms of the SMGF, 1995, and the EOIC, 1996.
[a]Employees include workers, management, and technical staff.

trained technical workers. However, in 1996, 70 percent of the women were concentrated in semiskilled or unskilled jobs, while 30 percent of them were classified as skilled workers. As to female cadres, they were very rarely found in middle- and high-level management.

More than 3,000 of the workers' households had dormitories allocated by the firm. The dormitory area was located opposite to the production area and separated by an avenue. All the conveniences of life, such as grocery stores and canteens, could be found within the compound. The factory buildings are all around 50 to 60 meters high and are filled with the roaring noise of the machines and workers laboring in a greasy environment. The production workers liked to dress in a simple style, usually in a blue-gray uniform, and to talk loudly.

The EOIF was established in 1958. It consists of several small, privately owned factories in instrumental processing and was under the control of the Bureau of Instruments and Meters of Guangzhou until the year 2000. Located on the south shore of the Pearl River, the EOIF covers an area of 30,000 square meters. It mainly produces optical instruments, including microscopes, lenses, and eyeglass frames. In 1996, 70 percent of its products were exported to Europe, North America, and Asia. The EOIF benefited from its flexible adjustment to market needs. Even in the period of economic depression beginning in 1990, the EOIF was profitable due to its export-oriented strategy.

In the EOIF, skilled female workers comprised about 60 percent of the entire skilled workforce in 1996. They were concentrated in optical jobs because factory management believed that women workers fit these jobs well because of their nimble fingers and patience. Nevertheless, positions in mechanical work, electroplate work, and maintenance, which require "highly trained skills," were still dominated by men. However, compared to the SMGF, the concentration of women workers in semiskilled and unskilled work was lower in the EOIF. Yet women were still the majority of behind-the-scenes service jobholders, working in cleaning and catering jobs, for example. Likewise, female cadres in the EOIF made up the minority in middle- and high-level management, except for the director of the EOIF who was, and continues to be, a woman.

Nearly 200 households of workers lived in the allocated dormitories of the firm. The firm had fulfilled about 60 percent of the workers' applications for housing. More than 80 percent of the firm's housing was built in 1988 and 1993 as the firm turned profitable. In comparison to the SMGF, women workers who held optical jobs in the EOIF dressed in a more fashionable style. They were permitted to wear skirts and leather shoes during working hours and could sit on chairs to work. The general working environment was clean and peaceful. The monthly salary of workers in the EOIF in the period of 1990–95 was usually 1000 yuan per month, which was 10 percent higher than that of the SMGF.

In this study of two firms, the research shows that the essential meaning behind the sex ratio of workers in the labor force is that it can reflect the significant role of women workers in skilled jobs. In the firm that identified women as being appropriate for skilled jobs, women workers were given more credit by management control; for example, women in the EOIF were given more positive comments about their work performance and skills than women in the SMGF.

WOMEN WORKERS IN THE PREREFORM ERA

Gendered Job Arrangements of Women Workers

First, the state's employment policy was gendered in its arrangement of female workers. When the state was in demand for workers, such as during the era of "The Great Leap Forward" in 1958 that symbolized a nationwide industrialization of China, a great mass of urban and town women began to join the labor force. Women's participation in paid labor was an outcome of a state socialist policy of industrialization. In addition, the state's guarantee of women's employment was taken to represent women's liberation and the superiority of socialism (Tan 1994).

Guided by the socialist ideology of emancipating women, the state government had ruled that state-owned and collective factories must employ women and had reprimanded factory managers for refusing to recruit women. In 1963 the Labor Department sent out notices several times that demanded that firms recruit women as much as possible if the positions were appropriate for both men and women; most firms complied with the order. However, the quota for the allocation of jobs was arranged on the principle of "good ones and bad ones are arranged in pairs." The undertone of the quota system was that men are "good ones" while women are "bad ones." Men and women were arranged in a certain ratio as "a heap" in the same work unit.[1] The factory could not choose employees according to their qualities, and neither could the employees choose jobs (Tan 1994:80–88).

Moreover, the ownership, occupation, and wages of work units were segregated by gender. National-level statistics show that the proportion of women in state-owned firms was lower than in collective firms. Nevertheless, state-owned firms were sought after by workers because of the welfare services and job security they offered. Researchers also found that women were concentrated in less prestigious occupations (Zheng 1995:70) and that they were in the lower hierarchy of the political system (Loscocco and Wang 1992:123–25). Lastly, women's overall wages were lower than those of men (Zheng 1995).

Second, besides the state's gender priority in employment, the division of labor in firms was also gendered. It sorted male workers into skilled jobs and female workers into semiskilled or unskilled jobs. The Division of Labor and Wage used educational levels and gender as two important measurements in arranging workers' positions. Because the SMGF and the EOIF have been technology-demanding factories, both of them have required that machine operators, to a certain extent, have a degree of education. Since the educational levels of women workers were generally lower than that of their male counterparts, they were more likely than males to be assigned to semiskilled or unskilled jobs.

According to my interviews with personnel in the two factories, there were fewer jobs requiring physical labor that were deemed to be more appropriate for women than for men; only 7 of the 25 technical jobs were perceived to be suitable for women in the EOIF, and in the SMGF, less than 20 of the 102 jobs were thought to be more appropriate for women. Women workers were thus more likely to engage in traditional "female jobs" such as tools coordinator, cleaning, teachers in child care centers, catering, nursing, and so forth. Thus, the segregation of jobs by gender was clearly defined, and control over the arrangement of skilled jobs became the underlying gendered control.[2]

However, the gendered arrangement of jobs established the role of women workers as being merely assistants to men. In return, most of the women internalized their low status in the labor process and accepted it as fact. This was manifested by women who gave more credit to the daily life jobs engaged in by men. Consequently, the nature of women's jobs predetermined that they would have fewer opportunities for promotion.

Among women workers who were eager to have skilled jobs but remained unsatisfied because the arrangement of gender consigned them to unskilled jobs, the frustrations faced by these career-conscious women lasted a lifetime. One woman, who graduated from high school, accepted a tool coordinator position reluctantly in 1973 and now has 22 years' tenure, said,

When I knew I was assigned to the tool room of the shop floor, I secretly cried many times, because I was eager to be a draftsman. I believed that I would do well in that position. But a tool coordinator? First, it requires no skill. Second, it has no future. Third, it is only daily routine work. But as I was eager to be perfect in all aspects, I did it well even if reluctantly. At that time, you could not disobey the Labor and Wage Division's command. The party advocated workers to "love your duty, to be an expert in whatever occupation you were pursuing." Moreover, I was a member of the Communist Youth League [an advanced youth group affiliated with the Communist Party]. This period of time attached much importance to propaganda, and the party emphasized being a model. I, myself, was a model who had "achieved extraordinary success in an ordinary post." I dared not ask to switch my job, since the factory had made me a model. Now 20 more years have vanished in a flash. You asked me if I am happy doing this job. I would be 100 percent unhappy even if I had been a team leader for 20 years! We, this generation, have been educated to embrace the party's education. We have been very obedient. What a time! Flowers will die, do what one may. Even the reform made it possible for workers to shift jobs. Your age doesn't permit you to think left and right.

Marginalization of Women Workers in the Firm's Political Control

The Maoism period was characterized by a reward system that was based on workers' political performance and has been discussed by Walder (1986). I found that management wielded political control by sorting according to gender, which I term "gendered political control." Gendered political control was embodied in the process of allocating political resources according to gender. These kinds of resources were revealed in two aspects: being appraised as a model worker and being granted membership in the Communist party. First, in assessing model workers at the firm level, shop floors would appraise the candidates and submit the list of names and their deed reports to the firm's general office or to the trade union. Usually, the gender ratio was restricted and more men were assigned than women. In spite of the model workers assessment, there was another specific prize for female workers called the "handler of three and eight red banner."[3] Essentially, the consequence of this prize for women was to label them as "the other" in contrast to men; it was an attempt to compensate women workers for their minority position by naming them model workers. Labor models beyond the firm level, such as at the industry, city and national levels, were appraised under the assigned gender ratio by the higher authority. I found in my interviews with model workers at the city and national levels that there were more male than female workers. It is an indicator, then, of women's marginalized status in political control.

Secondly, female party members made up a minority of the overall party members in the SMGF and the EOIF. Women were one third of all party members in the EOIF, while in the SMGF, less than one-sixth of the party members were women workers. Furthermore, the gender ratio of party members was lower than the gender ratio of workers in the two firms. Because party membership meant greater career opportunities during that political time, talented shop floor workers who were party members were more likely to be promoted to cadres compared to those who were not party members. However, this kind of identity transition was more often apt to be experienced by male workers with party membership. This situation more or less indicates women workers' inferior status in gaining political resources.

Being a party member enhanced one's good performance when pursuing political progress in China. However, it was common for women workers to be indifferent about their decision to join the party or not. I argue that there were two factors forcing them to keep away from political matters. One factor was the women's double burden of being responsible for work and family obligations when they reached a certain age (i.e., 23 or older).[4] This restricted them from positively engaging in the pursuit of political progress, such as by joining the party, being an activist, and striving for the honor of being a model worker. Men viewed party membership as a political investment, while women workers who were less educated regarded themselves as not being qualified "material to be a cadre." Women believed that being a party member would conflict with their family obligations, thus causing them to stay at home and to quell any internal motivation to be cadres. Although all women agreed that "a cadre is the best position in a factory without hard labor," they found it difficult to bear the dual responsibility of family and job. Consequently, they had no interest in joining the party. A woman worker represented this opinion clearly:

When I was young and unmarried, I performed well on the shop floor. Several party members tried to persuade me to join the party, but I didn't. I did not have any complex ideas. After getting married, I would have to bear children and would have no energy left. I knew a party member would have to do much more than the ordinary guys. You needed to be a model worker in every aspect and work harder than others. When I entered the factory, I was the team leader of the trade union. I was busy writing articles, writing wall newspapers.[5] I had to attend meetings six times every week. You see, four days for shop floor meetings, one day for the league member's community life, one day for youth study, the whole week was occupied. It was easy for me as a daughter to deal with these affairs, because I had my mom cook for me, but how could you handle that after you got married and had sons and daughters? So once I heard the invitation to join the party, I felt fear. When I quit the Communist Youth League, I was 25. I began to date after 24, and I made up my mind then to join the party, and it meant that I would have many things to do, but how could I handle them after I got married?

Women's commitment to the family, then, is much stronger than that of men, and their commitment to careers is quite weak. Women's housework duties and the responsibility of childbearing restricted them from actively participating in political matters as much as men did. They painted a dim picture of political performance when compared to men. Consistent with Chinese traditional culture, more hope is placed on a man having a successful career, and the firm works to nurture the man's hope to achieve success.

Gender Priority in the Firm's Provision of Housing

Gender priority was utilized in the allocation of political resources and was also manifested in the provision of housing, since the latter was a scarce and main welfare resource offered by state-owned firms. "Males are given primary status, females a secondary status" was an unwritten principle. There were no written files declaring this gendered principle clearly or even in ambiguous terms in either firm, but the hidden principle did work in practice. A woman worker was not qualified to apply for housing unless she had a certification from her husband's work unit to confirm that he did not already have a house through his work unit. Even so, under the same condition as the male applicant, the woman would be satisfied only after the male applicant's need had been met. A female administrative executive in the EOIF explained the reason for this principle when asked why the allocation of housing favored males. As she noted, "We are, after all, coming from the feudal system. Men are masters of the family. So men having the first priority in housing is reasonable. Our factory practices the principle of 'men have primary, women have secondary status.' Women's applications will be considered only after men's applications are satisfied." A male vice director of the factory, when asked the same question, answered, "It is difficult to give the reason clearly. All of the people do it this way. Probably it is influenced by traditional ideas."

Although resenting their secondary status in the work unit's allocation of housing, women workers had no alternative. They had to rely on their husbands' work units for housing, so they did not even bother to submit applications for housing in their own work units. "Submitting is meaningless," one woman said to me in a tranquil tone. Women were also not interested in the office for processing housing applications. When I asked a woman worker who had 26 years seniority in the SMGF to show me the way to the Division of Housing Administration of the SMGF, she said she didn't know where it was located.

The principle of male priority in the provision of housing had created an institutionalized effect on women's choice of a mate. A woman tended to choose a man who already had a house or whose status was higher than hers; this choice was essentially the same as the stereotype that the Chinese society had prescribed for women. Furthermore, because cadres received superior status in the provision of housing, male workers had greater institutional motivation and more chances to strive for promotion to be cadres. So, the priority for males in housing encouraged wives to be dependent on their husbands.

Hence, this finding suggests supportive evidence for Judith Stacey's argument about "patriarchy-socialism" (1983:227). Stacey argues that a socialist revolution utilizes and reforms patriarchy but leaves its foundation untouched. From the practice of allocating housing we see that women were always given secondary status in housing allocation, so women's participation in the state-owned system did not change their structural dependence on men in the family. Thus, the patriarchal system still worked in both the workplace and the family via women's dependence on men.

Moreover, I suggest that because of women's institutionalized dependence on men for housing, their dependence on the work unit was shaped differently than men's. Women's dependence on the work unit was achieved via their dependence on their husbands. I will describe and analyze this kind of dependence, which I have labeled "bifurcated dependence," in the following section.

Bifurcated Firm Dependence of Women Workers

While women had to depend on their husbands for housing after marriage, they still had to depend on their work unit for economic resources and welfare services (e.g., medical care and pension). Long before economic reform, men and women were merely eking out a living under the nation's low wage policy. Walder (1986) points out that "What separates prosperous urban families from the poor today is not the average wage of the employed family members, but the proportion of family members employed" (1986:197). One of his interviewees made the point that even though his wage had not changed for 14 years, life was not hard because his wife worked too (1986:198). This evidence indicates that women workers also shouldered a responsibility for family subsistence. Because both spouses had resources other than the work unit, they had to rely heavily on wages. Since men and women who worked in state-owned industries in the pre-reform era were paid wages according to the same regulation by the central government, men and women were able to contribute equally to the family's economy. However, by the beginning of the postreform era in 1978, workers' income became dependent upon the profit of work units, which disrupted men and women's equal contribution to the family economy.

Viewing women workers from a broad perspective, I deem that their dependence had a bifurcated structure. On the one hand, a woman worker was forced to depend on her work unit for wages and welfare services; on the other, she had to depend on her husband for housing, while her husband depended on his work unit for housing. Thus, women's structure of dependence had a double layer that did not exist for men who depended solely on their work unit. Because a woman's needs had to be fulfilled within and outside of the work unit, I describe her dependence as "bifurcated dependence."

Furthermore, because of women's bifurcated dependence, which in essence is an institutionalized dependence on the family, the reward system of the work unit did not function in the same way for women as it did for men. Women workers' behavior differed from the general pattern of workers' institutionalized behavior that was revealed by Walder (1986), in that workers were eager to perform well in political movements and to be promoted based mainly on political performance. However, this bifurcation resulted in women's indifference to politics as well as to their infrequent promotion. This fact indicates that even before the reform women were subjected to institutional bias and that the firm's gender strategy had been implemented in allocating resources, including jobs, political honor, and housing.

WOMEN WORKERS IN THE POSTREFORM ERA

As the state began in 1978 to shift its focus from political to economic construction after the end of the Cultural Revolution, the central point of urban reform was the reform of state-owned firms. Emphasizing efficiency and profitability became the top priority of state-owned firms, and the reform led to a different relation between the state and state-owned firms. First, the way that the state controlled state-owned firms had changed significantly. Beginning in 1988 with the nationwide practice of the "regulation of managerial responsibility," the state began to retreat from its role of owner and manager to being merely an owner. The relationship between the state and state-owned firms became based on limited delegate/agent credentials (Fan 1995). In other words, firms acted like agents of the state. Firms had to determine their orders from the market, because they were not being directed by the central government's planning. This change pushed women workers into a more disadvantaged status as firms gained autonomy in deciding the size and wages of their labor forces based on their profitability.

Second, the firm's system of control had also changed, and was now being guided by another principle of reward. While economic reform aimed at maximizing economic profit, political control in the prereform era yielded to economic stimulation. In the piece-rate system, which was utilized after the reform, workers got their return by calculating the quantity of their labor. The standard to assess a worker, then, had been changed from one's political performance to the worker's productivity and skill competence. The frequency of meetings had decreased from at least two times a week to once every six months. The cycle for appraising model workers was extended and became the firm's choice; for example, in the EOIF the schedule for the appraisal of model workers had been changed to once every three years.

However, the state government or local state government still had the final say for state-owned firms; the chief administrative branch was still in control of appointing the legal person of the firm, or the general manager. The general manager's political performance was assessed by sending a person to investigate the firm once a year. The person would report people's comments about the manager to the higher authority, and these reports determined the firm manager's future in the political hierarchy. Hence, to a great extent, the general manager of a state-owned firm was responsible for the state's interest rather than the firm's.

Managers had fallen into a dilemma based on the firms' requirements to remain profitable and "politically correct" at the same time. While firing inefficient workers was generally discouraged in the interest of political correctness, managers adapted this by focusing on internally restructuring the workforce. However, by utilizing a gendered perspective, it is seen that the internal restructuring resulted in managers putting women workers in a disadvantaged position. As the following shows, this affected recruitment, wages, and housing.

The Disadvantages of Women Workers in the Labor Market

As firms were permitted more and more autonomy in operation and production after the reform, the management of state-owned firms began to show a gendered priority favoring men in some areas. First, I will analyze the gender implications for recruitment. In the EOIF, although the management believed that some optical positions, such as grinding, assembling, and examining, were especially suitable for women because of their carefulness, management still preferred to recruit men because they believed that men were superior to women and would more easily concentrate on learning skills. However, at the same time, they admitted that under the piece-rate system, the ones who worked the most hours and were paid the most money in the EOIF were women. This shows that the management were contradicting themselves and failing to reconsider their preference for men in skilled positions. In the SMGF, skilled women workers comprised about one-third of the firm's skilled workers. Among skilled workers, according to the estimation of the vice general manager, one-third were core workers, and of the core skilled workers about one-fourth were women. However, the top core workers were all men. It can be readily deduced that, in the mind of the senior management, women workers received credit only after the men were given recognition for their performance. This discrimination determined women's secondary status in the firm's recruitment, and almost no women workers were recruited after 1989.

Another important factor that strengthened management's gender preference for men was the labor market's preference for men. In the period of 1988–92, due to the rise of private firms and joint venture firms in Guangzhou and in the Pearl Delta, male technology professionals and skilled workers found it easy to leave state firms for higher wages and better career opportunities elsewhere. Comparatively, women workers had no alternatives, so they had to stay at their original work units, which resulted in a relative increase of women in the labor force at the two research sites. This made management in both sites treasure male skilled workers who stayed with the firms more than their female counterparts. As a result, men received higher levels of promotion and more rewards in their jobs.

As the statistics show, the number of staff and workers in the SMGF decreased from 6,421 in 1983 to 4,563 in 1995 (including retired employees), which means the workforce had been reduced by 1,858 members in thirteen years. The number of women workers lessened from 1993 to 1995, yet their ratio in the workforce raised by 0.7 percent, and male workers' gender ratio decreased by 0.76 percent. Meanwhile, the data of the EOIF indicate that there were 79 more male workers than female workers in 1981; yet in 1995, there were 16 fewer male workers than female workers. The gender dynamics show that more men left than women during the reform process. This trend caused management to view male workers as a more important group than women workers.

Why has the labor market been unfavorable for female workers? The reason is that they have not dominated the popular skills in the market. For example, jobs carrying a higher market value have been fitter, welder, electrician, riveter, and technician for electroplating—all of which are thought to require greater skill and to be more difficult to grasp. Men, without exception, have dominated these jobs. In the EOIF, although optical jobs have been key skilled positions, their market value has not been as high as that of other jobs. There was no local competitor in Guangdong recruiting this type of skilled worker. Hence, women workers who held diplomas from optical secondary school or professional titles remained in the state system. Women's skills are generally non-marketable and garner lower wages in the market compared to the marketable skills usually held by men.

The non-state firms' requirements for workers were essentially based on a preference for males. In response to market forces, state firms needed to use that same preference to urge male workers to stay—especially core male workers. Due to varying characteristics of production in different industries, state firms did not use the same arrangements for new workers based on gender. For example, from my observation of the arrangement of workers' jobs in the EOIF, management preferred to offer marketable, skilled jobs to young male workers in order to retain their service. They tended to offer the less marketable, skilled jobs to young female workers, thus providing them with less mobility.

For those quasi-workers who were from the countryside of Canton and studied in the technological secondary school of the SMGF, the firm promised to register them for permanent residency in the city if they worked at SMGF after their graduation. However, these kinds of workers were mainly male because the school discouraged females from attending. Thus, it is clearly seen that women workers had a disadvantaged status in the internal labor market and external labor market of state-owned firms.

The Disadvantages of Women Workers in Skill-Related Payment and Housing Provision

After the reform, wages in the two firms were set to incline for production workers. The piece-rate system created different rates for different jobs. Women workers found themselves in a disadvantaged position, since women were concentrated in the lower paid piece-rate or un-skilled work, and the positions usually required women workers to make the products more quickly and in large amounts. In contrast, men were concentrated in positions that demanded quality, not quantity. The firm showed that it favored jobs that demanded quality by setting higher wage rates for them. Consequently, men's average wage was higher than that of women's.

According to Michael Burawoy, the negotiation power of workers would be determined by the degree of their working power independent of management's control (1985:171–90). His logic can also be applied to the present study. In both firms, people who dominated the jobs that were difficult to quantify, such as fitters, electricians, riveters, and technicians for electroplating, had more power to negotiate with the supervisor. Hence, these workers had autonomy over their work. The female interviewees frequently described these kinds of skilled jobs that were usually held by men as "difficult jobs," but women who had skilled jobs seemed to receive less credit and accepted lower recognition for their work.

Skilled and semiskilled women workers were more easily controlled because their jobs were easily quantified. In this sense, women workers were secondary to management control. In return, they were more dependent on management because they had less power to negotiate. The gender segregation of jobs before the reform had further contributed to the women's secondary position that was reflected in the distribution of wages after the reform.

After the reform the previous free housing provision was no longer provided but became based on credit assessment. Workers had to pay at a certain ratio for the allocated houses. Women whose husbands were in the same work unit usually contributed to the family's application by getting some credit as a spouse. Since housing was still a scarce resource, the firm especially favored core male workers, who were thus rewarded by getting houses that were larger and positioned better compared to those houses provided to the ordinary workers. The vice general manager of the SMGF told me that "If a worker is competent, he himself knows the point. The leaders would also like to treat him in a respectful manner, even by saying hello. Even if his credits are insufficient to get housing, he could get it because he is a core member. Otherwise, he gets nothing."

The vice-secretary of the Communist Party in the EOIF expressed the same logic saying, "The factory usually offers a discount to core workers when it collects money to build the houses. This is secret. Only that man knows that he is privileged." In comparison to core male workers' privileged status in housing, we can deduce that women workers as a group were still not favored by the housing provision system after the reform.

Control by Basic Level Management and the Routine Production of Gender

Besides management's disadvantageous treatment of women workers at the firm level, the control by basic level management over women was dependent upon their family's financial situations. Once the piece-rate wage system was put into practice in the production section, the section chief played an important role on the shop floor by distributing concrete, daily tasks to workers. However, the section chief had a special way of motivating women workers' labor activism. Arranging the quota by aiming at women's family financial situation was an effective way to get their cooperation. A male section chief of the rear service in the SMGF said,

> Women's personalities are very funny. If the wife and husband are both breadwinners, she would be obedient in the work unit. If her husband earns much more money than she, then she would be arrogant and care little about her own wage. This kind of woman is difficult to control. However, she doesn't dare do anything at work, other than just slow down and not cooperate behind your back. For example, two women workers in my section asked for a long sick leave. Their husbands gain a lot money in the nonstate institution, and they slow down at work on the shop floor. They just cook at home. They could get doctor's certifications, although you know that is ostensible. They said they have hepatitis. How can you deal with them?

This section chief often assigned more work with overtime pay for those women whose families were in a bad financial situation. In the SMGF, these women also received more bonuses in the second round of redistribution than those who were in good situations and slowed down at work.[6] Sometimes the latter got nothing in the second round of redistribution. Another example took place in the EOIF. A female kindergarten teacher was reassigned to the production position because of oversaturation. She relied on her wealthy husband and never went to work regularly but often pretended to be sick, so in 1993 management dismissed her. She was also the only one who was dismissed in the labor retrenchment after the reform.

The above cases in the two firms enable us to determine that women workers' family financial situation was an important factor in management's control. It was especially implemented in management's practice at the most basic level, such as selective assignment of the amount of labor, approving requests for long leave, and giving suggestions on workers' employment tenure. Comparing the working behavior of men with women, the explanatory power of the family's financial situation was weakly related to men's working behavior. The occurrence of a part-time job outside of the work unit influenced their working behavior decisively. The man whose wife was in a good situation usually did not slow down in the workplace. So the routine control of basic level management, especially the section chief's way of control, was especially effective for women workers. This can be understood as a routine production of gender.

THE TRANSFORMATION OF WOMEN'S DEPENDENCE: THREE TYPES

In addition to being discriminated against in various aspects of factory life, such gender inequalities were also unevenly experienced by different groups of women. In the prereform era, they shared more homogeneously gendered locations in relation to the firm. In the postreform era, two separate consequences for women emerged: greater inequality and more heterogeneity in patterns of dependence. Women workers as a group became diverse because their living sources were not homogeneous. Even if they were in the same section, had the same job, and the same skill level, women varied greatly in labor intensity, degree of caring about wages, and degree of obeying superiors.

If we term women's dependence in the prereform era as firm dependence, then in the postreform era their dependence can be differentiated into three types according to the combination of family's financial situation, their own marketable skills, network resources, and the firm's profitability. I have clarified and labeled women's dependence on the institution, which constitutes the main living source for them. The three types of situations for women workers (see table 7.2) are: firm dependence, family dependence, and market dependence.

Women with Firm Dependence

These women workers were the most common group and shared with their husbands responsibility for the family's economic survival. Women with firm dependence relied on their wages, especially when the firm's profit was high. Mainly skilled workers, they worked long hours, devoted all of their labor to the firm,

**Table 7.2. Social Characteristics of the Three Types
of Dependence for Women Workers**

Types	Marketable skills	Network resources	Family economic situation	Profitability of firms
Firm dependence	Strong/Weak	Few	Poor	High/Low
Family dependence	Weak	Few	Good	Low
Market dependence	Strong	Many	Poor	Low

never asked for leave during the year, and were obedient to their superiors. Their family economic situations were poor, their husbands usually worked in a badly managed work unit, and they had no social networks through which to seek other economic resources. Consequently, they had to rely on the work unit to survive. Due to the demands of housework duties, they lacked time and space to develop the social networks needed to find available alternatives in the market.

Women with firm dependence worked the longest hours and devoted themselves to both productive and nonproductive matters in the firm. Although workers were mostly indifferent to political honors after the reform, this type of women worker was often named the advanced productive worker of the firm, or the labor model. Some were even awarded the title of provincial and national labor model.

The women's dependence on the firm was increased because their husbands relied on them for wages or housing, or both—the men usually worked in badly managed state-owned firms or were paid wages comparable to their wives' in private or joint venture firms. One woman in the SMGF who was 42 years old often worked two extra hours before going back home. Her husband was working in another state-owned firm and was paid less. She said:

> Generally speaking, people who are old like me will shift to the second line jobs, say, semiskilled or nonskilled jobs, and don't desperately need to work every day in front of the machine. But there is no way for me—my husband earns less money than me, our family is dependent on both of us to survive. I think I will keep working hard until I retire.

Women with firm dependence focused not only on the economic benefits that could be gained from the firm but also on housing, medical treatment, and other benefits. They cared about the economic fate of their work units, attached importance to the security of state-owned firms, and were sentimentally attached to the character of those firms. A woman with firm dependence in the SMGF was prone to comparing the advantages and disadvantages of state-owned and private firms:

> A boss of a private firm would fire you if the firm was badly run, so you could not rely on the firm. But in the state-owned firm, you would always get the same number of granules of rice as your coworkers got. That means you won't die of

hunger. That means you are hungry together and full together. In the private firm, the boss evaluates you not only your performance, but also on the firm's orders. If there were not too many orders, he would fire you. However, it is different in state-owned firms, which would seek out orders here and there and arrange for workers to produce. The firm would try to maintain your status in the factory as long as you performed well. So we say that the state-owned factory reveals differences among individuals' work performance when there are many orders. However, when there were no orders, people would be free from work, but the manager still wouldn't fire a good worker.

Many of these women workers had to rely on the housing of firms, which shaped their relations with their work units. According to my fieldwork data, housing had a profound impact on workers' behavior, by enhancing the workers' feelings of falling within the authority of their work units. For example, a woman who received housing from her work unit and whose husband earned more money worked harder than a woman in the same economic situation but who did not have housing through her work unit.

Women with firm dependence relied on their work units for promotions and upward mobility, which encouraged them to develop harmonious relations with their supervisors and caring personal and cooperative relationships with co-workers. Therefore, these women workers were most effectively controlled by management. The firm controlled its labor rates by making use of the women's dependence on factory jobs and paid them enough to satisfy their survival needs. When the firm needed to rush an order, management looked to women with firm dependence to work the extra hours.

Women with firm dependence rarely took additional part-time jobs or moonlighted after office hours—not because they lacked the appropriate skills, but because they either did not have social networks to secure a job outside the firm or they gave up other opportunities in order to focus on their factory job when the firm was making a good profit. Housework also severely hampered their ability to moonlight. As one woman, who was a skilled worker and thought that it was not possible to juggle one's work unit, housework, and moonlighting, told me:

> I feel that I have insufficient energy. If you promise to do something outside of your work unit, then you will be exhausted when you go back to your work position because this profession relies much on physical energy and spirit. But if you focus on the work unit, then you cannot take an outside job. I think I can only guarantee 8 working hours in the factory per day [author's note: in actuality she usually worked 11 hours a day]. When I come home after work, I have to take care of all my family members. If I were to moonlight, I would be too tired—it would destroy my body. In addition, we are housewives who live under relentless pressures. When you get home from the shop floor, you turn into a housewife. Housework is always waiting there for me. It is impossible for me to take on so much responsibility, so I turned down several chances for a part-time job outside of the work unit.

The Chinese notion that women should not emerge too often in public society, which includes working outside of the work unit, was also a reason obstructing women from moonlighting. For example, men were not criticized if they didn't sleep at home when they worked too late at moonlighting jobs. Women, on the other hand, would be suspected of violating the "women's morality" if they didn't sleep at home. A woman worker in the SMGF told me,

> Two of my coworkers once took moonlighting jobs for a period of time but now they dared not do it again. They didn't come back home at night and were judged by others. How could you defend yourself that you weren't a prostitute if you didn't go back home to sleep? Their husbands didn't permit them to do the jobs again even if they trusted their wives. The women just could not stop the gossip.

Women with Family Dependence

For some women workers their primary source of economic and housing resources was the family rather than the work unit. These women were concentrated in firms making few profits, were mainly semiskilled or nonskilled workers, and had lower educational levels. Women with family dependence cared little about work hours and wages. They sluggishly labored and emphasized comfortable work. They tended to slow down and did not follow the directions of their superiors. They devoted much energy to nonproduction activities outside the workplace, frequently asked for leave, and were willing to endure harsh economic punishments.

The lack of concern over wages demonstrated by these women was possible because their husbands earned much more than they did. Having benefited from the economic reform, their husbands had become managers or executive officers in foreign investment or joint venture firms or worked part-time jobs that paid well. Men's wages were four to five times higher than women's—which indicates that women's wages were just for survival while men's wages guaranteed quality of life. In the prereform era these women had been breadwinners like their husbands, but when their husbands' wages rose, they lost the motivation to work hard.

Mostly non–party members, women with family dependence became indifferent to honors and social matters in the firms, such as being promoted. As a result, they rarely received the honor of becoming labor models or advanced producers like the women with firm dependence. Women with family dependence were most concerned about the benefits of medical care and pension provided by the firms. Housing was secured through their husbands's jobs.

The working behavior of women with family dependence was contingent on the profit situation of their firms. When the firm's profits were low, they tended to work slowly; when the firm's profits were high, they worked more diligently to earn a bonus given to all employees. A woman worker with firm dependence described how a female coworker with family dependence exploited an institutional weakness because she had a "money-earning husband":

> When we got a bonus of 50 yuan per month, she didn't care about this little bit of money and often asked for sick leave since her husband earned a great deal of money at the time. The rule of the factory for asking for leave was that if you took leave for five days, then you would have no bonus in the current month. Leave for two days, deduct 10 percent of the bonus; three days, deduct 20 percent; four days, deduct 40 percent. Thus she always asked for leave less than five days per month. She knew the doctor personally, so she could get the doctor's permission to rest, even though she was not sick. Then she was comfortably resting about five days each month while the rest of us just became busier.
>
> Nevertheless, when the firm did well and had 300 yuan of bonus for us each month, she came back to work every day and didn't ask for leave. What do you think about her behavior? Isn't it the factor of money working in her mind? I believe that even if her husband gets great money, she came back to get the bonus of 300 yuan. However, if the bonus was only 50 yuan, that was unreasonable to her, so she refused to work regularly. You see how good at calculating she is!

From the management's viewpoint, this kind of woman worker was the most difficult to control. Compared to the other types of women workers, women with family dependence didn't think it important to establish harmonious relations with their coworkers and superiors, mainly because they had no motivation to move upward or to get benefits in the work units. The firm had two primary ways of dealing with this kind of woman: one was to use the women's mentality of competition to motivate them to work hard, and the other was to permit them to take a long leave or to lay them off to decrease the cost to the firm. However, women over age 40 were within the "protection line"—a state mandate that state-owned firms could not fire them before retirement. Consequently, the authority of the firm was minimal for those women with family dependence whose ages were within the "protection line."

Women with family dependence rarely moonlighted. They had no ambition to earn an income equal to their husbands' since their husbands' incomes were high enough to maintain the family's quality of life. A 30-year-old woman in the EOIF, with a 3-year-old son, a monthly income of 1,000 yuan, and a husband with a regular monthly income of 3,000 yuan, said to me with an air of self-satisfaction,

> I don't like to think about doing a part-time job or moonlighting. I don't have that kind of need, either. My husband is capable of making much more money than me. The only important thing for me is to look after our son, take care of the family. My husband earns more than me and has a higher educational degree than me. Earning that kind of money is beyond what I can imagine.

Women with Market Dependence

In my interviews, women with market dependence were the least common type of female workers. This is not surprising because it was not easy for a woman to straddle the demands of the family and work unit. Although women with market dependence didn't enter into the market completely but kept work in state system, they did have some characteristics that had made them more diversified.

This kind of woman worker was concentrated in the EOIF from 1984 to 1993 and in the SMGF from 1994 to 1995 when both of the firms had dismal profits. They had abundant work experience, were competent in their professions, and could adapt to the market. Mainly skilled workers, these women had attained educational levels that were the highest among the three types, with most holding a high school degree. Noticeably, their parents were mostly cadres as opposed to workers. In addition, they had social networks that made getting jobs in the market easy. Personal relations cultivated both within and outside of the firm were important to these women; consequently, their relations with co-workers and superiors fell between the harmonious relations forged by firm-dependent women and the indifferent relations of family-dependent women. Their family economies were dependent on both them and their husbands. They possessed the significant ability to mobilize resources and capitalized on their talents in arts and crafts in order to improve their living standards.

Women with market dependence behaved similarly to women of firm dependence in the workplace, by devoting much to their work and laboring long hours. Their dependence on the market took one of two forms, depending on the woman's age. When the firm's profit, were low women workers older than 40 would seek economic resources outside the firm to compensate their insufficient income. Workers between 25 and 35 years of age also sought other job opportunities but did not give up their jobs in the state system. So compared to other women workers who struggled with the firm (firm dependence) or worked at their leisure (family dependence), women with market dependence were unwilling to work just inside the work units or were dissatisfied with their identities as workers.

A brilliant and skilled woman worker in SMGF who was divorced and lived with her 10-year-old daughter didn't stop operating her machine even when she talked to me on the shopfloor:

> I don't have time to talk with you. This period our firm's profits are very bad and we have nothing to do at work time. Every day I just come here to report my arrival and then I go to a part-time job. How can I survive if I don't work another job? In times of low profits, we skilled workers make less than those nonskilled workers because our rate of work is very low and they have the basement wage. So working here costs more than working outside. I calculated it and found that if I worked for a whole month here I could only get 200 yuan. I still have to make sure my daughter will survive, so I have to go out to do a part-time job.

The benefits you get outside is up to the individual's skill competence. It is not that everyone who wants a job outside can get it. I had friends introduce me. My original family has many relatives and social relations. I didn't tell the firm that I went out to work. The firm had nothing for me to do and could not stop me from going out.

Women with market dependence looked upon the firm as a place to wait or look for other opportunities. Usually, they received benefits from the market and used state-owned firms for retreat. State-owned firms provided security because they offered employee benefits. However, these women workers didn't regret parting from the state system despite its security. They were eager to be free from the limitations of the state-owned firms, such as the scarcity of administrative positions, the surplus of workers, and the inability to develop as individuals.

Women with market dependence yearned for upward mobility based on their own skills and intelligence and were interested in improving their social image and having a higher status in the family. Furthermore these women workers had a tendency to look down on their occupations. Their degree of occupational identity was the lowest among all of the women. They always tried to free themselves from the image of the manual worker and to realize their value through other means. For these reasons, the women moved outside the state-owned system in search of additional resources and the chance to develop themselves.

The state-owned firms were an important source for some material needs. For instance, these relied on the state for housing when their husbands left the state system. For those whose houses were not allocated by work units, who held relatively high degrees of education, and were under 30, the desire to change jobs and seek other chances was strong, causing them to sign only one- or two-year contracts with the work units.

Because this kind of worker composed the core of skilled workers, management, especially at the lowest level, viewed them as being very important. When profits were poor, the firm consented to their part-time jobs and management was powerless to control them. When profits were good, management would make them feel that they could earn more money inside the state firm and let them compete for the long working hours to meet rush orders.

One woman worker in the EOIF who graduated from a professional school of optimal specialty in 1965 took a technical consultant job for four years in a private firm in the mid-1980s when her work unit was earning poor profits. One of her friends introduced her to the second job. She had a part-time job on weekends, earning an income four times her wage in the EOIF. The income from the consultant job allowed her to pay 18,000 yuan—in one lump sum— to buy a house of her own and without any hesitation. For twenty years she had lived with her parents-in-law, but with her purchase she, her husband, and her son could live on their own.

From the above description and analysis, we may conclude that a woman worker's dependence on the firm was conditioned by her family's economic situation. Management responded to this fact by consenting to women's reliance on the family for subsistence. Management's solution was to grant men a generally superior status to women. Because women with family dependence held unskilled or semiskilled jobs, we can see the interaction between skill status and dependence on the family. Women's marginal status under management control was a two-way and interactive process constructed between women workers and the management.

CONCLUSION

The research shows first that male and female workers were subjected to different forms of resource allocation in aspects of economics, politics, and welfare even before reform, because of their gender. However, the structure of women workers' dependence was different from men's—it is a "bifurcated dependence." Men were able to depend on the work unit to satisfy their needs for wages and housing. Women, however, had to depend on the work unit for wages (like men), but on their husbands for housing.

The data also shows that management shifted its focus from political control in the prereform era to economic control in the postreform era. This enhanced women's disadvantaged status in the firms. Female workers were increasingly not favored in many areas, such as recruitment, distribution of wages based on job, and provision of housing. However, the change in women's family economic situations also affected their dependence. The basic level of management treated women differently according to their varied family financial situations, causing gender inequalities to be unevenly experienced by different groups of women. The reform had two separate consequences for women workers: more inequality and more heterogeneity in patterns of dependence. Three types of dependence were formulated after the reform: family dependence, firm dependence, and market dependence. This chapter has shown that there is a gender structure underlying women workers' situations in the two research sites. Hence, this study provides an alternative explanation for women workers' secondary status in state-owned firms.

This chapter enables us to question the gender blindness of the universalized model of workers' dependence represented by Walder (1986) by proposing that gender is an institutional principle used to construct women workers' secondary status in factory life. Moreover, through this process, the gendered arrangement of jobs in the prereform era played a crucial role in shaping women workers' labor experiences, market chances, and their relations with the work unit during the transition to a market economy. This study suggests that Walder's theory on authority and power in a socialist industry needs to reconsider gender.

NOTES

I would like to thank Professor Ching Kwan Lee, my thesis advisor, for her constructive comments and suggestions for the study. Thanks are also given to the anonymous reviewers who made useful comments and suggestions on the content and presentation of the paper. This study was partially supported by the South China Program, Dr. Cheng Ye-tung and Dr. Lee Shan-kee Student Fellowship (1995) of the Hong Kong Institute of Asia-Pacific Studies at the Chinese University of Hong Kong.

1. To "heap" means to pair a certain number of men with a certain number of women. For example, if the set number to recruit is 20, then there should be 12 men assigned and 8 women.
2. Although during the 1960s and 1970s the party advocated that "women hold up half the sky" and the state advocated an expansion of the range and quantity of women's employment, a minority of women held jobs conventionally worked by men, such as welding, benchwork, and milling, and had realized a certain degree of equality. Since women were still the majority of unskilled laborers on the shop floors and the majority of service workers in the dining halls and factory kindergartens, I can say that the arrangement of jobs is gendered in state-owned factories.
3. "Three and eight" represent March 8, which is International Women's Day.
4. The age that the state advocates for women's late marriage is 23.
5. It is a common practice to post newspapers or bulletins written by the workers on the walls in factories.
6. The second round of redistribution is a new regulation that the SMGF initiated after the reform. The section chief grasps a bonus amount that is independent of workers' wages and privately decides who will get how much.

Chapter 8

Gender Embeddedness of Family Strategies

Hong Kong Working-Class Families during Economic Restructuring

Vivien Hiu-tung Leung

As has happened in other global cities, Hong Kong has been undergoing economic restructuring on a massive scale over the past decade. Until the early 1980s, the Hong Kong economy was largely buttressed by the manufacturing sector; then the manufacturing base of Hong Kong began to dwindle rapidly. Within a decade's time, Hong Kong experienced a massive yet unprecedented scale of industrial relocation and manufacturing downsizing, resulting in a rapid decline of manufacturing employment. From 1985 to 1996, the labor force in the manufacturing sector decreased by two-thirds, or an absolute number of 550,000 (see table 8.1)—a rate of decline that has outnumbered that of many other advanced countries. To the previous manufacturing workers, this massive de-industrialization meant a loss of jobs, a loss of income security, job intensification, demoralization, and so on (see Chiu and Lee 1997). Little information, however, has shown us how these manufacturing workers and their families got by and responded to these macrolevel changes and, from a gender perspective in particular, how different responses of manufacturing workers and their families cast varying implications for men and women.

This chapter aims to tackle this lacuna by focusing on the family strategies of manufacturing workers under economic restructuring in Hong Kong. As I will illustrate, patterns of family strategies are formulated under the very specific contexts of two gender structures: (1) the type of gender structure in a family, and (2) a wider gendered employment opportunity structure. My study shows that different patterns of family strategies were formulated in households with different pre-existing gender structures, namely a traditional one and a flexible one, and that there was an interlocking effect between the gender structure in family and the gendered employment opportunity market. I argue that both gender structures are of equal importance in understanding how the employment structure changes under the context of economic restructuring.

ECONOMIC RESTRUCTURING IN HONG KONG

Hong Kong's economic take-off was led by export-oriented manufacturing, which began in the early 1970s. Until the early 1980s, Hong Kong's economy capitalized on labor-intensive light industry such as the manufacture of textiles and garments, electronics, and toys.

Since the mid-1980s, Hong Kong's economic structure has changed. Both labor and property costs increased sharply, and the manufacturing activities in Hong Kong, which leveraged cheap labor and production, lost their competitive advantage. With the opening policy of Mainland China, there has been a large-scale industrial relocation from Hong Kong to the mainland since the mid-1980s. The economy of Hong Kong, on the other hand, transformed itself to a regional service center, focusing on trade and business services activities. Within a decade's time, manufacturing employment was reduced to 375,800 by 1995 (12.9 percent of the total workforce; see table 8.1).

Manufacturing is still of significant importance to Hong Kong. However, unlike in the past, it no longer has a large production base in the local economy. Rather, its importance is revealed in the blossoming trade-related activities that have been supportive of the manufacturing base now in Mainland China. Hong Kong's remaining manufacturing base takes a "back-office" position, providing services such as distribution, sourcing, warehousing, and quality assurance. The remaining production base in Hong Kong, which is still dominated by small firms, adopted labor-market strategies such as replacing long-term permanent labor with part-time and casual workers to reduce cost (Chiu and Levin 1993; Lui and Chiu 1994).

To the manufacturing workers who were once employed in the local production processes, economic restructuring in Hong Kong means more intensified work, severed income and job insecurity, and demoralization of their work life (Chiu and Lee 1997; Chiu and Levin 1993; Lui and Chiu 1994). Moreover, the

Table 8.1. Manufacturing Employment in Hong Kong

	1985	1987	1989	1991	1993	1995	1997
Number of manufacturing workers (in thousands)	847.6	867.9	791.5	629.2	483.6	375.8	288.9
Male workers (in thousands) (% of manufacturing workforce)	424.8 (50.1%)	430.4 (49.6%)	410.9 (51.9%)	336.0 (53.4%)	267.3 (55.3%)	211.5 (56.3%)	166.5 (57.6%)
Female workers (in thousands) (% of manufacturing workforce)	422.8 (49.9%)	427.6 (50.4%)	380.6 (48.1%)	293.1 (46.4%)	216.3 (44.7%)	164.2 (43.7%)	122.4 (42.4%)
Number of establishments	45,915	49,403	50,566	44,388	36,847	30,761	25,724

Source: Hong Kong Monthly Digest of Statistics, December issues, various years

impact of economic restructuring does not fall on men and women to the same extent: opportunities for employment and changes in wages differ according to gender. Over the period 1987–97, female employment in the manufacturing sector was reduced by 70 percent, compared to a 60 percent reduction in male employment. A government survey in 1997 also showed that, under such a buoyant labor market, a higher percentage of women under 50 years of age had left the labor market than had a year earlier.[1] Within the period 1987–95, the real average daily wage of male workers increased by 8.0 percent whereas that of female workers decreased by 7.1 percent (Chiu and Lee 1997). Such gender differences in the wider job-opportunity structure certainly impact the family strategies of men and women.

FAMILY STRATEGY

Individuals seldom respond to macro socioeconomic changes in complete isolation from one another; rather, they are found to draw on family resources and assistance to respond to societal and community changes. In this regard, family strategy can offer an analytical construct to understand how individuals are affected by and, in turn, affect macro structures through the family setting. In particular, by investigating the process of repooling as well as reallocating family processes, family strategy offers the advantage of unraveling the workings of gender structure within the family, as well as how this gender structure is linked with the wider socioeconomic context. With this thematic focus, some existing studies have attempted to look into the participation of women workers during the process of industrialization, or the responses of men and women toward economic recession from their family settings (Hareven 1982; Lamphere 1987; Morris 1985; Pahl and Wallace 1985; Pratt and Hanson 1991; Roberts 1994; Tilly and Scott 1978).

Over the past decade, the concept of family strategy has been revised. Conflicts and power structure within the family have become the focus of analysis. This emphasis emerges from a flurry of criticisms against the approach known as new home economics, which regards family as a unitary, monolithic entity and assumes that its individual members share a common interest in maximizing the welfare of the family as a whole (see Becker 1981). This approach is criticized for ignoring power imbalances, diverse interests, negotiations, and conflict in the decision-making process of a household (Morris 1989, 1990; Pahl 1985; Wolf 1990, 1992). Contenders claim that decisions about the allocation of paid work and domestic work as well as about financial arrangements are processes as well as consequences of power negotiations, and even conflicts, between individuals along age and/or gender lines. In these studies, the distribution of duties and roles to fulfill family economic needs, and even what constitutes "family needs," are regarded as products of conflicting individual interests.

Another dimension for revision is to focus on the interdependence of the gender relationship inside a family and the wider gendered opportunity structure in the economy. Gender roles and household arrangements are found to have altered in response to changes in the employment statuses of the couple (Gallie, Gershuny, and Vogler 1994; McKee and Bell 1985; Morris 1985, 1989; Harris and Morris 1986; Pahl and Wallace 1985; Pratt and Hanson 1991; Redclift 1985; Wheelock 1990). Their findings illustrate that a traditional gender division of labor should not be assumed, but has to be explained, with regard to the employment status of the couple. To quote Lydia Morris (1994), family strategy has to be understood from the very type of gender hierarchy at home and the very opportunity structure in which individual actors are located. Arguing in a similar vein, Phyllis Moen and Elaine Wethington (1992) have pointed out that family adaptation strategies are subject to four interlocking social systems, of which economic opportunity structure and gender relationships are two.[2]

Family strategy also offers us a vantage point to understand how people in Hong Kong respond to the macro social changes of economic restructuring. On the one hand, as was found in various studies, the Hong Kong Chinese emphasize economic interdependence among familial members and use family in a pragmatic-instrumental manner to cope with a far-from-benign social environment as well as to strive for achievement (Lau 1982). The re-organization of household resources therefore fundamentally reveals how workers cope with changes in the economy and in the labor market. On the other hand, family strategy can provide a looking glass to understand how the gender structure within a family relates to the changing employment structure. It has been claimed that families in Hong Kong are not at all strictly traditional/patriarchal. While the husband/father is still the family head, changes have been found with respect to his authority and his control over family resources (Lee 1991; Wong 1981). The gender relationship in the Chinese family does not always follow a traditional, patriarchal type; rather, the type of relationship changes with respect to outside economic and social contexts. By bringing into focus the process of formulating and executing family strategies in Hong Kong families, this study aims to address the dynamism of familism as well as the fluidity of patriarchy in Chinese households.

In light of these themes, the research design of my study is as follows. Based upon materials collected from in-depth interviews with 34 households,[3] I will contrast family strategies across households with two types of gender structures— a traditional one and a flexible one—according to their pre-existing gender structure. Among these households, 23 of them were regarded as having a traditional gender structure, and eleven of them had the flexible type (see the appendix). In a traditional household, not only were roles of husband and wife rigidly split between breadwinner and caretaker, but gender hierarchy was also a strictly dyadic one. The husband's preferences have always predominated over his wife's on household matters such as the allocation of both waged and domestic labor and the distribution of household finances. In a flexible household, negotiations between the couple were common when deciding the allocation of labor and family finances even before restructuring.

For the purpose of this study, only nuclear households were chosen for interviews.[4] These in-depth interviews were conducted throughout the whole year of

1995, a year when the impact of industrial restructuring on the livelihood of workers was exacerbated and many informants experienced fluctuations in employment.

FINDINGS AND ANALYSIS

As industrial transformation unfolded at an unexpectedly fast pace, all of my informants experienced tremendous employment changes. In corollary to a gender difference in employment opportunities for manufacturing workers found in an earlier questionnaire survey,[5] my male and female informants exhibited different patterns of change in terms of employment status. Among the 20 men I interviewed, 10 of them managed to stay in the manufacturing sector, yet none of my 14 female informants could retain their manufacturing jobs.

As for the ten male informants who stayed in the manufacturing sector, they reported that their wages had not been adjusted to the annual inflation or had even decreased in absolute terms.[6] However, their employment, far from permanent and long-term, had changed to contract-based, and five of these ten manufacturing workers were actually underemployed. Two of them had already started moonlighting by taking up part-time taxi driving and waiting on tables. Another three survived by switching firms constantly and thus preempted wage and work cuts. For those who could switch out of the manufacturing sector, half ended with short-term employment in furnishing, plumbing or installing electronics equipment, while two others became doormen, earning a salary that could hardly sustain their personal livelihood. Only two of the men managed to switch to service jobs with a salary level that was comparable to that of their previous manufacturing jobs.

As for the women workers, none could retain their manufacturing jobs.[7] Only 8 out of my 14 female informants relocated to service jobs, whereas the remaining 6 were economically inactive at the time of the interviews. Among those who switched sectors, only 3 became shop assistants and waitresses with an income similar to what they had earned in the manufacturing industries; others ended up in menial service jobs doing office cleaning and street sweeping for a lower income.

In all of these households, the employment conditions of the couple and thus their household economic situations were affected to such an extent that waged and domestic labor, as well as household finances, had to be re-organized to subsist.

Family Strategy in Traditional Households:
Patriarchal Resource Remobilization

In the 23 traditional households, a distinctively patriarchal pattern of resource remobilization emerged in the re-allocation of waged labor, redivision of housework, repooling of household income, and redistribution of household finance. Even though the household budget was shrinking, the husband's personal interests regarding job preferences and consumption patterns prevailed over those of other household members. Moreover, the husband's own preferences shaped how "family needs" were defined and resolved. In the process of making and implementing family strategies, the authority of the husband in a traditional household was preserved and even strengthened.

In these households, the principle rule was that the re-organization of all household resources and labor centered around the husband's employment needs. In some families where savings were available, the most common family response was to channel these family resources, however scant they were, to finance the retraining of men, so as to secure their breadwinning role. Men from these traditional households were found to take courses on cloth cutting (as in the case of Kin-man), English and computer courses (as in the case of Kwok-keung), or translation courses (as in the case of Lai-yee's husband), funded by the family's limited savings, to enhance their employment in the manufacturing sector or to switch to the service sector. Expenses for taking these courses were actually very large compared to their average household expenditure. For instance, the translation courses of Lai-yee's husband cost H.K.$14,000 (around U.S.$1,750)—an amount that exceeded their household savings. Still, the family made do by borrowing from their paternal families. In the family of Yuk-chu, because he planned to take up part-time taxi driving, a lump sum of around H.K.$10,000 was needed for taxi rentals—an amount equal to the total family savings. In these households, the meager household savings were spent at the husband's request to redistribute finances in order to secure his employment opportunities.

Another observation was that the husband's preferences for employment were given primacy and not affected by the family's finance. In fact, all of the men in these households expressed a reluctance to switch to such service jobs as doorman and security guard, which in their eyes required no skills or physical strength. To avoid taking these unwanted jobs, the husbands rearranged household resources and labor in such a way as to safeguard their autonomy over work choices. Other than their aforementioned capability to reallocate household savings when preparing to switch to more favorable positions in the service sector, some male workers also asked their wives to work so as to prevent themselves from having to take low-ranking service jobs. Sai-hung, previously a contract-based worker in the garment industry, managed to avoid unwanted service positions by asking his wife to become a waitress. In doing so, he could stay with the manufacturing work he preferred, however slack his employment was. In Yuk-chu's family, his wife also took a paid job mainly to support his additional financial needs for taxi driving. Similarly, Kar-kui, previously an electronics factory supervisor, asked his wife to take a service job so that he could stay in the manufacturing sector, despite the fact that his earnings could no longer meet the family's needs. A similar story was found in Yiu-tung's family. When I interviewed him for the first time, he spoke strongly against the idea of asking his wife to work. In a few months' time, when I interviewed him for a second time, his wife had already begun to work as a dishwasher in a nearby restaurant, and he held onto his underemployed plumber job. When I asked why he did not consider switching to the service sector, he mentioned the low wages and low status and concluded that he preferred the present arrangement.

In all of these families, the husband's ability to safeguard his career preferences needs to be understood from his pre-existing dominant position in the family and from his unchallenged authority to re-arrange household labor. In these families, the wife's employment also has to be understood not only as a mere response to the family's financial upheavals but as a means to safeguard her husband's career preferences. The employment decisions of the wife in these families should not be explained by a mere fact of insufficient family income, but by her husband's ability to define how big of a burden the latter would shoulder.

In some traditional families where the husband could sustain the family with his own income, his wife would exit from the labor market.[8] The withdrawal of these women from the labor market can be understood by considering how their domestic roles constrain their job choices. In the past, when these women held full-time manufacturing jobs, it was still their responsibility to take care of the housework. In contrast to their previous manufacturing jobs, working in the service sector demanded a stricter schedule and longer hours. Some service jobs, such as those of waitresses and shop assistants, required shift duties, which clashed with such housework duties as cooking and taking care of the children. Even upon changes in their family finances, the husbands were reluctant to help with housework. For these women, then, taking up jobs in the service sector implied a further intensified double day, which led to their preference to retreat from the labor market if the situation allowed. It was this pre-existing traditional division of labor, underpinned by a gender hierarchy in allocating resources within the family, that pulled these women from paid work.

In all of the traditional families, a redistribution of the household budget was dominated by the preference of the husband to preserve his personal money and his personal consumption. As household financial situations became acute, the husband further tightened his control over household budgeting. In the families of Chi-wai, Kar-kui, Kin-ming, Sai-hung and Yuk-chu, the men took over their wives' obligation to allocate household finances. As the wives of Kar-kui, Sai-hung and Yuk-chu began to bring in paychecks, their wages were handed over to their husbands for re-allocation. Such shifts in responsibility for budget re-allocation was explained by Sai-hung, who noted, "My wife used to squander. She does not know how to skimp or well manage the household budget. It is for the sake of the family as a whole for me to have control, so I can check the flow of household expenditures more closely."

Very similar comments were made by Chi-wai. In fact, resuming control over the household budget served the personal interests of the husband in two ways: first, by taking control of household financial resources, he could cater to the extra financial needs of his aforementioned career preferences; second, control over the household budget allowed the husband to maintain his original patterns of consumption. Kim-hung, for instance, frankly stated that he reserved a fixed sum from the household budget for his personal spending before handing the remaining portion to his wife. By doing so, his personal consumption patterns would be less affected by the shrinking family budget. Similarly, Kin-ming, Kai-jang and Wang-ki also kept their expenditures on smoking, eating out, and gambling despite their more stringent household budgets, and their personal consumption alone took up an amount equivalent to half of the monthly household budget.

As a result of this male-dominated re-allocation of the household budget, the wives were the hardest and most obviously hit in terms of personal spending. While Wang-ki could keep a daily amount of H.K.$80 (around U.S.$10) as personal eating-out expenses, his wife was confined to self-made meals every day; she even picked up discarded cloth from nearby factories to make clothes for herself. During the interview, Wang-ki simply told his wife, "You can eat with H.K.$20 [U.S.$2.50] a day, but not me!" Hence, in order to meet an increasingly stringent budget, wives in traditional households made do by cutting their own personal expenses or even daily necessities. Yuk-ying told me that she stopped eating breakfast, and sometimes lunch, in order to reserve more money for her children. Similarly, Hon-ming's wife gave up taking computer courses so that the portion of money could be reserved for her children's tuition fees. Many women from traditional households said that they were the ones in their families who felt the most financial pressure:

> I am the one who suffers the most from the financial pressure. After giving me a monthly family allowance of H.K.$8,000 [around U.S.$1,000], my husband leaves me with the tremendous task of making ends meet, and even expects me to have savings left over. He never realizes how insufficient this sum is, he just thinks that he has done his part. He does not even have any long-term plans to cope with future changes in earnings. It is me, alone, who deals with such pressures. (Lai-yee)

> He thinks that his family allowance is more than enough. . . . He never cares how expensive electricity, water, gas, and other daily necessities can be. (Yuk-ying)

In these traditional households, even when the wife brought as much income home as her husband, her wages were regarded as the family's rather than her own personal money. Family responses in these traditional households were formulated and executed in such a way that gendered spending patterns became more discreet, and the husband's dominance over the household budget was intensified. Although the wife might also bring in wages, her weightier role in income pooling did not transform her subservient position in the family. Instead, the traditional gender hierarchy was intensified, and the domination of the husband became even more encompassing.

Family Strategy in Flexible Families: Resource Negotiation

Eleven households were found to have a pre-existing flexible gender structure. In these eleven families, more negotiations in the re-allocation of labor and the redistribution of household finance were involved in the formulation of family strategies and, in some cases, conflicts of interests were overt. In some families where women earned an income, the power relationship between couples could be transformed into a more egalitarian one. However, as we shall see, since women's service jobs were always unstable and short-term and their financial contribution to the family could not be secured, this egalitarian gender relationship could not persist and would return to a more traditional mode when the women in these families lost their paid work.

Instead of focusing on the husband's employment, in flexible households the wife's employment played a pivotal role in family responses. Different from those in traditional households, where decisions about the wife's employment were always subject to the husband's interests and preferences, the division of labor or other domestic re-arrangements in flexible households were re-organized around the needs of the wife's employment. The wife's initiative to take up full-time employment and her own preferences for types of jobs usually affected how other changes in a flexible family were carried out. Women in these households had a more significant role in defining how urgent the needs of their families were and even how the burden of supporting their families was shared with their husbands:

> My husband objected to my taking the restaurant job in the beginning, but I ignored him and tried. . . . Well, I did it just to confront him, although I did find the job very exhausting. Then our financial situation went so badly, and he could not afford to be so picky about my jobs. I worked in a restaurant, and asked my husband to come back from work earlier to prepare supper. (Yue-yee)

Similar to Yue-yee, Siu-wah, despite disapproval from her husband, also switched to waiting on tables when she recognized that his employment would become unstable. The job required her to wear a tight dress and to be amicable to customers' requests, however unreasonable they were, and her husband found these job requirements particularly unacceptable. During the interviews, she reiterated how uneasy she was with always pleasing customers and handling occasional sexual harassment at work. Still, she insisted that she had made the right choice for her family by disregarding the objections of her husband. A similar situation was found in Shun-mei's family. Shun-mei negotiated with her husband to keep her sales job, despite her husband's objections about the hours. In another case, Chi-bo complained to me about his wife who, despite his strong objections, kept her part-time work:

> I told her that I don't want her to keep this night-shift job. I thought it is better for her to stay home and take care of the children. Before she took the job, I had already asked her not to. But she insisted—okay then, I let her try. We have quarreled over her job, but she has not been persuaded. Then I proposed to find a part-time job myself instead, but she refused. I have no idea why she is so determined. (Chi-bo)

Some women even managed to re-arrange family resources and labor to accommodate their employment needs. In those flexible families where wives worked full-time, husbands took a noticeably larger share of housework. Because Yiu-kai's wife chose to work the night shift, most of the housework was left to Yiu-kai despite his reluctance and even objections. Yiu-kai became responsible for the daily routines of buying groceries, making meals, and doing the laundry. Also, when Yue-yee switched to a messenger job and enrolled in an English course to enhance her "marketability" in the labor market, she negotiated with her husband on both financial and domestic arrangements in order to meet her schooling needs. Yue-yee remarked that her husband was more "cooperative" in helping with household chores, although she realized that he did them reluctantly. Such redivision of housework was also found in the families of Lai-hing, Shun-mei and Siu-wah when these women took up service jobs that required longer hours of work. For instance, Lai-hing was required to work an evening and graveyard shift for a grocery assistant job, so her husband took over most of the housework. The husbands of Shun-mei and Siu-wah were also asked to care for their children as well as to prepare meals to accommodate the long hours of their service work.

In many of these families, the husband experienced job changes as well. Yet, compared to traditional families, men from flexible households did not have much control over the re-allocation of financial resources and domestic labor to accommodate their plans. In flexible households, men were more willing than those from traditional households to take up unfavorable service jobs.

In terms of financial re-arrangements within a family, in flexible households the wife's own needs took a more prominent part in the processes of repooling and redistributing the household budget. Instead of putting a substantial portion of the wife's wages toward the family budget as seen in traditional households, wives in flexible households managed to keep a portion for their own personal expenses. For instance, Chi-bo's wife sent her moonlighting wages back to her parental family in China, disregarding Chi-bo's disapproval and the fact that their family was still writing off their debt. A similar situation was found in the families of Wai-guen, Yue-yee, and Yiu-kai. In these families, wives controlled a portion of their wages that was put toward the family budget. As Yue-yee explained,

> My husband asks me for more money whenever he does not have enough—he says he "borrows" from me but in fact he never pays me back. Once I asked him to pay for more household items. He did, but he asked to "borrow" more from me again. Well, that means he has not contributed more. We quarreled over financial matters a couple of times, and now I refuse to lend him more money. I simply stopped being the "Buddha"—offering whenever he asks.

I also found that in these families the men were requested by their wives to contribute a larger proportion to the household budget. In some of these dual-wage households, the couple's financial management was transformed so that each became responsible for discrete items. In most cases, husbands were responsible for the rent, children's tuition expenses, electricity, gas, and other house maintenance fees, while wives paid for food and child care expenses. This re-arrangement of household labor and changes in gender positions, which centered around the wife's job choices and preferences, was affected, however, by the instability of women's employment in the service sector. Because the service sector that these women encountered was a fluid labor market (Chiu and Lee 1997), women experienced severe job insecurity. Even after successfully relocating into service, many women lost their jobs or found them to be too demanding after a period of several weeks or months. Especially in families where child care was required, women were more likely to resume being full-time housewives after being frustrated by the fluidity in employment and low pay. In these flexible households, as wives exited from the labor market, the division of waged and domestic labor soon reverted back to a traditional type.

In this regard, family strategies were marked by a flexibility in the re-organization of household labor depending on the employment situation of the couple. Their lived experiences show us that reliance on women's employment was constrained by the gendered opportunity structure in the labor market.

Family Strategies and Gender Inequalities

The family responses of the households mentioned above show that the patterns of family strategies were predicated upon types of gender structures in the family. The formulation and implementation of family strategies were not only shaped by the pre-existing gender power structure in the family but also transformed it.

In traditional families, caretaking responsibilities were always reserved for women, even though they pursued a paid job. Under a pattern of patriarchal resource mobilization, decisions about women's employment and the allocation of their wages revolved around the interests of their husbands. Not only was the traditional division of gender roles unaffected by women's entry into the workforce, but the dyadic gender hierarchy in the families was also reinforced. Women's control over family and personal resources remained as limited as in the past, if not reduced further. Their hard work only served to fortify the power of their husbands. In the course of re-organizing household resources to maintain the family's subsistence in a buoyant labor market, the pre-existing traditional gender structure was transformed into one even more patriarchal.

In flexible households, the strategy was one of resource negotiation. The processes of decision-making and implementing family strategies were marked by negotiations and conflicts in interests. Wives' personal opinions and interests in employment options took a pivotal role in the process of re-organizing household resources and labor. Gender relationships seemed to become more egalitarian, but change in this direction was limited by the buoyancy of the labor market that women were more likely to encounter than men. Even for some of the women who managed to relocate into the service sector and to re-arrange responsibility for household chores with their husbands, they too soon resumed domesticity. A return to domesticity occurred especially in households with small or school-age children. Hence, changes in the allocation roles and gendered responsibilities were transitional. Once women assumed their housewifery obligations, the division of labor returned to a male/breadwinner–female/caretaker split.

In view of this, family strategies were shaped both by employment opportunities (perhaps more specifically, constraints), which fell on the couple, and by the pre-existing gender structure. Under economic restructuring, both female and male workers found themselves in the quandary of reduced income, job and income insecurity, more intensified labor, and more adverse working conditions. However, the opportunities open to men and women differed. At the time of the interviews, men had more opportunities than women to remain in the manufacturing sector, while women had to either switch to low-ranking service jobs or exit from the labor market. The service jobs available to women, however, were often short-term and temporary in nature and required long hours. Therefore, aside from their own ability to find a job, the success of women's switch to the service sector often depended on the re-allocation of domestic labor—which depended on the support of their husbands. Under such a structural context, the pre-existing gender relationship in a family was of crucial importance to the family's response.

These patterns of family strategies illustrate how a gendered employment structure and a dyadic gender structure in the family reinforced each other and how a flexible gender structure could be transformed into a more egalitarian one and constrained by gendered employment opportunities. The gender structure of both the family and work underpinned the very redistribution of family resources as well as the process of household re-organization. In return, family strategies also affected the gender structure of the family.

CONCLUSION

Following the insights of feminist critiques of the new home economics approach, the analytical focus of family strategies is thus placed upon the divergent and even conflicting interests in a household. Family strategies, in the name of maximizing the welfare of the household as a whole, are the product of prioritizing the interests of different household members according to a pre-existing gender hierarchy in the family.

Instead of assuming that women are always inferior to their husbands, this chapter illustrates that there are different forms of power structure in a household, and women's position vis-à-vis their husbands' is not in all cases confined to a patriarchal form. By categorizing families as traditional or flexible according to their pre-existing gender structure, I have shown that patterns of family strategies differed according to a pre-existing form of gender hierarchy. The family's gender structure, therefore, affected how individuals and their families responded to economic restructuring. Family strategies, which concern the re-allocation of resources and redivision of roles, are embedded in a pre-existing gender hierarchy.

However, family strategies were also influenced by the employment opportunities available in the labor market. For these impoverished households, the employment options open to my informants—disregarding their gender, skills, and previous employment experience—included only low-ranking jobs in the service or manufacturing sectors. Yet, the men and women did face different market situations in terms of job security and type of work. I have illustrated that as families strived for survival, opportunities for employment and the couple's income security affected how domestic resources and labor would be organized. Furthermore, this chapter shows how gender structure interacted with employment opportunities and constraints. A traditional gender structure could be reinforced by a gendered employment opportunity structure, and in some cases, a flexible gender structure enabled women, by re-organizing limited household resources, to capitalize on employment opportunities. In other cases where women's employment became insecure, I found that changing from a flexible gender structure to a more egalitarian one could be limited by the fluidity of women's employment. Hence, to account for the different changes in livelihood that men and women encountered, both the wider gendered labor market structure and the family's gender hierarchy have to be analyzed.

My study examines the gender dimension in how family strategies were guided by both economic needs and the interaction of economic exigencies and cultural values, as claimed by Tamara Hareven (1991). I have illustrated that aspects of the gender structure in families and the gendered labor market *interacted* with each other to shape the various patterns of family strategies under specific contexts. While family strategies were guided by pre-existing gendered responsibilities and roles, the latter should not be conceptualized as a set of culturally defined practices per se; these cultural practices, patterned by a certain type of gender hierarchy, also changed in accordance with employment circumstances. Family strategies, which refer to the re-organization of various types of domestic resources, should be conceived as being derived from the operation of certain power structures. Therefore, a gender embeddedness in family strategies means that, in addition to other possible power structures, the dual structures of gender hierarchy in the home and gendered employment opportunities took a salient role in the re-organization of family resources and labor.

NOTES

1. Hong Kong Census and Statistics Department. 1997. *Special Topics No. 19:Labour Mobility and Related Topics.*
2. The four interlocking social systems that cast impacts on family adaptation, according to Moen and Wethington (1992), are: (1) the economic opportunity structure; (2) social status, caste, and educational stratification; (3) gender relationships; and (4) the age/generational hierarchy.
3. The interviewees were chosen from a telephone survey that covered 1,004 respondents drawn by random sampling. The survey was on the situation of women workers under industrial restructuring, and only nuclear households were chosen for in-depth interviews.
4. Family strategies can vary tremendously by family types; for instance, constraints and

resources faced by single-parent or empty-nest households can be very different from those from nuclear households. For the purpose of contrasting family strategies across households with different gender relations, I therefore restricted the sample to nuclear households, so as to control for variations due to family types.

5. It is found that in the questionnaire, while 81.6 percent of the previous male manufacturing workers managed to stay in the manufacturing sector or to switch to other sectors, 57.6 percent of the female respondents were unable to find the job or exit from the labor market (Chiu and Lee 1997).

6. As wages in electronics, clothing and textiles industries were counted on a piece rate, the remaining manufacturing workers experienced a substantial decrease in wages because of slack orders; in addition, according to many of them, the rate per order has not been raised for the past decade.

7. The gender difference in employment situations of my informants also corresponds with the aggregate scenario. As recorded in the earlier telephone interview, 30.9 percent of the women respondents exit from the labor market and 26.7 percent were unable to find jobs, whereas only 5.6 percent of male informants exit and 12.8 percent unable to find jobs (Chiu and Lee 1997).

8. In six households, household finance could still be maintained by the male breadwinners alone, and I found that the six women workers became economically inactive at the time of the interview.

Appendix: Profile of the Informants and of Their families

Traditional Families

Informants (Pseudonym)	Sex	Age[a]	Past Occupation[b]	Present Employment[c]	Spouse's Employment
Kai-jang	M	69	Operator, plastic machinery	Low-paid operator, plastic machinery	Retired since 1990 due to illness
Kar-kui	M	43	Factory supervisor, electronics	Temporary worker, installation of security equipment	Housewife
Kim-hung	M	45	Ironing worker, garment	Casual labor (saan-kung), ironing and collier	Housewife
Kin-ming	M	44	Technician, plastic molding	Unemployed (after checkered career)	Housewife
Sai-hung	M	44	Contract labor (bao-kung), buckling buttons	Underemployed (manufacturing worker)	Contract labor, buckling buttons (work with Sai-hung)
Sai-lung	M	54	Worker, cloth dyeing	Casual worker, furnishing	Housewife → Part-time messenger
Yiu-tung	M	52	Worker, metal hardware	Casual worker, plumbing and furnishing	Housewife → Restaurant service worker
Yuk-chu	M	45	Ironing worker, garment	Casual ironing worker, night-shift taxi driver	Worker, garment → Packaging worker, bakery
Wang-ki	M	66	Operator, plastic machinery	Doorman	Worker, garment → Part-time office caretaker
Chi-wai	M	58	Tailor, clothing	Cloth cutter	Housewife
Fan-leung	M	41	Quality controller, plastic casing	Team supervisor, cleaning company	Worker, garment → Clerk
Kin-man	M	36	Worker, cloth cutting	Worker, cloth cutting and part-time night-shift waiter	Housewife

Traditional Families (continued)

Informants (Pseudonym)	Sex	Age[a]	Past Occupation[b]	Present Employment[c]	Spouse's Employment
Kin-sang	M	42	Production supervisor, watch band fabrication	Production supervisor, watch band fabrication	Housewife and baby-sitter, seeking employment
Kwok-keung	M	46	Foreman, torch fabrication	Driver → Clerk	Housewife → Office caretaker
Ho-wah	M	46	Head of maintenance section, metal hardware	Head of maintenance section, metal hardware	Housewife
Hon-ming	M	40	Technician, plastic molding	Technician, plastic molding	Housewife and part-time domestic helper
Fung-tai	F	41	Worker, garment	Housewife	Self-employed technician, electrical wiring
Lai-tao	F	46	Line supervisor, knitwear	Housewife	Quality controller, clothing, work in China
Lai-yee	F	39	Worker, cotton spinning	Housewife, seeking employment	Accounts clerk, construction company
Mo-king	F	35	Worker, garment	Housewife	Contract labor (*bao-tao*), marble work
Yuk-chun	F	38	Worker, spinning	Housewife	Taxi driver
Yuk-ying	F	34	Worker, garment	Receptionist→ Housewife	Worker, metal welding
Sau-guen	F	45	Worker, textiles	Hawker	Worker, textiles → Doorman

Flexible Families

Informants (Pseudonym)	Sex	Age[a]	Past Occupation[b]	Present Employment[c]	Spouse's Employment
Yiu-kai	M	52	Supervisor, cotton spinning	Doorman	Assistant shop manager, Pizza Hut
Chi-bo	M	46	Worker, watch casing	Worker, electroplating	Worker, metal work and night-shift cleaning woman
Ah-wah	M	50	Technician, plastic molding	Unemployed	Factotum, garment
Hing-yim	M	56	Operator, brewery	Messenger, after five years' unemployment	Engineering worker → Housewife
Ai-ngo	F	40	Worker, garment	Housewife, seeking employment	Driver
Kam-lin	F	41	Factotum, cotton weaving	Messenger, checkered career in the service sector	Security guard
Lai-hing	F	46	Weaver, knitwear	Night-shift shop assistant, checkered career	Hotel cook
Siu-wah	F	30	Worker, garment	Restaurant service worker → Housewife and baby-sitter	Technician, electrical and water supply
Yue-yee	F	40	Weaver, knitwear	Office cleaner and part-time saleswoman during weekends	Self-employed herb seller
Wai-guen	F	40	Worker, clothing	Street cleaner and baby-sitter	Factotum of a factory
Shun-mei	F	30	Worker, garment	Checkered career in the service → Housewife and a part-time network sales agent	Lorry driver

[a]"Age" is from the time of the first interview in 1995.
[b]"Past Occupation" refers to the type of full-time regular employment as well as the industrial sector in the manufacturing sector.
[c] "Present Employment" refers to present employment status, job position, and industrial sector of employment.

Part IV

Migration, Household, and Gender Strategies

Chapter 9

Guests from the Tropics
Labor Practices and Foreign Workers in Taiwan

Anru Lee

Facing competition from newly industrializing countries, like China and those in Southeast Asia, and beset by problems with rising wages and labor shortages in the country, industrial producers in Taiwan have resorted to various adaptive strategies in order to reinvigorate the process of capital accumulation. Since the late 1980s many of them have sought offshore production sites where labor is cheap and abundant, or rearranged their production organization in the country. The government of Taiwan also lifted the ban on foreign labor employment in 1991 to alleviate the labor shortage (see table 9.1).

The introduction of foreign workers has had a multifarious impact on Taiwanese society; this chapter focuses on the economic aspect of the impact. While much of the recent literature on gender and international migration in Asia focuses on the structural change of Asian countries in the global economic system and the experience of migrant women as domestic workers (Chin 1998; Constable 1997), this chapter looks at issues of industrial migrant workers and emphasizes the view of capital owners and workers from labor-receiving countries.[1]

Drawing from my observation of the textile industry in Hai-kou, a small town in central Taiwan, and conversations with local factory owners and workers, this chapter explores four issues. First will be the socioeconomic transformations, especially the change in gender roles and gender ideologies, in Taiwanese society that set forth Taiwan's economic restructuring and the import of foreign workers after the late 1980s. Second will be the policies of the Taiwanese government and public debates in the larger society with regard to foreign labor, which tend to see foreign labor not only as a temporary yet urgent solution for Taiwan's continuous economic prosperity but also as a potential cause for labor dislocation and sociocultural disruption. The third issue is the labor practice on the shop floor in Hai-kou's textile factories, which fully exploits the vulnerable legal status of foreign workers. Fourth will be the varying perceptions Hai-kou's residents have about female foreign labor in the context of their different economic situations and needs.

Table 9.1. Foreign Labor Force in Taiwan[a]

	Quota Available	Quota Approved	Actual Number in Taiwan
1992	35,864	14,707	15,924
1993	124,900	93,039	97,565
1994	212,254	140,696	151,989
1995	257,226	181,463	189,051
1996	270,131	226,868	236,555
1997	302,014	226,202	248,396
1998	337,430	251,893	270,620
10/1999	349,137	273,287	291,437
Agricultural (sailors)	1,310	866	959
Industrial	199,783	164,058	171,744
Textiles[b]	38,456	32,607	33,839
Construction	56,753	45,472	48,752
Service	91,291	62,891	69,982

Source: EVTA (2000b)
[a]Data provided by EVTA do not differentiate the sex of foreign workers.
[b]The textile industry employs the second largest number of foreign workers.

Treasure Island, the textile company whose dormitory housed me in my recent fieldwork, will serve as the primary example of my discussion. Nevertheless, I will also draw on my observations from other factories to broaden the scope of this chapter.

GENDER, GLOBAL INDUSTRIALIZATION, AND TAIWAN'S RECENT ECONOMIC RESTRUCTURING

Changes in gender roles and gender ideologies are the keys to understanding Taiwan's recent economic restructuring and the subsequent introduction of industrial foreign workers to the country. Gender has long been acknowledged to be an important factor in understanding the processes of global industrialization, as it is fundamental to the organization of production and labor (Fernandez-Kelly 1989, 1994; S. K. Kim 1997; Nash 1988; Nash and Fernandez-Kelly 1983; Ong 1987, 1997; Ward 1990). Pioneering studies on Chinese women and industrialization also elucidate how the young women's roles in the family made them an ideal source of cheap labor that was essential to Taiwan's early export industrialization (Arrigo 1980; Cheng and Hsiung 1992; Diamond 1979; Gallin 1984, 1990; Kung 1994[1978]; Salaff 1995[1981]). While young girls constituted the majority of the earlier industrial work force that made Taiwan's "economic miracle" possible, at present they are no longer available due to several reasons. First, the birth rate in Taiwan dropped dramatically after the 1960s, resulting in a smaller pool of prospective labor after the 1980s that was available while the economy continued to expand (Lin 1994). Second, general living standards in Taiwan have greatly improved as a result of the successful export economy, giving daughters more options than working in factories to make money for their families. Nowadays, Taiwanese women stay in school longer than did those of previous generations; many of them are able to pursue high school or vocational school education, and even continue to junior colleges (Chou, Clark, and Clark 1990). Subsequently, upon graduation, they prefer to find jobs in the rapidly expanding service sector,[2] which they consider to be cleaner, easier, more comfortable, more modern and prestigious, and with a better chance for upward mobility (Lee 1999).

Despite continuous efforts to upgrade technologically and invest capital, most Taiwanese industrial producers still rely on cheap labor for profit. Accordingly, many of them see the short supply of young women workers as a major drawback to remaining competitive in the world market, particularly when they are facing more competition from other newly industrializing countries in Asia. To amend their problems, Taiwanese industrial producers have developed cost-effective strategies such as reorganizing the division of labor on the shop floor, reducing factory size, or upgrading the quality of production (Lee 1999). During the course of my recent fieldwork (Lee 1999), I also observed an increase in employment opportunities for married women, who were previously considered to be less dependable because of their domestic responsibilities, but are being regarded as more reliable now that young women are no longer available.[3] Many small factory owners also rely on their own family members to make up for the short labor supply (Lee 1996, in print).[4] In addition, Taiwanese manufacturers have explored new sources of cheap labor overseas (see table 9.2), adopting more radical practices such as relocating their production abroad and importing foreign workers to their shop floor (Chang and Chang 1992; J. H. Wang 1995). With capital outflow and the introduction of foreign workers to the country, Taiwanese economy has become increasingly internationalized and transnationalized (Lee 1999; Schive 1992, 1995).

FOREIGN LABOR POLICY IN TAIWAN

International migration is a ubiquitous phenomenon in human history, increasing particularly after the European expansion in the 16th century. Whether coerced or spontaneous, population movements from one location to another in recent times demonstrate a structural interconnectedness of societies under global economic forces (Goss and Lindquist 1995; Kearney 1986; Massey et al., 1993; Sassen 1984, 1988). Although Europe and North America have been historically the primary destinations for most international migrants, other regions with high economic growth or expanding labor markets also are experiencing a major influx of migrant workers; such regions include oil-exporting Arab and newly industrialized East Asian countries like Taiwan (Cheng 1999; Raghaven 1996).

In addition, there has been a surge in the number of female migrants. Asian women have been identified as the most rapidly growing group of individuals in

Table 9.2. Average Hourly Wage in Selected Asian Countries (in U.S. dollars)

Country	Average Hourly Wage
Taiwan	$5.10
Hong Kong	$4.51
South Korea	$4.18
Thailand	$1.06
Philippines	$0.62
Indonesia	$0.34
China	$0.28

Source: Smithsonian Institution (1999).

international (and intra-Asian) migration. Most of them are hired as domestic or industrial workers in their host countries, but there is also an increasing number of them working in the sex industry (Raghaven 1996). Again, this recent phenomenon must first be understood in the context of the global economic restructuring that began in the 1960s. The result was a "new international division of labor" (Fröbel, Heinrichs, and Kreye 1980) that recruited primarily young women from developing countries to work in labor-intensive industries across the globe. The latest development of intra-Asian migration indicates a continuation of the process, yet with different destinations for laborers. Affluent East Asian economies have now joined the ranks of advanced capitalist societies in the importing of cheap female foreign labor as a solution to the problem of rising production costs in industrial sectors and as domestic laborers who fulfill the child care and domestic duties of married women working paid, full-time jobs outside the home.

A system of migrant labor is characterized by the separation of processes of renewal from those of maintenance. Certain costs of renewing the labor force are externalized to an alternate economy and/or state (Burawoy 1976:1050), thereby increasing "the level of profits of certain firms and [of] capital as a whole by lowering the cost of labor and the cost of the reproduction of the labor force" (Sassen 1984:181). In the case of international migration, this separation is often facilitated by the governments of labor-receiving countries (Cheng 1999:52) that intervene in the functioning of the market by enforcing specific legal and political mechanisms which regulate geographical movement, impose restrictions on occupational mobility, and control the migrants' length of residence (Burawoy 1976:1050). The political status of migrant laborers is a key factor here. It is their relation to the state—that is, the denial of legal, political, and civil rights—that distinguishes them from native workers. As a result, migrant workers are deprived of the rights and abilities, as individuals or as a group, to influence the institutions that subject them to the employer as well as to other factions of the labor force (Burawoy 1976:1061).

The recent legalization of foreign workers in Taiwan faithfully reflects the general pattern discussed above. It has been clear since the very beginning that foreign workers are primarily introduced to ease Taiwanese employers' need for cheap and disposable labor, resonating the phenomenon of capital outflow, as a strategy to reinsure surplus accumulation. Nevertheless, it is also the general public's consensus that the stay of foreign workers has to be short and temporary; they cannot become a permanent burden to society. Consequently, underlying the Taiwan government's foreign labor policy is a concern with protecting the job security of Taiwanese, particularly disadvantaged groups such as the aborigines or the disabled, and with preventing foreign laborers (legal and illegal) from becoming permanent residents and a cause of social problems (The Liberty Times 1998).

In order to regulate the inflow of foreign laborers efficiently, the government of Taiwan signed bilateral agreements with several foreign governments (mainly in Southeast Asia), and only allows citizens from those countries to be legally employed in Taiwan. The Taiwan government, as well as the governments that signed the bilateral agreements, license a limited number of labor recruitment agencies to be in charge of related matters such as recruitment, health examination, and other measures designed to screen for disqualifications before a foreigner is allowed to enter Taiwan as a legal worker (Sobieszczyk 1999). Also, under the current policy, the number of foreign workers hired in one single factory cannot exceed 30 percent of the total work force in that factory. The percentage can be up to 35 percent if an employer also hires aborigines or disabled individuals (EVTA 2000a). However, because the unemployment rate has been on the rise since the early 1990s (EVTA 2000b), the government's Council of Labor Affairs also announced its intention to gradually reduce the number of foreign workers. Each foreign worker is allowed to work in the country only once for two years, with an extension of another year. During their tenure in Taiwan, foreign workers are prohibited from changing employers; they can only work for the employer who brought them to the country. They are not permitted to marry a Taiwanese citizen, nor would such a marriage grant them permanent resident status or citizenship; they still have to return to their countries of origin at the end of their contract (EVTA 2000a).

These legal and political measures have a profound impact on foreign workers' experiences both in Taiwan's wage-labor market and on the shop floor. In the following section, I will illustrate the impact through a discussion of labor practices in the textile industry in the Hai-kou area, using the Treasure Island company as a primary example.

ON THE SHOP FLOOR

Among all industries, textiles are the least favored by young Taiwanese women, for several reasons. To begin with, as I have constantly been told by both young and older workers and by factory owners, the conditions in the workplace are terrible. It is particularly hot in summers, due to the heat generated by the looms and worsened by Taiwan's natural climate; needless to say, very few employers are willing to spend money on air conditioners to make workers comfortable. If cotton is the primary raw material used in production, the air inside the factory is always full of cotton fibers and thus very polluted. Once again, not many employers are willing to spend money on ventilation to improve the situation. It is also extremely noisy on the shop floor because of the loud noise made by looms; degradation of hearing ability is one of the vocational hazards textile workers have to bear. In addition, many local people have told me that the work schedule in textiles is horrible. To make maximum use of machinery, it is the local convention that textile factories run 24 hours per day, 7 days per week, and nearly 365 days per year except for the few days off around the Chinese New Year. To accommodate this, textile workers are divided into three shifts around the clock, with 8 hours per shift, and they are required to change shifts. This is hard on the circadian rhythm and unnatural for one's body, as I have been told by many workers. It also becomes difficult for a textile worker to arrange activities in her leisure time, for she may be off at odd hours. To use my informants' words, to switch shifts "disrupts one's life order."

The work itself has been identified as laborious by most of my informants. A textile worker is usually assigned 20 to 30 looms, depending on the scale of the factory. The major responsibility of a loom tender is to keep an eye on looms so that the machines will operate smoothly. When a loom stops (for various reasons), she must fix the situation as quickly as possible so that the loom is back on line quickly. Since most of the textile factories in Hai-kou adopt a piece-rate system—to ensure workers' efficiency—it is also in the worker's best interest to act instantly when a loom pauses. To do a good job, she dare not take a break. She also has to watch all her looms with equal attention, which entails constantly walking around the area where her machines are stationed. It is said that a weaver would have to walk dozens of miles in an eight-hour shift; this requires much physical strength. Ironically, the more advanced a loom is, the fewer problems it may cause, but the bigger the loom will be. Therefore, a worker may choose to work in a factory with advanced looms, but the number of looms she has to tend as well as the area of her designated responsibility is likely to increase.

All things considered, textile employment has lost its attraction, particularly among young women. As a result, textiles is considered to be one of the industries facing the most serious problem of labor shortage.

Life and Work at Treasure Island

Treasure Island is atypical in many respects among Hai-kou's textile companies. Primarily, the size of the company is comparatively large by local standards. The company employed roughly 150 shop floor workers in the mid-1990s, a number far exceeding the number of workers (usually fewer than 30) hired in most of the local settings. Benefiting from its relatively large size, the company is still able to attract young single women who are absent in small factories. At the end of my fieldwork, Taiwanese workers constituted two-thirds of the company's work force, with half of them young, single women and the other half married women with children. The remaining one third of the work force in the company were foreign workers from Thailand. Most of these Thai workers were women, but a few of them were men.

Although the management never explicitly explained to me why they hired more Thai women than men, it was implicit in the many conversations I had with them that women were considered to be more conventional and appropriate workers for the jobs involved. This was evident in the ways work was assigned. The Thai workers were divided into small groups and assigned to both the weaving and spinning sections as well as to different shifts. Their tasks varied, but the division between men and women mainly followed the traditional pattern in textiles, i.e., men maintained and repaired machines or carried heavy objects, and women tended looms or assisted loom tenders. However, the management would occasionally ask Thai men to assist in loom-tending.

By and large, Thai workers played an auxiliary role. In particular, they were not involved in the last phase of production, which has a decisive effect on the quality of final products and therefore was assigned to the Taiwanese only. Taiwanese workers were believed to be more skilled, for many of them had many years of experience and had learned to do the job from their line leaders and peers. In contrast, the language barrier between the Taiwanese and Thais inhibited effective communication and thus the transfer of knowledge between the two groups. The management at Treasure Island were unable to speak directly with the Thais—or vice versa. Both sides relied on the few ethnic Chinese Thais to be their mediators and translators. Yet, these ethnic Chinese Thais were also foreign workers at Treasure Island; they were hired to be production workers but not translators.[5] They had their own duties to perform and could not possibly keep up with the needs of management. Hence, communication between management and Thai workers was indirect and constantly delayed. Many important messages and subtle pieces of information were lost in the process. As a result, the delivery of commands and transmission of technological know-how were difficult and incomplete, which in turn prevented the company from placing trust in its foreign workers for important tasks.

Given the fact that the majority of foreign labor in Chaug-hua County, where Hai-kou is located, came from Thailand, the Bureau of Industry at the county government offered some Thai language classes to factory managerial personnel in the county. Yet, no one at Treasure Island seemed eager to take this opportunity, probably because the company did not provide enough incentive for an individual to invest the considerable amount of time needed to master this language.

The Thai workers lived in the company's dormitory during their two-year stay. The company did not build the dormitory specifically for the Thais; it has been part of the company's facility since its founding days in the late 1970s, to house its workers from out of town as well as those who finished night or graveyard shifts and needed a place to sleep before going home. In the company's peak days, the dormitory was the home for a few hundred young women. However, since the number of female workers had shrunk rapidly in recent years, and most of the remaining employees possessed motorcycles and thus preferred to commute daily, the Thais were almost the only regular residents in the dormitory. The women resided on the third floor of the women's dormitory. Male Thai workers resided in the men's dormitory, to which I had no access.

In their off hours the Thais liked to go out shopping, visiting night markets, or meeting and socializing with friends who were also guest workers in Taiwan. But they were not encouraged to stay out overnight. The company kept a close eye on them and checked their whereabouts every night. Thai workers needed to have permission from their direct supervisor in order to leave the company even in their off hours, although their requests were rarely turned down. One of the functions of the security office by the company's front gate was to stop unauthorized foreign workers from going out.

Thai workers had very little spare time to spend, however. Textile workers do not have weekends. They work seven days a work. The only extended time off that textile workers have, Taiwanese and Thais alike, is between the hours when they end the day shift on Saturday afternoon and return to work on the graveyard shift at midnight on Monday, which gives them thirty-two hours for recuperation (see table 9.3). For the Taiwanese at Treasure Island, this was their "grand weekend" (*Ta li pai*), a time for sleeping late or catching up with personal and family duties. But the Thais usually preferred being busy. They rarely took the time off and often asked the management for overtime work.

One of the major differences between the Taiwanese and foreign workers at Treasure Island was the way they were paid. The former was on a piece-rate wage system and the latter was paid at a fixed monthly rate. Without overtime pay, a Taiwanese loom tender, almost exclusively female, made around N.T.$22,000 in Taiwanese dollars (approximately U.S.$814, with an exchange rate of N.T.$27 to U.S.$1 in the mid-1990s prior to the Asian financial crisis) to N.T.$30,000 (U.S.$1,111) per month depending on the nature of her work. The monthly wage of a mechanic, usually a male, ranged from N.T.$30,000 (U.S.$1,111) to N.T.$40,000 (U.S.$1,481). In comparison, regardless of gender, a Thai was paid around N.T.$14,000 (U.S.$518). This amount was originally required by the Labor Standards Law to be the minimum wage for all workers, domestic and foreign, but it often became the standard wage for foreign workers. The wages have increased since the time I conducted my research (see table 9.4). However, the

Table 9.3. Shift Change in Textile Factories, Hai-kou Area

Shift Change	Time Change	No. of Off Hours
Graveyard to Night	(Sun) midnight–8 A.M. to (Sun) 4 P.M.–midnight	8
Night to Day	(Sat) 4 P.M.–midnight to (Sun) 8 A.M.–4 P.M.	8
Day to Graveyard	(Sat) 8 A.M.–4 P.M. to (Mon) midnight–8 P.M.	32 (24+8)

Table 9.4. Wage in the Taiwanese Textile Industry in 1999
(in N.T. dollars/U.S. dollars)

	Average	Minimum
Skilled labor	$25,875 (U.S.$958)	$20,700 (U.S.$767)
Non-skilled labor	$22,508 (U.S.834)	$18,000 (U.S.$667)

Source: EVTA (2000a)

practice of paying foreign workers minimum wages largely remains unchanged. Foreign workers come to Taiwan primarily to make money. Since their monthly wage is fixed under the system, the only way they can make more money is to work overtime. The Thais at Treasure Island frequently worked two consecutive shifts (i.e., 16 hours), without a break in between.

The differences in pay and work assignment between Taiwanese and foreign workers usually became the subject of complaint among the Thais. Conflicts and struggles between management and Thai workers played out on the shop floor in various forms on a daily basis. Although most of the Thais (except for the few ethnic Chinese Thais) did not speak Mandarin or Minanese/Taiwanese and could not understand the conversation among their Taiwanese coworkers, they were not deprived of the ability to watch and observe. It did not take them long to realize the differential, and often discriminatory, practices toward them. They complained about the differences in pay scale and work assignments from time to time. The Thais at Treasure Island, as in many other companies, were often allocated night and graveyard shifts because most Taiwanese were not willing to work at night. As a result, foreign workers had to work two night shifts, which consumes more physical strength and rarely gave them the chance to see sunlight because they would sleep during the day.

It was usually the ethnic Chinese Thais who, understanding both Mandarin and Minanese/Taiwanese, picked up information on the shop floor and informed their Thai compatriots about the discriminatory practices. They also negotiated with the company on behalf of the Thai workers. From my limited conversation with the management of Treasure Island on this subject, I was given the impression that managers had an ambivalent attitude toward their ethnic Chinese Thai employees. For one thing, ethnic Chinese Thais were usually better workers because they communicated with management directly and learned the essential production knowledge more quickly. They were also indispensable for their language skills. Yet, they were often considered trouble makers and leaders of dissent among foreign workers.

In spite of all the grievances they had against the company, foreign workers could not do much to change their situation. The company always had the power to send them home if they were alleged to be slow workers or trouble makers. Subsequently, their protest and resistance were often in covert form, but were able to cause continual disruption to the daily routine of production. Mr. Chen, a foreman of Treasure Island, said to me, "They complained, complained, and complained. [It] gave me a big headache! Sometimes they also slow down their work and stagnate the whole production process. They even threatened to have a strike once." When asked what he did then, he responded, "Well, I warned them if they didn't keep quiet and work hard, I would bar them from any opportunity of working overtime. You know they all love to work overtime. That's the only chance they have in order to make more money [other than their monthly wages]. They can't afford to lose that."

Mr. Chen continued to explain that the Thais came from different regions of Thailand. They were not a unified group. The management of Treasure Island often played on the fact that there were factions among them and gave overtime work only to those considered to be cooperative. This strategy aggravated ill feelings among the Thais and prevented them from forming solidarity. It also created competition among them, which in turn forced them to drop their grievances and cooperate with management.

Foreign Labor Across the Region

The situation of foreign workers at Treasure Island is neither a norm nor universal. Great variations exist among factories in the Hai-kou area with regard to the number of foreign workers hired, their national origin, sex ratio, work assignment, living arrangement, food preparation, and life after work. Not every factory has a ready-made dormitory to accommodate foreign labor. Some firms put together temporary huts, and others—particularly the family-centered, small factories—set aside unused space in owners' houses to board these workers.

The sex ratio of foreign labor varies greatly from factory to factory, depending on the nature of production and products. Some factory owners hire only men or only women, but most others have a mixture of both. Although the tasks assigned to male and female foreign workers mainly follow tradition, it seems that more factory owners have discovered the advantage of using foreign males to do both "men's" and "women's" jobs. Among Taiwanese, the sexual division of labor in textiles is strictly prescribed, though more so for men than for women. Women may occasionally become mechanics, but men will never choose to tend looms; neither would any sensible factory owner ask his male employees to do such tasks. "That's a woman's job," I was often told. Nonetheless, the introduction of foreign labor began to introduce new ways of labor deployment. During the course of my research, I observed more than once that factory owners assigned their male foreign workers to tend looms, without shame or hesitation. When asked the reason, their answers were usually simple and straightforward: "It's perfect. Men can do both, tending looms and uploading and downloading fabric," or, "But why not? They don't complain."

Sometimes I was told that men were just as good as women. Yet a close look beyond this phenomenon reveals a strong economic incentive that did not exist when the workforce was merely Taiwanese. The labor market in Taiwan is gender biased. Men's labor is usually valued more than women's, even if they are performing the same task. A textile factory owner will have to pay much more to hire a Taiwanese man to tend looms, assuming that there are willing candidates. Hence, based on both cultural sanction and economics, it is a better deal for Taiwanese factory owners to hire a female loom tender and a male mover. The introduction of foreign labor presents a more flexible as well as cheaper option. Because male and female foreign workers are paid the same wage, it appears to be a shrewd business decision to have foreign men perform both tasks. The concept that loom-tending is a woman's job does not apply to foreign workers.

Nevertheless, assigning foreign male workers to do "women's" work was still rare. While I was in the field, factory owners who did so often had to answer questions from fellow employers about this unusual work arrangement. This suggests that economic incentives alone do not dictate employers' decisions about production. Although recognizing the potential benefit they might get from rearranging the sexual division of labor on the shop floor, industrial employers are still influenced by the culture that shapes one's perception of appropriate gender roles. It is yet to be observed whether deploying foreign males to do "women's work" will become a trend or "convention" in the near future.

Aside from the differences, there are common patterns underlying foreign workers' situation in Hai-kou. First of all, like the management of Treasure Island, employers across the region generally do not entrust their foreign employees with crucial production procedures. Foreign workers are frequently assigned to the dirtiest, most laborious (and smelly), and least skillful tasks like dyeing that very few Taiwanese are willing to do nowadays. In the textile industry, in which machines operate 24 hours per day but where fewer and fewer Taiwanese are willing to endure the hardship of changing shifts or working late shifts, foreign workers have become the main workforce for night or graveyard shifts; this is also true in many local factories. Also, although policy varies from company to company, most employers have developed strict codes for regulating the movement of their foreign workers. The Thais at Treasure Island were required to report to their immediate superior before leaving the company in their off hours. This was a rather benevolent rule compared to some of the harshest in the area. A Taiwanese weaver told me that foreign workers in her workplace were prohibited from leaving the company at all. She said:

My company has very rigid rules toward foreign workers. The company hired a couple [husband and wife] to keep an eye on the Thais. The couple lives in the dormitory, so they can watch the Thais 24 hours a day. Day and night! The Thais resent it. They are not allowed to go out—not on any occasion. The company doesn't want them to communicate with foreign workers in other companies. They don't want the foreign workers to exchange information and compare with others. ["Are they allowed to have visitors?" I asked.] Only if the visitor is their brother, sister, or spouse. The Thais like to drink. They drink a lot.

A Model Company in Foreign Labor Management

How to effectively manage foreign workers emerges as one of the newest challenges not only to Taiwanese factory employers but also to government officials in related agencies such as the Council of Labor Affairs. The phrase "foreign labor management"— *Wai chi lao kung kuan li* or *Wai lao kuan li*—widely used in the manufacturing circle, government guidelines, and scholarly literature of labor and human resources exemplifies their collective concern and anxiety about being in control. Two issues are frequently emphasized in the general discussion of foreign labor management: the custody of foreign labor and enhancement of their productivity. The fact that all companies have developed policies to control foreign workers' movement shows the magnitude of the former's concern. As to the issue of productivity, factory employers commonly complained that two years is too short, because their foreign workers can only reach a satisfactory level of productivity after six months or longer on the job. By the time foreign workers have familiarized themselves with their tasks, they are almost about to go home. Taiwanese employers constantly complained that they will have to hire new foreign workers and start the training cycle all over again. Also, many factories have adopted a fixed wage system like that of Treasure Island, which impedes the incentive for foreign workers to be quick learners and efficient producers; they do not have much to gain from improving their productivity. How to motivate foreign workers to learn and yield a high efficiency has, therefore, become an urgent issue for the companies involved.

E & P, which stands for "Excellence and Prosperity" and refers to one of Taiwan's largest tire-producing companies with a predominantly male workforce (due to its type of products), was chosen by the Council of Labor Affairs to be a model company in foreign labor management and was listed on the emulation tour for factory owners and managers in central Taiwan. According to a manager of Treasure Island who participated in the tour, foreign workers at E & P (also from Thailand) could apply to the company only once a week regarding their time off for the following week. Otherwise, they would have to be escorted by their fellow Taiwanese workers if they were leaving the company's grounds. The Taiwanese served both to protect the Thais from trouble and to prevent them from escaping. Also, the management of E & P enforced the rule that those living in the same room were held jointly responsible for one another's actions— a traditional East Asian control measure. All of the roommates would be sent back to Thailand as a punishment if any fleeing occurred among them. This strategy turned foreign workers into their own guards. In fact, this strategy was so effective that none of the Thais at E & P had run away in recent years.

In contrast to most of the local companies in Hai-kou, foreign workers at E & P were on a piece-rate wage system. Instead of paying a fixed monthly salary for all, the company only rewarded a full wage and bonus to those who accomplished a prescribed, target production quota. Also, their pay was reduced for any products that might be of substandard quality in order to compensate for the company's loss. The company also expected them to reach a satisfactory level of productivity within a given time, and the workers were told that they would be sent back to Thailand if they failed to do so.

Amazed by the rigor of E & P's codes, I asked the manager at Treasure Island how E & P's management could afford to send back their workers even for the purpose of enforcing the rules, given my understanding that it took both time and money—and time in particular—to obtain foreigners for work in Taiwan. The manager answered that the company's forcefulness was the key to its successful management of foreign labor. He said that E & P's policy was to send back a few foreign workers to set an example. Not many would risk their jobs to challenge the company's authority. Nevertheless, the manager at Treasure Island also pointed out the fact that E & P has had an established, overseas firm in northern Thailand for a decade. The company knew the region and drew workers to Taiwan mainly from there. Unlike most Taiwanese employers who relied on recruitment and placement agencies to facilitate hiring and were blind regarding the selection process, "they [E & P] get to choose better workers," said the manager at Treasure Island.

The case of E & P presents a new phase in the global economy. The company's very pattern of capital and labor flow exemplifies a recomposition of world capital, in which Taiwan gradually becomes a major player in shaping the structure of the Asian-Pacific regional economy, if not the global economy. As more and more Taiwanese companies invest or relocate their production overseas, hiring practices like that of E & P are becoming increasingly common. The transnational link between Taiwanese companies and their overseas plants not only signals the most recent development of Taiwan's capital accumulation, but also facilitates a flow of labor in both directions. For those who manufacture in both Taiwan and abroad, workers are drawn from these investment regions to supplement or reduce the labor cost back home. Some of the foreign workers hired under these circumstances have already worked for their Taiwanese employers in Thailand before being transferred to Taiwan. They have been familiarized with the production and discipline codes of their factories, so that they should be able to fit in their new workplaces without much disruption. Furthermore, since Taiwanese companies usually move the least complex and most mass-produced parts of their production overseas and leave the more technologically advanced and complicated procedures in Taiwan, their Taiwanese operations often serve as a training ground for employees from overseas. Taiwanese manufacturers recruit foreign workers and train them in Taiwan. After they complete their two-year contract, these foreign workers go home and become line leaders or foremen in the overseas factories of their Taiwanese employers.

The Runaway Incident of the Summer of 1994

The vulnerability of foreign workers is particularly evident when they transgress the legal boundaries set up by their receiving country's government. The runaway incident I witnessed while staying at the dormitory of Treasure Island was a clear illustration. According to the Taiwan government's regulations, each foreign worker is allowed to work in Taiwan once for two years. After that they cannot renew their contracts and must return to their countries of origin. Some of the Thai workers at Treasure Island came in the early fall of 1992. In 1994, the company had to send them back.

I was away for one weekend in late July. When I came back on Sunday evening, Mrs. Lin, the chaperon of the women's dormitory, informed me that something "big" had happened. Over the weekend two Thai women went out but did not return. "They must have gone to look for other jobs," Mrs. Lin said, "They have to go back in a few months. But they want to stay. They want to make more money." Mrs. Lin then pointed out to me the photos of the two women who ran away from the chart of pictures she had placed on her desktop, and said, "This one! This one is particularly a troublemaker. She constantly came in late after going out. We have looked for her for several times in the past. I always had a hunch sooner or later she was going to cause us a serious problem."

Mrs. Lin continued to tell me that this was not the first time foreign workers at Treasure Island ran away before their contract ended. A male worker, also from Thailand, had run away a year earlier. He had been recently caught by the police and sent to a detention center for illegal migrants waiting for deportation. "Life is not easy [in the detention center]. They are treated like criminals!" Mrs. Lin shook her head, expressing her incomprehension of the runaway behavior of Thai workers. She informed me that the company had acted quietly this time and hired a private investigator to look into the whereabouts of the two Thai women. According to the government's rules, employers of runaway foreign workers have to report the missing to their local police stations at once, so that the police are able to assist in the search. Missing foreign workers are considered to be potential law offenders and seen as posing a serious threat to the society at large. Nonetheless, many Taiwanese companies choose not to report to the police, mainly out of concern that they will be held responsible and even sanctioned for the runaway behavior. The government may take away a company's foreign labor quota if such a missing person case occurs. Thus, the management of Treasure Island decided to act on its own.

A week passed. A rumor spread in the company saying that the two runaway workers were seen working in a factory in an industrial park nearly Hai-kou. Before the weekend was over, however, the two women came back. Employees at Treasure Island gossiped that the factory owner who hired them a week ago was concerned with their illegal status and decided to fire them. They had nowhere else to go. At any rate, they quietly sneaked back in the dormitory and reappeared on the shop floor at their presumed working hours, as if they had always been there.

Life went on at Treasure Island for two peaceful days. On the third morning, while typing up field notes in my room, I heard swift steps and men's voices in the hallway. Men were not allowed in the women's dormitory! I stuck my head out of the window and saw several Thai men carrying luggage and walking down the stairs. They were leaving the dormitory, followed by the two runaways and some other Thai women. I followed the group to the front gate of the company and saw that a crowd of Thai workers was waiting. The two runaways went to see the personnel manager for the last time. After they came out of the office they were immediately taken away by staff from the recruitment and placement agency that had facilitated the hiring of these Thai for Treasure Island. There was only time for the crowd gathering at the front gate to say good-bye.

Later that day the general manager of Treasure Island informed me that the two runaways were flying back to Thailand, at their own expense, that afternoon. The staff from the recruitment agency would see to their departure. "We have to act quickly," the general manager said,

> We have no other choice. We don't want to turn them in to the police [which we are supposed to do according to the law]. We don't want to send them to the detention center. It's like a prison! But we can't keep them in the company, either. We couldn't confine them. If we don't send them back right away, who knows what other troubles they might bring us? They have run away once. They will try again.

VOICES OF THE TAIWANESE

The "deportation" of the runaways became a popular topic in the company's conversation for days to come. None of the Taiwanese employees were affected by the incident, but it provided them with an entertaining break in their daily routine and gave a researcher like myself an excellent opportunity to ask about their opinions on foreign labor. In addition to the runaway incident, several other events related to the Thais had occurred around that time. One woman requested the company to terminate her contract and send her back to Thailand. She had received a letter from home, telling her that her husband was having an affair. "Why should I work so hard here and make money for him to have fun in Thailand?" she said to the company. Another man, who was considered a troublemaker by the company and who was said not to take orders from his superior, had been sent back not long before the runaway incident. A close working relationship with the recruitment and placement agency on these events seemed to indicate that Treasure Island as a customer was entitled to full warranty for their purchase of foreign labor. The recruitment agency had to agree to replace the returned goods with satisfactory commodities. They supplied Treasure Island with new workers to replace those who failed to follow the rules.

Factory Owners/Employers

Foreign labor that runs away is a potential problem faced by all factory owners who employ guest workers. They are, thus, interested in and sympathetic to other owners when runaway incidents occur. After listening to my recitation of the incident, a friend who owned a local weaving factory and hired fifteen Thai workers quickly responded:

Did they have to go back soon? [I nodded yes.] That will do. It's in fact very bad for foreign workers themselves that they try to run away. Their employers will only develop stricter rules to control their movement. The best strategy [for foreign workers] is to stay where they are. [If they do so,] their employers won't restrict them that much, and both sides will be happy.

He spoke from his own experience. The Thai workers in his factory were not restrained from moving around. They moved freely among their workplace, living quarters, and shopping areas in downtown Hai-kou. By granting his workers unconstrained freedom, this friend seemed to be able to establish mutual trust with his workers, thereby exempting himself from the worry that they might attempt to flee.

Middle-Level Management

The middle-level management at Treasure Island—those who are themselves employees of the company, but who are in charge of shop-floor production and have direct contact with foreign workers—had the most negative things to say about foreign labor. Primarily because of their supervisory role and responsibility for efficiency and productivity, middle-level management tended to see Thais as slow, lazy, and stubborn workers who did not want to learn. Mr. Huang, a foreman at Treasure Island, said to me in a conversation after the runaways were deported,

If it were up to me to decide, I wouldn't like to hire any foreign labor. See how many of them have been sent back since your short stay here? [I raised four fingers.] That's right. Four! They say foreign labor won't cause any problems because they will go back after two years. It's ok only when there are a few of them. Now their number has increased to such an extent that we will have many problems to come.

One of the criticisms made by the middle-level management at Treasure Island was that Thais did not learn the proper ways of taking care of production. Mr. Huang continued,

As I said, when there are only a handful of them, they follow your instructions. When their number increases, they stop listening to you [and instead] start teaching one another wrong ways to do things. They don't learn the good things, but only the bad. When our company began to hire foreign workers, we lost money on them in the first few months on the job. Their products were only of inferior quality. Now they don't even bother to learn from you. They don't care whether their final products are in perfect shape. We completely rely on the Taiwanese [who work in the packing section and serve as the last gatekeeper before the products leave the company] for quality control.

Nevertheless, the language barrier was the key to the problem here. As stated earlier, unable to communicate directly with the Thais, management had to rely on a few ethnic Chinese Thais to translate for them. As a result, communication was indirect and constantly delayed, adding more barriers to already existing cultural misunderstandings.

"But how do you feel about foreign workers? Do you resent their presence here in Taiwan? Are they replacing Taiwanese in textile factories?" I always asked my informants. Given the popular impression that foreign workers are taking over Taiwanese jobs, these questions were of great importance. When I asked the middle-level managers at Treasure Island this question, instead of expressing their concerns over the potential replacement effect of foreign labor, some chose to make comments on the problem of labor shortage and the decline of the work ethic among the "new new generations" (*hsin hsin ren lei*—i.e., young Taiwanese who were born after the 1970s) as its major cause.[6] They lamented that young people nowadays liked to take jobs that were easy-going and high paid, with regular days off on weekends and national holidays, and that also allowed them to dress well. They moaned that the society had lost its virtue of diligence and that this foretold the downfall of the Taiwanese economy.

Shop-Floor Workers

Young female workers at Treasure Island—that is, the "new new generation" that has been criticized by their elderly for having a decreased work ethic—had very different views about themselves, their future, and foreign workers. Most of them were going to vocational school at night while working during the day. They considered their jobs in textile factories as temporary and expected to move on to better ones upon graduation. In answering my questions regarding foreign labor, one of the young workers thought hard for a while, as though answering an exam question, and replied, "For now, no. But I think they will replace the Taiwanese eventually." But this was not a problem that concerned her: she intended to find a white-collar job as soon as she was out of school.

It was middle-aged women workers who revealed the most anxiety about the presence of foreign labor, especially if they had observed a gradual substitution of Taiwanese with foreign workers in their workplaces. This was the group of people who formed the core workforce in Taiwan's earlier export industrialization. Many of them had begun working at a very young age, sacrificing their own chance for schooling to support their families or to pay for their younger siblings' education. Without having the much needed education and skills necessary for jobs in Taiwan's fast growing service sector, these women would not have many alternatives if they were pushed out of their current jobs. As a result, they were the most vulnerable group of industrial workers. In one interview my informant, a weaver in her late 30s, repeatedly pleaded for an answer to the impact of foreign labor. She was very anxious to know whether employment of foreign workers would one day reach a point where all Taiwanese would lose their jobs to foreigners. In her workplace, Thais had gradually become the main labor force. She said that the owner of her company had explicitly expressed his preference for foreign workers over Taiwanese:

> He said that the Taiwanese take [factory] jobs only when their families have extra needs. When the extra needs are met, they quit their jobs immediately. He feels it takes him too much just to keep up with all these hassles. It's much simpler to deal with foreign workers. Now, my manager relies on us to teach the foreign workers. He will fire us all as soon as the foreign workers have learned what we know. I no longer feel I have any job security.

Counting the cost of hiring a foreign worker became a favorite exercise for my informants and me. According to our calculations, despite the fact that a foreign worker was paid a monthly wage of N.T.$14,000 (U.S.$518), the total cost to an employer was almost as much as for a Taiwanese worker. An employer has to pay for their foreign employees' lodging, food, health insurance, airplane tickets for home visits once or twice during their two-year contracts, and a special fee to the Council of Labor Affairs. In the end it would amount to at least N.T.$20,000 (U.S.$740) per month to hire a foreign worker, not much cheaper than hiring a Taiwanese. Yet there are other benefits. First and foremost, from an employer's viewpoint, it saves him the headache of labor shortages. It also assures the stability of a workforce for at least two years, since foreign workers would not and could not change jobs. Second, it is easier for Taiwanese employers to enforce a strict discipline code when their employees are foreign and under a constant threat of being sent back. Finally, it saves employers from paying retirement pensions and annual bonuses. The pension issue has increasingly become a serious problem for many Taiwanese companies established in the 1970s, because they face an aging labor force but have, until now, failed to save for their workers.

CONCLUSION

The introduction of foreign labor to Taiwan, first and foremost, resonates with the global strategy of capital accumulation that includes seeing women as secondary wage earners and as disposable laborers who can be paid less than men. While young Taiwanese single women are no longer available to work in the industrial sector due to recent socioeconomic transformations, Taiwanese manufacturers turn to women from less industrialized countries as a source of cheap labor. The introduction of foreign labor also parallels an age-old strategy of capital to control labor that is facilitated by the state. It increases the employers' profit by lowering workers' wages and by separating labor renewal processes and those of maintenance, thereby externalizing certain costs of labor reproduction to the home countries of foreign workers. The Taiwan government's legal and political measures to prevent foreign workers from becoming permanent residents and the denial of their rights to geographical and occupational mobility as well as to union organization further extends the power of Taiwanese employers. Foreign workers are under constant threat of "deportation" if they do not comply with the employers' needs and demands. The government's tight regulation of foreign labor also gives the larger society a sense of security and control, although it has been increasingly criticized as insufficient and inefficient. The fear of labor displacement and the presence of unfamiliar faces have made it to newspaper headlines from time to time. Yet for the time being, these largely remain latent social concerns rather than a focus of public outcry.

The introduction of foreign labor to Taiwan, however, is more than a simple replication of an old strategy. It signifies a new phase of articulation between international capital and labor flows (Sassen 1984:185). On the one hand, there has been an acceleration of direct foreign investment of Taiwanese enterprises in China and Southeast Asia, primarily in the form of manufacturing capital, and on the other hand, there has been a large influx of Southeast Asian migrant workers to Taiwan. Both of these are strategies developed by Taiwanese industrial producers in hopes of maintaining their competitiveness in the global economy. Notably, in an increasingly sophisticated world system of production, there is no clear demarcation between those who invest overseas, thus directly exploiting cheaper labor in other countries, and those who continue to produce in Taiwan, thereby hiring foreign workers to reduce production costs in their own country. Many Taiwanese manufacturers have carefully divided the production process into parts that are distributed to different sites, in order to maximize the comparative advantage provided by each locality. Labor is thereby contracted to move in multiple directions in this intensified process of capital accumulation.

NOTES

This article emerged from fieldwork in Taiwan between September 1993 and January 1996. I am grateful for the generous support of grants from the Wenner-Gren Foundation for Anthropological Research, and the Institute of Ethnology, Academia Sinica in Taipei. This article has benefited from the feedback of Keith Markus, Kim Haslinger, Michael Blim, Joan Mencher, June Nash, Murray Rubinstein, Esther Ngan-ling Chow, and Ching Kwan Lee, and the editorial comments of Thomas Swift. I am indebted to them all for their valuable criticisms. To keep the confidentiality of my informants, the name of the town, the town's companies and residents in this article are all pseudonyms.

1. This is not to say that industrial foreign workers are the only group recently introduced to Taiwan's wage labor market. There are also large numbers of foreign workers in construction industries and in domestic service, and they each have a very different impact on the preexisting, native workforce in their respective sectors. Due to the nature of my research, however, I chose to focus on the industrial sector.

2. As a result of past economic expansion, Taiwan is no longer a blue-collar society. Thirty-five percent of the working population had manufacturing jobs in 1987. Since then, the percentage of the labor force in manufacturing has declined gradually. At

the same time, the proportion of the workforce in the service sector has increased substantially. By the end of 1995, half of the working population held jobs in the service sector (*Monthly Bulletin of Labor Statistics*, the Council of Labor Affairs, The ROC Administration Yuan, Republic of China 1995).

3. This trend has also been indicated in *Report on the Manpower Utilization Survey, Taiwan Area, Republic of China, 1990*, published by the Directorate-General of Budget, Accounting, and Statistics and the Council for Economic Planning and Development, the ROC Executive Yuan, Republic of China 1991.

4. Family members have always been a core workforce in Taiwan's small-scale, family-centered industries (Harrell 1985; Hsiung 1996; Li and Ka 1994; Niehoff 1987). Under the recent predicament of labor shortages, however, family labor has become even more important than ever before. In particular, the labor of daughters is often considered to be crucial for the survival of family businesses.

5. Aside from their Chinese language ability, ethnic Chinese Thais are largely perceived, and treated, the same as their fellow Thai workers. Institutionally, I did not observe a difference in work arrangement or in pay between these two groups of Thai workers—only between Thais and Taiwanese. Nationality, rather than ethnicity, plays a more significant role in determining one's position in the company. At the personal level, however, Taiwanese employees of the company may have had more interaction with the ethnic Chinese because they could intercommunicate.

6. The term "new new generation" is an adaptation of the "new generation," a term coined in the mid-1980s by Japanese writer Sakaiya Taichi. He was referring to the generation of Japanese born after 1965, who came of age when the Japanese economy and society had become highly prosperous and who were able to enjoy life without laboring hard, like their parents' generation. In Taiwan, however, where the phenomenon of rich and carefree urban youth occurred a bit later, the term "new new generation" mainly refers to those born after the 1970s. I have discussed the issue of the "new new generation" moral discourse elsewhere (Lee 1997).

Chapter 10

Fleeing Poverty

Rural Women, Expanding Marriage Markets, and Strategies for Social Mobility in Contemporary China

Christina Gilmartin and Lin Tan

Since the first years of China's economic reform, alarming stories have appeared from time to time in Chinese and Western newspapers about women falling prey to kidnappers and being sold as wives to poor farmers. Traffickers usually targeted women from poor rural areas who were quite young, unsophisticated, and easily duped, but in a few instances they also snared educated, urban women. Transported hundreds of miles from their homes, these women found themselves imprisoned in villages where everyone in the community sympathized with the men who had spent much of their life savings to acquire these wives. In many cases, the birth of a child transformed these abducted women from virtual captives to permanent residents of their new communities. Deemed trustworthy, they were released from surveillance, allowed to communicate with their distraught natal families, and encouraged to assume normal lives in their new families.[1]

While this type of involuntary marriage migration is generally regarded as an unfortunate consequence of the introduction of market forces in China, government officials and social science researchers hailed the emergence of a much larger voluntary female marriage migratory pattern as a tribute to the benefits of the economic reforms. Spurred by the same demographic and economic factors that fueled the illegal trafficking, millions of women in the mid-1980s opted to trek great distances from their homes in order to marry. In many ways, this pattern of marriage migration seemed to be closely connected with the vast internal labor migrations that had proved so critical to the start of market reforms. Thus, as has happened in many other places in the world, women's migration in contemporary China has experienced a marked increase as of late (Chattopadhyay 1997).

This chapter aims to explore the character, causes, and social implications of this large-scale marriage migration in order to shed light on the ways in which economic reforms have shaped women's opportunities and spurred social change.[2] Preliminary in nature, it considers whether marriage migrations can be seen as a form of female agency and whether they are contributing to greater female social equality. The evidence for this study is mainly drawn from demographic data—particularly the 1990 population census data and the 1987 One Percent Sample Survey.[3] We have supplemented our analysis of these data with some relevant case studies, the most useful of which was done by Hesheng Zhang (1994). In addition, we have included some data collected from marriage registrations in 1996 in certain counties of the Tianjin Municipality, from interviews with women workers in the Tanggu Special Economic Zone and from focus groups of women in Zhangjiagang, Jiangsu in 1998.[4]

A DISTINCTLY FEMALE AND RURAL PHENOMENON

In sharp contrast to the era of Mao Zedong (1949–1976), when migrations were increasingly impeded by the enforcement of the population control (*hukou*) system, the introduction of economic reforms in the late 1970s unleashed large-scale economic migrations. Although young women participated in internal circular migrations in order to secure short-term employment and were particularly evident in certain occupations, such as nannies in large cities or workers in some light industries in the special economic zones, they did not constitute a major group of the newly emerging flexible workforce of the 1980s. Rather, the floating population (*liudong*), as these temporary labor migrants came to be called, was primarily composed of men.[5] But as the publication of the findings of the 1987 One Percent Sample and the 1990 Census revealed, there was one type of permanent migration (*qianyi*) in the economic reform era in which women predominated—marriage migration. Totaling 4,325,747 in the 1990 census data, these female marriage migrants comprised 28 percent of the overall female migration in China.[6]

What kind of women migrated to marry in the first decade of economic reform? The great bulk of marriage migrants came from agricultural backgrounds. In one Jiangsu case study, Zhang (1994:35) found that 97.2 percent of female marriage migrants originally farmed for a living. In this respect they differed from female migrants as a whole, who according to the 1990 census, came only somewhat disproportionately from farming and factory backgrounds. That is to say, approximately 40 percent farmed for a living and roughly 30 percent were employed in factories before they migrated (Li 1994). Marriage migrants have not, for the most part, been able to switch their rural residences for urban ones through the migration process. Their destinations have primarily been rural, in large part because of the limitations imposed by the hukou system of residence registration. Those who have successfully penetrated the boundaries of the great metropolitan areas of Beijing, Tianjin, and Shanghai have not ended up in the urban areas, but in their outlying rural districts.

Another general characteristic of these marriage migrants was their youth. The only comprehensive data on the age structure of female marriage migrants have been obtained from the China Migration of 74 Cities and Towns Sampling Survey, which was conducted in 1987 by the Population Institute of the Chinese Academy of Social Sciences. These data show that in the first decade of the economic reform era female marriage migration was clustered in the age groups of 15- to 29-year-olds, with the main concentration in the 20- to-24-year-old cohort (Rolland 1994). Those who gained entry to the rural areas of large metropolitan areas of Beijing, Tianjin or Shanghai may have been a bit older. For instance, Lin Tan's Tianjin survey (1997) of 2,645 rural marriage migrant women who legally registered their marriages to Tianjin men in 1996 shows that the average age of these women at the time of marriage was 25.19 years old, which was higher than that of Tianjin women with agricultural household registrations (23.03) and lower than that of Tianjin women with nonagricultural household registrations (26.93).

In contrast to the millions of rural women who migrated to marry, the 1990 census reported that only 427,287 men migrated for this reason, constituting a mere 2 percent of all male migrants. The main reason for such low male participation in this type of migration is due to the tenacity of patrilocal marriage patterns in rural communities. Even after the establishment of a communist state in 1949, government initiatives were unable to motivate large numbers of men to undertake virilocal marriages (Johnson 1983).[7] Those few men who moved to another village and took up residence in the homes of their wives were not accorded full rights and social status in their new communities (Lavely 1991).

Women, on the other hand, have almost always moved at the time of marriage in China. Village exogamy was held up as a norm and only a small percentage of women defied this custom, opting to stay in their natal villages at the time of marriage. The great majority of rural women who observed the strong taboos against same-village marriages, however, married within a radius of 20 *li* (ten kilometers), and usually in the same county (Gu 1991).[8] William Lavely (1991) found that the distances women moved at the time of marriage varied depending on economic factors. His study showed that one prosperous Sichuan county at the end of the Mao era attracted women from quite a distance, while indigenous women who were reluctant to leave married out of their communities. Moreover, those who married into the area generally ended up with husbands from the poor strata of the community, indicating that these men were less able to attract local women. This pattern clearly revealed the existence of a marriage market even at a time when economic forces were weak and marriage decisions were greatly influenced by political factors (Lavely 1991).[9]

The marriage market of the Mao era was radically expanded with the introduction of economic reforms in 1978. As a result, the distances some women traveled for marriage increased dramatically. Larger numbers of women began to cross county and provincial borders, thereby attracting the attention of census takers. Within a few years, some women began to venture hundreds and even thousands of miles in order to marry.

MAPPING MARRIAGE MIGRATION PATTERNS

Marriage migrations in the economic reform era have tended to follow certain distinct geographical patterns. The general pattern is that migrants originate in the poorer areas of the southwest and travel to the rural areas of the richer sections of the eastern coast, especially Jiangsu and Zhejiang. Yunyan Yang (1992) in his analysis of the 1990 census noted that the largest number of marriage migrants travel to east and north China, especially to the more economically developed counties and cities. He also pointed out that the net migration for Jiangsu province was positive, amounting to approximately 160,000. In certain areas of Zhejiang, the settlement patterns of these female marriage migrants have been quite pronounced. For instance, in the more developed counties of Xiaoshan city in Zhejiang in 1989, in every 51 households, there was one female marriage migrant. In Huzhou, Yang reported that the situation was similar. Furthermore, Yang calculated that 71 percent of the female marriage immigrants of Jiangsu came from the four provinces of Sichuan (29 percent), Guizhou (16 percent), Anhui (13 percent), and Yunnan (13 percent). He showed that a similar pattern existed for Zhejiang, where 69 percent of the female marriage immigrants came from the five provinces of Guizhou (17 percent), Hunan (14 percent), Jiangxi (14 percent), Sichuan (13 percent), and Guangxi (11 percent). He also highlighted the net negative marriage migration patterns in the southwest of China, especially Sichuan, Guizhou, and western Yunnan. In Sichuan, for instance, the net female marriage migration was –240,000 (Yang 1992:41).

A study by Hua Tian (1991) supported Yang's findings. His work on female marriage migration from the southwestern rural areas to east China showed that from 1982 to 1986 there were about 766,800 interprovincial marriage migrants and among them, 59.98 percent (that is, 459,900) were from rural areas. His study shows that many women from the poverty-stricken rural areas of Sichuan, Yunnan, Guizhou, and Guangxi first moved eastward. Then in the next wave, marriage migrants fanned out a bit, pushing into the richer eastern seacoast provinces and also into the rural areas of the southeastern coastal area of Guangdong and the northern plains (Tian 1991). As a result, the most common destinations for interprovincial marriage migrants were Jiangsu, Hebei, Guangdong, Shandong, Anhui, and Zhejiang. Another striking aspect of the 1990 census figures is the high level of intraprovincial marriage migrations in some provinces. Sichuan stands out in this respect, with almost half a million women crossing county lines for marriages.

These geographical trends reflect specific economic realities. Jiangsu, Zhejiang, Guangdong, and Hebei are among the richest provinces in China, while the southwestern provinces of Sichuan, Yunnan and Guizhou are among some of China's poorest. Even as early as 1989, the per capita net income in rural Zhejiang was more than 400 yuan above the national average, approximately 450 yuan above Hunan level, and more than double that of the rural areas of Guizhou, Guangxi, and Sichuan (Li 1995).

THE PROCESS AND CAUSES OF EXPANSION

These long-distance marriage migrations were slower to develop in the economic reform era than either the labor migrations or the illegal trafficking in brides. The demographic data show that they began in a gradual manner in the mid-1980s. For instance, Wang Jinling, using data from a 1990 survey of Zhejiang rural areas conducted by the Hangzhou University Population Institute, demonstrates that in the 1980s more than 100,000 women migrated into Zhejiang for the purpose of marriage. But only 7 percent came between 1979 and 1985; 10.5 percent in 1986; 23.2 percent in 1987; 31.2 percent in 1988; and 28.1 percent in the first nine months of 1989 (Wang 1992). In his 1992 survey, Zhang (1994:34) found that 90.67 percent of the female marriage migrants were unmarried when they came to Huaiyin, whereas 3.07 percent were married, 4.14 percent were divorced, and 2.12 percent were widows. It is possible that the group of married women participated in this migration pattern because they were unhappy with their original marriages or had been lured by illegal marriage traffickers.

Some studies have shown that over the course of the 1980s and 1990s, there was also a significant shift in the marital status of female in-migrants. In the early years, it appears that single rural women were not as able to overcome family constraints and participate in the migrations. According to Xiong Yu and Lincoln H. Day's study (1994) of the 1987 Migration Survey data, 61 percent of female permanent migrants (qianyi) were married at the time of migration, whereas only 35 percent were unmarried. But with the passage of time, we see distinct shifts in this pattern. Fang Cai (1997), for instance, found that by 1995 that proportion of married women in the migrant population of Jinan was only 13.4 percent. We also find that by 1995 all the factory girls who had migrated from rural areas to the urban areas of Guangdong were unmarried (Yintao Chen 1997:39). This is also true for many of the export processing factories in the special economic zones such as Shenzhen and Tanggu (Tan and Gilmartin 1996). It may well be that the female labor migrations helped to stimulate marriage migrations. As small companies run by local rural governments, joint ventures and foreign companies increasingly preferred to hire young unmarried female workers; the customary constraints against any type of unmarried female migration began to weaken in the rural areas. This changed attitude may well have provided a more conducive atmosphere for unmarried female migration, both for the purposes of work and marriage.

Labor migrations were intertwined with marriage migrations in other ways as well. Ten Mile Inn (Shilidian), a village in Henan, for instance, began to recruit Sichuan men to work in its mines because of the unwillingness of local people to continue doing such dangerous work. These Sichuan men soon began to arrange for their female relatives to be married into the families of Ten Mile Inn. By the end of 1996 there were 20 Sichuan brides in the community, and by 1999 the number had doubled.[10] It was more difficult for rural women who were working in factories in a special economic zone near large municipalities to find local men willing to marry them, and only a small percentage were successful.

The illegal marriage trafficking may also have spurred the emergence of a legal, voluntary marriage migration. It is worth noting that these kidnapped women made up a sizable cohort of marriage migrants themselves. According to Zhang (1994), they constituted 14.21 percent of the almost 18,000 female marriage migrants in his survey. Once these young women produced children, they generally became resigned to their circumstances and no longer sought to return to their natal communities. In order to reduce their isolation in their new communities and create a more supportive network in an unfriendly environment, they began to encourage other women from their natal villages to migrate to their new communities. Such an enclave of Yunnan women started in Huiyang county, Henan in 1990 when one kidnapped woman persuaded a group of her fellow Yunnan friends to migrate into this faraway central Chinese province.[11]

The marriage migrations owed their existence to the sex ratio imbalances that existed in rural communities. To be sure, the imbalances of the 1980s and 1990s were of a different nature and scope than those that had been produced as a result of the social impact from the one-child family policy when it was instituted in 1979. Indeed, the 1990 census data show that the sex ratio of the total rural population in the 15- to 39-year-old group was relatively normal. But local women leaving the countryside to work in urban areas or in the special economic zones led to a shortage of women of marriageable age in many rural areas. As a result, the sex ratios for the unmarried rural population were adversely affected, as table 10.1 shows.

This unbalanced sex ratio shows the difficulty of young, rural, unmarried men in the marriage market. They experienced a great deal of difficulty finding a wife, either because many women married early or had gone into the towns and cities. In table 10.1, among unmarried rural people between 20 and 24, there were almost 162 unmarried men for almost every 100 unmarried women. In the older age groups, there were essentially no unmarried women in the rural areas (Guojia Tongjiju 1992:210). In such circumstances, the prevailing bias against the acquisition of an "outsider" as a bride dissolved among those families who were unable to secure a local woman.

Table 10.1. The Sex Ratios of Chinese Rural and Unmarried Rural Populations

Age	Sex Ratio of Rural Population	Sex Ratio of Unmarried Rural Population
15–19	105.14	108.91
20–24	102.27	161.97
25–29	103.21	508.91
30–34	108.12	3,119.29
35–39	105.71	5,244.08

Source: Guojia Tongjiju Renkou Tongjisi (Department of Population Statistics, Statistics Bureau), 1990 *China Census Data* 1993.

FACILITATING FACTORS OF MARRIAGE
MIGRATION DYNAMICS

For most Chinese, the common saying *"Shui wang dichu liu; ren wang gaochu zou"* (water flows downward, but people aspire upward) seems more than adequate to explain the motivation of women marriage migrants. Perhaps the self-evident nature of this phenomenon explains why the survey data concerning the motivation of women who migrate for marriage are not very specific. But the compelling desire to use marriage as a means to achieve social mobility is clearly revealed in the survey data. According to Zhang's survey (1994:34), 52.16 percent of the women who migrated to Huaiyin City, Jiangsu did so because of *jiating kunnan* (family difficulties), which implies that they were trying to escape family economic difficulties. In the neighboring province of Zhejiang, at the Hangzhou University Population Institute, there was a similar finding that 51.8 percent of the female marriage migrants surveyed migrated in order to *zhao ge hao duixiang* (to find a better husband). According to Huijing Li, who analyzed some of these data, the term *hao duixiang* for these women refers to the husband's economic conditions (Li 1995).

Economic factors are also critical in the decisions of those men who marry female migrants. The bride price paid for immigrant women is usually significantly less than what is required for a local bride. In Zhejiang, for instance, the bride price for local women has gone up precipitously since 1982. From the engagement of the couple to the wedding party, the bride price is at least 10,000 yuan and might be as high as 100,000 yuan. But female marriage immigrants only ranged from 300 to 3,000 yuan (Xu and Ye 1992).

For a sizable percentage of the men's families, this type of marriage might be the only possibility, as no woman in the local community would be willing to marry into a poor family. According to Zhang's data (1994), the majority of female immigrants married local men who were not particularly well-off: 44.87 percent married into households that are characterized as *yiban* (denoting that they are considered to be average income families in the locality), and 21.16 percent married men who were experiencing very difficult financial circumstances.[12] In comparison with the husbands' families, Zhang (1994) found that 42.8 percent women's natal families were worse off, while 28.2 percent of the women's families enjoyed a comparable standard of living with that of the men they had married, and 28.8 percent of the natal families actually lived at a higher standard of living than the men's families. Most of the women in this last group did not voluntarily participate in the marriage migration, but were victims of traffickers (Zhang 1994:123).

Whether illegal or legal, most marriage immigrants make use of *tong xiang* (people from their indigenous communities) networks to locate a husband in a faraway place. In China today, it is almost inconceivable for an unmarried woman to show up in a distant rural village as a stranger and try to arrange for her own marriage. According to Tian's survey data (1991) of 21,587 female marriage migrants in Zhejiang, only 2.15 percent were impulsive enough to violate the well-established cultural norms and arrive in a new community without any social connections. In stark contrast is the fact that 83.77 percent of the female marriage migrants into Zhejiang in the 1980s utilized family or hometown connections to find a husband in an unfamiliar community. However, men often make their own arrangements and bring or arrange for the new wife to be brought back. In some cases, a man working in a distant locality will find his own wife and bring her back to his hometown. Other times poor men go to remote areas and encourage the parents of a prospective wife to accompany her to the new locality so they can see with their own eyes what type of place she will be living in. According to Zhang, (1994:34), 53.5 percent of the female marriage migrants to Huaiyin City, Jiangsu chose to migrate as a result of these kinds of direct male solicitations. But Tian's study (1991) of a community in a neighboring province revealed a much different pattern, where only 9.8 percent (21,587 female marriage migrants) were brought back by the man.

Another "modern" way for a man to find a wife is to place an advertisement in a magazine or newspaper, a practice that began in Chinese cities with the onset of economic reforms and which slowly gained acceptability in rural communities. Such an advertisement would include information about the man's age, housing situation, height (he should be 1.65 meters), household registration (urban or rural), marriage status (single, divorced, or widowed), and the number and sex of his offspring. According to Zhang's Jiangsu study (1994), 4.92 percent of the female marriage migrants responded positively to this type of advertisement.

The role that the educational level of female marriage migrants plays in this process is quite difficult to determine. Based on Lavely's study (1991) of marriage patterns in a Sichuan village in the Mao era, which found that better-educated women moved into more prosperous villages while lesser-educated women ended up living in poorer areas, it seems likely that education is a major factor in determining or influencing the ability of female migrants in the post-Mao era to gain entry into wealthier localities. While no study to date has shown this to be the case, the information that has been gathered on this issue suggests that some kind of sorting process based on educational criteria does occur.

Unfortunately, we could not locate any comprehensive data on the educational level of these women migrants. There are, however, some national statistics derived from the 1990 Census by Zhuzhuo Li which compare the educational level of female migrants (*qianyi*) as a whole to the total female population. This study reveals that the proportion of the migrant (*qianyi*) women (that is, all qianyi migrant women, including the married migrants) who graduated from junior high, high school, college, and university is higher than is true for the total female population. At the same time, the proportion of female migrants who graduated from primary school and were classified as semiliterate and illiterate was lower than the total female population (Li 1994). However, as most female marriage migrants are rural women, their average educational level should be lower than the total female migrants as a whole.

Some studies of marriage in-migrants to relatively prosperous communities in Zhejiang claim that women migrants are generally better educated than the destination population (Li 1995; Jinling Wang 1992). In these findings, only educated migrants are able to participate in these long-distance migration patterns due to the formidable challenges that need to be met. But Zhang's examination of the educational background of female marriage migrants in Huaiyin city reveals a different profile. According to his survey, the proportion of those women who graduated from primary school or who were semiliterate or illiterate was very high, 76.1 percent. And the female marriage migrants who had attended junior high constituted 21.5 percent, while those who attended high school or above only made up 2.4 percent of the female marriage migrants (Zhang 1994).

The survey data for Tianjin show a fairly substantial gap between the number of school years of the female marriage in-migrants who marry Tianjin residents and local women. It was found that the educational level of in-migrant women who registered their marriages was 8.80 years, much lower than the average level of education for Tianjin city women, which is 11.15 years, or of Tianjin women who are not involved in rural production (*Tianjin feinong*), which is 12.55 years. However, when the educational background of these marriage migrants is only compared with that of women in Tianjin who hold a rural residence permit, the discrepancy is not as glaring—8.80 years as compared to 8.89 years (Tan 1997; see table 10.2 for details).

Clearly more research is needed in order to determine if any definitive conclusions can be drawn on the relationship between educational levels of female marriage migrants and their final destination points. In order to gain a better

Table 10.2. Comparative Analysis of the Educational Level of Female Marriage In-Migrants with Tianjin Women

	Illiterate	Elementary School	Junior High School	High School	College	Post-Graduate	Total
Marriage Migrants	44	346	1,988	243	22	2	2,645
Ratio	1.66%	13.08%	75.16%	9.19%	0.83%	0.08%	100%
Tianjin Farming Women	47	584	7,925	606	22	3	9,187
Ratio	0.51%	6.36%	86.26%	6.60%	0.24%	0.03%	100%
Tianjin Nonagricultural Women	112	473	5,415	12,366	4,814	201	22,382
Ratio	0.50%	2.11%	24.19%	55.25%	21.50%	0.90%	100%
Tianjin City Women	159	1,057	13,340	12,972	4,836	204	32,569
Ratio	0.49%	3.25%	40.96%	39.83%	14.89	0.63%	100%

Source: Tianjin survey data (Tan 1997).

grasp of the relevant issues, it may prove useful to also consider the evidence that exists about the educational levels of temporary labor migrants. According to Anan Shen (1995), the average educational level of female temporary migrants (*liudong*) is rather low, but their literacy rate is rather high. When Shen compared the literacy rate of the *liudong* population with that of Shanghai residents, she found that the proportion of illiterate or semiliterate females in the liudong population in 1993 (14.2 percent) was lower than it was among the Shanghai female residents in 1990 (20.1 percent) (Shen 1995:48). These figures are most likely influenced by differences in the age structure of the two populations, as younger Chinese, including migrants, are more likely to receive a basic education than older people.

Fang's study (1997) reveals that women in-migrants in Jinan, although on average six years younger than male migrants (*qianyi* and *liudong*), have about the same level of education. Given the fact that in China, women on average have two years less education than men, this finding is interesting. Yintao Chen's survey of female *liudong* worker populations in four cities in Guangdong Province—Guangzhou, Dongguan, Zhaoqing, and Shenzhen—found that the average education level among 15- to-29-year-olds in this group was 9.42 years, which is much higher than for the same age group in the total population in 1990 (Y. Chen 1997:39). That means that these female migrant workers attained a much higher level of education than that of the general local population from which they came.

While much of the educational data are intriguing, indicating some of the complexities of the marriage migration process that need further exploration, they also suggest the role that politics has played in shaping the representations of these marriage migrants. That is to say, at least some researchers seem to have chosen to stress the high level of educational attainment of some marriage migrants in order to offset some of the ways in which the experiences of marriage migrants reveal troubling dimensions of the economic reform era. In this and in other ways, the power to represent these marriage migrants is totally in the control of the researchers, who are very much influenced by the political context in which they work.

THE POLITICS OF REPRESENTATION

With female marriage migrants refraining from representing themselves in public discourse, it has been left to social scientists, especially demographers and sociologists, to document their existence and experiences. Accordingly, the unarticulated agendas, assumptions, and apprehensions of the researchers have shaped the subjective construction of these migrants in the scholarly literature. A quick perusal of the various publications reveals that in many respects these marriage migrants constitute a troubling category. For instance, most researchers avoid discussing the links between illegal marriage trafficking and voluntary marriage migrations. Rather, they seem intent on emphasizing the positive aspects of this form of migration and glossing over or ignoring the problematic facets.

An examination of the portrayal of the age structure of marriage migrants provides a good illustration of the politics involved in these representations. All of the studies mention the youthfulness of these female migrants. Zhang (1994:32), in his 1992 Huaiyin City, Jiangsu survey noted that four-fifths of the almost 18 thousand women marriage migrants he surveyed were under 25 years of age, as table 10.3 shows. Similarly, the 1987 migration survey data indicated that a fairly high proportion of these migrants marry at an age less than 20.

According to Jinling Wang's analysis (1992) of the Zhejiang survey of 780 marriage migrants, 7.3 percent were less than 20 years of age. Zheng Guizhen also estimates that 36 percent of the women in the floating population marry below the legal age, including some 15- and 16-year-olds. Yet none of these researchers point out that women below 20 years of age are not legally entitled to marry. Similarly, they are unwilling to interrogate the accuracy of these figures, even though it is well-known that it is relatively easy for people in China to inflate their ages, and even to prevail on local authorities to change legal documents. Thus it is quite likely that the age-structure data collected in these surveys underestimates the percentage of marriage migrants below the legal age of marriage.[13] One obvious reason for this failure to discuss the full ramifications of age issues is that they have a direct bearing on the ability of the government to uphold its population control policies. According to our calculations, the reported rate of early marriages among marriage migrants suggests that fertility rates are higher in the destination areas. It is thus not surprising that at least some officials regard migrant women, particularly marriage migrants, as a potential threat to the population control program (Tan, Li, Bowen, Chen, and Sun 1998).

The power of the researchers to represent the realities of these women migrants could be challenged by the women themselves. However, thus far they have had little to say about their subjective experiences. Not only have they been reluctant to speak out about their difficulties in public forums, but they also go to great lengths to avoid detection. Indeed, even the reported size of this group is suspect as many of these women evade government scrutiny as much as possible. Zhang's case study (1994), for instance, reveals that only 25 percent of marriage migrants register their marriages in Huaiyin City, Jiangsu. Given that much of the female marriage migration data are based on permanent registration figures, the census and sampling surveys only provide a partial indicator of the total

Table 10.3. Age Structure of Women Marriage Migrants in Huaiyin City

Age Groups	Proportion
Under 20	19.52%
20–24	60.78%
25–29	12.78%
30 and over	6.92%

Source: Hesheng Zhang 1994.

female marriage migration in the 1980s. It is possible that the number of female marriage migrants reached 17 million by the early 1990s and most likely has grown significantly larger since then.

These female migrants often seem to provide incomplete and misleading information to researchers. A case in point is the answers that are commonly given about the quality of their marriages, an issue critical to their emotional health. Generally they report that the quality of these marriages is quite good. Zhang (1994:137) reports in Huaiyin that 76.5 percent of the women said that they enjoyed very or fairly good marriages and 18.4 percent said okay (*yiban*), while only 5.1 percent of the women said that their marriages were very bad, and 1.1 percent of this group indicated that they planned to leave almost immediately. Jinling Wang's data from the survey conducted by the Hangzhou University Population Institute obtained similar results (Jingling Wang 1992).

However, it is unlikely that most women are answering this part of the survey in a frank manner. Village studies have shed some light on the problematic aspects of these types of marriages. For instance, Liping Zhang and Ping Fan (1993) found through their conversations with a whole range of people in Lingxian, Shandong, that only around half of the marriages between local men and the female in-migrants were stable. The countless reports of wife battering and female suicides in the rural areas that have been published in both the journalistic and scholarly literature raise some concerns as well. It also seems likely that there is some correlation between marriage migrations and recent reports of high suicide rates among rural women in China. It has been reported that more than half of the suicides in China between 1990 and 1994 were committed by rural women.[14] This is an unusual phenomenon because in most other countries in the world more men than women commit suicide, and more suicides occur in cities than in rural areas.

Regardless of the general problems faced by rural women, it is clear that female marriage migrants have few if any resources at their disposal in their destination localities. Thus, it is not surprising that many of them are less than candid about their personal situations when researchers randomly stop by for an hour to ask a few questions. Marriage in-migrant women in Zhangjiagang were willing to acknowledge their lives were more difficult than had been the case in their home localities, but they were not inclined to provide specifics about the internal dynamics of their family situations (Tan et al. 1998). Rather, they talked with some emotion about the difficulties they faced as outsiders in their new communities. It appears that the discriminating treatment of fellow villagers tends to make them cling to their newfound families. Indeed, many of these female marriage migrants seem to lead fairly solitary existences, refusing to assume jobs in the public domain (Tan et al. 1998). The relatively hostile environment coupled with the lack of nearby relatives means that the main source of emotional and economic support for these women is their husbands' families. Thus, it is understandable why many of these marriage migrants are reluctant to offend their husbands or mothers-in-law by revealing problematic aspects of family dynamics.

CONCLUDING REMARKS

The dynamics of the economic reform era have not only given rise to the emergence of a flexible workforce, but also to a flexible marriage force. That is to say, women are now willing to travel hundreds or even thousands of miles in order to respond to the ever-expanding marriage markets that have emerged in the past twenty years. Although much remains to be known about these migrations, from the available data and case studies it is clear that rural women generally enter into these marriage migrations in order to improve their economic well-being. In so doing, they are treating the selection of a husband as a type of market activity in which they are using demographic advantage to maximize their economic benefits. Unfortunately, we know little about the quality of these marriages. While it has been argued that women's participation in these marriage migrations constitutes a type of female agency, it seems unlikely that their actions are contributing to the creation of more egalitarian marriages. By relying on their roles as wives and mothers to effect this shift from the poorer to the richer regions of China, they are in fact tending to reinforce male power within marriage relationships. Without the support of their natal familial networks that can be tapped to combat abuse or to provide emotional support in times of crisis, these women are less able to assert their own rights in the context of paternal power. Not only are these migrant women more vulnerable to verbal and physical abuse, but it seems quite possible that they also can easily suffer from feelings of isolation and depression.

The expansion of this marriage market in the economic reform era has been strongly influenced by the entry of large numbers of rural women into lucrative employment as factory workers in the special economic zones, as nannies in large urban areas, and as prostitutes. The demographic imbalances and the resulting higher bride prices can be compensated for in richer communities by accepting women from faraway places as brides. Men living in poorer regions of the country are subjected to a marriage squeeze and many are unlikely to find a spouse. It seems inevitable that this situation will intensify in the coming decades with the increasing gender ratio imbalances that exist among children today.

NOTES

The authors would like to thank the editor of this volume and Ching Kwan Lee for their insightful critiques of earlier drafts of this chapter. Our revisions were also aided by the comments and criticisms of participants of three conferences: The International Conference on Gender and Development, at the Chinese University of Hong Kong, November 27–29, 1997; Re-evaluation and Repositioning: Gender, Women's Agency, and Development in China at the Threshold of the New Century, at Tufts University and Harvard University, March 10–11, 1999; and the Modern China Seminar at Columbia University, March 16, 2000.

1. For examples of Western accounts of these Chinese news reports, see Christopher S. Wren (1983); Sheryl WuDunn (1991); Paul Watson (1995); and Seth Faison (1995).
2. In 1997, when we first presented our findings on this topic at the International

Conference on Gender and Development in Hong Kong, no other Western studies existed on this topic. Since then two relevant studies have been published: C. Cindy Fan and Youqin Huang (1998) and Delia Davin (1999).

3. The 1987 One Percent Sample Survey covered the five year period 1982–1987 and was the first survey to yield systematic marriage migration data. The 1990 census compiled data for the years 1985 to 1990 (Guojia Tongjiju Renkou Tongjisi 1993; Quanguo Renkou Chouyang Diaocha Bangougshi 1987).

4. The interviews that we conducted in 1996 with young rural Shandong women working in Tanggu factories were useful in helping us explore the issues related to one cluster of women who ultimately became marriage migrants. That is to say, a small percentage of temporary women workers who migrate to the special economic zones are successful in finding a local man or a male worker from another region of China to marry, and thus translate their status as a migrant industrial worker into that of a marriage migrant. We have also included some of the findings from a study conducted by Lin Tan et al. (1998).

5. For a discussion of the floating population in the economic reform era, see Dorothy Solinger (1999).

6. To be more precise, marriage migrants composed 21.64 percent of the total female intraprovincial migrants and 29.90 percent of the female inter-provincial migrants.

7. An anthropological study of Linxian by Nancy Jervis (1987) has shown that more men were willing to undertake virilocal marriages in the late Mao and early economic reform eras than scholars like Johnson have supposed, but even still the percentages are not high.

8. A slightly different figure has been given by Hua Tian, who found that women in the southwest of China normally married within a 25-kilometer radius. According to his figures, 85 percent of the population in rural communities married within their county and 57 percent married within the same township. Thirty percent married within the same village (Tian 1991:41).

9. Political factors refers to how a person's class status was an important criteria for marriage. In the countryside, it was very difficult after the land reform for the male children of people who had been labeled as landlords to marry. Male children from rich peasant households also experienced difficulty in marrying.

10. These figures are in a letter from a local cadre in Ten Mile Inn (Shilidian) to Isabel Crook, a teacher at Beijing Foreign Languages University, who has maintained close ties with this village ever since she conducted research on communist economic initiatives there in the 1950s.

11. This information was supplied by Xiaojiang Li and Jun Liang, December 1996.

12. Zhang (1994) also showed that 16.10 percent of the women married men who were fairly well-off financially and another 10.35 percent married into well-off households.

13. The most frequent occasions when false information is provided about age are to gain entrance to a school, to comply with legal age requirements for marriage, and to gain employment.

14. A study by Chinese doctors at the Clinical Epidemic Disease Research Office of Huilonguan Hospital revealed that between 1990 and 1994, 324,711 Chinese committed suicide, of whom 173,230 were rural women. Owen Brown, "China Ranks Third in Suicides by Women," Nationwide General News, Overseas News, September 20, 1998.

Chapter 11

Women's Work in International Migration

Janet W. Salaff

INTRODUCTION: FAMILY EMIGRATION AS GENDERED WORK

The explosion of international migration has amazed many observers. Migration streams draw from all social groups; women and men, married and single, investors, the middle class with degrees, and laborers move within the third world and from the third world to the first and back again (Ong, Chang, and Chew 1995). In 1993, 15 million of the estimated 100 million migrants were within Asia and the Middle East (Low 1995). To bring this home, in 1994 four Asian nations (China, the Philippines, Vietnam, and India) accounted for 42.7 percent of the 430,441 immigrants from the top ten countries sending to the United States (Suro 1994). How can families move so readily, when it takes so much work? Some think first of wars, depressions, and other large shifts that push people out of a country. For others, migration results from the calculations that men make to get jobs after deliberating their economic interests. But the view of migration as either a mass movement rooted in tragedy or as an individual decision grounded in market opportunity cannot explain the many moves people make that are not "rational" at all (Portes and Borocz 1989). I believe that migration is embedded in social structure, and that common place activities help explain such near universal movement. In this chapter, I look at the work Hong Kong women do every day to spur the long distance projects of their families across the seas.

I look at migration "work" as gendered. Just as women do a lot of unpaid family, community, and societal work, so, too, the labor that underlies migration work is both gendered and unpaid (Boyd 1989; Daniels 1987; DeVault 1991; Massey 1990; Pedraza 1991). I will argue that Hong Kong women often subordinate their own interests to the care of their families, thereby making their migration work largely unpaid and unnoticed. The embeddedness of migration in social relations also suggests that the family's social class position casts the range, meaning, and content of migration work. Women negotiate to get resources for the family, and these are shaped by their social class position. I thus view women's migration work as a crucial exchange that draws on the same kinds of resources that their other work does.

In the pages that follow I first describe the global issues that promote the migration of women and their families. I recount a range of unpaid migration labor that Hong Kong women do, grouped as economic exchanges and support-ing kin. I point out differences by social class. That women who negotiate these exchanges differ by their class-based access to resources is seen in case studies of families in three main class groups.

Why Do Hong Kong Families Leave?

Hong Kong is a key migration area, yet neither formal migration data nor empir-ical studies reveal women's roles in family migration. World economic develop-ments, Western manpower and immigration policies, political events, and international Chinese networks change the specifics of work in different periods. Women's migration work changes with the contours of history.

After the colonial order linked Hong Kong to the West in the early part of the century, South Chinese working-class men often sought work abroad (Glenn 1983; Liu 1992). Women, unable to join their husbands, had to maintain the family's reproductive center at home. After World War I, many rural New Terri-tories, working-class, Hong Kong men entered England as part of the Common-wealth (Watson 1975). When England cut off the flow, migrants followed Commonwealth ties into Canada and Australia. As nation-state policies relaxed to allow family members to join these early emigrants and do important repro-ductive work, women joined family class migration.

Migration, long a way of life for Hong Kong families of all backgrounds, has increased at the century's end (Lai 1975; Ng and Cheng 1994; Sinn 1995a, 1995b; Skeldon 1994a). Broader forces that propel these moves start with the global political economy, with its elaborate multidirectional movements of capi-tal, goods, knowledge, and jobs that create cross-national social spaces (Harvey 1989). Commodity chains link Pacific Rim countries to firms in the West (Gereffi 1998). Transnational corporations transfer employees across the seas to Asia and back, while local professionals also seek independent business opportunities in the West (Bartlett and Goshal 1989; Fielding 1993; Salt 1988). Students and employ-ees follow these chains abroad, and women are part of these chains. Local, inner-Asian migration systems involve Hong Kong sojourners. Hong Kong families have kin, jobs, and investments in South China, its wider socioeconomic region.

Global reasons for international migration start with Western workforce poli-cies. American firms hire low-cost, nonunionized labor, prompting working class, often illegal migration (Kwong 1997). At the same time, states court human cap-ital, thereby contributing to middle-class migration (Ishi 1987; Richmond 1992). Familiarity with conditions abroad also contributes to migration. Global-ization of the media, glossy images of Western life, and mass-produced consumer goods also stimulate international moves (Anderson 1983). As migration gained momentum, those who knew other emigrants like themselves followed suit if they thought they could better their living conditions in another land (Shu and Hawthorne 1996; Yoon 1993). Failing to do so, some remigrated to earn an income back home. These remigrants are mainly middle-class men who keep their jobs in Hong Kong, while the wives and children build a life in the new country. They are called "astronauts" because they fly frequently to mesh the families on both sides of the seas. Women have special roles to play in astronaut families, for they remain behind to do the family work.

Global institutions ease people's moves, and colonial Hong Kong's schools have long reproduced Western educational systems. Young people continue their studies abroad. Many travel for short-term training or business and perceive knowledge as international. As a result, middle-class professionals can access collegial networks in different lands.

A study of Chinese migrants cannot overlook political factors. Asian women as well as men, especially those of the middle class, lean toward Western democracies. The June 4, 1989, Tianenmen Square massacre prompted a swell of applicants, many of whom applied to leave prior to Hong Kong's reversion to China in July 1997. The political heritage of middle-class Hong Kong families made most of them inclined to emigrate. Parents, dispossessed of property, taught their children never to forget their past suffering (Salaff, Wong, and Fung 1997). On the eve of Hong Kong's transition to China, Great Britain and other countries eased the entry of those in sensitive jobs, opportunities that were particularly attractive to female and male civil servants. Yearning for political security, women as well as men saw emigration as a strategy to confront Hong Kong's uncertain future.

There are more than global issues at play. Family decision making also contributes to migration. Many Chinese families are run as economic units that sometimes place members abroad. How they do so depends on their resources. While working-class families use family labor to run family enterprises abroad, the Chinese elite more widely spreads its capital risks in a number of countries (Chan 1996; Lever-Tracy, Ip, and Tracy 1996; Liu 1992; Mitchell 1995; Thrift and Olds 1996; Wong and Salaff 1998). Like their brothers, daughters can also shore up family fortunes and forge alliances abroad. Finally, social networks link people in many locales. Since people like those we study get help from others to go abroad, international migration no longer involves the immense, once and for all uprooting characteristic of earlier eras (Massey, Goldring, and Durand 1994; Salaff, Fong, and Wong 1998; Tilly 1990). Nevertheless, women work hard to maintain these migration networks. Although migration work takes on different meanings and activities for each class group, women work hard to secure their family's well-being before and after migration.

GENDERED MIGRATION WORK

Women were half of the Hong Kong immigrants to Canada from 1986 to 1993. They were not only migrants themselves; they also played specific migration roles. For instance, while nearly half these new female Canadians immigrated as "spouse," hardly any men did (Man 1996:70, 72). Although women less often assume leadership in their family emigration project, they are enablers. They are backstage more than centerstage workers that maintain the reproductive household in the wider society. Family migration adds new tasks to their formal paid work and to their reproductive and family maintenance activities. I group these forms of labor generally as exchanges related to economics and to kinship work. It is important to stress variations in women's roles. Women's gendered work reflects their family heritage, and their migration labor also varies with social class resources.

Gendered Work Related to Economic Exchanges

Distinct assets available to emigrant families of different social classes shape women's work. Women from different sectors not only have very different amounts of money and contacts they can draw on to migrate; their resources also come from distinctive realms. Whereas the working class rely on kin, the middle class with considerable education and money can draw on their cultural capital (Wong and Salaff 1998).

Jobs. Women and men plan careers to ease migration. They may take particular jobs that earn immigration points or are likely to succeed in the new country. Both husbands and wives may undergo extra training for career transition. However, women, whose careers are often contingent on family outcomes, must generally be the more flexible spouse (Bonney and Love 1991; Partridge 1996). Their work patterns differ. Married women are one-third less likely to work than unmarried women in the same age group; and some are unpaid working partners in their husband's businesses (Chiu 1998; William K. M. Lee 1996:283). This contingency is in part due to women's lower earnings: they averaged 85 percent of men's wages in Hong Kong in 1991. As the designated flexible partner, women do much work linking family to society. Some quit their jobs when they migrate. In a contemporary variant of the split household, the astronaut's wife plays an extreme role that can only occur because she is willing to flexibly rearrange her personal schedule to do more family work. This family work is part of women's reproductive role, albeit unpaid. I will refer to these connecting activities as "linking work." It reinforces gender positions when women give up further education and careers.

Purchases. Families that plan to leave often have to save money for migration (Grasmuck and Pessar 1991; Hondagneu-Sotelo 1994). They may defer upgrading their homes or postpone buying major consumer purchases. Since the home is seen as the woman's work place, skimping on consumer purchases affects the quality of her daily environment.

Kin-Related Gendered Work

Kin responsibilities. Hong Kong Chinese women and men keenly feel their kin responsibilities, and both get and give considerable help. This help is crucial for daily survival for the working class and for a more flexible and comfortable life for the middle class. The Hong Kong Indicators of Social Development surveys find that people seeking help for family needs turn more to kin than to friends, neighbors, or the market. In the six months prior to the 1993 survey, the proportion that got help from kin ranged from 42 percent for child care to 33 percent for financial problems; 27 percent sought the help of kin when someone was sick. Women get and give more help to kin than men give. Men gave kin money, women gave time (M. K. Lee 1992, 1995:15, 17). Apart from material exchanges, families also maintain kin connections as emotional resources. Although these studies do not explore class differences, I believe that resource exchanges are patterned by class.

Maintaining social networks. Women also do connecting work to build social support networks of a wide variety. Reciprocity is expected in women's family support work (Antonucci 1990; Antonucci and Akiyama 1987; Beutel and Marini 1995; Lye 1996). To get the help they and their families need at work and at home, migrants move close to kin and friends and keep up ties on both sides of the ocean. Maintaining these relations takes work, which many consider women's work. While men actively build employment links, women connect the different kin strands on both sides of the family. They keep the flow of goods, advice, support, and other intergenerational exchanges that are essential migration structures going (Basch, Schiller, and Szanton-Blanc 1994; Boyd 1989; Massey 1990; Pedraza 1991).

At home in Hong Kong, women organize informal gatherings, lunches, phone chats, and other social occasions that nurture networks. They keep up with friends or colleagues that have migrated and returned to town. Those that intend to emigrate often devote family vacations to familiarize their families with life abroad. Some make initial forays abroad during the application process.

Emigration increases stress and threatens kinship unity, and migrant women do more work on an emotional level. Family needs are harder to meet in a new setting, and many emigrant men find themselves without work. It is women who give emotional support when their family or husbands face strains (Luxton 1983; Menaghan 1991).

This social meshing continues when immigrants cross borders. To maintain the fabric of social life abroad, some go where their kin are. Yet even a settlement of several kin cannot duplicate the complex web of support that the full family and friends left behind once gave. Women now take on tasks that other family members had once undertaken for them. They also continue from afar to help those left behind and find substitutes for the help they had once given to kin. Migrant women often return home creating multiple cross-national links (Hondagneu-Sotelo 1994). At the same time, women are often reluctant to emigrate due to the needs of their kin at home. Thus, responsibilities to kin not only propel families abroad, but may also tie women to their home.

Child rearing. Migration affects family life at its most intimate level. Some may plan how many children to have and when to have them to ease the impending trans-Pacific move. Migration also affects how parents raise children. Hong Kong mothers help their children with what is reputed to be the heaviest homework load in Asia. Since most Hong Kong women work, and child care services are rudimentary, they get help from their kin or servants (Constable 1997). Migrants must take over this work and more. To ensure they will fit into the new world, women educate their children for change, raising them to fit into both the new world and the one left behind. Immigrant children try new sports and other social activities and encounter new ways of thinking about the world. Transmitting ethnic culture is also part of women's work. Mothers try to continue the children's local language as well as training them in a foreign tongue. Although all families share in an ethnic culture, there are social class variants. Thus, I anticipate class differences in how emigrant women adjust their child rearing and reproductive work.

Kinscripts. Different voices, loud and small, can be heard in family decisions. Researchers debate the degree to which Hong Kong women align their claims with the family's. Will Hong Kong women hold out for their own interests, or subordinate them to their husbands'? May Partridge (1996) finds that the views of middle-class Hong Kong women toward a wide variety of issues may be subordinated to, negotiated with, or given precedence over those of their partners, children and wider kin groups. I explore this in migration work; I look to see in which households husbands and wives work together in pursuit of emigration goals. What happens when wives disagree with the value their husbands set on emigration?

There is one important reason for a lack of unity in family views. Different demands on a couple to meet their respective families' goals easily give rise to conflicts, since the two partners come from different kin lines. Carol Stack and Linda Burton (1994) use the term *kinscripts* to refer to the transmission of family goals across generations. In migration, a spouse's kinscript demanding displacement can conflict with their partner's kinscript that demands stability. For instance, the family of one spouse may have long aimed to emigrate, whereas the other spouse's family has not. If one partner honors his kinscript, he prevents the other from honoring hers. Women's dual gender roles of caring for spouse and seniors can collide. This is not to say that women will refuse to emigrate. In such a collective family culture, women often acquiesce to keep the family united. In emigration, too, they will join the flow.

The nature of kinscripts seems to be patterned by class. Working-class parents greatly desire a united hearth and a united family economy and urge their children to emigrate if they can reunite abroad. Their kinscript is economic. Middle-class families, however, commonly press children to regain the class standing lost in the 1949 Chinese Revolution. Their kinscript is political (Salaff et al. 1997).

In sum, we find that although women do migration work that we can call gendered, their social class resources and social exchanges nuance what they do. These give rise to class-based alternatives. Although they honor them, women with economic resources depend less on kinship exchanges, whereas those with little money are more dependent on kin. I thus explore how social class and kinship interact to affect the nature of women's migration work. The cases that follow suggest how women's diverse migration work is differently distributed among those of different classes.

THE SAMPLE

We learned how Hong Kong women help their families migrate from a two-phase study our team conducted in Hong Kong, from 1991 through 1997. In 1991, we surveyed 1,552 families on the topic of "Emigration from Hong Kong" to understand emigration plans as Hong Kong reverted to China. We drew the sample randomly by street address, to include the broad range of emigrant statuses. As all the women in this study come from Hong Kong Chinese backgrounds, there are no ethnic differences. But the questions did uncover diverse demographic, socioeconomic, and attitudinal patterns associated with migration (Wong 1995). Few working-class and many middle-class families planned to leave before 1997, although in each sector families with more kin abroad were also more likely to hope to emigrate. There were social class differences as well in the political and civic attitudes associated with the decision to emigrate.

These findings argued for an understanding of migration as embedded in social structure. However, the short interview could not detail the full range of a household's kin or friends, let alone more elaborate questions about the social organization of migration. Least of all could we discern the meaning of migration to women. To learn about the every day activities that people undertake to migrate, we needed a lengthier and more sensitive format, and we chose qualitative interviews and naturalistic fieldwork.

My colleagues and I reinterviewed 30 representative families from three main social classes chosen from the survey list. By social class, we refer mainly to occupational groups. We included 10 working, 10 lower-middle-class, and 10 upper-middle-class families. Unfortunately, the upper class survey respondents, who did not respond to our follow up requests, were not included. We spoke with emigrants and nonemigrants in each class to understand the types of resources used when they anticipated leaving Hong Kong. To do so, we oversampled those in the working-class that applied.

The designation *emigrant* refers to applicants, whether or not they got accepted, remained in, left or returned to Hong Kong. I have chosen this broad definition in the belief that women figure in all migration plans, whether they succeed or fail. Of the 30 families studied intensively, 16 had applied and 14 had not applied to emigrate: there were 4 working-class, 4 lower-middle-class, and 8 upper-middle-class emigrant families. Success varied by class. The 4 working-class couples that applied to emigrate were all rejected, but all 8 middle class applicants had gotten their papers.

Twenty-eight of the 30 respondents were married, and we thus count 58 adults, aged from 28 to 78, in our sample. Our research team tried to talk to most yearly from 1992 through 1997 on a range of topics. In some cases, we joined their social activities. We placed the experiences of these families in their wider kinship and friendship circles because we were interested in how people take kin and friends into account when they plan to leave. These households are not connected to each other, and each described their personal kin and friendship communities. They recounted the circumstances of the applications of their emigration and how they settled in. Through this "naturalistic" means, we learned about gendered roles in migration.

We used this detail in several ways. First, we got a clearer contextual and comparative picture of our respondents' kin structure. Next, information on respondents' siblings, parents, and children that have emigrated broadened our understanding not only of how some leave, but also how they settled. The 58 spouses enumerated 400 emigrant and nonemigrant siblings, and told of the circumstances of their applications. These are the basis of what I term "emigration chains." To explain briefly, I refer to the emigrants whose kin paved the way for them to leave as "kin-dependent emigrants." In contrast, those who followed friendship or other non-kin links to apply are "kin-independent emigrants." We also can learn about the gender of the person who started a chain, having sponsored or invited others to leave. By calculating the numbers of women and men who follow emigrant kin in each social group, we have an indicator of how migration chains are organized around gender roles. Such a rough measure of social networks that lead abroad helps us learn if women lead emigration chains as much as men do.

Our transcribed interviews amount to 100 megabytes of text, which we entered on a relational database. For this paper, I searched for themes on what women do in the course of their families' emigration forays abroad.

CASE STUDIES: THE CLASS BASE
OF GENDERED MIGRATION WORK

Typical cases of real families we talked with illustrate how different economic and social resources shape women's emigration work.

Gendered Migration Work of the Working Class

Kin are important in the daily life of the working class. Their social structural position is integrated with their families in many areas, and maintaining ties with kin entails a lot of work for women. As their main focus in social reproductive work, kin responsibilities also shape working-class women's migration activities and views. This close interdependence with kin is seen in the economic and kinship exchanges of migrant people.

Work related to economic exchanges. Working-class families, whose money and human capital are limited, rely on kin for economic help. Migration decisions also revolve around jobs kin can give. Learning how these couples find jobs opens a window onto the large place kin hold in the everyday lives of the working-class. Husbands and wives do manual labor, much of it arduous. They have few credentials or capital and speak little English. They have mainly their labor power to exchange. Personal ties expand scarce resources and a lot of work is put into their maintenance. Since many people qualify for jobs like theirs, they often find work through an inner track to which kin and close contacts provide access. That many pool labor and capital, get jobs from, and work side by side with kin underlines the importance of mutual help. Nearly all working-class adults in our study had gotten jobs through kin. Few enjoyed "careers" or the regular internal progression through a bureaucracy. Instead, they followed dense networks to enter and leave jobs. All had initially worried that they could not find jobs were they to emigrate and leave behind their kin networks.

The men in our study worked at such occupations as ivory carver, construction laborer, garment cutter, cook, taxi or bus driver, butcher, bank "office boy," and prison guard. Some, whose parents before them had tiny sideline family firms, were keen on starting businesses. Three ran petty enterprises and drew on their family members' labor. One petty proprietor with skills, tools, and a local reputation in car repair did not even own his shack. He inherited his firm from his father, who still lends a hand. When his wife lost her job driving a school bus, she became his unpaid helper.

The women had all worked, and six still earned money, most in the service sector in truck and van driving, part-time restaurant work as clerks in a dry cleaning as store and supermarket, and in baby-sitting. Four still cared for youngsters at home; their work did not stop with paid labor. The mainly male-run, petty enterprises of the poor draw on the unpaid labor of women, and kin often called upon them to help in their small enterprises (Chiu 1998). No wives owned their own firms.

Women's interaction with kin also shaped their major household purchases, especially housing. When the homes they shared with parents or kin grew too crowded, most of the working-class families rented public housing flats. Only half the Hong Kong populace can afford to buy even the average 500-square-foot apartment on their own. Two of the three that had bought homes shared costs and a roof with kin. When their kin emigrated, they could enlarge their space by gaining access to their rooms. When their kin returned, they relinquished this space. In many ways, the larger migration plans of their kin group affected their housing plans.

Emigration plans did not affect most consumer goods purchases. These working-class families bought televisions, VCRs, and computers for their young children. Nearly all had refrigerators and semiautomatic washing machines to help women do their chores. They considered these household items basics and were not likely to reduce expenditures on them to save money to migrate. They spent little on home renovation; however, those in construction did their own interior design work with the help of kin and friends.

Kin-related gendered work. Working-class women give services and care to their elders. They give little more than "red packets" of small sums of money to their elders on holidays. Few we met currently lived with their elders, although many had. Hong Kong has been redeveloped often, and only five of the 20 husbands and wives lived where they grew up. While they provided little monetary support, they gave other help, such as caring for the ill elderly, and visited kin often. Children had grown up under their grandparents' care. Transportation is good, and they drop in often. (Visiting cements caretaking and women's feeling that they can count on kin for a host of things.) Potential migrants tried to meet their kin responsibilities, and concern over depriving the elderly of this care and sociability deterred emigration.

Their kin help with many household activities. They especially depend on kinswomen for help in child care, and realize that their reproductive labor would increase should they emigrate. The most senior woman in our sample had seven children; her own mother-in-law had helped her in the past, and she now cared for an infant granddaughter. And while younger mothers have from one to three, they still get help from relatives. Six mothers got help from kin when their children were young. Four have themselves cared for nieces, nephews, and grandchildren. Although money changes hands, they define child care as helping kin, not paid work. They also see child care as a suitable way to earn money for people like themselves. In contrast, friends did little baby-sitting, and only three mothers turned to schools for day care; these latter cases, too, were special: a sheltered workshop for a handicapped lad, tutorial classes for children.

Few knew how to shape their children's education, whether at home or abroad. If their children were doing poorly, they paid for tutoring classes and encouraged them to do their homework. But the women were poorly educated and it was not part of their job to arrange extra courses of study or make efforts to change the school of the child. They mainly depended on the routines of the Education Department. Those with prospects of going abroad did not change their education work with their children, as they did not know what the foreign school system demanded in detail. Relatives abroad mainly told them that the system was easy for children and parents. For instance, those who planned to go to Canada heard that the neighborhood they lived in determined their children's school, and they did not have to take admission tests. Women's preparatory migration work in the area of education was not extensive. Those who did go abroad sought out the city's heritage language programs. Few women could themselves effectively teach characters to their young charges.

Some decided against emigrating because their children still needed care from their kin. For instance, a couple whose only child has always lived with kin had applied to emigrate to Singapore, but eventually dropped the application because they had no kin there to find them jobs or care for their daughter. Some were part of larger family unions and had a mother or mother-in-law to help them with their children. Where they could not, women's work increased considerably, usually requiring them to leave their jobs. If they were in Hong Kong, they would have had access to greater kin help.

With kin as the central focus of their daily social interaction, the women tried hard to fulfill their kinscripts. They took kin into account in deciding whether to leave or remain in Hong Kong. Three of the four working-class applicants applied in order to join siblings abroad. However, siblings do not meet the official immigration requirements for family unification, and they were turned down. None had enough personal resources to pass as independent professionals on their own. Thus, enmeshed in family and wider kin circles, they take kin into account in migration plans (Salaff et al. 1998). They cannot leave without kin support. The majority that did not apply to emigrate have few close kin abroad, and if kin remain in Hong Kong or China, couples are unlikely to migrate.

As kin-dependent emigrants, the working-class respondents form "emigration chains" of several family members on a single application or apply under the same narrow conditions. Siblings emigrate together. Husbands and wives pool scarce resources to apply and can usually only apply to one place. To get kin support, it is advantageous for them to apply only to one place—the country where their kin live. The disadvantage lies in having few alternative options should this application fall through (see the case example below).

Working-class women are as likely to apply as men. However, their sponsors are most likely to be male. Only 30 percent of the respondents and their brothers and sisters applied through kinswomen, while 70 percent applied as part of male-led chains. At the same time, these densely interwoven emigration interdependencies rely on "women's work." As spouses and mothers, women in these accounts added their work to the family emigration forays that relied on kin.

Case example. We met a couple whose husband came from a family of four sons in a small working-class butcher business catering to traditional eateries. Gawai, a truck driver, delivered meat for the shop. The parents made considerable demands on the couple, who worked long hours for a low wage. The husband recalls that he had to complete the deliveries for the store even on the morning of his wedding.

Gawai and her 11 siblings had worked together on the family pig farm and turned to each other for help to move to a new house, raise money for a business, or house among other help. Her Hong Kong jobs in the market had all come from maternal kin plus local networks. One child had lived with an aunt during the week, while the couple worked in the family shop. They kept up their visits. At times, I joined the kin group for family dinners held in a small restaurant that spilled into the narrow street, where they commandeered two large tables for two dozen kin.

The husband's younger brother had attended high school in Toronto and sponsored their parents. The parents sold the meat store and with the profits opened a small hardware store in Toronto that specialized in interior renovation for new Chinese immigrants. Initially Gawai and her husband intended to join them, thereby reuniting the brothers and parents in Toronto. The husband's parents hoped Gawai, their daughter-in-law, would do their housework in Canada while the son worked in the store. The son was keen to try this chance at a new career, and in preparation, he studied home renovation in Hong Kong from catalogs and books. Their emigration plans unfolded a bit haphazardly, however.

In contrast to her spouse, Gawai was reluctant to emigrate. Although her brother, of whom she was fond, had moved to Toronto to join his wife's kin, Gawai

was loath to leave her female kin in Hong Kong. Unable to speak English, she thought she could not easily find a job abroad. Further, she thought their living standard in Hong Kong was all right. "If you have a day's life, just live it. It's not bad in Hong Kong. If you can work and can eat, let it be." Worst of all, without a job that paid enough to free herself from their demands, she anticipated being on call for her needy in-laws in Canada. Although she was not keen on it, she appeared to have had no say in the emigration project of her husband and his kin.

During this period, Gawai kept up her kin work. The elderly parents lived in Canada for only six months of each year, while they were qualifying for citizenship. This was Gawai's respite. Then she resumed care for them during their winter sojourns in Hong Kong. After becoming Canadian citizens, the senior parents returned permanently to Hong Kong. Needing our Gawai to care for them in Hong Kong, they withdrew sponsorship for the couple to emigrate.

The move abroad could not have happened without the input of the wife, Gawai, whose farm background and marriage experience prepared her well to maintain kinship circles. Gawai worked hard to accomplish a project for which she had faint enthusiasm. She met the needs of her husband's parents, and her emigration work included helping her husband cope with the demands of his parents. If they had required that the family emigrate, she had to concur despite her objections. She would have continued to give them emotional support and daily care in Canada as she had done in Hong Kong. Although her husband retrained for the new job abroad, Gawai anticipated losing a chance to find work altogether.

She did not try to prepare her children for life abroad and gave no thought to their Canadian education—"The government assigns them to a school, you don't have to work so hard to enroll our children like you do in Hong Kong"—nor were their leisure activities part of their training. The family visited Toronto while the husband was making his application, and on another occasion the children visited their grandparents in Toronto. This was seen as a visit, but it was also a form of socialization for the move.

Kin become particularly important for working-class migration because of their importance in general. Women and men both powered emigration forays, but they do different emigration work. This kin dependence sets the stage for women's emigration work, since women are specialists in working with kin. However, there are costs. Whereas in Hong Kong access to support of her own natal kin buttresses the wife's standing, in Canada, she expected to be at the beck and call of the elders and other in-laws. In this case, because the social organization of emigration is mainly through kin work, the woman's dependence on others is reinforced.

Gendered Migration Work of the Lower Middle Class

The lower middle class pride themselves on their independence from kin. Although most have a solid education, many studied part-time in polytechnics, which gave them diplomas rather than recognized degrees. With careers as white collar employees, low-level bureaucrats and wage earners, their livelihood is generally stable, and they can expect pensions. However, two immigrant men from China with degrees that are not recognized in Hong Kong lost their jobs over the time we knew them, plummeting into working-class jobs; and while the rest were not doing poorly, they were on the margin with little funds or productive property. Because of their limited earnings, the lower middle class are referred to as the "sandwich class," squeezed between the working class, which qualifies for a subsidized social safety net, and the better off, who can afford to pay for what they need. While they do engage in social exchanges with kin, they define these mainly as expressive, ancillary to building their careers. The migration work of women is more to build cultural capital and collegial contacts than to find ways to continue relations with kin.

Work related to economic exchanges. The men worked at such occupations as technician, civil servant, clerk, teacher, and police officer. Their wives held such positions as civil servant, teacher, nurse, police clerk, factory seamstress, and hotel cleaner. There were no self-employed among them. Friends were as likely to help them get jobs as kin, but they found more of their jobs by responding to ads or taking civil service exams.

Nevertheless, they discussed and offered job advice and even held similar positions to those of their siblings. Pairs of siblings were technicians, civil servants, and nurses. These kin did not inherit the jobs from each other, but shared an understanding of the right kind of job and the limited alternatives for people in their position when they entered the job market.

Kin-related gendered work. The lower-middle-class respondents had mainly grown up in poverty and recalled mutual sacrifices warmly. They helped support their younger brothers and sisters and gave mutual support. Brothers and sisters pooled resources for life events. Older siblings lent younger siblings money for tuition, paid off a sibling's debt or lent money to start a business. A technician concocted joint investment plans with his brothers for emigration purposes. To get housing, three couples got help from both sides of the family for down payments in apartments. When they later sell the apartments, they are likely to sell them at reduced cost to younger siblings, adding in furniture and appliances. Siblings jointly bought or repaired ancestral homes in China for their parents' retirement. They help fund a sister's wedding. Although only one of our couples lived with parents, employed siblings joined to support elderly parents and dependent siblings. While six couples had child-care support from kin for periods of time, they also got child-care help from friends and servants; most children had several different caregivers at different times. Apart from monetary exchanges, our respondents also spent their leisure time with kin. Their kinship improved their families' livelihood, gave moral support, and opened wider flows of information. Nevertheless, the lower middle class maintains a self-image as independent actors; they downplay the material importance of kin.

Credentials and information are key to lower-middle-class migration applications. Their exit depends on qualifications achieved through study and legitimated by diplomas. Women with certain designated careers can contribute to migration "points." Four of the ten lower-middle-class couples applied to seven countries, under the categories of independents, business applicants, and the right of abode. None formally applied to emigrate as kin dependents. Two were accepted, and one has since emigrated. Nevertheless, lower-middle-class families who have worked their way up and got their skills on the job cannot easily move where they lack the necessary licenses or certificates to find work. Likewise, those with a local customer base fear they cannot find clients abroad. Nurses and other semiprofessionals would have to compete in the North American market, where ethnic politics can create hardship.

The 26 lower-middle-class emigrants and their siblings took part in 23 separate chains. More applied on their own than with kin. This near one to one ratio of emigrants and emigrant networks reveals their independence from kin in the application process. For those who applied to emigrate through kin, 67 percent formally applied through men's networks. In the end, however, few had the financial resources to succeed, and only one left Hong Kong.

Nevertheless, kin do figure in emigration plans. Compared with those that had never applied, families that applied to emigrate have markedly more siblings who were also emigrants. Four of the seven applications were to places where kin lived. People seek to move near kin because they trust kin to give them reliable information. Having kin abroad means enjoying their support, but not necessarily getting jobs from them. To migrate, women must still keep up family ties.

Case example. A telecommunications technician and his spouse, a former nurse, were bent on emigrating. The well-to-do parents on both sides had lost property and were politically attacked in Mainland China. As the wife, Waikei, explained, "The Communist government regarded him [the wife's father] as a capitalist and sent him to labor in the countryside. Father was treated worse than a beggar and our family suffered a lot. Once China condemned someone as guilty, that person cannot have a new life again. How could Hong Kong lie under such a government?"

This lower-middle-class couple had both come from families that set emigration as a goal. They took over this kinscript and sought to emigrate before Hong Kong's reversion to China. Their brothers and sisters, with the same family background and sentiments, likewise applied to emigrate. The couple worked in concert to organize their migration project. Waikei, whose mother had emigrated to Canada, applied to join her when she was still single so she could care for her better, while the husband applied with his brothers for visas to New Zealand and Australia. Both applications were rejected. Then, the Canadian consulate recommended that since nurses had immigration priority, the wife return to school to requalify. In the end, Waikei's upgraded credentials made her eligible for a job in a Hong Kong hospital, and she was satisfied with a nursing job as an end in itself.

The wife worked hard to help the family migrate. She learned about emigration policies and settlement from colleagues, friends, and relatives living in Hong Kong and overseas. She kept up the children's English and gave them books on foreign countries. She hoarded scarce household resources. They lived in an old walk-up apartment and did not buy a new apartment because they were saving money to emigrate. The wife's nursing retraining also was a form of emigration work; she amassed cultural capital to qualify for a credential. This case illustrates how lower-middle-class women develop their cultural resources, interact with but are not dependent on kin, and help bring migration plans to fruition.

Gendered Migration Work of the Affluent Middle-Class

More affluent couples see themselves as independent of kin obligations. Although they try to cater to their material and emotional needs, their colleagues are their role models. Women's chief migration work is networking with friends and colleagues, training their children for the new world, and arranging the support of kin who are left behind.

Work related to economic exchanges. These professionals and managers of middle class grew up in modest circumstances. Several parents had lost property in China, and our respondents studied hard to recoup their family's lost standing. By the end of our study, they all enjoyed comfortable livelihoods. Economically independent of kin, all had surpassed their parents' standard of living. Among the men's occupations, were business manager, accountant, computer consultant, engineer, and university lecturer. The sole man who worked in a family firm had trained for that line at technical college and only after marriage was he invited to manage his spouse's parents' firm. He considered himself an independent decision maker, and not beholden to kin. The upper-middle-class wives were well educated, but many put their families before their careers. Half gave up their jobs to care for their families, the rest worked as primary school teacher, manager, salesperson, and senior civil servant. Nearly all considered their jobs as substantial additions to the family economy, but saw their spouses as the main earner. Only one, a company manager, earned as much as her spouse. Immigrant wives reduced their work commitment even further so that their families could more easily move abroad.

The affluent respondents got jobs mainly by applying to newspaper ads and from university contacts and coworkers. They saw themselves as highly "independent." They needed information from colleagues more than help from kin, and kept in contact with classmates and workmates over the years.

Kin-related gendered work. These high-income earners felt responsible for kin, who figure broadly in their lives. Women did the caring and integrating part of their family work, offered help and advice to siblings and other kin. Because maintaining independence is important, they interpreted giving advice as exchanging information and personal experiences, while they defined asking for help as getting a handout.

Most remit more than H.K.$3000 a month to parents on each side which, when added to their siblings' shares, can support them. The affluent women need not do daily physical elder care and none lived with their elders. Instead, three paid the monthly mortgage for an apartment for their mother. Women also worked hard to meet the elders' needs, driving them to doctor's appointments or taking them shopping and to lunch.

These women did not turn to their seniors for child care help. Three briefly had help from kin which they combined with the help of servants and nursery schools, in the children's early years. Wives closely supervised their children's homework and extracurricular training. Kin take the children on excursions, but mothers explain that the grandparents mainly want to enjoy the youngsters, cannot be counted on to babysit, and do not know enough to teach them. Further, the seniors go to community centers, travel, and have their own activities.

Siblings enlarge available opportunities and are turned to because they can be trusted. For instance, one woman with Canadian papers whose brother was a Hong Kong resident regularly deposited sums of family money into his Hong Kong bank account, so that she need not declare it. When he landed in Canada for the first time, as part of his assets he was able to bring in the money tax free for her.

Five of the eight married couples saw their parents and other kin more than they saw friends. Many communicated nearly daily with at least one close relative, a parent or sister. For such "communicators," visits to kin are ends in themselves. There is considerable variation in which a sibling will support the parents—a choice that mostly turns on life cycle and personal lifestyles. For instance, a senior civil servant thought that after her marriage the importance of friendship dropped. Every Sunday she visited her mother but spent little time in gatherings of or even phone contact with friends.

Others spent more time with their friendship networks, beginning with schoolmates. Although now well-off, many had struggled to complete school, often in evening courses. Their schoolmates went through a lot with them, cooperating when studying and helping each other find jobs. They felt they could depend on them. They not only had extensive circles of friends at home, but also abroad. They kept contact, visit and holiday together, greet, and exchange e-mail. Women worked at maintaining their friendship ties and those of their husbands.

Eight couples applied for visas, and four of them emigrated. However, two returned and only two remain abroad. Most affluent couples, whether emigrant or not, have kin abroad: over one-half of the 98 affluent spouses and their siblings had applied to emigrate. However, they did not emigrate as dependents of kin; instead, the upper-middle-class saw emigration as an investment. They accounted for their exodus by referring to their family political history, lifestyle, and economic strategies. They belonged to many network chains. Affluents typically are part of more than one network. They felt that they should spread out their applications like an investment. The eight affluent applicants applied for papers to 15 countries, as business class immigrants, "other independents," or the British nationality categories. Some invested in partnerships with colleagues. Newcomers turned to former schoolmates, colleagues, and other friends in the same trade for leads (see also Bian 1999; Granovetter 1985). They did not feel that this is a form of dependence, for they had their own funds and diverse contacts to help them. Most applied through the man's jobs and contacts. Only one couple got papers to Singapore through the wife's senior civil service job; but even in this case the husband was principle applicant to two other countries, and in the end they stayed in Hong Kong.

Women, however, lay the groundwork by organizing disparate strands of personal networks. Few actually lived with parents, yet this did not absolve women of caregiving work. As emigrants, they had to ensure that kin on both sides were physically cared for. Women also line up colleagues and friends to help them in the new land. In turn, they will help other newcomers later on. The friends fetch them at the airport, help them fill out forms, open bank accounts and do other paper work, put them up, recommend a realtor and drive them to look at real estate, arrange for driving lessons, and connect them to schools and friends with possible jobs. To ensure that these kin are available is women's central migration work.

Case example. A site engineer and his wife, a software saleswoman, emigrated to Canada to avoid the chaos they expected that Hong Kong's reversion to China would usher in. Their parents on both sides had been wealthy landowners who fled to Hong Kong in the 1950s when they lost their property. They bequeathed to their children the goal of avoiding life under communism. As the only sibling to have achieved a solid living standard, the couple was able to carry out their family kinscript. Yet they did not move rashly. Like a personal investment, they saw emigration as having gains and costs. The greatest concern was making the right life decisions.

They invested their resources. The husband, Chen Chun, contrasted his approach with that of his father, years before. Expecting the communist takeover to be brief, the father had not tried to adapt. As the son tells it, "My father had his lands and his property taken away. He waited for years to have this rescinded and didn't take a job. Because of that, I didn't go to school until I was 10. Then when I was finished, I had to go to work, and give half my earnings to my younger brothers to go to school. I never had a chance to finish college." Determined to recoup, the son studied hard, and it was his dream to finish college in Canada.

Their style of living was consistent with an interest in planning. The husband married late, when he was financially sound. He saved $10,000 every year in foreign currencies for his daughter's educational fund. "Every three to five years, I change my plan. It's true I have a serious life with a tight schedule, but it's a must. When the world changes so fast, we can't wait," he advised. They invested widely in property. Their condominium in Vancouver symbolized their future presence in Canada. They bought few household goods that might encumber their emigration plan. They did not repair their audio equipment when it broke although they maintained the VCR for their daughter.

Chen Chun's friends were former classmates from the building trades—his own classmates and the classmates of other engineers who were coworkers. Employed by a large Hong Kong construction firm, he also ran a small interior design firm on the side, with classmates as shareholders. Yet another polytechnic classmate immigrated to Vancouver, and noted, "I bought my Vancouver house there with his help. I never even went there; he helped me care for it. Then when I was ready to sell it, he helped me too. My classmate told me not to immigrate to Vancouver because the economy for construction is so bad. But if I do, I'll probably work with him at the start." Colleagues find positions for each other on both sides of the ocean.

In his leisure activities, Chen Chun gambled or played cards while his active wife joined her former colleagues, her daughter, and other friends in hiking, swimming, and aerobics. If his work was to support the family, hers was to network.

As the best off in his family, the husband took economic responsibility for his mother while his wife looked after the social and emotional needs of three parents. She spent many days with her relatives on both sides, taking them to see a doctor and having their prescriptions filled, organizing outings, taking them shopping, brings their daughter to visit the grandparents, and arranged family celebrations and ritual occasions. When they applied to emigrate, she prepared her sister-in-law to become "successor" to this work.

Chen Chun's wife, Leui Ying, preferred to remain in Hong Kong with her kin and enjoy the city's convenient lifestyle. Nevertheless, pulled into her husband's strong emigration kinscript, her work was essential to it. For as long as I knew them, her life was organized around migration as a career. In order to fit their emigration plans, Leui Ying put off returning to school to complete her degree and took undemanding jobs. Expecting to emigrate, they also postponed having children. But because the wife had to care for their parents, and the husband had projects to finish, they delayed the move and had a daughter. The June 4 Tianenmen Square massacre in 1989 and their new family member spurred them to apply for emigration.

Before their emigration foray, the wife arranged many reunions of emigrant friends to get their experiences. She organized family travels abroad to explore different conditions until they ultimately invested in Canada. Emigrant friends helped them formulate views on their chosen country. Others offered their own negative advice. A colleague phoned them from Canada, warning them of the bad economy; he could not understand how a country so rich in minerals and raw products was doing so poorly: "It is said that's because Canadians do not like to work." They pointed out a Vancouver friend who had assimilated, noting, "He was very active in Hong Kong, bought houses and made lots of money. In Vancouver, he changed 100 percent. He says, 'Why bother?' He has enough money. He doesn't care anymore. The local environment did it. In Hong Kong, you have to struggle, and be commercial minded, keep up and go out with your friends." Another counseled them on how to answer immigration officials' questions. They took these friends' advice, but in contrast, found "our relatives are not useful" adding, "We have cousins in Vancouver and Toronto, but they didn't even answer my fax. They are afraid if they get involved, they can never get rid of us. Friends are more reliable." In the end, this engineer got a visa independently as an "independent applicant," and his Canadian kin did not help at all.

Curious about our research project, Leui Ying tried to help with stories of astronauts and invitations to meet astronaut friends. At a barbecue party, in a well-to-do mixed Chinese and expatriate community, I was introduced to "typical emigrant cases." Their family meal was luxurious. Three of the four families had gotten their papers, and talk centered on the personal costs of emigration. The hosts, a construction engineer and his wife, had gone to middle school with Chen Chun. "We've 30 years of friendship!" Chen Chun said proudly. The host offered that it was too costly to get emigration papers for Canada, noting, "There is no reason to emigrate. It is a crisis of confidence. If you get a passport to leave and then return it's a waste of time. You might as well stay here. I can send my children to England to study without a passport. It's not necessary to have a passport. If things are really bad, you can go as a refugee." However, he acknowledged that he had the right of abode: "It was the cheapest way, only cost us $2,000. 'One country, two systems' is impossible. Nevertheless, we still think China will want Hong Kong to make money." In contrast, a colleague that had studied engineering with the host was an early emigrant with a different tale. He had gone to Canada in early 1989, remained the three years needed for emigration papers in Toronto, and found his qualifications were not recognized: "Hong Kong people build high buildings, and they are quite complex, but Toronto builds mostly low buildings, and few high rises. All construction is in the hands of Italians, and they are very skillful; I didn't even send out résumés." His wife, whose relatives are all in Canada, got a good provincial government engineering job. He returned to Hong Kong, and she had to quit to follow him, leaving her relatives behind in Toronto. When he returned to Hong Kong, he got a contract in our respondent's firm. He had little problem getting work, but he took a cut in pay. "I'd read up on all the changes in [Hong Kong's] laws." he said. "No, there wasn't much I could learn from Canada. In fact in Canada the rules are so slow, you take three years to apply for all the paper work, within that time the Hong Kong building would have been finished."

The husband's reproductive work was to support the family, and he soon realized he could not quit his Hong Kong job. After emigrating to Toronto, he returned to Hong Kong as an "astronaut." He left his wife and daughter to put in the year they needed to qualify for their citizenship hearing. Then they returned to Hong Kong and reunited the family. The wife maintained her Canadian home without the paid and kin household help she had had before (Man 1997). She also did considerable linking work with others. She maintained her husband's Canadian networks and entertained their kin who visited them. She organized outings for her immigrant friend. "If I didn't arrange these things, nobody would," she proudly complained. However, her migration work in Toronto was mainly directed toward their daughter, and she ensured their daughter had as many sports and leisure activities as could be fit in after school, and that she benefited fully from this learning experience. The astronaut venture ended after a year, as the parents were reluctant to keep their daughter out of the Hong Kong school system for much longer. Although the chief applicant was the husband, the wife prepared both of them for the move abroad, before and after. She worked at keeping up links between emigrant classmates and colleagues.

SUMMARY

Just as spouses' family roles differ, so does their emigration work. Men have property and access to capital. They organize large and small patrilineal enterprises and initiate more emigration applications than their wives. While women may not be listed as immigration leaders, however, they contribute to the migration project by drawing on their social and gender positions. I group these tasks as: economic exchanges and supporting kin. The case studies of respondent families from different class backgrounds show the varied ways women negotiate these exchanges. Underlying the content of their work are women's activities as integrators of the family unit and linkers with others, or *network building*. Central to the social integration of the family and as links to kin and other contacts, women are a crucial part of the family migration process.

There are gendered forms of mobilization of kinship and economic resources in each social class. In the working class, kinship relations are central to the family, not only to emigration. This makes the working class most dependent on kin. Further, as kin mobilizers, women may want to be close to their kin, while their husbands expect them to further their patrilineage. Women's role as kin integrator in the working class appears to reinforce their lack of equity in meeting the needs of their kinswomen.

In contrast is the negotiated interdependency of the middle class. The lower middle class, with less money but with organizational independence, is like a pivot, taking part in working- and middle-class social frames. They support their kin in life skills, they give money and advice, but they do not find work for kin.

While the more affluent women are not "freed" of the responsiveness to kin, they also mobilize other resources of cash, information, or help from with friends and other non-kin. These middle-class couples look for economic support elsewhere, however, developing ties to friends and classmates and other non-kin. The women's contribution is valued most in this sphere as linkers to others that replace kin's help, which the affluent do not depend on. While both women and men are important in these activities, these behind-the-scenes activities are the barely visible but crucial aspect of women's migration work. In these ways, women's economic and kin integration work vary by class.

Women's migration work has implications for their position of power. While emigration work draws on women's behind-the-scenes strength, there are costs. The migration project undermines Chinese women's support from kin that stay behind. The project overrides and co-opts women's chance to seek goals on their own in Hong Kong other than migration. Finally, Hong Kong working women sacrifice the social support when they go elsewhere. At base, however varied the means and resources, women do much of the social organization of migration work.

NOTE

This paper forms part of the wider Emigration from Hong Kong Project. The sociological research was conducted jointly with Professor Siu-lun Wong of the Centre for Asian Studies, University of Hong Kong (see Skeldon 1995a). An early version of this paper appears in the *Asian and Pacific Migration Journal* 6, nos. 3–4 (1997):295–315. I gratefully acknowledge support for this project from the following bodies: Hong Kong Universities and Colleges Grants Association; the Canada and Hong Kong Project, Joint Centre on Asian Pacific Studies, University of Toronto/York University; the Initiatives Fund, Institute for International Programmes, University of Toronto; the Office of Research Services, University of Toronto; and the Centre of Urban and Community Studies, University of Toronto. I am also grateful to our contacts, with whom I talked at length, visited, and at times lived with. They generously shared their goals and plans, gave us much privileged information, and were willing participants. I thank Christine Inglis, Ching Kwan Lee, Esther Ngan-ling Chow, Evie Tastsoglou, and anonymous readers of this volume for their comments.

References

Abelmann, Nancy. 1996. *Echoes of the Past, Epics of Dissent: A South Korean Social Movement.* Berkeley and Los Angeles, CA: University of California Press.

Acker, Joan. 1990. "Hierarchies, Jobs, Bodies: A Theory of Gendered Organizations." *Gender & Society* 4:139–58.

Adkins, Lisa. 1995. *Gendered Work: Sexuality, Family and the Labour Market.* Buckingham: Open Press.

Afshar, Haleh, ed. 1998. *Women and Empowerment.* New York: St. Martin's Press.

Afshar, Haleh, and Stephaine Barrientos, eds. 1998. *Women, Globalization and Fragmentation in the Developing World.* New York: St. Martin's Press.

Alexander, M. Jacqui, and Chandra Talpade Mohanty, eds. 1997. *Feminist Genealogies, Colonial Legacies, Democratic Futures.* New York: Routledge.

Alford, Robert R. 1998. *The Craft of Inquiry: Theories, Methods, Evidence.* New York: Oxford University Press.

All-China Federation of Trade Unions. 1997. *The Status of Women Workers in China.* Beijing: Chinese Workers Press.

All-China Federation of Trade Unions, Women's Workers Department. 1998a. "An Investigation into the Difficulties of Women's Re-Employment." *Zhongguo Gongren* [*Chinese Workers*] 3:14–16.

———. 1998b. *Zhongguo nu zhigong zhuangkuang* [*The Status of Chinese Women Workers*]. Beijing: Chinese Workers Press.

Amsden, Alice. 1989. *Asia's Next Giant: South Korea and Late Industrialization.* New York: Oxford University Press.

Anderson, Benedict. 1983. *Imagined Communities: Reflections on the Origin and Spread of Nationalism.* New York: Verso.

Anderson, Sarah, ed. 2000. *Views from the South: The Effects of Globalization and the WTO on Third World Countries.* Oakland, CA: Food First Books.

Andors, Phyllis. 1983. *The Unfinished Liberation of Chinese Women, 1969–1980.* Bloomington, IN: Indiana University Press.

Antonucci, Toni C. 1990. "Social Supports and Social Relationships." Pp. 205–26 in *Handbook of Aging and the Social Sciences*, edited by R. H. Binstock and L. K. George. 3d ed. New York: Academic Press.

Antonucci, Toni C., and Hiroko Akiyama. 1987. "Social Networks in Adult Life and a Preliminary Examination of the Convoy Mode." *Journal of Gerontology* 42:519–29.

Appadurai, Arjun. 1990. "Disjuncture and Difference in the Global Cultural Economy." Pp. 295–310 in *Global Culture: Nationalism, Globalization and Modernity*, edited by M. Featherstone. Newbury Park, CA: Sage.

Arrigo, Linda Gail. 1980. "The Industrial Work Force of Young Women in Taiwan." *Bulletin of Concerned Asian Scholars* 12, 2:25–38.

Association for the Advancement of Feminism (AAF). 1993. *The Hong Kong Women File.* Hong Kong: AAF.

Athukorala, Prema-chandra, and Chris Manning. 1999. *Structural Change and International Migration in East Asia: Adjusting to Labor Scarcity.* New York: Oxford University Press.

Bai, Moo Ki, and Woo Hyun Cho. 1996. "Women's Employment Structure and Male-Female Wage Differentials in Korea." Pp. 165–206 in *Women and Industrialization in Asia*, edited by Susan Horton. London: Routledge.

Balassa, B. 1988. "The Lesson of East Asian Development: An Overview." *Economic Development and Cultural Change* 36:S273–90.

Bandarage, A. 1984. "Women in Development: Liberalism, Marxism, and Marxist Feminism." *Development and Change* XV:495–515.

Bardhan, Kaplana, and Stephen Klasen. 1999. "UNDP's Gender-Related Indices: A Critical Review." *World Development* 27:985–1010.

Baron, James N., and William T. Bielby. 1984. "The Organization of Work in a Segmented Economy." *American Sociological Review* 49:454–73.

Bartlett, Christopher A., and Sumantra Goshal. 1989. *Managing Across Borders: The Transnational Solution*. Boston: Harvard Business School Press.

Batliwala, Srilatha. 1994. "The Meaning of Women's Empowerment: New Concepts from Action." Pp. 127–38 in *Population Policies Reconsidered: Health, Empowerment, and Rights*, edited by Gita Sen, Adrienne Germain, and Lincoln Chen. Cambridge, MA: Harvard University Press.

Basch, Linda, Nina Glick Schiller, and Cristina Szanton-Blanc. 1994. *Nations Unbound: Transnational Projects, Postcolonial Predicaments and Deterritorialized Nation-States*. Amsterdam: Gordon and Breach.

Basu, Amrita, ed. 1995. *The Challenge of Local Feminisms: Women's Movements in Global Perspective*. Boulder, CO: Westview Press.

Bauer, John, Feng Wang, Nancy E. Riley, and Xiaohua Zhao. 1992. "Gender Inequality in Urban China: Education and Employment." *Modern China* 18:330–70.

Becker, Gary S. 1964. *Human Capital*. New York: Columbia University Press.

———. 1981. *A Treatise on the Family*. Cambridge, MA: Harvard University Press.

Bell, Daniel. 1956. *The Coming of Post-Industrial Society*. New York: Basic Books.

Bello, W., and S. Rosenfeld. 1990. *Dragons in Distress: Asia's Miracle Economies in Crisis*. San Francisco, CA: The Institute for Food and Development Policy.

Benería, Lourdes, and Shelley Feldman, eds. 1992. *Unequal Burden: Economic Crises, Persistent Poverty, and Women's Work*. Boulder, CO: Westview Press.

Benería, Lourdes, and Amy Lind. 1995. "Engendering International Trade: Concepts, Policy, and Action." Pp. 69–86 in *A Commitment to the World's Women: Perspectives on Development for Beijing and Beyond*, edited by Noeleen Heyzer. New York: United Nations Development Fund For Women.

Benería, Lourdes, and Martha Roldan. 1987. *The Crossroads of Class and Gender*. Chicago, IL: University of Chicago Press.

Benería, Lourdes, and Gita Sen. 1981. "Accumulation, Reproduction, and Women's Role in Economic Development: Boserup Revisited." *Signs* 7:279–98.

Beutel, Ann M., and Margaret Mooney Marini. 1995. "Gender and Values." *American Sociological Review* 60:436–48.

Bian, Yanjie. 1987. "Preliminary Analysis of the Basic Features of the Life Styles of China's Single-Child Families." *Social Sciences in China* 8:189–209.

———. 1994. *Work and Inequality in Urban China*. Albany, NY: State University of New York Press.

———. 1999. "*Guanxi* and the Allocation of Urban Jobs in China." *China Quarterly* 140:971–99.

Bielby, William T., and James N. Baron. 1986. "Men and Women at Work: Sex Segregation and Statistical Discrimination." *American Journal of Sociology* 91:759–99.

Blau, Peter. 1964. *Exchange and Power in Social Life*. New York: John Wiley & Sons.

Blumberg, Rae Lesser. 1994a. "Introduction: Engendering Wealth and Well-Being in an Era of Economic Transformation." Pp. 1–14 in *EnGENDERing Wealth & Well-Being: Empowerment for Global Change*, edited by R. L. Blumberg, C. A. Rakowski, I. Tinker, and M. Monteon. Boulder, CO: Westview Press.

Blumberg, Rae Lesser. 1994b. "Women's Work, Wealth, and Family Survival Strategy: The Impact of Guatemala's ALCOSA Agribusiness Project." Pp. 117–41 in *Women, the*

Family, and Policy: A Global Perspective, edited by E. N. Chow and C. W. Berheide. Albany, NY: State University of New York Press.

Bonney, Norman, and John Love. 1991. "Gender and Migration: Geographical Mobility and the Wife's Sacrifice." *Sociological Review* 39, 2:335–48.

Bose, Christine E., and Edna Acosta-Belen, eds. 1995. *Women in the Latin American Development Process.* Philadelphia, PA: Temple University Press.

Boserup, Ester. 1970. *Women's Role in Economic Development.* London: George Allen and Unwin.

Boyd, Monica. 1989. "Family and Personal Networks in International Migration: Recent Developments and New Agendas." *International Migration Review* 23, 2:638–71.

Braverman, Harry. 1974. *Labor and Monopoly Capital.* New York: Monthly Review Press.

Brecher, Jeremy, Tim Costello, and Brendan Smith. 2000. *Globalization from Below: The Power of Solidarity.* Cambridge, MA: South End Press.

Brinton, Dana M. 2000. "The Epistemology of the Gendered Organization." *Gender & Society* 14:418–34.

Brinton, Mary C. 1988. "The Social Institutional Bases of Gender Stratification: Japan as an Illustrative Case." *American Journal of Sociology* 94, 3:300–34.

———. 1993. *Women and the Economic Miracle: Gender and Work in Postwar Japan.* Berkeley and Los Angeles, CA: University of California Press.

Brinton, Mary C., Yean-Ju Lee, and William L. Parish. 1995. "Married Women's Employment in Rapidly Industrializing Societies: Examples from East Asia." *American Journal of Sociology* 100:1099–1130.

Brown, Owen. 1998. "China Ranks Third in Suicides By Women." Nationwide General News, Overseas News, September.

Burawoy, Michael. 1976. "The Functions and Reproduction of Migrant Labor: Comparative Material from Southern Africa and the United States." *American Journal of Sociology* 81:1050–87.

———. 1985. *The Politics of Production: Factory Regimes under Capitalism and Socialism.* London: Verso.

Burrell, G. 1984. "Sex and Organizational Analysis." *Organizational Studies* 5:97–100.

Butler, Judith. 1993. *Bodies that Matter.* New York: Routledge.

Cai, Fang. 1997. "Qianyi Juece Zhong De Jiating Juese He Xingbie Tezheng" [The Role of Family and Gender Characteristics in Migration Decision-making]. *Renkou yanjiu* [*Population Research*] 21, 2:7–12.

Calas, Marta B., and Linda Smircich. 1992. "Re-writing Gender into Organizational Theorizing: Directions from Feminist Perspectives." Pp. 227–51 in *Rethinking Organization*, edited by M. Reed and M. Hughes. Newbury Park, CA: Sage.

Cardoso, Fernando H., and Enzo Faletto. 1979. *Dependency and Development in Latin America.* Berkeley and Los Angeles, CA: University of California Press.

Chan, Anthony B. 1996. *Li Ka Shing: Hong Kong's Elusive Billionaire.* Toronto: Macmillan.

Chan, Audrey, and Jean Lee. 1994. "Women Executives in a Newly Industrialized Economy: The Singapore Scenario." Pp. 127–42 in *Competitive Frontiers*, edited by N. J. Adler and D. N. Izraeli. Cambridge, MA: Blackwell.

Chan, Kam-Wah, and Ng Chun-hung. 1994. "Gender, Class and Employment Segregation in Hong Kong." Pp. 141–70 in *Inequalities and Development: Social Stratification in Chinese Societies*, edited by Siu-kai Lau, Ming-kwan Lee, Po-san Wan, and Siu-lun Wong. Hong Kong: Hong Kong Institute of Asia Pacific Studies, Chinese University of Hong Kong.

Chang, Chin-fen. 1996. "Economic Rewards and the Determination Process for Female Workers in Export-Oriented Industries in the 1980s: Using Taiwan as an Example." *Taiwan: A Radical Quarterly in Social Studies* 22:59–81.

Chang, Kai. 1994. "Urban Women's Employment in Transformation toward a Market Economy." *Jingji Ribao* [*Economic Daily*], August 14, p. 7.

Chang, Kai. 1995. "The Investigation and Study of Women's Unemployment and Re-Employment in the Enterprises of Public Ownership." *Shehuixue Yanjiu* [*Sociological Studies*] 3:83–93.

Chang, Raymond J. M., and Pei-Chen Chang. 1992. "Taiwan's Emerging Economic Relations With the PRC." Pp. 275–98 in *Taiwan: Beyond the Economic Miracle*, edited by D. Simon and Y. M. Kau. Armonk, NY: M. E. Sharpe.

Chattopadhyay, Arpita. 1997. "Gender Differences in the Effect of Family Migration on Occupational Mobility in Malaysia." Ph.D. dissertation, Department of Sociology, Brown University, Providence, Rhode Island.

Chen, Fang. 1998. "Market Economy and Women's Employment." *Zhongguo Funu Yundong* [Chinese Women's Movement] 1:33–34.

Chen, Michael C., and Wen-Shan Yang. 1994. "Decomposition of Wage Differences Between Male and Female in Taiwan: A Sociological Analysis." *Business and Law Journal* 29:305–31.

Chen, Xueming. 1997. "The Achievements Brought about by the Re-Employment Project in Shanghai." *Shanghai Gaige* [*Shanghai Reform*] 12:23–26.

Chen, Yintao. 1997. "Dagongmei De Hunlian Guannian Jiqi Kunrao" [Anxieties and Notions about Marriage and Love among Women Who Have Migrated from Rural to Urban Areas]. *Renkou Yanjiu* [*Population Research*] 21, 2:39–44.

Cheng, Lucie, and Ping-chun Hsiung. 1992. "Women, Export-Oriented Growth, and the State." Pp. 233–66 in *States and Development in the Asian Pacific Rim*, edited by R. P. Appelbaum and J. Henderson. Newbury Park, CA: Sage.

———. 1998. "Engendering the 'Economic Miracle': The Labor Market in the Asia-Pacific." Pp. 112–36 in *Economic Dynamism in the Asia-Pacific: The Growth of Integration and Competitiveness*, edited by G. Thompson. New York: Routledge.

Cheng, Shu-Ju Ada. 1996. "Migrant Women Domestic Workers in Hongkong, Singapore and Taiwan: A Comparative Analysis." *Asian and Pacific Migration Journal* 5:139–52.

———. 1999. "Labor Migration and International Sexual Division of Labor: A Feminist Perspective." Pp. 38–57 in *Gender and Immigration*, edited by G. A. Kelson and D. L. DeLaet. New York: New York University Press.

Cheng, Tun-jen. 1990. "Political Regimes and Development Strategies: South Korea and Taiwan." Pp. 139–78 in *Manufacturing Miracles*, edited by G. Gereffi and D. Wyman. Princeton, NJ: Princeton University Press.

Cheng, Wei-yuan, and Lung-li Liao. 1994. "Women Managers in Taiwan." Pp. 143–59 in *Competitive Frontiers*, edited by N. J. Adler and D. N. Izraeli. Cambridge, MA: Blackwell.

Chin, Christine B. N. 1998. *In Service and Servitude: Foreign Female Domestic Workers and the Malaysian "Modernity" Project*. New York: Columbia University Press.

Chinese Women's Daily [*Zhongguo Funubao*]. 1998. "Jiangsu Finds Ways to Place Xiagang Workers." June 15, p. 3.

Chiu, Catherine. 1998. *Small Family Business in Hong Kong: Accumulation and Accommodation*. Hong Kong: Chinese University of Hong Kong Press.

Chiu, Stephen. 1994. *The Politics of Laissez-faire: Hong Kong's Strategy of Industrialization in Historical Perspective*. Occasional Paper no. 40. Hong Kong: Hong Kong Institute of Asia-Pacific Studies, Chinese University of Hong Kong.

Chiu, Stephen, and Ching Kwan Lee. 1997. *Withering Away of the Hong Kong Dream? Women Workers Under Economic Restructuring*. Occasional Paper no. 61. Hong Kong: Hong Kong Institute of Asia-Pacific Studies, Chinese University of Hong Kong.

Chiu, Stephen, and David Levin. 1993. "The World Economy, State, and Sectors in Industrial Change: Labour Relations in Hong Kong's Textile and Garment-Making Industries." Pp. 187–222 in *Organized Labor in the Asia-Pacific Region*, edited by S. Frenkel. Ithaca, NY: Cornell University, School of Industrial and Labor Relations, ILR Press.

Chiu, Stephen, and Tai-lok Lui. 1994. *Horizontal Expansion and Spatial Relocation: Production and Employment Restructuring of the Electronics Industry in Hong Kong*. Unpublished manuscript, Department of Sociology, Chinese University of Hong Kong.

Chong, Yon-Ju. 1990a. "(Company M) Factory Ajumma Goes to the U.S.A. to Protest." *The Hankyoreh*, April 6, p. 10.

———. 1990b. "(Company M) Workers Demonstrate In front of the Headquarter Building In Korean Traditional Way." *The Hankyoreh*, April 24, p.10.

—. 1990c. "(Company M) Workers' Persistent Fighting for a Month Now." *The Hankyoreh*, May 15, p. 5.

Chongqing Women's Federation. 1997. "Implementing the Re-employment Project for Xiagang Women Workers." *Funu Yanjiu Luncong [Forum of Womens Studies]* 23:34–36.

Chosun Ilbo. 1989. "The Police Indiscriminately Assault the Protesting Workers," March 23, p. 15.

—. 1990. "What the Company Has Done to the Company M's Incident," Editorial, July 15, p.3.

Chou, Bi-ehr. 1994. "Changing Patterns of Women's Employment in Taiwan, 1966–1986." Pp. 330–53 in *The Other Taiwan*, edited by M. A. Rubinstein. Armonk, NY: M. E. Sharpe.

Chou, Bi-ehr, Cal Clark, and Janet Clark. 1990. *Women in Taiwan Politics: Overcoming Barriers to Women's Participation in a Modernizing Society*. Boulder, CO: Lynne Reinner.

Chow, Esther Ngan-ling. 1994. "Asian American Women at Work." Pp. 203–27 in *Women of Color in U.S. Society*, edited by M. Baca-Zinn and B. Thornton Dill. Philadelphia, PA: Temple University Press.

—. 1996. "Making Waves, Moving Mountains: Reflections on Beijing '95 and Beyond." *Signs* 22:185–92.

—. 1997a. "Economic Development, Patriarchy, and Intrahousehold Dynamics Among High-Tech Workers in Taiwan, Republic of China." Pp. 145–81 in *Advances in Gender Research, Volume II*, edited by M. Texler Segal and V. Demos. Greenwich, CT: JAI Press.

—. 1997b. "Globalization, Gender, and Social Change." Presented at the International Conference on Gender and Development in Asia, Chinese University of Hong Kong.

—. 1998. "Economic Reforms, Gendered Migration, and Women's Employment in the Manufacturing Industries of Southern China: A Preliminary Analysis." Presented at the XIVth World Congress of the International Sociological Association, held in Montreal, Canada.

—. 2000. "Gender Discrimination Revisited: From a Gendered Organization and Embodiment Perspective." Presented at the Annual Meeting of the American Sociological Association, Washington, D.C.

Chow, Esther Ngan-ling, and Catherine White Berheide, eds. 1994. *Women, the Family, and Policy: A Global Perspective*. Albany, NY: State University of New York Press.

Chow, Esther Ngan-ling, and Ray-May Hsung. 2000. "Gendered Organizations, Management Regimes, and Employment: A Comparative Study of Japanese- and American-Managed Manufacturing Firms in Taiwan." Presented at the Annual Meeting of the American Sociological Association, Washington, D.C.

—. 2001. "Linking Globalism with Localism: Gender Embodiment and Labor Practices of Transnational Corporations in Taiwan." Presented at the Annual Meeting Of the American Sociological Association held in Anaheim, California.

Chowdhury, Anis, and Iyanatul Islam. 1993. *The Newly Industrising Economies of East Asia*. New York: Routledge.

Cockburn, Cynthia. 1991. *In a Way of Women: Men's Resistance to Sex Equality in Organizations*. London: Macmillan.

Cohen, Myron L. 1976. *House United, House Divided: The Chinese Family in Taiwan*. New York: Columbia University Press.

Cohen, Lisa E., Joseph P. Broschak, and Heather A. Haveman. 1998. "And Then There Were More? The Effect of Organizational Sex Composition on The Hiring and Promotion of Managers." *American Sociological Review* 63:711–27.

Collinson, David L., and Jeff Hearn. 1996. "Breaking the Silence: On Men, Masculinities and Managements." Pp. 1–24 in *Men as Managers, Managers as Men: Critical Perspectives As Men, Masculinities and Managements*, edited by D. L. Collinson and J. Hearn. London: Sage.

Committee for Asian Women. 1995. *Silk and Steel: Asian Women Workers Confront Challenges of Industrial Restructuring*. Hong Kong: Committee for Asian Women.

Company M Labor Union. 1989. "Pride of a Nation." Union Leaflet, June 9.

Connell, Robert. 1987. *Gender and Power*. Oxford: Polity Press.

Constable, Nicole. 1997. *Maid to Order in Hong Kong: Stories of Filipina Workers.* Ithaca, NY: Cornell University Press.

Dalsimer, Marilyn, and Laurie Nisonoff. 1984. "The New Economic Readjustment Policies: Implications for Chinese Urban Working Women." *Review of Radical Political Economics* 16:17–43.

Daniels, Arlene Kaplan. 1987. "Invisible Work." *Social Problems* 34, 5:403–15.

Davin, Delia. 1999. *Internal Migration in Contemporary China.* New York: St. Martin's Press.

Day, Lincoln, and Ma Xia, eds. 1994. *Migration and Urbanization in China.* Armonk, NY: M. E. Sharpe.

de Leon, Corinna T., and Suk-Ching Ho. 1994. "The Third Identity of Modern Chinese Women: Women Managers in Hong Kong." Pp. 43–56 in *Competitive Frontiers,* edited by N. J. Adler and D. N. Izraeli. Cambridge, MA: Blackwell.

Deng, Xiaobao. 1998. "Township Cadres Eat Up Xiangang Woman's Restaurant." *Zhongguo Funubao* [*Chinese Women's Daily*], June 10, p. 1.

DeVault, Marjorie L. 1991. *Feeding the Family: The Social Organization of Caring as Gendered Work.* Chicago, IL: University of Chicago Press.

Deyo, Frederic C., ed. 1987. *The Political Economy of the New Asian Industrialism.* Ithaca, NY: Cornell University Press.

———. 1989. *Beneath the Miracle: Labor Subordination in the New Asian Industrialization.* Berkeley and Los Angeles, CA: University of California Press.

Diamond, Norma. 1979. "Women and Industry in Taiwan." *Modern China* 5:317–40.

Dwyer, Daisy, and Judith Bruce, eds. 1988. *A Home Divided: Women and Income in the Third World.* Stanford, CA: Stanford University Press.

Edwards, Richard C. 1979. *Contested Terrain.* New York: Basic Books.

Elson, Diane. 1992. "From Survival Strategies to Transformation Strategies: Women's Needs and Structural Adjustment." Pp. 26–48 in *Unequal Burden,* edited by L. Beneria and S. Feldman. Boulder, CO: Westview Press.

Elson, Diane, and Ruth Pearson. 1981. "Nimble Fingers Make Cheap Workers: An Analysis of Women's Employment in Third World Export Manufacturing." *Feminist Review* 7: 87–107.

Employment and Vocational Training Administration, Council of Labor Affairs (EVTA). 2000a. "Foreign Labor." August 26, 2000 (http://www.evta.gov.tw).

———. 2000b. "Statistic Indice." August 26, 2000 (http://www.evta.gov.tw).

Erickson, Bonnie. 1996. "Culture, Class, and Connection." *American Journal of Sociology* 102:217–51.

Evans, Peter. 1995. *Embedded Autonomy: States and Industrial Transformation.* Princeton, NJ: Princeton University Press.

Faison, Seth. 1995. "Women as Chattel: In China, Slavery Rises." *New York Times,* September 6, A:1.

Fan, C. Cindy, and Youqin Huang. 1998. "Waves of Rural Brides: Female Marriage Migration in China." *Annals of the American Association of American Geographers* 88, 2:227–51.

Fan, Gang. 1995. "Zhong Hua Wen Hua Yu Jing Ji Fa Zhan" [Chinese Culture and Economic Development]. *Xin Hua Wen Zhai* [*New China Digest*] 7:148–52.

Fang, Hong. 1998. "The Plight of Unemployed Female Workers." *Zhongguo Gongren* [*Chinese Workers*] 3:10–11.

Feng, Tongqing, and Xiaojun Xu. 1993. "Zou Xiang Shi Chang Jing Ji de Zhong Guo Qi Ye Zhi Gong Nei Bu Guan Xi He Jie Gou" [The Internal Relationship and Structure of Chinese Employees in Its Way toward the Market Economy]. *China Social Sciences* 3:101–19.

Fernandez-Kelly, M. Patricia. 1989. "Broadening the Scope: Gender and International Economic Development." *Sociological Forum* 4, 4:611–35.

———. 1994. "Making Sense of Gender in the World Economy: Focus on Latin America." *Organization* 1:249–76.

Ferree, Myra Marx, Judith Lorber, and Beth Hess. 1999. *Revisioning Gender.* Thousand Oaks, CA: Sage.

Fielding, Alan. 1993. "Mass Migration and Economic Restructuring." Pp. 7–18 in *Mass Migration in Europe*, edited by R. King. London: Belhaven.

Findlay, Allan M., Huw Jones, and Gillian M. Davidson. 1998. "Migration Transition or Migration Transformation in the Asia Dragon Economies?" *International Journal of Urban and Regional Research* 22:643–63.

Foucault, Michel. 1980. *Power/Knowledge: Selected Interviews and Other Writings, 1972–1977.* New York: Pantheon Books.

Frank, Andre Gunder. 1967. *Capitalism and Underdevelopment in Latin America.* New York: Monthly Review Press.

———. 1998. *Re-Orient: Global Economy in the Asian Age.* Berkeley and Los Angeles, CA: University of California Press.

Frank, Arthur W. 1991. "For a Sociology of Body: An Analytical Review." Pp. 36–102 in *The Body: Social Process and Cultural Theory*, edited by M. Featherstone, M. Hepworth, and B. S. Turner. London: Sage.

Frenkel, Stephen, ed. 1993. *Organized Labor in the Asian-Pacific Region.* Ithaca, NY: Cornell University School of Industrial and Labor Relations, ILR Press.

Fröbel, Folker, Jürgen Heinrichs, and Otto Kreye. 1980. *The New International Division of Labor.* New York: Cambridge University Press.

Gallie, Duncan, Jonathan Gershuny, and Carolyn Vogler. 1994. "Unemployment, the Household and Social Networks." Pp. 231–63 in *Social Change and the Experience of Unemployment*, edited by D. Gallie, C. Marsh, and C. Vogler. Oxford, England: Oxford University Press.

Gallin, Rita. 1984. "Women, Family and the Political Economy in Taiwan." *Journal of Peasant Studies* 12, 1:76–92.

———. 1990. "Women and the Export Industry in Taiwan: The Muting of Class Consciousness." Pp. 179–192 in *Women Workers and Global Restructuring*, edited by K. Ward. Ithaca, NY: Cornell University School of Industrial and Labor Relations, ILR Press.

Gereffi, Gary. 1990. "Paths of Industrialization: An Overview." Pp. 3–31 in *Manufacturing Miracles: Paths of Industrialization in Latin America and East Asia*, edited by G. Gereffi and D. L. Wyman. Princeton, NJ: Princeton University Press.

———. 1998. "Commodity Chains and Regional Divisions of Labor: Comparing East Asia and North America." Presented at the Annual Meeting of the International Sociological Association, Montreal.

Gereffi, Gary, and Donald Wyman. 1990. *Manufacturing Miracles.* Princeton, NJ: Princeton University Press.

Giddens, Anthony. 1990. *The Consequences of Modernity.* Cambridge: Polity Press.

Glenn, Evelyn Nakano. 1983. "Split Household, Small Producer and Dual Wage Earner: An Analysis of Chinese-American Family Strategies." *Journal of Marriage and the Family*, 35–46.

Gold, Thomas B. 1986. *State and Society in the Taiwan Miracle.* Armonk, NY: M. E. Sharpe.

Goodkind, Daniel. 1997. "The Vietnamese Double Marriage Squeeze." *International Migration Review* 31:108–27.

Goss, Jane D., and Bruce Lindquist. 1995. "Conceptualizing International Labor Migration: A Structuration Perspective." *International Migration Review* 29, 2:317–51.

Granovetter, Mark. 1985. "Economic Action and Social Structure: The Problem of Embeddedness." *American Journal of Sociology* 91:1094–1133.

Grasmuck, Sherri, and Patricia R. Pessar. 1991. *Between Two Islands: Dominican International Migration.* Berkeley and Los Angeles, CA: University of California Press.

Greenhalgh, Susan. 1985. "Sexual Stratification." *Population and Development Review* 11, 2:265–314.

Gu, Yaode. 1991. "Dui Bianyuan Diqu Nüxing Renkou Yongru Zhejian Qianjian" [A Rudimentary Perspective on the Women Marriage Migrants from Remote Areas]. *Renkou Yu Jingji* [*Population and Economics*] 1:33–36.

Gui, Shixun, and Liu Xian. 1992. "Urban Migration in Shanghai, 1950–88: Trends and Characteristics." *Population and Development Review* 18:533–48.

Guojia Tongjiju Renkou Tongjisi [Department of Population Statistics, State Statistics Bureau], ed. 1991 and 1992. *Zhongguo Renkou Tongji Nianjian* [*Yearbook of Population Statistics in China*]. Beijing: China Statistics Press.

———. 1993. *1990 Nian Zhongguo Renkou Pucha* [*1990 China Census*]. Beijing: China Statistics Bureau.

Guowuyuan Renkou Pucha Bangongshi and Guojia Tongjiju Renkou Tongjisi [Population Census Office under the State Council and Department of Population Statistics, State Statistics Bureau], ed. 1993. Zhongguo Disici Renkou Pucha Ciliao [*Data of the Fourth Population Census in China*]. Beijing: China Statistics Press.

Hagestad, Gunhild O. 1986. "The Family: Women and Grandparents as Kinkeepers." Pp. 141–60 in *Our Aging Society*, edited by A. Pifer and L. Bronte. New York: W. W. Norton.

Haggard, Stephan. 1990. *Pathways from the Periphery: The Politics of Growth in the Newly Industrializing Countries.* Ithaca, NY: Cornell University Press.

Hamilton, Gary G., and Nicole W. Biggart. 1988. "Market, Culture, and Authority." *American Journal of Sociology* 94, supplement:S52–94.

Harcourt, Wendy, ed. 1994. *Feminist Perspectives on Sustainable Development.* London: Zed Books.

Hareven, Tamara. 1982. *Family Time and Industrial Time.* Cambridge: Cambridge University Press.

———. 1991. "The History of the Family and the Complexity of Social Change." *American History Review* 96:95–124.

Harrell, Stevan. 1985. "Why Do the Chinese Work So Hard? Reflections on an Entrepreneurial Ethic." *Modern China* 11:203–26.

———, ed. 1995. *Chinese Historical Microdemography.* Berkeley and Los Angeles, CA: University of California Press.

Harris, Christopher, and Lydia Morris. 1986. "Households, Labour Markets and the Position of Women." Pp. 86–96 in *Gender and Stratification*, edited by R. Crompton and M. Mann. Cambridge, England: Polity Press.

Hartmann, Heidi. 1976. "Capitalism, Patriarchy, and Job Segregation by Sex." Pp. 137–69 in *Women and the Workplace*, edited by M. Blaxall and B. Raegan. Chicago, IL: University of Chicago Press.

Harvey, David. 1989. *The Condition of Postmodernity: An Enquiry into the Origins of Cultural Change.* Oxford, England: Blackwell.

Heng, Geraldine. 1997. "'A Great Way to Fly': Nationalism, the State, and the Varieties of Third World Feminism." Pp. 30–45 in *Feminist Genealogies, Colonial Legacies, Democratic Futures*, edited by M. Jacqui Alexander and Chandra Talpade Mohanty. New York: Routledge.

Heyzer, Noeleen, ed. 1995. *A Commitment to the World's Women: Perspectives on Development for Beijing and Beyond.* New York: United Nations Development Fund for Women.

Hochschild, Arlie. 1989. *The Second Shift.* Berkeley and Los Angeles, CA: University of California Press.

Hondagneu-Sotelo, Perrette. 1994. *Gendered Transitions: Mexican Experiences of Immigration.* Berkeley and Los Angeles, CA: University of California Press.

Hong Kong Census and Statistics Department. 1961. *Census Report.* Hong Kong: Government Printer.

———. 1981. *1981 Population Census: Main Report.* Hong Kong: Government Printer.

———. 1991. *1991 Population Census: Unpublished Tables.* Hong Kong: Government Printer.

———. 1996. *1996 Population By-Census: Main Report.* Hong Kong: Government Printer.

———. Various Years. *Annual Digest of Statistics.* Hong Kong: Government Printer.

———. 1990–1997a. *Hong Kong Monthly Digest of Statistics*, December. Hong Kong: Government Printer.

———. 1997b. *Special Topics No. 19: Labour Mobility and Related Subjects.* Hong Kong: Government Printer.

Horton, Susan, ed. 1996. *Women and Industrialization in Asia.* New York: Routledge.

Hsiao, Michael Hsin-Huang. 1987. "Development Strategies and Class Transformation in Taiwan and South Korea: Origins and Consequences." Pp. 183–217 in *Bulletin of the Institute of Ethnology*, no. 6. Taipei, Taiwan: Academia Sinica.

———. 1997. *Asia-Pacific Transformation, Regional Growth Triangles and Sustainable Development.* Occasional paper no. 55. Hong Kong: Hong Kong Institute of Asia-Pacific Studies, Chinese University of Hong Kong.

Hsiung, Ping-chun. 1996. *Living Rooms as Factories: Class, Gender, and the Satellite Factory System in Taiwan.* Philadelphia, PA: Temple University Press.

Hsu, Tsung-Kuo. 1989. *The Nature of Work and Gender Role: The Quality of Work Life for Female University Teachers in Taiwan.* Taipei, Taiwan: Chi-Yie Publications.

INSTRAW (United Nations, International Research and Training Institute for the Advancement of Women). 1994. *The Migration of Women: Methodological Issues in the Measurement and Analysis of Internal and International Migration.* Santo Domingo, Dominican Republic: INSTRAW.

International Labour Organization (ILO). 1998. *The Social Impact of the Asian Financial Crisis.* Technical report for discussion at the High-Level Tripartite Meeting on Social Responses to the Financial Crisis in East and South-East Asian Countries, Bangkok, April 22–24, 1998. Bangkok, Thailand: ILO Regional Office for Asia and the Pacific.

Ishi, Tomoji. 1987. "Class Conflict, the State, and Linkage: The International Migration of Nurses from the Philippines." *Berkeley Journal of Sociology* 32:281–312.

Islam, Iyanatul, and Anis Chowdhury. 1997. *Asian-Pacific Economies: A Survey.* New York: Routledge.

Jabeer, N. 1994. *Revised Realities: Gender Hierarchies in Development Thought.* London: Verso.

Jackson, Cecile, and Ruth Pearson, eds. 1998. *Feminist Visions of Development: Gender Analysis and Policy.* New York: Routledge.

Jahan, R. 1995. *The Elusive Agenda.* London: Zed Books.

Jayawardena, Kumari. 1994. *Feminism and Nationalism in the Third World.* Atlantic Highlands, NJ: Zed Books.

Jefferson, Gary H., and Thomas G. Rawski. 1992. "Unemployment, Underemployment, and Employment Policy in China's Cities." *Modern China* 18:42–71.

Jervis, Nancy. 1987. "Retracing a Chinese Landscape: The Interaction of Policy and Culture in a North China Village." Ph.D. dissertation, Department of Anthropology, Columbia University, New York.

Johnson, Chalmers. 1982. *MITI and the Japanese Miracle: The Growth of Industrial Policy, 1925–1975.* Stanford, CA: Stanford University Press.

Johnson, Kay Ann. 1983. *Women, The Family and Peasant Revolution in China.* Chicago, IL: University of Chicago Press.

Kabeer, Naila. 1994. *Reversed Realities: Gender, Hierarchies in Development Thought.* New York: Verso.

Kandiyoti, Deniz. 1988. "Bargaining with Patriarchy." *Gender & Society* 2:274–89.

Kanter, Rosabeth. 1977. *Men and Women of the Corporation.* New York: Basic Books.

Kearney, Michael. 1986. "From the Invisible Hand to Visible Feet: Anthropological Studies of Migration and Development." *Annual Review of Anthropology* 15:331–61.

Kempadoo, Kamala, and Jo Doezema, eds. 1998. *Global Sex Workers: Rights, Resistance, and Redefinition.* New York: Routledge.

Kerfoot, Deborah, and David Knights. 1996. " 'The Best is Yet to Come?' The Quest for Embodiment in Managerial Work." Pp. 78–98 in *Men as Managers, Managers as Men: Critical Perspectives as Men, Masculinities and Managements*, edited by D. L. Collinson and J. Hearn. London: Sage.

Kim, Chong-Bae. 1990. "Go to the United States for Negotioation." *Joong Ang Ilbo*, April 12, p. 18

Kim, Hyun Mee. 1997. "Gender/Sexuality System as a Labor Control Mechanism: Gender Identity of Korean Female Workers in a U.S. Multinational Corporation." *Korea Journal* 37, 2:56–70.

Kim, Son-Gyu. 1990. "Three Union Representatives Returninh Home." *The Hankyoreh*. July 19, p. 14.
Kim, Seung-Kyung. 1997. *Class Struggle or Family Struggle? The Lives of Women Factory Workers in South Korea*. Cambridge, England: Cambridge University Press.
Kim, Tae Hui, and Kyung Hee Kim. 1995. "Industrial Restructuring in Korea and its Consequences for Women Workers." Pp. 106–55 in *Silk and Steel*, edited by the Committee for Asian Women (CAW). Hong Kong: CAW.
Koo, Hagen. 1987. "The Interplay of State, Social Class, and World System in East Asian Development: The Cases of South Korea and Taiwan." Pp. 165–80 in *The Political Economy of the East Asian Industrialization*, edited by F. C. Deyo. Ithaca, NY: Cornell University Press.
Korea Update. 1990. "Company M's Korean Union Representatives Bring the Korean Labor Struggle to the U.S." May–June, pp. 8–9.
Korean Women's Development Institute. 1994. *Social Statistics and Indicators on Women*. Research Report. 128–29, 143. Seoul: Korean Women's Development Institute.
Kung, Lydia. 1983. *Factory Women in Taiwan*. Ann Arbor, MI: University of Michigan Press.
———.1994 [1978]. *Factory Women in Taiwan*. New York: Columbia University Press.
Kwong, Peter. 1997. "Manufacturing Ethnicity." *Critique of Anthropology* 17:365–87.
Lai, Ada Pui-yim. 1999. "Working Daughters in the 1990s." Unpublished master's thesis. Hong Kong: University of Hong Kong.
Lai, Ah Eng, and Keong Yeoh Lam. 1988. "The Impact of New Technology on Women Workers in Singapore." Pp. 356–95 in *Daughters in Industry*, edited by N. Heyzer. Kuala Lumpur: Asian and Pacific Development Centre.
Lai, Chuen-Yan. 1975. "Home Country and Clan Origin of Overseas Chinese in Canada in the Early 1990s." *BC Studies* 27:3–29.
Lamphere, Louise. 1987. *From Working Daughters to Working Mothers*. Ithaca, NY: Cornell University Press.
Landolt, Patricia. 1997. "Salvadoran Transnationalism: Toward the Redefinition of the National Community." Working Paper no. 18, Program in Comparative and International Development, Department of Sociology, Johns Hopkins University, Baltimore, Maryland.
Lau, Siu-kai. 1982. *Society and Politics in Hong Kong*. Hong Kong: Chinese University Press.
Lauby, Jennifer, and Oded Stark. 1988. "Individual Migration as a Family Strategy: Young Women in the Philippines." *Population Studies* 42:473–86.
Lavely, William. 1991. "Marriage and Mobility under Rural Collectivism." Pp. 286–312 in *Marriage and Equality in Chinese Society*, edited by R. S. Watson and P. Buckley Ebrey. Berkeley and Los Angeles, CA: University of California Press.
Lederman, Joanne, and Esther Ngan-ling Chow. 1996. "Gender-Based Violence and International Human Rights: Women Claim their Humanity." Presented at the Annual Meeting of the American Sociological Association, New York.
Lee, Anru. 1996. "A Tale of Two Sisters: Gender in Taiwan's Small-Scale Industry." Pp. 67–79 in *Anthropology For A Small Planet: Culture and Community in a Global Environment*, edited by A. Marcus. St. James, NY: Brandywine Press.
———. 1997. "The Waning of a Hard Work Ethic: Moral Discourse in Taiwan's Recent Economic Restructuring." Presented at the Annual Meeting of the American Anthropological Association, November 19–23, Washington, D.C.
———. 1999. "In the Name of Harmony and Prosperity: Labor and Gender Politics in Taiwan's Recent Economic Restructuring." Ph.D. dissertation, Department of Anthropology, City University of New York, New York.
———. 2002. "Between Filial Daughter and Loyal Sister: Global Economy and Family Politics in Taiwan." In *Women in New Taiwan: Gender Roles and Gender Consciousness in a Changing Society*, edited by C. Farris, A. Lee, and M. A. Rubinstein. Armonk, NY: M. E. Sharpe.
Lee, Bun Song. 1993. "Sex Differential in Labor Force Participation in Korea." Working Paper no. 9304, Korea Development Institute.
Lee, Ching-kwan. 1995. "Engendering the Worlds of Labor: Women Workers, Labor

Markets, and Production Politics in the South China Economic Miracle." *American Sociological Review* 60:378–97.

———. 1998a. *Gender and the South China Miracle.* Berkeley and Los Angeles, CA: University of California Press.

———. 1998b. "The Labor Politics of Market Socialism: Collective Inaction and Class Experiences among State Workers in Guangzhou." *Modern China* 24:3–33.

Lee, Hyo-chae. 1988. "The Changing Profile of Women Workers in South Korea." Pp. 329–55 in *Daughters in Industry,* edited by N. Heyzer. Kuala Lumpur: Asian and Pacific Development Centre.

Lee, Ming-kwan. 1991. "Family and Social Life." Pp. 41–66 in *Social Indicators of Social Development,* edited by Siu-kai Lau. Hong Kong: Hong Kong Institute of Asian-Pacific Studies, Chinese University of Hong Kong Press.

———. 1992. "Family and Gender Issues." Pp. 1–32 in *Indicators of Social Development: Hong Kong 1990, Hong Kong 1993,* edited by Siu-kai Lau, Ming-kwan Lee, Po-san Wan, and Siu-lun Wong. Hong Kong: Hong Kong Institute of Asia Pacific Studies, Chinese University of Hong Kong.

———. 1995. "The Family Way." Pp. 1–19 in *Indicators of Social Development; Hong Kong 1993,* edited by Siu-kai Lau, Ming-kwan Lee, Po-san Wan, and Siu-lun Wong. Hong Kong: Hong Kong Institute of Asia Pacific Studies, Chinese University of Hong Kong.

Lee, Sharon M. 1996. "Issues in Research on Women, International Migration and Labor." *Asian and Pacific Migration Journal* 5:5–26.

Lee, William K. M. 1996. "Women Employment in Hong Kong." Pp. 277–306 in *The Other Hong Kong Report, 1996,* edited by Mee-kau Nyaw and Si-ming Li. Hong Kong: Chinese University of Hong Kong.

Leong, Sow-Theng. 1997. *Migration and Ethnicity in Chinese History: Hakkas, Pengmin, and their Neighbors.* Stanford, CA: Stanford University Press.

Lever-Tracy, Constance, David Ip, and Noel Tracy. 1996. *The Chinese Diaspora and Mainland China: An Emerging Economic Synergy.* London: Macmillan.

Li, Huijing. 1995. "Cong Zhejiang 'Wailainü' Kan Nongcun Funü Diwei De Bianhua" [Changes in the Status of Rural Women from the Perspective of Zhejiang's 'Female Marriage Immigrants']. Pp. 179–86 in *Dangdai Zhongguo Funü Diwei* [*The Status of Women in Contemporary China*], edited by S. Jicai. Beijing: Beijing University Press.

Li, Shuzhuo. 1994. "Bashi niandai Zhongguo nüxing renkou qianyi de xuanzexing tantao" [A Discussion of Characteristics of the Migration of Female Population in China in the 1980s]. *Fünu yaniu luncong* [*A Collection of Women's Research*] 2:26–28.

Li, Yueh Tuan, and Chih Ming Ka. 1994. "Hsiao Hsing Chih Ye De Ching Ying Yu Hsing Pieh Fen Kung: Yi Wu-Fen-Pu Cheng Yi Yeh She Chu Wei An Li De Fen Shi." [Sexual Division of Labor and Production Organization in Wufepu's Small Scale Industries] *T'aiwan She Hui Yen Chiu Chi Kan* [*Taiwan: A Radical Quarterly in Social Studies*] 17:41–81.

Liang, Zai. 1997. "Market Transition, Government Policies and Interprovincial Migration in China: 1983–1988." *Economic Development and Cultural Change* 45 (January):321–39.

Liang, Zai, and Michael J. White. 1996. "Internal Migration in China, 1950–1988." *Demography* 33, 3:375–84.

Liberty Times. 1998. "Wai Lao Wei Ch'i Suo. Cheng Yuan T'ung Kuo," February 20.

Liew, Geok Heok, and Chooi Peng Leong. 1993. "Legal Status." Pp. 252–83 in *Singapore Women,* edited by A. K. Wong and W. K. Leong. Singapore: Times Academic Press.

Lim, Hyun-chin. 1985. *Dependent Development in Korea.* Seoul: Seoul National University Press.

Lim, Lin Lean, and Nana Oishi. 1996. "International Labor Migration of Asian Women: Distincitve Characteristics and Policy Concerns." *Asian and Pacific Migration Journal* 5:85–116.

Lim, Linda Y. C. 1983. "Capitalism, Imperialism, and Patriarchy." Pp. 70–91 in *Women, Men, and the International Division of Labor,* edited by J. Nash and M. P. Fernandez-Kelly. Albany, NY: State University of New York.

———. 1990. "Women's Work in Export Factories: The Politics of a Cause." Pp. 101–19 in

Persistent Inequalilties: Women and World Development, edited by I. Tinker. New York: Oxford University Press.

Lin, Chung Cheng. 1994. "T'aiwan Fang Chi Kung Yeh Fa Chan Chi Yen Chiu" [A Research Report on the Development of Taiwan's Textile Industries]. Unpublished manuscript. Institute of Economics, Academia Sinica, Taiwan.

Liu, Bohong. 1995. "The Situation of Women's Employment in China." *Shehuixue Yanjiu* [*Sociological Studies*] 2:39–48.

Liu, Haiming. 1992. "The Trans-Pacific Family: A Case Study of Sam Chang's Family History." *Amerasia Journal* 18:1–34.

Loomba, Ania. 1991. "Overwording the Third World." *Oxford Literature Review* 13:164–91.

Loscocco, Karyn A., and Xie Wang. 1992. "Gender Segregation in China." *Sociology and Social Research* 76:118–26.

Low, Linda. 1995. "Population Movement in the Asia Pacific Region: Singapore Perspective." *International Migration Review* 29:745–64.

Lu, Jian Ming. 1999. "Self-Employment: Another Way to Solve Women's Employment Problems." *Shanghai Gongyun* [*Shanghai Labor Movement*] 4:14–16.

Lui, Tai-lok, and Stephen Chiu. 1994. "A Tale of Two Industries: the Restructuring of Hong Kong's Garment-making and Electronics Industries." *Environment and Planning* 26:53–70.

Luxton, Meg. 1983. *More than a Labour of Love.* Toronto: Women's Press.

Lye, Diane N. 1996. "Adult Child-Parent Relationships." *Annual Review of Sociology* 22:79–102.

Ma, Laurence J. C., and Chusheng Lin. 1993. "Development of Towns in China: A Case Study of Guangdong Province." *Population and Development Review* 19 (September):583–606.

Maass, Peter. 1989. "Foreign Firms a Target in South Korea Workers at Overseas-Owned Companies Grow Increasing Militant." *Washington Post*, May 21, H3.

MacKinnon, Catharine A. 1979. *Sexual Harassment of Working Women.* New Haven, CT: Yale University Press.

Mallee, Hein. 1995. "China's Household Registration System Under Reform." *Development and Change* 26:1–29.

Man, Guida C. 1996. "The Experience of Women in Middle-Class Hong Kong Chinese Immigrant Families in Canada: An Investigation in Institutional and Organizational Processes." Ph.D. dissertation, Department of Sociology in Education, University of Toronto.

———. 1997. "Women's Work is Never Done: Social Organization of Work and the Experience of Women in Middle-Class Hong Kong Chinese Immigrant Families in Canada." *Advances in Gender Research* 2:183–226.

Manguno, Joseph P. 1989a. "Company M's Abrupt Exit from South Korea Could Inflame Anti-American Sentiment." *Wall Street Journal*, Eastern Edition, March 30, p. A8 (E).

———. 1989b. "Plant's Closing Tensions in South Korea; Plant Closing Aggravates Anti-Americanism in Korea." *Asia Wall Street Journal*, March 30, pp. 1, 7.

Martin, Karin. 1998. "Becoming a Gendered Body: Practices of Preschools." *American Sociological Review* 63:494–511.

Martin, Patricia Yancey. 1992. "Gender, Interaction, and Inequality in Organizations." Pp. 208–31 in *Gender, Interaction, and Inequality,* edited by C. L. Ridgeway. New York: Springer-Verlag.

Massey, Douglas S. 1990. "Social Structure, Household Strategies and the Cumulative Causation of Migration." *Population Index* 56:3–26.

Massey, Douglas S., Joaquin Arango, Graeme Hugo, Ali Kouaouci, Adela Pellegrino, and J. Edward Taylor. 1993. "Theories of International Migration: A Review and Appraisal." *Population and Development Review* 19:431–66.

Massey, Douglas S., Luin Goldring, and Jorge Durand. 1994. "Continuities in Transnational Migration: An Analysis of 13 Mexican Communities." *American Journal of Sociology* 99:1492–1533.

Matsui, Yayori. 1996. *Women in the New Asia.* New York: Zed Books.

McKee, Lorna, and Colin Bell. 1985. "Marital and Family Relations in Times of Male Unemployment." Pp. 387–99 in *New Approaches to Economic Life*, edited by B. Roberts, R. Finnegan, and D. Gallie. Manchester, England: Manchester University Press.

Mehra, Rekha, Simel Esim, and Margorie Sims. 2000. *Fulfilling The Beijing Commitment: Reducing Poverty, Enhancing Women's Economic Options*. Washington, D.C.: International Center for Research on Women.

Menaghan, Elizabeth G. 1991. "Work Experiences and Family Interaction Processes: The Long Reach of the Job?" *Annual Review of Sociology* 17:419–44.

Menahem, Gila, and Shima E. Spiro. 1999. "Immigration in a Restructuring Economy: A Partial Test of Theories." *International Migration* 37:569–86.

Meng, Xianfan. 1995. *Gai Ge Da Chao Zhong de Zhong Guo Nü Xing* [*Chinese Women in the Tide of the Reform*]. Beijing: Chinese Social Science Press.

Mies, Maria. 1986. *Patriarchy and Accumulation on a World Scale*. London: Zed Books.

Mills, C. Wright. 1959. *The Sociological Imagination*. New York: Oxford University Press.

Ming Pao Daily (Ming Pao). 1999. "Massive Layoffs, Rampant Corruption." February 27, p. A16.

Mitchell, Katharyne. 1995. "Flexible Circulation in the Pacific Rim: Capitalism in Cultural Context." *Economic Geography* 71:364–82.

Moen, Phyllis, and Elaine Wethington. 1992. "The Concept of Family Adaptive Strategies." *Annual Review of Sociology* 18:233–51.

Moghadam, Valentine M. 1999. "Gender and the Global Economy." Pp. 128–60 in *Revisioning Gender*, edited Myra Marx Ferree, Judith Lorber, and Beth B. Hess. Thousand Oaks, CA: Sage.

Mohanty, Chandra Talpade. 1997. "Women Workers and Capitalist Scripts: Ideologies of Dominiation, Common Interest, and the Politics of Solidarity." Pp. 3–29 in *Feminist Genealogies, Colonial Legacies, Democratic Futures*, edited by M. Jacqui Alexander and Chandra Talpade Mohanty. New York: Routledge.

Mohanty, Chandra Talpade, Ann Russo, and Lourdes Torres. 1991. *Third World Women and the Politics of Feminism*. Bloomington, IN: Indiana University Press.

Molyneux, Maxine. 1985. "Mobilisation Without Emancipation? Women's Interests, the State and Revolution in Nicaragua." *Feminist Studies* 11:227–54.

Moore, Gwen. 1990. "Structural Determinants of Men's and Women's Personal Networks." *American Sociological Review* 55:726–35.

Moore, Hannah. 1989. "South Koreans Riot over Departure of US Company." *Journal of Commerce*, March 23, pp. 1A, 5A.

Morgan, David. 1998. "Sociological Imaginings and Imagining Sociology: Bodies, Auto/Biographies and Other Mysteries." *Sociology* 32:647–63.

Morris, Lydia. 1985. "Renegotiation of the Domestic Division of Labour in the Context of Male Redundancy." Pp. 221–44 in *Restructuring Capital*, edited by H. Newby, J. Burja, P. Littlewood, G. Rees, and T. Rees. London: Macmillan.

———. 1989. "Household Strategies: The Individual, the Collectivity and the Labour Market: The Case of Married Couples." *Work, Employment and Society* 3:447–64.

———. 1990. *The Workings of the Household*. Cambridge, England: Polity Press.

———. 1994. "Informal Aspects of Social Divisions." *International Journal of Urban and Regional Research* 18:112–26.

Moser, Caroline. 1989. "Gender Planning in the Third World: Meeting Practical and Strategic Needs," *World Development* 17:1799–1825.

Moser, Carolyn O. N. 1993. *Gender Planning and Development: Theory, Practice, and Training*. London: Routledge.

Mosse, Julia Cleves. 1994. *Half the World, Half a Chance: An Introduction to Gender and Development*. Oxford, England: Oxfam, Alden Press.

Nash, June. 1977. "Women in Development: Dependency and Exploitation." *Development and Change* 8:161–82.

———. 1988. "Cultural Parameters of Sexism and Racism in the International Division of Labor." Pp. 11–38 in *Racism, Sexism, and the World System*, edited by J. Smith, et al. New York: Greenwood Press.

Nash, June, and M. Patricia Fernandez-Kelly, eds. 1983. *Women, Men, and the International Division of Labor*. Albany, NY: State University of New York.

Ng, Sek-hong, and Soo-may Cheng. 1994. "The Affluent Migrants as a 'Class' Phenomenon: The Hong Kong Case." Pp. 171–204 in *Inequalities and Development: Social Stratification in Chinese Societies*, edited by Siu-kai Lau, Ming-kwan Lee, Po-san Wan, and Siu-lun Wong. Hong Kong: Hong Kong Institute of Asia Pacific Studies, Chinese University of Hong Kong.

Ngo, Hang-Yue. 1989. "The Situation of Women's Employment: A Comparison of Hong Kong, South Korea, Singapore, and Taiwan." *Hong Kong Journal of Business Management* VII:71–83.

Niehoff, Justin D. 1987. "The Villager as Industrialist: Ideologies of Household Manufacturing in Rural Taiwan." *Modern China* 13:278–309.

Ogasawara, Yuko. 1998. *Office Ladies and Salaried Men: Gender, Power and Work in Japanese Companies*. Berkeley and Los Angeles, CA: University of California Press.

Ong, Aihwa. 1987. *Spirits of Resistance and Capitalist Discipline: Factory Women in Malaysia*. Albany, NY: State University of New York.

———. 1991. "The Gender and Labor Politics of Postmodernity." *Annual Review of Anthropology* 20:279–309.

———. 1997. "The Gender and Labor Politics of Postmodernity." Pp. 61–97 in *The Politics of Culture in the Shadow of Capital*, edited by L. Lowe and D. Lloyd. Durham, NC: Duke University Press.

Ong, Jin Hui, Chang Kwok Bun, and Soon Beng Chew, eds. 1995. *Asian Transmigration*. Upper Saddle River, NJ: Prentice-Hall.

Onis, Z. 1991. "Review Article: The Logic of Developmental State." *Comparative Politics* 24:109–26.

OECD (Organization for Economic Cooperation and Development). 1999. *Labor Migration and the Recent Financial Crisis in Asia*. Social Issues/Employment. Paris: OECD.

Osirim, Mary J. 1996. "The Dilemmas of Modern Development: Structural Adjustment and Women Microentrepreneurs in Nigeria and Zimbabwe." Pp. 127–46 in *The Gendered New World Order: Militarism, Development and the Environment*, edited by J. Turpin and L. A. Lorentzen. New York: Routledge.

Pahl, Ray E. 1985. "The Restructuring of Capital, the Local Political Economy and Household Work Strategies." Pp. 368–86 in *Social Relations and Spatial Structure*, edited by D. Gregory and T. Urry. London: MacMillan.

Pahl, Ray E., and Claire Wallace. 1985. "Household Work Strategies in Economic Recession." Pp. 189–227 in *Beyond Employment: Household, Gender and Subsistence*, edited by N. Redclift and E. Mingione. New York: Basil Blackwell.

Pan, Ying-hai. 1993. *Tai-pei hsien wai chi lao kung wen ti yen chiu pao kao [A Research Report on the Issues of Foreign Labor in Taipei County]*. Taipei: Bureau of Labor Affairs, Taipei County Government.

Park, Kisu. 1990. "A Story of Stolen Justice." *Korea Report*, August/September, pp. 17–19.

Park, Kyung Ae. 1995. "Women Workers in South Korea." *Asian Survey* 35, 8:740–56.

Parker, Andrew, Mary Russo, Doris Sommer, and Patricia Yaeger, eds. 1992. *Nationalisms and Sexualities*. New York: Routledge.

Parreñas, Rhacel Salazar. 2000. "Migrant Families Domestic Workers and the International Division of Reproductive Labor." *Gender & Society* 14: 560–580.

Partridge, May. 1996. "Strategies of Employment and Family: University-Educated Women in Canada and Hong Kong." Ph.D. dissertation, Department of Sociology, University of Hong Kong.

Pasternak, Burton. 1986. *Marriage and Fertility in Tianjin, China: Fifty Years of Transition*. Honolulu, HI: East-West Center.

Pedraza, Sylvia. 1991. "Women and Migration: the Social Consequences of Gender." *Annual Review of Sociology* 17:303–25.

Pessar, Patricia R. 1982. "The Role of Households in International Migration and the Case of U.S.-Bound Migration from the Dominican Republic." *International Migration Review* 16:342–64.

Phongpaichit, Pasuk. 1988. "Two Roads to the Factory." Pp. 151–63 in *Structures of Patriarchy*, edited by B. Agarwal. London: Zed Books.
Pleck, Elizabeth. 1976. "Two Worlds in One: Work and Family." *Journal of Social History* 10, 2:178–95.
Population Institute of the Academy of Social Sciences. 1987. *The China Migration of 74 Cities and Towns Sampling Survey*. Beijing: Academy of Social Sciences.
Policy Research Institute, All-China Federation of Trade Unions. 1999. *Survey of the Status of Chinese Workers in 1997*. Beijing: Xiyuan Publishing House.
Porter, Marilyn, and Ellen Judd. 1999. *Feminist Doing Development: A Practical Critique*. New York: Zed Books.
Portes, Alejandro, and Jozsef Borocz. 1989. "Contemporary Immigration: Theoretical Perspectives on Its Determinants and Modes of Incorporation." *International Migration Review* 23:606–30.
Pratt, Geraldine, and Susan Hanson. 1991. "On the Links between Home and Work: Family-Household Strategies in a Buoyant Labour Market." *International Journal of Urban and Regional Research* 15:55–74.
Presser, Harriet B., and Gita Sen, eds. 2000. *Women's Empowerment and Demographic Processes*. New York: Oxford University Press.
Price, Janet, and Margrit Shildrick, eds. 1999. *Feminist Theory and the Body*. New York: Routledge.
Pringle, R. 1989. *Secretaries Talk: Sexuality, Power and Work*. London: Verso.
Pyle, Jean L. 1994. "Economic Restructuring in Singapore and the Changing Roles of Women, 1957 to Present." Pp. 129–44 in *Women in the Age of Economic Transformation*, edited by N. Aslanbeigui, S. Pressman, and G. Summerfield. London: Routledge.
Qian, Wenbao. 1996. *Rural-Urban Migration and its Impact on Economic Development in China*. Aldershot, England: Avebury.
Quah, S. T. 1998. "Singapore's Model of Development: Is It Transferable?" Pp. 105–25 in *Behind East Asian Growth: The Political and Social Foundation of Prosperity*, edited by H. S. Rowen. New York: Routledge.
Quanguo Renko Chouyang Dialcha Bangogshi, comp. 1989. 1987 Nian Quanguo 1 percent Renkou Chouyang Diaocha Ziliao (1987 One percent Sample Survey on population). Beijing: Chinese Statistical Publishing House.
Quibria, M. G. 1997. "Labour Migration and Labour Market Integration in Asia." *The World Economy* 20:21–42.
Raghaven, Chakravarthi. 1996. "Asian Female Migrant Workers Require Protection, Says ILO." *Third World Resurgence* 67:32–34.
Rai, Shirin. 1992. " 'Watering Another Man's Garden': Gender, Employment and Educational Reform in China." Pp. 20–40 in *Women in the Face of Change: The Soviet Union, Eastern Europe and China*, edited by S. Rai, H. Pilkington, and A. Phizacklea. London: Routledge.
Rathgeber, Eva M. 1990. "WID, WAD, GAD: Trends in Research and Practice." *Journal of Developing Areas* 24:489–502.
Redclift, Nanneke. 1985. *The Contested Domain: Gender, Accumulation and the Labour Process*. In *Beyond Employment: Household, Gender and Subsistence*, edited by N. Redclift and E. Mingione. Thousand Oaks, CA: Sage.
Redding, S. G. 1993. *The Spirit of Chinese Capitalism*. New York: de Gruyter.
Research Institute of All China Women's Federation and Research Office of Shanxi Women's Federation. 1991. *Statistics on Chinese Women: 1949–1989*. Beijing: China Statistical Publishing House.
Reskin, Barbara F., and Debra Branch McBrier. 2000. "Why Not Ascription? Organizations' Employment of Male and Female Managers." *American Sociological Review* 65:210–33.
Reskin, Barbara F., and Irene Padavic. 1994. *Women and Men at Work*. Thousand Oaks, CA: Pine Forge Press.
Richmond, Anthony H. 1992. "Immigration and Structural Change: The Canadian Experience, 1971–1986." *International Migration Review* 26, 4:1200–1221.

Roberts, Brian. 1991. "Household Coping Strategies and Urban Poverty in a Comparative Perspective." Pp. 135–68 in *Urban Life in Transition*, edited by M. Gottdiener and C. G. Pickvance. *Urban Affairs Annual Review*, vol. 39. Newbury Park, CA: Sage.

Roberts, Bryan. 1994. Informal Economies and Family Strategies. *International Journal of Urban and Regional Research* 18:6–23.

ROC Executive Yuan, Council of Labor Affairs. 1995. *Monthly Bulletin of Labor Statistics*. Taipie; DGBAS

ROC Executive Yuan, Directorate-General of Budget, Accounting, and Statistics and the Council for Economic Planning and Development . 1991. *Report on the Manpower Utilizing Survey, Taiwan Area, Repulic of China, 1990*. Taipei: DGBAS

———. Accounting and Statistics. 1996. *Yearbook of Manpower Survey Statistics 1996*. Taipei: DGBAS.

———. 2000. (http://www.dgbasey.gov.tw/dgbas03/STAT-N.HTM).

ROC Ministry of the Interior. 1997. *1996 Taiwan-Fukien Demographic Fact Book*. Taipei: MOI.

Rodney, Walter. 1981. *How Europe Underdeveloped Africa*. Washington, D.C.: Howard University Press.

ROK Administration of Labor Affairs. 1978. *Yearbook of Labor Statistics*. Seoul: ALA.

ROK Economic Planning Board, National Bureau of Statistics. 1962. *Korea Statistical Yearbook*. Seoul: EPB.

———. 1984. *Korea Statistical Yearbook*. Seoul: EPB.

ROK Ministry of Labor. 1995. *Yearbook of Labor Statistics*. Seoul: MOL.

ROK National Statistical Office. 1992. *Korea Statistical Yearbook*. Seoul: NSO.

———. 1997a. *1996 Annual Report on the Economically Active Population Survey*. Seoul: NSO.

———. 1997b. *The Economically Active Population Survey*. Taejon, S. Korea: NSO.

———. 1997c. *Korea Statistical Yearbook*. Seoul: NSO.

Rolland, D. T. 1994. "Family Characteristics of the Migrants." Pp. 129–53 in *Migration and Urbanization in China*, edited by L. H. Day and M. Xia. Armonk, NY: M. E. Sharpe.

Rowen, Henry S., ed. 1998. *Behind East Asian Growth: The Political and Social Foundations of Prosperity*. New York: Routledge.

Rowlands, Jo. 1997. *Questioning Empowerment: Working with Women in Honduras*. Oxford, England: Oxfam Publications.

———. 1998. "A Word of the Times, but What Does it Mean? Empowerment in the Discourse and Practice of Development." Pp. 11–34 in *Women and Empowerment*, edited by Haleh Afshar. New York: St. Martin's Press.

Rueschemeyer, Dietrich, and Peter Evans. 1985. "The State and Economic Transformation: Toward an Analysis of the Conditions Underlying Effective Intervention." Pp. 44–77 in *Bringing the State Back In*, edited by P. Evans, D. Rueschemeyer, and T. Skocpol. New York: Cambridge University Press.

Saith, Ashwani. 1999. "Migration Process and Policies: Some Asian Perspectives." *Asian and Pacific Migration Journal* 8:285–311.

Salaff, Janet. 1995 [1981]. *Working Daughters of Hong Kong*. New York: Columbia University Press.

Salaff, Janet W., Siu-lun Wong, and Mei-ling Fung. 1997. "Hong Kong Families' Views of 1997." Pp. 149–75 in *The Challenge of Hong Kong's Reintegration with China*, edited by M. K. Chan. Hong Kong: Hong Kong University Press.

Salaff, Janet W., Eric Fong, and Siu-lun Wong. 1998. "Paths out of Hong Kong: Social Class and Contacts of Emigrant and Nonemigrant Families." Pp. 299–330 in *Networks in International Perspective*, edited by B. Wellman. Boulder, CO: Westview Press.

Salt, John. 1988. "Highly Skilled International Migrants, Careers and International Labour Markets." *Geoforum* 19:387–99.

Sassen, Saskia. 1984. "Labor Migration and the New Industrial Division of Labor." Pp. 175–204 in *Women, Men, and the International Division of Labor*, edited by J. Nash and M. P. Fernandez-Kelly. Albany, NY: State University of New York Press.

————. 1988. *The Mobility of Labor and Capital: A Study in International Investment and Labor Flow.* Cambridge, England: Cambridge University Press.

Savage, Mike, and Anne Witz, eds. 1992. *Gender and Bureaucracy.* Oxford, England: Blackwell.

Scharping, Thomas, ed. 1997. *Migration in China's Guangdong Province: Major Results of a 1993 Sample Survey, Migrant and Floating Population in Shenzhen and Froshan.* Hamburg, Germany: Mitteilungen des Instituts Für Asienkunde.

Schilling, Chris. 1996. *The Body and Social Theory.* Thousand Oaks, CA: Sage.

Schive, Chi. 1992. "Taiwan's Emerging Position in the International Division of Labor." Pp. 101–22 in *Taiwan: Beyond the Economic Miracle,* edited by D. F. Simon and M. Y. M. Kau. Armonk, NY: M. E. Sharpe.

————. 1995. *Taiwan's Economic Role in East Asia.* Washington, D.C.: Center for Strategic and International Studies.

Schoenberger, Karl, and Nancy Yoshihara. 1989. "L.A. Firms Shuts S. Korea Unit; Claims Left Hanging." *Los Angles Times,* March 30, pp. 2, 15.

Scott, Catherine V. 1995. *Gender and Development: Rethinking Modernization and Dependency Theory.* Boulder, CO: Lynne Rienner.

Scott, Joan Wallach. 1988. *Gender and the Politics of History.* New York: Columbia University Press.

Scott, S., and David Morgan, eds. 1993. *Body Matters: Essays in the Sociology of the Body.* London: Falmer Press.

Scott, W. Richard. 1998. *Organizations: Rational, Natural, and Open Systems,* 4th ed. Englewood Cliffs, NJ: Prentice-Hall.

Sen, Gita, and Caren Grown. 1987. *Development, Crises, and Alternative Visions: Third World Women's Perspectives.* New York: Monthly Review Press.

Sen, Gita, and Srilatha Batliwala. 2000. "Empowering Women for Reproductive Rights." Pp. 15–36 in *Women's Empowerment and Demographic Processes,* edited by Harriet B. Presser and Gita Sen. New York: Oxford University Press.

Shad, Nasra M., and Indu Menon. 1997. "Violence Against Women Migrant Workers: Issues, Data and Partial Solutions." *Asian and Pacific Migration Journal* 6:5–30.

Shen, Anan. 1995. "Shanghai Nüxing Liudong Renkou De Tezheng Yu Cunzai De Wenti" [Characteristics and Existing Problems of the Shanghai Female Floating Population]. *Renkou [Population]* 4:47–53.

Shen, Jianfa. 1996. *Internal Migration and Regional Population.* Oxford, England: Elsevier.

Shu, Jing, and Lesleyanne Hawthorne. 1996. "Asian Student Migration to Australia." *International Migration* 34, 1:65–95.

Si, Mingshen. 1995. "Working is Beautiful: Chinese Women's Economic Status." *Renmin Ribao [People's Daily]* August 17, p. 1.

Simone, Vera, and Anne Thompson Feraru. 1995. *The Asian Pacific: Political and Economic Development in a Global Context.* New York: Longman.

Singapore Department of Statistics. 1993. *Singapore Census of Population 1990: Economic Characteristics.* Singapore: SNP Corporation.

————. 1998. *Yearbook of Statistics Singapore 1997.* Singapore: SNP Corporation.

Singapore Ministry of Labor, Research and Statistics Department. 1995. *Profile of the Labor Force of Singapore, 1983–1994.* Singapore: SNP Corporation.

Singapore Ministry of Manpower, Research and Statistics Department. 1998. *1997 Yearbook of Manpower Statistics.* Singapore: SNP Corporation.

————. 1999. *Report on the Labor Force Survey of Singapore 1998.* Singapore: SNP Corporation.

Singapore Ministry of National Development. 1967. *Singapore Sample Household Survey, 1966.* Singapore: Government Printing Office.

Sinn, Elizabeth. 1995a. "Emigration from Hong Kong before 1941: General Trends." Pp. 11–34 in *Emigration from Hong Kong,* edited by R. Skeldon. Hong Kong: Chinese University of Hong Kong.

————. 1995b. "Emigration from Hong Kong before 1941: Organization and Impact."

Pp. 35–50 in *Emigration from Hong Kong*, edited by R. Skeldon. Hong Kong: Chinese University of Hong Kong.

————, ed. 1994a. "Hong Kong in an International Migration System." Pp. 21–52 in *Reluctant Exiles? Migration from Hong Kong and the New Overseas Chinese*, edited by R. Skeldon. Hong Kong: Hong Kong University Press.

————. 1994b. "Turning Points in Labor Migration: The Case of Hong Kong." *Asian and Pacific Migration Journal* 3:93–118.

————, ed. 1995a. *Emigration from Hong Kong*. Hong Kong: Chinese University of Hong Kong.

————. 1995b. "Emigration from Hong Kong, 1945–1994: The Demographic Lead-Up to 1997." Pp. 50–77 in *Emigration from Hong Kong*, edited by R. Skeldon. Hong Kong: The Chinese University University Press of Hong Kong.

Skrobanek, Siriporn, Nattaya Boonpakdi, and Chutima Janthakeero. 1997. *The Traffic in Women: Human Realities of the International Sex Trade*. London: Zed Books.

Smith, Dorothy. 1990. *The Conceptual Practices of Power: A Feminist Sociology of Knowledge*. Toronto: University of Toronto Press.

Smithsonian Institution. 1999. "Between a Rock and a Hard Place: A History of American Sweatshops." December 31, 1999 (http://americanhistory.si.edu/sweatshops).

So, Alvin, Y. 1990. *Social Change and Development: Modernization, Dependency, and World-System Theory*. Newbury Park, CA: Sage.

So, Alvin, and Stephen W. K. Chiu. 1995. *East Asia and the World Economy*. Thousand Oaks, CA: Sage.

Sobieszczyk, Teresa. 1999. "Official and Unofficial Methods of Recruitment of Thai Labor for Overseas Employment." Presented at the Annual Meeting of the Association for Asian Studies, Boston.

Social Statistics and Indicators on Women. 1994. Seoul: Korean Women's Development Institute.

Solinger, Dorothy. 1999. *Contesting Citizenship in Urban China: Peasant Migrants, the State, and the Logic of the Market*. Berkeley and Los Angeles, CA: University of California Press.

Spivak, Gayatri C. 1988a. *In Other Worlds: Essays in Cultural Politics*. New York: Routledge.

————. 1988b. "Can the Subaltern Speak?" Pp. 271–311 in *Marxism and Interpretation of Culture*, edited by G. Nelson and L. Grossberg. Chicago, IL: University of Illinois Press.

Stacey, Judith. 1983. *Patriarchy and Socialist Revolution in China*. Berkeley and Los Angeles, CA: University of California Press.

Stacey, Judith, and Barrie Thorne. 1985. "The Missing Feminist Revolution in Sociology." *Social Problems* 32:301–16.

Stack, Carol B., and Linda M. Burton. 1994. "Kinscripts: Reflections on Family, Generation, and Theory." Pp. 33–44 in *Mothering: Ideology, Experience and Agency*, edited by E. N. Glenn, G. Chang, and L. R. Forcey. London: Routledge.

Stahl, Charles W. 1999. "Trade in Labour Services and Migrant Workers Protection with Special Reference to East Asia." *International Migration* 37:545–68.

Stalker, P. 1994. *The Work of Strangers: A Survey of International Labor Migration*. Geneva: International Labour Office.

Stark, Oded. 1988. "On Marriage and Migration." *European Journal of Population* 4:23–37.

State Statistical Bureau, People's Republic of China. 1998. *China Statistical Yearbook*. Beijing: China Statistical Publishing House.

Staudt, Kathleen, ed. 1997. *Women, International Development, and Politics: The Bureaucratic Mire*. 2d ed. Philadelphia, PA: Temple University Press.

Suen, Wing. 1994. "Labour and Employment." Pp. 149–64 in *The Other Hong Kong Report, 1994*, edited by D. H. McMillen and Si-wai Man. Hong Kong: Chinese University Press.

Summerfield, Gale. 1994. "Economic Reform and the Employment of Chinese Women." *Journal of Economic Issues* 28:715–32.

Sun, Chengshu, Chen, Guozi Gao, and Chenggong Liu. 1998. *How the Miracle Was Created: A Study of Shanghai's Re-Employment Project*. Shanghai: Fudan University Press.

Suro, Robert. 1994. "Watching America's Door: The Immigration Backlash and the New Policy Debate,"table 2.1. Boston, MA: Electronic Policy Network. (http://www.epn. org/tef/surointr.html).

Tan, Lin. 1997. "Tianjinshi 1996 Wailaihun Qingkuang Diaocha Fenxi Baogao" [An Analysis of a Survey on the Situation of Migrant Marriages in Tianjin in 1996]. Unpublished manuscript. Population and Development Research Institute, Nankai University, Tianjin, China.

Tan, Lin, and Chris Gilmartin. 1996. Interviews with "Dagongmei" the Dingyi Limited Corporation, Tanggu, Tianjin, on December 10.

Tan, Lin, Li Xinjian, Bowen Huang, Mingzhu Chen, and Shumin Sun. 1998. "Nüxing Hunyin Gianru Dui Qi Zishen Fazhan Yingxiang De Yanjiu: Guangyu Jiangsu Zhangjiagangshi de diaocha" [Research on the Impact of Female Marital Migration on Personal Development: A Survey of Jiangsu's Zhangjiagang City]. *Funü Yanjiu Luncong* [*A Collection of Women's Studies*], April:13–17.

Tan, Lin-Ti, and Ruoh-Rong Yu. 1996. "An Application of the Dual Labor Market Model: Structural Change in Taiwan's Female Employment." *Taiwan Economic Review* 24:275–311.

Tan, Shen. 1994. "Dang Dai Zhong Guo Fu Nü: You Zheng Fu An Zhi Gong Zuo Huo Jing Ru Lao Dong Li Shi Chang" [Career Women in Present China: Accepting Jobs or Entering the Labor Market Arranged by the State Government]. Pp. 78–92 in *Xing BieYu Zhong Guo* [*Engendering China*], edited by X. J. Li, H. Zhu, and X. Y. Dong. Beijing: Life, Reading and New Knowledge Bookstore.

Tang, Ning, and Shizhen Sun. 1997. "Take Off Right After Xiagang." *Xinmin Wandbao* [*Xinmin Evening News*], March 20, p. 12.

Thompson, Grahame, ed. 1998. *Economic Dynamism in the Asia-Pacific: The Growth of Integration and Competitiveness*. New York: Routledge.

Thrift, Nigel, and Kris Olds. 1996. "Refiguring the Economic in Economic Geography." *Progress in Human Geography* 20, 3:311–37.

Tian, Hua. 1991. "Xinan Nongcun Funü: Dongqian Hunpei Taishi Tanxi" [Preliminary Analysis of the Trends of Eastward Female Marriage Migration from Southwestern Villages]. *Nanfang Renkou* 1:39–42.

Tiano, Susan. 1987. "Gender, Work, and World Capitalism." Pp. 216–43 in *Analyzing Gender*, edited by B. Hess and M. M. Ferree. Beverly Hills, CA: Sage.

———. 1994. *Patriarchy on the Line: Labor, Gender, and Ideology in the Mexico Maquila Industry*. Philadelphia, PA: Temple University Press.

Tilly, Charles. 1990. "Transplanted Networks." Pp. 79–95 in *Immigration Reconsidered: History, Sociology and Politics*, edited by E. Yans-McLaughlin. New York: Oxford University Press.

Tilly, Louise, and Joan Scott. 1978. *Women, Work and Family*. New York: Methuen.

Townsend, Janet, Emma Zapata, Jo Rowlands, Pilar Alberti, and Marta Mercado, eds. 1999. *Women and Power: Fighting Patriarchies and Poverty*. New York: St. Martin's Press.

Tsai, Shu-Ling. 1987. "Occupational Segregation and Educational Attainment: The Comparative Analysis by Gender." *Chinese Sociological Journal* 11:61–91.

Tsui-Auch, Lai Si. 2000. "Taking Stock of Global, Regional and Local Perspectives to Development and Change of ANICs." Presented at the Annual Meeting of the American Sociological Association, Washington, D.C.

United Nations. 1995. *The World's Women 1995: Trends and Statistics*. New York: United Nations.

———. 2000. *The World's Women: Trends and Statistics*. New York: United Nations.

United Nations, Division for Economic and Social Information. 1980. *Women: 1980*. Conference booklet for the World Conference of the United Nations Decade for Women, Copenhagen, July 1980.

United Nations Development Programme (UNDP). 1995. *Human Development Report 1995*. New York: Oxford University Press.

———. 1999. *Human Development Report 1999*. New York: Oxford University Press.

USAID, Office of Women in Development. 2000. "Working Without a Net: Women and the Asian Financial Crisis." *Gender Matters Quarterly* 2:1–8.

U.S. Bureau of the Census. 1997. *Statistical Abstract of the United States: 1997.* Washington, DC: U.S. Government Printing Office.

Visanathan, Nalini, Lynn Duggan, Laurie Nisonoff, and Nan Wiegersma, eds. 1998. *The Women, Gender & Development Reader.* London: Zed Books.

Wade, Robert. 1990. *Governing the Market.* Princeton, NJ: Princeton University Press.

———. 1992. "East Asian Economic Success: Conflicting Perspectives, Partial Insight, Shaky Evidence." *World Politics* 44:270–320.

Walder, Andrew G. 1986. *Communist Neo-Traditionalism: Work and Authority in Chinese Industry.* Berkeley and Los Angeles, CA: University of California Press.

Wallerstein, Immanuel. 1979. *The Capitalist World-Economy.* New York: Cambridge University Press.

Wan, Guang Hua. 1995. "Peasant Flood in China: Internal Migration and its Policy Determinants." *Third World Quarterly* 16:173–96.

Wang, Chengjing. 1998. "Beijing Forms an Employment Services System." *Zhongguo Laodong Bao [Chinese Labor News]*, February 24, p. 1.

Wang, Jenn Hwan. 1995. "Yu Nan Hsiang Cheng Tzo, Wo Men Ko Yi Kan Tao Sho Mo?" [Comment on 'The Imperialist Eye': What Does the South Bound Policy Tell Us?]. *Tai-Wan Sho Hui Yen Chiu Chi Kan [Taiwan: A Radical Quarterly in Social Studies]* 18:225–30.

Wang, Jiafeng. 1992. "Women's Employment in the Transitional Period." *Shanghai Funu [Shanghai Women]* 49:6–7.

Wang, Jinling. 1992. "Zhejiang Nongmin Yidi Lianyin Xin Tedian" [New Characteristics of Interprovincial Marriage Migrants into the Rural Areas of Zhejiang]. *Zhehuixue Yanjiu [Sociological Research]* 4:92–95.

Wang, Lih Rong. 1995. *Fu Nu Yu She Hui Zheng Ce [Women and Social Policy].* Taipei: Chuliu.

Ward, Kathryn. 1988. "Women in the Global Economy." Pp. 17–48 in *Women and Work no. 3*, edited by B. Gutek, A. Stromberg, and L. Larwood. Beverly Hills, CA: Sage.

———, ed. 1990. *Women Workers and Global Restructuring.* Ithaca, NY: ILR Press.

———. 1993. "Reconceptualizing World System Theory to Include Women." Pp. 43–68 in *Theory in Gender/Feminism on Theory*, edited by Paula England. New York: Aldine De Gruyter.

Watson, James L. 1975. *Emigration and the Chinese Lineage: The Mans in Hong Kong and London.* Berkeley and Los Angeles, CA: University of California Press.

Watson, Paul. 1995. "China's Abuse of Women Condemned." *Toronto Star*, June 30, A21.

Watts, Susan J. 1983. "Marriage and Migration, A Neglected Form of Long-Term Mobility: A Case Study from Ilorin, Nigeria." *International Migration Review* 17:682–98.

Waylen, Georgina. 1996. *Gender in Third World Politics.* Boulder, CO: Lynne Rienner.

Weaver, James H., Michael Rock, and Ken Kusterer. 1997. *Achieving Broad-Based Sustainable Development: Governance, Environment, and Growth with Equity.* West Hartford, CT: Kumarian Press.

Wen, Xianliang. 1993. "Women's Adaptation to the Market Economy." *Funu Yanjiu Luncong [Forum of Women's Studies]* 2:8–14.

West, Candace, and Don Zimmerman. 1987. "Doing Gender." *Gender & Society* 1:125–51.

Westwood, Robert I. 1997. "The Politics of Opportunity: Gender and Work in Hong Kong, Part II." Pp. 101–56 in *En-Gendering Hong Kong Society*, edited by F. M. Cheung. Hong Kong: Chinese University Press.

Wharton, Amy S., and James N. Baron. 1987. "So Happy Together? The Impact of Gender Segregation on Men at Work." *American Sociological Review* 52:574–87.

Wheelock, Jane. 1990. "Capital Restructuring and the Domestic Economy: Family Self Respect and the Irrelevance of 'Rational Economic Man.'" *Capital and Class* 41:103–41.

Wilson, Tamar Diana. 1994. "What Determines Where Transnational Labor Migrants Go? Modifications in Migration Theories." *Human Organization* 53:269–78.

Witz, Anne, Susan Halford, and Mike Savage. 1996. "Organized Bodies: Gender, Sexuality and Embodiment in Contemporary Organizations." Pp. 173–90 in *Sexualizing the Social: Power and the Organization of Sexuality*, edited by L. Adkins and V. Merchant. New York: St. Martin's Press.

Wolf, Diane. 1990. "Daughters, Decisions and Domination: An Empirical and Conceptual Critique of Household Strategies." *Development and Change* 21:43–74.

———. 1992. *Factory Daughters: Gender, Household Dynamics and Rural Industrialization in Java.* Berkeley and Los Angeles, CA: University of California Press.

Wolf, Margery. 1985. *Revolution Postponed: Women in Contemporary China.* Stanford, CA: Stanford University Press.

Women's Committee of Zigong Party. 1998. "Different Impact of Xiagang on Men and Women." *Zhongguo Funubao [Chinese Women's Daily]*, May 28, p. 3.

Women's Federation of Hubei Province. 1998. "Use Policy and Legal Means to Forcefully Push Forward the Development of Re-Employment Project." *Lilun Yuekan [Theory Monthly]* 2: 18–20.

Women's Federation of Luwan District, Shanghai. 1997. "Develop District Services to Open More Employment Channels." *Shanghai Funu [Shanghai Women]* 3: 25–27.

Wong, Fai-Ming. 1981. "Effects of the Employment of Mothers on Marital Role and Power Differentiation in Hong Kong." Pp. 217–34 in *Social Life and Development in Hong Kong*, edited by A. King and R. Lee. Hong Kong: Chinese University Press.

Wong, Lloyd. 1997. "Globalization and Transnational Migration: A Study of Recent Chinese Capitalist Migration from the Asian Pacific to Canada." *International Sociology* 12, 3:329–51.

Wong, Siu-lun. 1995. "Political Attitudes and Identity." Pp. 147–76 in *Emigration from Hong Kong*, edited by R. Skeldon. Hong Kong: Chinese University of Hong Kong.

Wong, Siu-lun, and Janet W. Salaff. 1998. "Network Capital: Emigration from Hong Kong." *British Journal of Sociology* 49:258–74.

Woo-Cumings, Meredith. 1999. *The Developmental State.* Ithaca, NY: Cornell University Press.

Woon, Yuen-fong. 1993. "Circulatory Mobility in Post-Mao China: Temporary Migrants in Kaiping County, Pearl River Delta Region." *International Migration Review* 27:578–604.

World Bank. 1993. *The East Asian Miracle: Economic Growth and Public Policy.* New York: Oxford University Press.

———. 2001. *Engendering Development: Through Gender Equality in Rights, Resources, and Voice.* Washington, D.C.: World Bank.

Wren, Christopher S. 1983. "China Still Fighting an Old Abuse: Women for Sale." *New York Times*, January 6, A:2.

Wu, Rose. 1995. "Women." Pp. 121–56 in *The Other Hong Kong Report, 1995*, edited by S. Y. L. Cheung and S. M. H. Sze. Hong Kong: Chinese University Press.

WuDunn, Sheryl. 1991. "Feudal China's Evil Revived: Wives for Sale." *New York Times*, August 4, A:11.

Xia, Lingxiang. 1995. *Women's Role Development and Role Conflict in China.* Beijing: Pearl Publishing House.

Xiao, Yang, Xiuhua Jiang, and Yukun Hu. 1997. "The Impact of Economic Transition on SOE Women Workers." *Funu Yankiu Luncong [Forum of Women's Studies]* 3:28–29.

Xiong, Yu, and Lincoln H. Day. 1994. "Demographic Characteristics of the Migrants." Pp. 103–28 in *Migration and Urbanization in China*, edited by L. H. Day and M. Xia. Armonk, NY: M. E. Sharpe.

Xu, Tianqi, and Ye Zhendong. 1992. "Zhejiang Wailai Nüxing Renkou Tanxi" [Exploration of Female Marriage Migrants in Zhejiang]. *Renkou Xuekan [Population Journal]* 2:45–48.

Xue, Zhaojun. 1998. "Some Suggestions on Xiagang Workers' Re-Employment." *Renmin Ribao [People's Daily]*, May 4, p. 1.

Yang, Xiushi. 1993. "Household Registration, Economic Reform and Migration." *International Migration Review* 27:796–818.

Yang, Yiqing, Yue Wu, and Ping Chang. 1993. *Nobody Can Keep the "Iron Rice Bowl."* Chengdu, China: Sichuan University Press.

Yang, Yunyan. 1992. "Woguo Renkou Hunyin Qianyi De Hongguang Liuxiang Chuxi" [A Macroscopic Study of the Trend of China's Marriage Migration]. *Nanfang Renkou* [*Southern Population*] 4:39–42.

Yeoh, Brenda S. A., Shirlena Huang, and Joaquin Gonzalez III. 1999. "Migrant Female Domestic Workers: Debating the Economic, Social and Political Impacts in Singapore." *International Migration Review* 33:114–36.

Yeung, Yue-man. 1999. "Globalization and Regional Transformation in Pacific Asia." Occasional Paper no. 103, Hong Kong Institute of Asia-Pacific Studies, Chinese University of Hong Kong.

Yi, Hyo-Jae. 1990. "Company M's Union Visits the U.S.A" *Chosun Ilbo*, April 13, p. 15.

Yi, Sang-yong. 1990. "Han guk oeja kiop nodong undong ui hyonhwang Kwa kwaje" [The Current Situation of the Labor Movement in Foreign Firms]. *Tagukchok Kiop Kwa Nodong Undong* [*Multinational Corporations and Labor Movement*]. Seoul: Paeksan Press.

Yoon, In-Jin. 1993. "The Social Origins of Korean Immigration to the United States from 1965 to the Present." *Papers of the Program on Population* 121. Honolulu: University of Hawaii, East-West Center.

Young, Kate. 1992. *Gender and Development Reader.* Ottawa: Canadian Council for International Cooperation.

Young, Kate, C. Wolkowitz, and R. McCullagh, eds. 1981. *Of Marriage and the Market.* London: CSE Books.

Yu, Chom-Sun. 1990. "I'd Like to Take My Pride Back, Not Money." *The Hankyoreh*, July 11, p. 7.

Yu, Xiong, and Lincoln H. Day. 1994. "Demographic Characteristics of the Migrants." Pp. 103–28 in *Migration and Urbanization in China*, edited by Lincoln H. Day and Ma Xia. Armonk, NY: M. E. Sharpe.

Yu, Xiu. 1998. "Walking Over; There is Sky. . . ." *Remin Ribao* [*People's Daily*], June 6, p. 6.

Yuval-Davis, Nira. 1993. "Gender and Nation." *Ethnic and Radical Studies* 16, 4:621–32.

Zang, Xiaowei. 1995. "Labor Market and Rural Migrants in Post-Mao China." *American Asian Review* 13:78–108.

Zhang, Hesheng. 1994. *Hunyin Daliudong: Wailiu Funü Hunyin Diaocha Jishi* [*The Great Marriage Migration: A Survey of Female Marriage Migrants*]. Shenyang: Liaoning People's Press.

Zhang, Houyi, and Lizhi Ming. 1999. *A Report on the Development of China's Private Sector.* Beijing: Social Science Classics Publishing House.

Zhang, Liping, and Ping Fan. 1993. "Chuantong Nongye Diqu De Hunyin Tezheng Shandong Shen Lingxian Diaocha" [Marriage Characteristics in the Traditional Agricultural Regions of China—An Investigation of Lingxian County in Shandong]. *Shehuixue yanjiu* [*Research on Sociology*] 5:92–100.

Zhao, Pinghe. 1997. "Developing Skill Training Programs to Help Off-Duty Women." *Zhonghua Nuzi Xueyuan Xueba* [*Journal of the Chinese Women's College*] 26:40–43.

Zheng, Xiaoying, ed. 1995. *Zhong Guo Nü Xin Ren Kou Wen Ti Yü Fa Zhan* [*The Problems and Development of Female Population*]. Beijing: Beijing University Press.

Zhongguo 1990 Nian Renkou Pucha Ziliao [*Tabulations on the 1990 Population Census of the People's Republic of China*]. Beijing: China Statistical Press.

Contributors

Esther Ngan-ling Chow is Professor of Sociology at American University, Washington, D.C. She is a feminist scholar, researcher and community activist. Her research interests include gender and development; globalization and social change; industrial sociology; work and family; migration/immigration; state theories; the intersection of race, class, ethnicity, gender, and sexuality; social inequality and global feminism. She is the guest co-editor of a special issue of *Gender & Society* on Race, Class, and Gender (1992). She is the co-author and co-editor of *Women, the Family and Policy: A Global Perspective* (1994) and *Race, Class and Gender: Common Bonds, Different Voices* (1996); the latter book was a recipient of the Myers Center Award for the Study of Human Rights in North America in 1997.

Yin-Wah Chu is Assistant Professor in the Department of Sociology at the University of Hong Kong. She is interested in various aspects of social and political development of East Asia. Her publications include various journal articles on the democratic transitions in Taiwan and South Korea, labor conditions and labor movements in the two societies, and the social organization of industrial production in Hong Kong. She has been revising her work on Taiwan and South Korea's democratization and has recently started a project on Hong Kong's emerging information economy.

Christina Gilmartin is Associate Professor of History and Director of the Women's Studies Program at Northeastern University. She is the author of *Engendering the Chinese Revolution: Radical Women, Communist Politics, and Mass Movements in the 1920s* (1995). She has also co-edited *Engendering China: Women, Culture, and the State* (1994) and *Feminist Approaches to Theory and Methodology: An Interdisciplinary Reader* (1999).

Ting Gong is Associate Professor of Political Science at Ramapo College of New Jersey. She received her Ph.D. in political science from the Maxwell School of Citizenship and Public Affairs, Syracuse University. She is the author of *The Politics of Corruption in Contemporary China: An Analysis of Policy Outcomes* (1994); and a dozen articles on China's political issues. Her articles have appeared in *Problems of Post-Communism, Communist and Post-Communist Studies, Crime, Law and Social Change, China Information*, and *Journal of Communist Studies and Transition Politics*. She has received grants and awards from a number of foundations, including the National Endowment for the Humanities and the American Association of University Women. She has been a visiting scholar at Hong Kong University and at Syracuse University's Hong Kong Program.

Ray-may Hsung is Professor of Sociology at Tunghai University in Taiwan. She has been working on research in gender and development, institutions, social capital, urban policy networks, social support networks, migration, and mobility. She is currently editor of *Taiwanese Sociological Review*. Her major recent publications are: "Institutions and Networks Constructing Gender Inequality in Factories: The Case of Taiwan's Export Processing and Industrial Zones" (co-authored with Esther Ngan-ling Chow, 2001); The Analyses on Action System of Urban Events: the Case of Taichung City," *Journal of Sociology*, 2001; "Transition and Restructuration in a German City," *Journal of Population Studies*, 1998; and "Factors Influencing Emotional and Financial Support Networks," *Journal of Humanities and Social Sciences*, 1994.

Hyun Mee Kim is Assistant Professor in the Department of Sociology, Yonsei University, Seoul, South Korea. She received her Ph.D. in cultural anthropology from the University of Washington. As a cultural anthropologist, she is interested in interpreting Korean women's working experiences through their own narratives. Her areas of interest also include globalization and women's labor, feminist cultural theories, and postcolonialism. Recently, she has been interested in doing comparative studies on Asian women's experience of modernization and global modernity.

Anru Lee is Assistant Professor of Anthropology and Asian Studies at California State University, Sacramento. She has focused on issues of global economic development and Asian-Pacific regional integration and conducted research in Taiwan. She is co-editing an anthology on *Women in New Taiwan: Gender Roles and Gender Consciousness in a Changing Society*, 2002. She is also working on a book entitled *In the Name of Harmony and Prosperity: Labor and Gender Politics in Taiwan's Recent Economic Restructuring*.

Vivien Hiu-tung Leung is now working for the Boston Consulting Group. The study on gender embeddedness of family strategies herein was part of her M. Phil. thesis while she studied at the Chinese University of Hong Kong. She then moved to Oxford, where she received another M. Phil. degree in sociology and studied the growth of self-employment in Britain. Though having left academia for a while, Vivien is still very interested in sociological studies, especially those on labor market segmentation and social stratification.

Deanna M. Lyter is a doctoral candidate in sociology at American University in Washington, D.C. and is working on her dissertation, entitled "Tools of Domination and Forums for Resistance: The Impact of AFDC and Tribal Codes on Seneca and White Mountain Apache Women, 1934–1960." Her areas of research include globalization, gender, poverty, and law. Currently, she is a research associate with the Institute for Socio-Financial Studies in Virginia.

Ping Ping received the B. Law degree in sociology from Zhongshan University, Guangzhou, China in 1990 and the M. Phil. Degree in sociology from the Chinese University of Hong Kong in 1996. She works at the Institute of Sociology and Demography of the Guangzhou Academy of Social Sciences. Currently, she is a Ph.D. candidate in Sociology at the Chinese University of Hong Kong. Her research interests are in sociology of gender, industrial sociology, economic organization, and firm theory.

Janet W. Salaff has received her degrees in sociology from the University of California at Berkeley, and has done research on the relationship between the Chinese family and the economy. In her current work on international migration, she looks at family economies and the decision to move across the seas. A Professor of Sociology, she teaches at the University of Toronto and is affiliated with the Centre of Asian Studies, University of Hong Kong and the Asia-Pacific Research Centre (A-PARC), Stanford University.

Lin Tan holds a Ph.D. degree in demography. She is currently Professor and Director of the Center for Women and Development Research at the Nankai University. She is also working as Professor and Associate Director of the Institute of Population and Development Research. Her recent research interests are in gender and work, gender and migration, and gender and health in China. She is currently working on her project "Gender Inequality in the Work Place: How China Should Build Its Labor Market" as a Fulbright Scholar at Brown University.

Index

Acker, Joan, 84
Agricultural economies, 28
Ajumma workers, 114–119
Anti-Americanism, Korean workers and, 114–119
Antrobus, Peggy, 41
Appadurai, Arjun, 9, 19
Asian dragons; *see also* East Asia; *specific country*
  dependency theory and, 32
  economic miracle of, 10–11
  HDI and GDP of, 27
Asian financial crisis, 19, 34–35
  women and, 2, 35
Association of Southeast Asian Nations (ASEAN), 15
Athukorala, Premo-chandra, 19

Balassa, Bela, 28
Bello, W., 32
Bian, Yanjie, 141
Blumberg, Rae Lesser, 81
Boserup, Ester, 38
Brandt Commission (1980), 26
Burawoy, Michael, 154
Bureaucratic paternalism labor system, 75
Burrell, G., 85
Burton, Linda, 222

Cai, Fang, 207
Capitalism, 82
  patriarchy and, 84
  women and, 71, 119–121
Chaebols (industrial conglomerates), 12, 74
Chiang Kai-shek, 11
China, 1, 14–15, 48–49
  economic restructuring of, 15, 125–127, 203
  impact on labor, 125–131
  Re-employment Project, 131–132

women's reemployment (*zaijiuye*), 131–134
GEM and, 34
HDI and GDP of, 27, 33
marriage migration, 203–204
  age structure of, 213
  educational levels and, 211–212
  factors of, 209–212
  as female/rural phenomenon, 204–205
  geographical patterns of, 205–206
  politics of representation, 212–214
  process and causes of expansion, 206–208
migration and, 20, 51
"one party, two systems" policy, 14
prereform era, gendered job arrangements, 146–148
state-owned firms, 144–146
underemployment and unemployment, 126–131
women workers
  control and production of gender, 155–156
  disadvantages of, 152–155
  family dependence, 143, 159–160
  firm dependence and, 143, 151, 156–159
  gender priority in housing, 149–150
  gendered job arrangements, 146–148
  marginalization of, 148–149
  market dependence, 161–163
  postreform era, 151–156
  prereform era, 146–151
  self-employment, 134–137
xiagang (unemployment), 127–131
Chiu, Stephen, 17, 28–29
Chow, Esther Ngan-ling, 1, 9, 13, 25, 47, 49, 81
Chu, Yin-wah, 47–48, 61
Classism, 39, 118
Colonialism, 12, 29

Women; *see also specific country*
Asian economic crisis and, 2
capitalism and, 71, 119–121
Confucian culture and, 36
economic development and, 2
employment structure of, 61–65, 70–72
exploitation thesis of, 16, 61
industrialization and, 13, 72
labor force participation, 13, 21, 62–65
labor market as liberating, 16
as laborers, 108–110, 118–119
marriage and, 65, 74–76
marriage migration; *see* China
migration and, 20–22
occupational representation and status,
   77–78
private/public dichotomy of, 36–37
self-employment of, 134–137
as "super proletariat," 18
Third World women, 40–41, 45
undervaluation of work of, 33

union-organized labor struggles and, 37
working mothers, 107–108
workplace violence and, 110–114
Women and development (WAD), 38–39
Women in development (WID), 38
Women's Role in Economic Development
   (Boserup), 38
Woo-Cumings, Meredith, 31
World Bank, 1, 26, 30, 45
World system theory, 31–32, 35
World Trade Organization (WTO), 45

Xiagang (unemployment), 127–133

Yang, Yunyan, 206
Yu, Xiong, 207

Zaijiuye (women's reemployment), 131–134
Zhang, Hesheng, 204, 207–210, 213–214
Zhang, Liping, 214
Zimmerman, Don, 43